IN SEARCH OF MODERN ARCHITECTURE

IN SEARCH OF MODERN ARCHITECTURE

A TRIBUTE TO

HENRY-RUSSELL HITCHCOCK

EDITED BY HELEN SEARING

THE ARCHITECTURAL HISTORY FOUNDATION
NEW YORK

—

THE MIT PRESS
CAMBRIDGE, MASSACHUSETTS
LONDON, ENGLAND

Frontispiece: Henry-Russell Hitchcock and Philip Johnson, 1979.

Designed by Nora Sheehan

Acknowledgments

I would like to express my gratitude to the following: the members of my Editorial Board—John Coolidge, John M. Jacobus, and Thomas McCormick—for their sage counsel; Philip Johnson and John Loeb for their unfailing generosity; Henry-Russell Hitchcock, Robert Schmitt, and Kitty for their unflagging hospitality; Victoria Newhouse, Julianne Griffin, Moira Duggan, and Karen Banks of the Architectural History Foundation for their editorial guidance; Ann Swain Landreth for the photograph of Messrs. Hitchcock and Johnson; Dennis Doordan for caption information; Erna Huber for her donation of typing time; my husband, David Burres, for his sustained and sustaining support; and the contributors for their patience during the lengthy process of bringing this volume to completion.   *Helen Searing*

CONTENTS

To a Festschrift such as this, I—a practicing artist and only an amateur historian of architecture—can provide but a small contribution. I am only proud that I was right in 1929 to claim that Russell Hitchcock is the leading historian of architecture in the world today. My judgment has not changed.

It was through an article on J. J. Oud by Russell that a "Saul-Paul" conversion changed my life from one of philosophy to one of architecture. It was working for Russell in 1930–32 that gave me my artistic direction. It was again Russell's leadership that brought not only me but my generation to face the end of the International Style with fortitude and delight. His latest books I can confess with pleasure have had direct influence on the latest tall buildings of the Johnson/Burgee office.

From the architect's point of view, what stands out in Russell's scholarship is his use of primary visual sources. I can bear personal witness that from his first travels in 1930, to the latest for his German Renaissance book, Russell saw every extant building he writes about. He is an "eye" scholar.

Not having a genuine scholarly background, I can perhaps all the better appreciate without envy Russell's great contribution to both the practice of architecture and its history.

Philip Johnson
July 1982

INTRODUCTION

HENRY-RUSSELL HITCHCOCK: ARCHITECTURA ET AMICITIA*

Helen Searing

T HESE ESSAYS ON MODERN ARCHI-
tecture presented here to Henry-Russell
Hitchcock celebrate only a few of the accomplishments of this protean man, just as
they allude to only a portion of his scholarly
contributions. Museum director (Fig. 3),[1] traveler, curator,[2] collector, supporter of the avant-
garde in music and theater as well as in art and
architecture,[3] reviewer of Marcel Proust, Virginia Woolf, and 1928 movie magazines,[4] epi-
cure and chef, oenophile and ailurophile (Fig.
2), designer and dandy (Fig. 1),[5] Professor
Hitchcock is here honored in his roles as stimulating teacher,[6] intrepid critic,[7] and esteemed
historian.[8] Most of all, perhaps, we cherish him
as mentor and friend, for no less important than
his erudition as a scholar is his rare gift for
friendship, a theme that forms a leitmotif in
Hitchcock's career.[9] Students of all ages, whether
beginners or mature scholars, have benefited as
much from the geniality of his company and his
generous willingness to share intellectual discoveries as from the breadth of his knowledge. Some
of us have listened to him in the undergraduate
classroom and graduate seminar, some have produced dissertations and books inspired and directed by him; all have been touched professionally and personally by the publications, lectures,
exhibitions, and conversations that have led to
new explorations of architecture and its history.

Restricted to the modern period as it has come
conventionally to be defined (mid-eighteenth
century to the present),[10] our *Festschrift* pays
homage to but one area of Hitchcock's expertise,
although the one that at the outset established his
reputation as an architectural historian of the first
rank. But as the bibliographies attest, his publications span more than one thousand years of
architectural history. Initially committed to explaining contemporary architecture to an international audience,[11] Hitchcock in his interests
has moved steadily backward, chronologically,
from Early Victorian architecture to German Rococo to the architecture of the seventeenth and
sixteenth centuries in Germany and the Netherlands, though all the while he remains involved
with the current architectural scene.

Those familiar with his earliest writings have
not been surprised by the temporal range of
Hitchcock's studies. His career began in 1927
with the publication of "The Decline of Architecture," in which he sought to interpret, in somewhat Spenglerian terms, the meaning of modernism in contemporary buildings, and demonstrated,
especially for an American, a precocious familiarity with Le Corbusier (Fig. 4) and Erich Men-
delssohn (*sic*), together with a more predictable

*The Latin subtitle of this essay was inspired by the name of a
Dutch architectural organization, *Architectura et Amicitia*,
founded in 1855, which played a seminal role in the development
of architecture in the Netherlands during the late nineteenth century and throughout the first forty years of the twentieth. I have
summarized its importance in my dissertation, *Housing in Holland and the Amsterdam School* (New Haven, 1971), which
owes so much to Professor Hitchcock's encouragement and to
his own penetrating analyses of twentieth-century Dutch architecture.

acquaintance with "Mr. Loew's picture palaces and Mr. Cram's cathedral on the Hudson."[12] Yet in 1927 he also wrote "Banded Arches before the year 1000,"[13] a consideration of brick arcades from Roman times forward to the first millennium, indicating in a footnote his desire to search still further back for origins in Ur and ancient Egypt!

This essay grew out of his intention of compiling a comprehensive history of brickwork, but after Hitchcock's second trip to Europe, in 1924/25, he abandoned that somewhat daunting project in order to focus on the architecture of his own time.[14] Yet the initial goal was significant, for Hitchcock has never ceased to place modern architecture within its historical context and to forge relevant connections with the past. In an engaging little essay of 1928, "Four Harvard Architects," he traced formal and theoretical continuities between the work of Charles Bulfinch and that of his friend, Peter van der Meulen Smith.[15] In the same essay he adumbrated the notion that twentieth-century architecture can be perceived as a dialectical contest between traditional architecture[16] and the type of design that "has lost all traditional features and depends on the expression of functional needs in terms of scientific materials," represented by Smith. In noting that the latter was "the first to develop an American version of what is . . . an international style," Hitchcock launched the term that would soon become synonymous with orthodox modern architecture.[17] While the phrase was suggested by the title of Walter Gropius's Bauhaus book, *Internationale Architektur* (Munich, 1925), it was not fortuitous that Hitchcock took what was meant to be an inevitable, *Zeitgeistlich* phenomenon and through a linguistic substitution made of it a style with deliberate aesthetic ends.[18]

This point of view was made explicit in Hitchcock's first magnum opus, *Modern Architecture: Romanticism and Reintegration* (New York, 1929). While admiring the structural and material innovations of self-proclaimed functionalists like J.J.P. Oud and Gropius, he had immediately seen through their technologically deterministic protestations: "It is a point worth stressing, since it is a point frequently denied by its theorists, that the new manner constitutes essentially an aesthetic and not necessarily particular methods of construction."[19] Hitchcock went on to observe that "however much there may be progress technically, aesthetically there is only more or less sequential change."[20] Thus he saw that the international style, like every other, "will be in its turn superseded,"[21] though he did not attempt to prophesy when this would happen.

In this book, too, Hitchcock introduced his

categories "The New Pioneers" and "The New Tradition" (see the essay by Vincent Scully immediately following). The entire volume is an astonishingly bold venture for a twenty-six-year-old; its authoritative tone and audaciously comprehensive sweep successfully belie the author's age.[22] Hitchcock decisively took the beginnings of modern architecture back not just to Romanticism, a crucial movement which he saw commencing "at a date considerably anterior to that customarily given,"[23] but all the way back to the Flamboyant Gothic period, arguing that

> the phases through which European architecture has passed since the culmination of the High Gothic in the thirteenth century are not to be considered as constituting successive independent styles comparable to those of the earlier past, the Greek or Egyptian, for example, but rather as subsidiary manners of one Modern Style.[24]

Also characteristic of Hitchcock's synthetic approach is the fact that he understood that the Classical Revivals of the mid-eighteenth century were fully as much a product of Romanticism as the revivals of medieval and exotic modes,[25] just as he followed the pervasive impact of the Picturesque ideal from the eighteenth century down to 1929.[26] In the awe-inspiring thirteen-page appendix which concludes the book, Hitchcock offered a breathtaking survey of architecture from the thirteenth century onward, one which he has ever since been amplifying in detail. His most recent book is *German Renaissance Architecture* (Princeton, 1982) and who knows on what flights further back in time he may yet lead us?

The chronicler of current architecture must be an astute critic and Hitchcock has consummately played both parts in innumerable articles which subsequently appeared in professional and scholarly journals. These constituted a useful resource when he again took up the task of providing an integrated consideration of modern architecture. In 1958 there appeared his magisterial Pelican volume, *Architecture: Nineteenth and Twentieth Centuries*, where he shortened the chronological reach in favor of a more encyclopedic view of the last two hundred years (an introduction covers the second half of the eighteenth century; the first chapter commences with 1800). Everyone who has ever tried to make sense of the diverse productions of this immensely rich period must be indebted to the coherent and logical organization that he constructed without sacrificing the complexity that actually exists.

Like life, architecture is dynamic, a condition that Hitchcock has recognized more readily than many of those who seek to be interpreters, if not apologists, for the buildings of their own time. His evaluations and opinions have never become frozen and, thanks to an unquenchable curiosity and an enduring commitment to architecture, he has remained abreast of changing developments. At the same time his early work remains prescient; in 1982, with the tension between traditionalism and modernism once more a factor, his categories of the New Pioneers and the New Tradition are again useful. Similarly, it was his maiden monograph which suggested the organizing principle for this group of essays in his honor.

This volume is dedicated to the Hitchcock who, throughout numerous scholarly incarnations, has continued to wear the mantle of the historian of the modern period and instruct all of us who labor in that fertile field. Herein some of the prominent heroes of his first work on modern architecture— Sir John Soane, Henry Hobson Richardson, Le Corbusier—are reexamined by Dorothy Stroud, John Coolidge, and H. Allen Brooks, respectively; the latter has uncovered a hidden Le Corbusier who once revered the urbanistic traditions he later set out to destroy. The work of some whose achievements were redefined in the Pelican volume—McKim, Mead & White and Antonio Gaudí—has been illuminated further by Mosette Broderick and George Collins. In the same 1958 compendium, Hitchcock introduced new figures for some of us to pursue. Accordingly, Edgar Kaufmann, jr. has cast new light on the architectural activities of the Italian theorist, Carlo Lodoli; David Van Zanten has deepened our under-

standing of the sociopolitical no less than artistic goals of such French Romantic figures as Félix Duban; Henry Millon has provided a detailed account of the process of design of the church of St. Paul's Within the Walls in Rome by the English Victorian, G. E. Street; and I, at Hitchcock's urging, have explored activities in the office of the Dutchman Eduard Cuypers, the "godfather" of the Amsterdam School. Two of the essays relate particularly to Frank Lloyd Wright (Fig. 5), at whose invitation Hitchcock wrote *In the Nature of Materials*. Neil Levine has brought fresh insights into Wright's planning practices, and Thomas McCormick has recovered the early work of Wright's first mentor, Joseph Lyman Silsbee.

Some of the contributors have made a gift of new characters, whose designs, writings, and buildings support Hitchcock's historical assumptions. David De Long has demonstrated that Bruce Goff, a modern maverick who never entered the pages of Hitchcock's surveys, has inherited that Picturesque ideal whose persistence down to the present day Hitchcock had anticipated, and John Harris, J. Mordaunt Crook, and Mark Girouard,

respectively, have exhumed C. H. Tatham, T. G. Jackson, and William Sharp Ogden. Others have chosen themes which supplement Hitchcock's investigations. His methodology has been followed by Richard Carrott, who refines certain terms indispensable to the historian of modern architecture, while Hitchcockian breadth is evoked by William MacDonald, who traces connections between the architecture of ancient Rome and Fascist Italy. Sarah Landau has revised the history of a familiar American building type, the tall office building, and William Jordy has traced the survival into the 1920s of a familiar American interior space, the living hall.

Editing these essays has been a stimulating and fruitful challenge, and one of the special delights is the way that material in one interacts with the topics in another. Such resonances are part of the excitement of the story of modern architecture, which has been so definitively elaborated by Henry-Russell Hitchcock.

Notes

1. Mr. Hitchcock was director of the Smith College Museum of Art from 1949 to 1955. Among his notable acquisitions were *A Cavern, Evening*, 1774, by the British Romantic painter, Joseph Wright of Derby; a landscape, c. 1879, by Paul Gauguin; and a portrait of Jean-François Millet by William Morris Hunt. He and his associate, Mary Bartlett Cowdrey, were responsible for various exhibitions, of which the most notable were *Winslow Homer, Illustrator*, 1951, sparked by the acquisition of *Shipbuilding at Gloucester*, 1871, by Homer, and *Edwin Romanzo Elmer*, 1953, which was followed by the acquisition of *A Mourning Picture*, Elmer's most renowned painting. There was also a centenary exhibition on the London Crystal Palace, done in association with the Massachusetts Institute of Technology, where Hitchcock held a visiting lectureship.

2. In 1931, Hitchcock, with Philip Johnson, began work on his first exhibition, for the Museum of Modern Art (MOMA) in New York (see n. 17). This was followed in 1933 by *Early Modern Architecture: Chicago, 1870*, also done in collaboration with Johnson for MOMA. In 1934 he prepared four circulating architectural exhibitions (three on European subjects, one on "Early Museum Architecture:

1770–1850"); in 1935 he mounted the first exhibition devoted to a selective survey of the building history of an American city, in this case Springfield, Massachusetts. Subsequently he put together similar shows for Worcester and Buffalo. In 1939 Hitchcock prepared *Rhode Island Architecture*, which was the basis for his book of the same title. His *Painting Toward Architecture* (New York, 1948) is essentially a catalogue of the Miller Company Collection of Abstract Art, a collection which circulated nationally and thus in a sense also constitutes an exhibition. Other exhibitions arranged by Mr. Hitchcock are noted in the printed bibliographies.

3. In his autobiography, Virgil Thomson, an old and valued friend, attributes to Hitchcock the major initiative in getting his first opera performed (*Virgil Thomson* [New York, 1966], *passim*). This was *Four Saints in Three Acts* (book by Gertrude Stein), written in 1927 and heard on the piano by Hitchcock in Paris; its world premiere was in 1934 at the Wadsworth Atheneum in Hartford, Connecticut. In his review of that premiere for the *New York Herald Tribune*, Lucius Beebe wrote, "Professor Hitchcock of Wesleyan smashed his opera hat with gay abandon and called for Mr. Thomson. . . . [Then] Mr. Hitchcock tore open his collar and shouted for Mr. [A. Everett, Jr., "Chick"] Austin [director of the Atheneum and another friend of Hitchcock's]." This passage is quoted in John Houseman, *Run-Through* (New York, 1972), p. 118. In a footnote on the same page, Houseman observed that "Russell Hitchcock's enthusiasm must have been prodigious that evening for another reporter described him as 'red-bearded . . . running up and down the aisle screaming bravos and tearing his stiff-bosomed shirt into shreds with each huzzah.'"

4. "Marcel Proust 1927," *The Hound and Horn* I, no. 3 (March 1928): 254–260; "Orlando. A Biography, by Virginia Woolf," *The Hound and Horn* II, no. 2 (January–March 1929): 184–186; "Movie Magazines," *The Hound and Horn* II, no. 1 (September 1928): 95–98.

5. Hitchcock acted as designer when in 1936 he remodeled the colonial house of James Thrall Soby, the art critic and collector. The house still stands in Farmington, Connecticut. As the photo made in Soby's redesigned library attests, Hitchcock cut a dashing figure. His elegant clothes no less than his beard and his enjoyment of fine food and wine made him a most appropriate biographer of Richardson, whose appreciation of fashion led him for his tailoring to Poole's in London (Hitchcock, *The Architecture of H. H. Richardson and His Times*, New York, 1936; rev. ed., New York, 1961, p. 61).

6. Hitchcock began his teaching career as an instructor at his alma mater (Harvard, Class of 1924; M.A., 1927). He was an assistant professor at Vassar College (1927/28), and an assistant and finally full professor at Wesleyan College from 1929 to 1948. He moved to Smith College in 1949 and held the Sophia Smith Professorship there from 1961 until his

retirement in 1968. He then taught for one year at the University of Massachusetts in Amherst. He has been a visiting lecturer at M.I.T. (1946–1948), Yale University (1951/52, 1959/60, 1970), Cambridge University (1962, 1964), and the Institute of Fine Arts of New York University (1940, 1951, and 1957), where since 1968 he has held the post of Adjunct Professor.

7. He is an honorary member of the Royal Institute of British Architects, and received the award of merit of the American Institute of Architects in 1978.

8. Hitchcock's honorary degrees include the D.F.A. from New York University (1969), the D. Litt. from Glasgow University (1973), and the D.H.L. from the University of Pennsylvania (1976) and Wesleyan (1979). He was a Guggenheim fellow (1945/46) and in 1961 received an award from the American Council of Learned Societies. He was Katherine Asher Engel lecturer at Smith in 1965 and Mathews Lecturer at Columbia University in 1971; in 1970 he received the Benjamin Franklin Medal of the Royal Society of Arts. He served as president of the Society of Architectural Historians from 1952 to 1954 and of the Victorian Society in America from 1969 to 1974.

9. The union of architecture and friendship seems especially appropriate in connection with Hitchcock, whose acquaintance is treasured by architects as well as historians and critics. The architect Oscar Stonorov, in his review of *Modern Architecture: Romanticism and Reintegration* (New York, 1929; reprint ed., New York, 1970), which appeared in *Architectural Record* 67 (June 1930): 586, observed that the author's "long journeys and European friendships are happily connected with architecture."

10. In his delightful "Modern Architecture—A Memoir" (*Journal of the Society of Architectural Historians* 27 [December 1968]: 227–233), Hitchcock dispassionately discusses the historiographical questions involved with defining modern architecture's chronological boundaries. While in the nineteenth century "modern" meant the period from the Renaissance onward (as distinct from Antiquity and the Middle Ages), in our century the standard date for the commencement of the modern period has been 1750. Thus in *The History of Architecture* (New York, 1918) by Fiske Kimball and G. H. Edgell, the chapter on modern architecture commences with Soufflot's Pantheon (1757 ff.) and ends with Behrens's Turbine Factory (1909). In a later book, *The American Architecture of To-day* (New York, 1928), Edgell noted that the word *modern* meant to some "contemporary," to others "radical." He proposed that one use *modernist* when the connotation was "radical"; he himself would employ *modern* always to mean current building, which included both "the conservative and the radical, the archaeological and the original" (p. 3). Hitchcock solved the problem in the same year by terming the former The New Tradition, the latter The New Pioneers. Modern for him had immediate sources in the mid-eighteenth century but could indeed be traced back another five hundred years;

here he was in accordance with the nineteenth-century notion.

11. Thus early articles include "America-Europe," published in *i 10* IV, no. 20 (1929): 149–150, an international review based in Amsterdam dedicated to avant-garde movements. For the Paris-based *Cahiers d'Art* he wrote monographs on Frank Lloyd Wright (1928) and J.J.P. Oud (1931).

12. *The Hound and Horn* I, no. 1 (September 1927): 28–35. The same article had appeared a few months earlier in an Advance Issue of this Harvard-based "little review."

13. *Art Studies*, 1928, pp. 175–191.

14. Hitchcock, "Modern Architecture—A Memoir."

15. *The Hound and Horn* II, no. 1 (September 1928): 41–47. Smith, a graduate of Harvard College who briefly attended the Harvard School of Architecture, was one of the friends with whom Hitchcock could most knowledgeably discuss advanced European architecture. He worked in Paris for André Lurçat and also knew Le Corbusier. Hitchcock dedicated his first book to Smith, who died prematurely in 1928.

16. To illustrate traditional architecture, Hitchcock chose the Colonial Revival dormitories by the firm of Ames & Dodge. Both John W. Ames and Edwin Sherrill Dodge were graduates of Harvard College; Dodge attended as well the Harvard School of Architecture and M.I.T. Felicitously, in light of Hitchcock's later teaching career, the dormitories form the "Quadrangle" of Smith College, Northampton, Massachusetts.

17. "Four Harvard Architects," p. 47. In his entry, "The International Style," in the *Encyclopedia of Modern Architecture* (ed. G. Hatje, London, 1963), Hitchcock noted with characteristic objectivity that although the term has been "recurrently under attack since it was first introduced . . . it has become—in considerable part by default—perhaps the most useful name for the dominant architectural current of the second quarter of the 20th century." With Philip Johnson, another Harvard acquaintance, Hitchcock prepared *The International Style: Architecture Since 1922* (New York, 1932; paperback ed., 1966) concurrently with MOMA's (and Hitchcock's) first architectural show, *Modern Architecture: International Exhibition*, but it is *not* the catalogue. Rather, there is a separate volume, with contributions by Lewis Mumford, Alfred Barr, Johnson, and Hitchcock. Confusingly, some copies are titled *Modern Architecture*, while others are called *Modern Architects* (the latter carry the name of W. W. Norton and Company on the title page). Johnson wrote the entry on Mies van der Rohe, while Hitchcock was responsible for the other participants, viz., Wright, Oud, Le Corbusier, Raymond Hood, Howe & Lescaze, Richard Neutra, and the Bowman Brothers.

18. See, for example, my essay, "The Crimson Connection," *Progressive Architecture*, February, 1982: 88–91.

19. *Modern Architecture: Romanticism and Reintegration*, p. 161.

20. Ibid., p. 210.

21. Ibid., p. 219.

22. I cannot resist quoting a comment made by Alfred Barr in his favorable review of *Modern Architecture: Romanticism and Reintegration* for *The Hound and Horn*: "The author's style is perhaps a little too much influenced by the German and his spelling by the French. . . . But these idiosyncracies are to be pardoned one whose first and second names have suffered voluntary post-baptismal hyphenation" (III, no. 3 [April–June 1930]: 435).

23. So noted Donald Drew Egbert in his review of the book for the *Art Bulletin* 13 (March 1930): 98–99. Although in starting the main part of his story in the mid-eighteenth century Hitchcock was following an established convention (see n. 9), by the time *Modern Architecture* was published it had become more common in works on architecture described as "modern" to dispense with all references to buildings constructed much before 1890 (see, for example, Gustav Adolf Platz, *Die Baukunst der Neuesten Zeit* [Berlin, 1927], and Bruno Taut, *Modern Architecture* [London, 1929]); however, in his "Bibliographical Note" Hitchcock refers to Peter Meyer's *Moderne Architektur und Tradition* (unknown to me) which, "like the present book [his own], attempts to bridge the gap between the Hameau de Trianon and Les Terrasses at Garches" (p. 241).

24. *Modern Architecture*, p. xvi.

25. Siegfried Giedion had earlier made the connection in his *Spätbarocker und Romantischer Klassizismus* (Munich, 1922), coining the useful term "Romantic Classicism" (cf. Richard Carrott's essay below). This book is not cited in the bibliographical note to *Modern Architecture*, although it appears in the bibliography for *Architecture: Nineteenth and Twentieth Centuries* (Baltimore, 1958) and in note 1 of the Introduction. In "Modern Architecture—A Memoir," Hitchcock noted that "later, basing myself on pointers from Giedion and Kimball, I could recognize a synthetic style or style phase that could be called Romantic Classicism" (p. 231).

26. Shortly after *Modern Architecture* was completed, Hitchcock embarked on a study of landscape architecture—or more precisely, a history of gardens—for the same publisher. It was not published, due to the demise of the publishing firm; the manuscript is in Hitchcock's possession.

HENRY-RUSSELL HITCHCOCK
AND THE NEW TRADITION

Vincent Scully

IN 1939, WHEN HENRY-RUSSELL Hitchcock published the W. G. Low House (Fig. 1) of 1887 in Bristol, Rhode Island, by McKim, Mead & White as plate 67 of his *Rhode Island Architecture*,[1] he set in train a series of events that were to affect the course of American architecture in the second half of the twentieth century. Hitchcock's earliest work had been directed toward the emerging modern architecture of Europe. His first book on that subject, *Modern Architecture, Romanticism and Reintegration*, of 1929,[2] had identified two important and highly different modes within that architecture, one of which Hitchcock called the New Tradition, the other, the New Pioneers. To us today, the first mode probably seems even more important than it did to Hitchcock in 1929. It comprises, in fact, the progressive twentieth-century architecture that had grown out of the intrinsic development of the nineteenth-century vernacular and academic traditions, its roots deep in history but consistently alive and in process of articulation throughout the complex urbanistic growth of the modern period. Against this architecture and its vernacular development, Hitchcock's New Pioneers—Gropius, Mies, Oud, Le Corbusier, et al—had resolutely set their iconoclastic faces, condemning *in toto* the traditional vernacular and urbanistic achievements of the recent past. In 1929, Hitchcock was able to preserve a balance of judgment between the ruthlessly revolutionary and the more traditional points of view, although his term, "The New Pioneers," was, especially for an American, emotionally weighted enough. But by 1932, under the brilliant, impatient, and persuasive influence of his collaborator, Philip Johnson, Hitchcock had swung wholly over to the revolutionary camp. Instinctively, though, he and Johnson academicized the more inchoate, visionary, and activist aspects of the modern movement into a clear, prescriptive canon of design, and they named it in terms which many of its major protagonists found most distasteful: in terms of style—hence, The International Style.

That done, Hitchcock, as if driven once more by his deeply scholarly instincts to keep a balance and to redress exaggerations, set out to dig back into the roots of what amounted to the New Tradition—not, it should be noted, into the sources of his New Pioneers. In so doing, he made another significant shift; he turned to nineteenth-century America, not to Europe. Out of all this came his book, *The Architecture of H. H. Richardson and His Times*,[3] of 1936, written in conjunction with an exhibition of Richardson's architecture which he prepared for the Museum of Modern Art. Here indeed another new tradition was set, wherein the museum at intervals over the years would step beyond the merely contemporary and the canonically "modern." This precedent was to have important effects later, as in Arthur Drexler's Beaux-Arts show of 1975,[4] which was intended to fill out, as Hitchcock had begun to do, the true history of nineteenth-century architecture in order to replace the Modern movement's mythologized image of it.

In the book on Richardson, Hitchcock repeatedly referred to the strengths of the vernacular and academic traditions, and he was drawn in domestic architecture toward the Shingle Style, which he called "Suburban Richardsonian." From this interest he was led to the shingled cottages of Rhode Island, and he published some of the best of them in 1939: the Watts Sherman, the Robert Goelet, and the Isaac Bell houses in Newport, and the Low House itself. In the caption for

the Low House he wrote: "A masterpiece among American summer houses, purged of the extreme picturesqueness of the 'Queen Anne,' but not bound by the academic discipline of the colonial revival. To be compared with Richardson's and Wright's best wooden houses." And in the text (p. 60), he said of it and its kind, "But what is really early American is the spirit: the ease, the breadth, the relation to the site." He noted also that "the detail is reduced almost to zero." To him at that time this last quality was an especially important and desirable one, and he pursued it in the short series of rather dreary twentieth-century houses which he sought out and included among his illustrations. Despite his admiration for the Low House, the International Style still represented for him not only the immediate present (which it was only in part) but the future as well. Of the best and most ambitious of that

group, the house by Richard Neutra for John Nicholas Brown, of 1937/38—which had to be dragged in more or less by force because it was built on Fisher's Island in New York—Hitchcock said in part: "Here is a house developed from the interior outward, not the other way around, yet it adapts itself to the ocean site as do none of the Newport houses."

Nevertheless, when one opened the Rhode Island book it was the Low House that caught one's eye, and for those of us who knew at that time only as much about American architecture as was then available in publication, the Low House destroyed most of our preconceptions and started our interest up again. At least it did so for me when I first saw it in the late 1940s; almost alone it persuaded me to write my doctoral dissertation on American nineteenth-century domestic architecture in wood. Since there was no one at Yale

2. Robert Venturi, project for a beach house, 1959. Elevation drawing. (Drawing: Venturi, Rauch & Scott Brown, Philadelphia.)

who was especially interested in that subject, George Heard Hamilton very generously put me in touch with Professor Hitchcock, and he, though teaching at Wesleyan, most kindly consented to serve as an unofficial adviser. In that role he opened to me the extensive file of photographs and drawings of American architecture that he had collected and made me free of his library as well. Among his books was Sheldon's *Artistic Country Seats*,[5] not then available at Yale. From these and related materials the position of the Low House in American architecture soon began to emerge: it stood between, for example, the gabled houses by Bruce Price at Tuxedo Park, of 1885/86 and Frank Lloyd Wright's own house in Oak Park, of 1889. My dissertation of 1949 ("The Cottage Style") and various publications during the fifties, among them "The Stick Style" and "The Shingle Style," "American Villas," and *The Shingle Style*,[6] all essentially derived from this beginning, which was due to Hitchcock's example and assistance.

What happened thereafter is well known. In 1959 the Low House triggered the famous Project for a Beach House (Fig. 2) by Robert Venturi, the pioneer of what I came to call "the Shingle Style today."[7] It was the first of a new vernacular or a restoration of the old. The process reversed that by which Wright had transformed the Shingle Style into the forms of his own early maturity, out of which in some considerable measure the International Style itself had taken shape. Venturi's design moved backward, as it were, toward the revival, in the Trubek and Wislocki houses on Nantucket, not only of the Shingle Style but also of the whole vernacular tradition out of which the Shingle Style had originally developed. It cut through three generations of

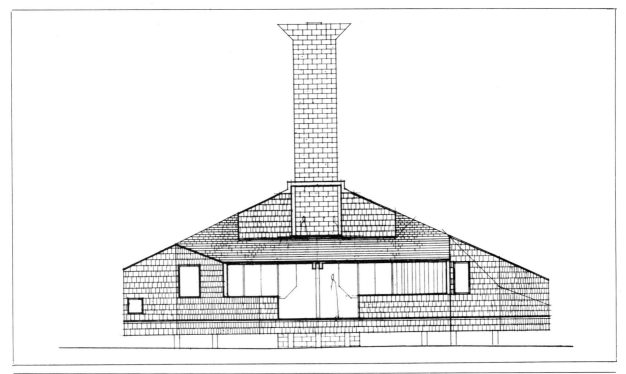

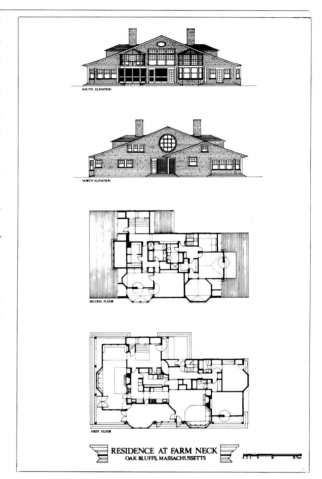

3. House, Oak Bluffs, Martha's Vineyard, Massachusetts. Robert A. M. Stern, 1980/81. Plans and elevations. (Drawing: R.A.M. Stern Associates, New York City.)

architectural adventures to historical roots and symbolic realities. By 1980 the work of numerous architects, from Charles Moore to Robert A. M. Stern, himself a prolific critic and historian of American architecture, had moved wholly into the vernacular strain, traditional details and all—farther into it, perhaps, than the Low House itself, with its "detail . . . reduced almost to zero." Stern's design (Fig. 3), now being built on Martha's Vineyard, is an advanced example.

It therefore follows that Hitchcock, himself a Pioneer in the establishment of the International Style, also acted as an historical precursor of what has come to be called Post-Modernism but which might in this instance better be described as the resurrection of that New Tradition which had been perceived in his earliest work (see above p. 5).

Notes

1. H.-R. Hitchcock, *Rhode Island Architecture* (Providence, R.I.: Rhode Island Museum Press, 1939; reprint ed., New York: Da Capo Press, 1968).
2. Hitchcock, *Modern Architecture: Romanticism and Reintegration* (New York: Payson and Clark, 1929; reprint ed., New York: Hacker Art Books, 1970).
3. Hitchcock, *The Architecture of H. H. Richardson and His Times* (New York: Museum of Modern Art, 1936; rev. ed., Cambridge, Mass.: M.I.T. Press, 1966).
4. Arthur Drexler, ed., *The Architecture of the Ecole des Beaux-Arts* (New York: Museum of Modern Art, 1977).
5. George Sheldon, *Artistic Country Seats*, 2 vols. in 5 parts (New York: D. Appleton, 1886–1887).
6. Vincent J. Scully, Jr., "Romantic Rationalism and the Expression of Structure in Wood: Downing, Wheeler, Gardner and the 'Stick Style' 1840–1876," *Art Bulletin* 35 (June 1953); "The Shingle Style," in Antoinette F. Downing and Vincent J. Scully, Jr., *The Architectural Heritage of Newport, Rhode Island* (Cambridge, Mass.: Clarkson N. Potter, 1952); "American Villas: Inventiveness in the American Suburb from Downing to Wright," *Architectural Review* 115 (March 1954): 168–179; and *The Shingle Style* (New Haven: Yale University Press, 1955; rev. and exp. ed., New Haven: Yale University Press, 1971).
7. Scully, *The Shingle Style Today, or, The Historian's Revenge* (New York: George Braziller, 1974).

THE AGE OF ROMANTICISM RATIONALISM, REVIVALISM, AND ECLECTICISM, 1740-1900

REVIVALS AND ARCHAISMS

Richard G. Carrott

THIS ESSAY IS AN ATTEMPT TO PRO-pose some degree of specificity and precision in the use of two art-historical terms that often are used so loosely as to seem more or less interchangeable.[1] I refer to the terms "revival" and "archaism." In considering the perplexing problems of eclecticism,[2] a wide-ranging phenomenon we have only begun to chart, these two concepts emerge as distinctly different. Nor should this come as any surprise. After all, we have been shown that a "renaissance" is not the same thing as a "renascence," upper-class British pronunciation notwithstanding.[3] "Historicism," which refers to a related but certainly separate problem, is another term currently being examined by contemporary scholarship.[4]

Although a revival is not the same as an archaism, there are, nevertheless, close parallels between them, and it is these similarities—particularly the idea of "a copy"—that lead to the confusion of the two designations. Both archaizing and revival artists have a passionate enthusiasm for, and a technical as well as scholarly knowledge of, the art of a previous era. In formal terms, both attempt to re-create, or at least recall, a style of the past, preferably of a rather distant past. But whereas the archaizing artist attempts to mirror that style as closely as he can, the revival artist seeks to produce new interpretations of that past mode, albeit copying specific architectonic forms and decorative motifs. Thus, the latter puts new wine in old bottles, to use Wölfflin's metaphor, while the former attempts to rebottle old wine in old bottles.[5] An archaism, therefore, *seems* to be a copy, whereas a revival monument can never be considered a copy—not even a not-very-good-copy-at-that type of copy.

Perhaps the two phenomena are more closely related in terms of iconography. Both attempt to evoke an idea associated with the past. But for the revival artist there is a new ingredient, namely, the application of contemporary associational ideas to the recalled forms, regardless of whether those ideas actually were part of the symbolic language of the original culture or merely seem to have been so.

Thus, archaisms in later Hellenistic sculpture may have attempted to re-create what appears to be an actual Greek archaic work and to evoke the aesthetic, and perhaps ethical, ideas of that earlier period.[6] A nineteenth-century revival building, on the other hand, could never be mistaken for an example of the "original" period, not even by a layman. Furthermore, the associations involved may not have been evident in the structures of that original era. Thomas Jefferson's Virginia State Capitol in Richmond (1785–1796) (Fig. 1) was certainly not intended to call forth thoughts of Roman religious paganism, as would the Maison Carrée at Nîmes (c. A.D. 1),[7] the very monument that inspired it. Or, in reversed historical perspective, an Egyptian Ptolemaic tem-

1. (left) Virginia State Capitol, Richmond. Thomas Jefferson, 1785–1796. Model, 1785. (Photo: Virginia State Library.)

2. Medical College of Virginia, Richmond. Thomas S. Stewart, 1844. (Photo: Virginia Historic Landmarks Commission.)

ple complex, in its day, must have elicited some kind of awesome religious feeling, whereas the revival building based on such temple forms but serving as a medical college (Fig. 2) calls up ideas, not of religion, but of the ancient medical knowledge that has been associated with Egypt since long before the time of Herodotus. Another example would be the New York City Halls of Justice and House of Detention complex (1835–1838) (Fig. 3), also based on ancient Egyptian

temple forms but serving a secular, albeit lofty, purpose.

Another difference between an archaism and a revival is that the former arrives on the scene fully developed, whereas the revival goes through a series of evolutionary stages.[8] Thus, in the revivification of classical antiquity that took place in the late eighteenth and early nineteenth centuries, one may trace a linear series of phases: Pseudo-Classicism, Romantic Classicism,[9] and

Classical Revival. In painting, the Pseudo-Classical is represented by works of Josèphe-Marie Vien, Angelica Kauffmann, and Anton Raffael Mengs. However much influence the discovery of Pompeian wall paintings may have had in terms of subject matter, organization, and archaeologically correct trappings, Vien's *Sale of Loves* (1763), with its soft, curving forms, pretty colors, and choice of subject matter, betrays far more than a hint of the Rococo. It is only seemingly classical and thus is more properly called Pseudo-Classical.

A truer classical spirit is apparent in Jacques Louis David's *Oath of the Horatii* (1785). The hard, severe forms of this painting, the simple geometry of its composition, the precise linearism of its technique, its restricted and direct color schemes, as well as its subject matter, all constitute a parallel in the figural arts to architecture's Romantic Classicism.

The third phase may be exemplified by later Davidian works such as *Leonidas at Thermophylae* (1814), in which a sense of Romantic Classical severity of form and organization is replaced by a compulsive interest in archaeological correctness and enriching detail. Here we have the full-fledged Classical Revival, the achievement of scholarly exactitude.

These same points can be made about the architecture of the period. The sequence of protagonists would be Ange-Jacques Gabriel and Richard Mique for the first phase, Claude-Nicolas Ledoux and Etienne-Louis Boullée for the second, and Thomas Jefferson, Pierre Vignon, and J.-F.-T. Chalgrin for the third. While Pseudo-Classicism bespeaks a classicizing taste within a governing Rococo style, Romantic Classicism, with its will toward solid geometric shapes, additive organization, severity of decoration, eccentric proportions, and intraplay of forms, is a new style in itself. The third phase, Classical Revival, somewhat vitiates these principles, mostly through its obsession with "archaeological" correctness and its increasing appetite for rich and heavy decoration, yet it is still a part of or related to Romantic Classicism.

Gabriel's Petit Trianon (1762–1764), frequently tagged as an example of Neo-Classicism or *le style Louis Seize*, can for our purposes be denominated as Pseudo-Classical. It might seem "classically" simple when contrasted with the architecture of the preceding century in France (e.g., Château de Cheverny), but when compared to Ledoux's Petit Château at Eaubonne (1776) (Fig. 4) of some ten years later, its elegant proportions and Corinthian decorative accents project a Rococo fragility. The Ledolcian example, on the other hand, indicates the true appearance on the scene of that radical new style, Romantic Classicism, which is as geometrically severe and simple as David's *Oath of the Horatii*.[10]

The final phase in this system, when fully mature, gives us such overwhelming monuments of the First Empire as Vignon's Madeleine (completed by J.-J.-M. Huvé,) and Chalgrin's Arc de Triomphe de l'Etoile (completed by G. A. Blouet). Whereas in their basic temple and triumphal-arch forms these enormous monuments certainly recall usually more diminutively scaled structures of the Roman Empire, the essential formal quality that identifies this phase is the taste for a rich and ponderous profusion of "archaeologically" correct decorative motifs.

The initial impulse and simpler realization of this cycle can be witnessed in the familiar example of Jefferson's Virginia State Capitol (1785–1796) (Fig. 1), in which a sense of archaeological correctness certainly plays a dominant role. But the Richmond building exhibits significant differences from its Maison Carrée prototype: the change from Corinthian to Ionic; the abandonment of the pseudoperipteral half-columns; a different elevation and interior; and, as we have noted, a different purpose. This particular monument, coming as it does from the earliest years of the Classical Revival phase, retains some of the simplicity of the Romantic Classical phase (which could have been a contributing factor to the change from Corinthian to Ionic, a mutation rather contrary to the elaboration of ornamental *embonpoint* that distinguishes the more mature examples of this phase). But it is important to note that it is modeled on a distinct antique monument and that, at the same time, there are unabashed divergences from that paradigm.

Thus, Classical Revival, even when considered alone, is a revival in the evolutionary sense we have discussed above, and not an archaism. Suffice it to say, all three phases when taken together in their cyclical development are, of course, a revival.

There is a similar progression in the Egyptian Revival of this same period.[11] Initially, Nilotic motifs provided part of the vocabulary for late Rococo *bizzarria*. This is seen, for example, in the remarkable fireplace designs of G. B. Piranesi (1769) (Fig. 5), in an ice house—of all things—by P.-F.-L. Dubois (c. 1800), and in an astonishing swing by J.-B. Kléber (1787) (Fig. 6), items which hardly recall pharaohnic Egypt.[12] In this late-eighteenth-century fascination with

a culture *plus antique que l'antiquité*, we have a group of architectural objects which can easily be identified as "Egyptian" but which, stylistically, we recognize as being Rococo. In other words, just as we have the "Pseudo-Classic," we have a category that might be called the "Pseudo-Egyptian."

The origin of the true Egyptian Revival occurs with the appearance of the great Napoleonic archaeological publications on Egypt: Dominique Vivant Denon's privately produced *Voyage dans la Basse et la Haute Egypte pendant les compagnes du général Bonaparte*, and the staggering official undertaking of the Commission des Monuments d'Egypte, *Description de l'Egypte, ou Recueil des observations et des recherches*

qui ont été faites en Egypte pendant l'expedition de l'armée françqise, publié par les ordres de Sa Majesté l'empereur Napoleon le Grand. The former, initially three volumes, appeared in 1802 and quickly ran through several editions in both French and English (Fig. 7). The latter's twenty-odd volumes were produced over a nineteen-year span, 1809 to 1828 (Figs. 8, 9). These publications were remarkably thorough in their treatment of Egyptian antiquities, although, of course, the later work was considerably more expanded than the Denon undertaking.

It was through these generously illustrated publications that American and European architects could gain a clear understanding of ancient Nilotic architecture and note how conveniently and effectively this style could express the revolutionary ideals of Romantic Classicism—as it does in John Haviland's New York City Halls of Justice and House of Detention (Fig. 3) and T. S. Stewart's Medical College of Virginia (Fig. 2). Thus, as opposed to the Pseudo-Egyptian mode, we have a true revival in clear and unadulterated form.

Parallels to the Classical Revival are not so easily found in the development of revived Egyptianism, although there is in the later phases of the Egyptian Revival a preoccupation with heavy forms and decorative richness based on "proper" Egyptian motifs. These structures may resemble their Egyptian prototypes far less than Napoleon's monuments for the *grandeur*-ization of Paris resemble their Roman paradigms, but there is the same kind of ponderous and elaborate ornamentation that can be discerned in such works as Minard Lafever's project for a monument to George Washington in New York City (1854) (Fig. 10) or Stephen Decatur Button's cemetery entrance in Philadelphia (1849) (Fig. 11). Yet even these retain an aesthetic of simple geometric forms no matter how heavy or decorated they are. This is one of the principles of Classical Revival architecture.

Certainly the beginnings of the Egyptian Revival are to be found in the *bizzarria* of a fading Rococo style, but the true manifestation of the movement is to be seen in later works that reflect an irreducible final statement of Romantic Clas-

sicism. Even as the "purity" of the Ledolcian phases of the latter breaks down in favor of a more meretricious taste with the Classical Revival, so, too, do we find a similar evolution within the more conflated Egyptian Revival.

It should be noted, of course, that there have been other "revivals" of the Egyptian taste (vis-à-vis style) than that discussed above.[13] Some might cite as a first Egyptian Revival those works commissioned by the Emperor Hadrian, to which we owe the only hideous statue of the beautiful Antinoüs ever created. Egyptian-type artifacts, including obelisks, were produced in Rome up until the Christian era.[14] But since they represent an attempt to re-create as exactly as possible the style, subject matter, and spirit of an earlier age, it would seem that they are examples of archaisms, renascences of Egypt rather than a renaissance. In other words, the so-called Hadrianic Egyptian Revival is in reality not a revival at all,

at least not as we have defined the term.[15]

Perhaps the most essential point about a revival is that exact copies of monuments of the original culture do not exist; the architects of a revival are neither interested in, nor committed to, making copies of prototypical structures. Yet it is only in the last thirty years that architectural historians and critics have begun to liberate themselves fully from the shackles of a strange and perverse prejudice which denied the qualities of artistic imagination and creative originality (so necessary to any valid aesthetic movement) to the architectural revivals of the nineteenth century.[16] Thus, while we recognize the sources for revival monuments, it is necessary to be aware of the new and different treatment accorded such structures. We might apply that treatment to some of the major Egyptian Revival monuments in order to establish the validity of the movement as indeed a revival for reasons beyond that of its having a cyclical evolution similar to the revival of classical antiquity. By explicating more fully this revival and its similarities in treatment and theory to another revival—namely, the Classical—we may be able to see a cohesive-

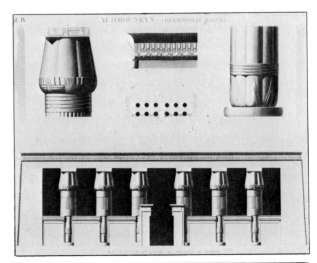

10. *Minard Lafever, project for Washington Monument, New York City, 1854. (Illustration: M. Lafever,* The Architectural Instructor, *pl. C.)*

11. *Odd Fellows Cemetery, Philadelphia. Stephen Decatur Button, 1849. Entrance. (Illustration:* Ballou's Pictorial Drawing Room Companion, *X, 1856, p. 25.)*

ness in the concept of revivals in general.

Formally, Egyptian Revival architecture diverged from the strict canons of plan, composition, organization, and elevation[17] inherent in pharaohnic monuments, all the while providing a final crystallization of Romantic Classical forms (as Professor Hitchcock has remarked).[18] In terms of iconography, it served as a singularly effective vehicle for the expression of the sublime as well as for the more literal facets of *l'architecture parlante*, which in the nineteenth century emerged in the guise of associationism. Thus, what was called for was an architecture that in both form and detail evoked the image of ancient Egypt without replicating it. The requisite sources, of course, were provided by Denon's *Voyage* and the *Description*.

Sometimes the sense for the sublime, however, could be evoked by less archaeologically precise sources, as in the case of Louis-François Cassas's *ex ante facto* Aïdian temple (1799) (Fig. 12). Naturally this was meant to be a reconstruction, even if fanciful, of a "typical" ancient Egyptian temple, not a project for a contemporary building. But it is important for us to realize that such quasi-archaeological fantasies served, in an especially effective manner, to provide a kind of *esprit du style* which could be used as a source for the iconographical attributes a revived style hoped to evoke. Etienne-Louis Boullée's megalomaniacal pyramid-cenotaph projects of the late eighteenth century are similar examples of this.

By the 1830s in America, standard professional practice demanded that revival architects concern themselves with a stricter adherence to archaeological prototypes even though a sublime effect was desired. Joseph Bigelow, an architect by avocation, designed the Mount Auburn Cemetery entrance in Cambridge, Massachusetts, in

12. *Restoration of an Egyptian Temple. (Illustration: L.-F. Cassas,* Voyage pittoresque . . . , *pl. 96.)*
13. *Mount Auburn Cemetery, Cambridge, Massachusetts. Jacob Bigelow, 1831. Entrance. (Photo: University of California at Riverside Photo Collection.)*

1831 (Fig. 13), using a plate from the *Description* as his source. The sublime scale of the prototype obviously has been reduced, but the structure is impressive nonetheless. The ultimate sublime experience, after all, is death itself (symbolized in a necropolis), and the funerary associations with ancient Egypt are apparent. What is non-Egyptian is the composition of the whole, with its interior colonnades and gate lodges. The elements are properly Egyptian, but the arrangement is not. Equally significant is the Biblical inscription on the rear lintel of the gate, "Then Shall Dust Return to Earth As It Was"; exorcizing-of-paganism motifs like this are found in almost all Egyptian Revival cemetery gates.

The same may be said of New Haven's Grove Street Cemetery portal (1844) by Henry Austin (Fig. 14) (whose scriptural quotation, "The Dead Shall Be Raised," has undoubtedly been lost on countless generations of Yale students). Again we have a convincing Egyptian structure based on a plate from Austin's copy of the *Description* (Fig. 9), although there is no example of any actual Egyptian gate given *distyle in antis* treatment. One might further note that although the order is different—papyrus open-flower rather than papyrus bud—the general proportions and treatment of cornice areas seem more like an illustration of the temple at Esne (Fig. 7) in Denon's *Voyage*, a work that certainly was known to Austin. The point to emphasize here is that not one but two specific monuments can serve as eclectic sources for a revival structure, thus further transforming the concept of "a copy."

As to nonfunerary architecture, contemporary critics considered Egyptian Revival fitting for a variety of building types, but particularly for prisons. Curiously, this was not because of the stout walls and reduced fenestration that prisons required, but because the mode symbolized the sublimity of justice and the timelessness of legal codes. Very specifically, these structures, which were all reform prisons, were not intended to call forth ideas of "gloominess and retribution" (which Gothic dungeons evoked), but rather feelings of "awesomeness and repentance."[19]

John Haviland's New Jersey State Penitentiary at Trenton (1832–1836) (Fig. 15) certainly looked Egyptian and even used hieroglyphics copied from a plate in the *Description* (A. vol. 1, pl. 35). Yet in spite of this, and of the pylon forms, cavetto cornices, battered walls, and torus moldings, we know of no Egyptian building that actually looked like this. The Nilotic forms were organized around such functional elements as the raised dock to accommodate prisoners disembarking from vans. Similarly, the Piranesi stepped-corbel windows (Fig. 1) above the entrance — a

"revived" pseudo-Revival motif—are not found anywhere in ancient Egyptian architecture.

The New York City Halls of Justice and House of Detention complex (1835–1838) (Fig. 3), also by Haviland—later nicknamed "The Tombs," thus missing the point—is also an example of a convincingly Egyptian style that resembles no ancient structure. One may be struck, of course, by the simple, solid block forms, especially in contrast with neighboring buildings; even the idiosyncratic awnings, shrubbery, and ivy trellises (added later) could not disguise the Romantic Classical aesthetic. But equally striking is its departure from antique Egyptian forms in terms of plan, elevation, interior and exterior spaces, and the like. The most striking divergence might well be that of the axes.

Thomas S. Stewart's Medical College of Virginia of 1844 (Fig. 2) betrays even more of a

THE DEAD SHALL BE RAISED.

Romantic Classical bias with its virtually unrelieved lofty cubic simplicity. Its more vertical proportions (in comparison to "The Tombs") are, of course, more typical of the 1840s rather than of the 1830s. The fact remains, however, that no specific copy was intended, despite the association of medical science with ancient Egypt. Thus we are presented with an elegant yet monumental structure which can only be read as Egyptian in style (even the fence posts, for example, are in the form of mummies), but which in no way can be mistaken for a Ramesside palace or a Ptolemaic temple.

Finally, with the later phase of the Egyptian Revival (Figs. 10, 11), already mentioned, it can be seen how truly eclectic the movement became in that specific borrowings are almost impossible to identify. Nevertheless, for all of its heavy surface decoration, Lafever's projected monument to Washington (1854) certainly was based on a simple Egyptian obelisk, though of colossal proportions. Button's Odd Fellows' Cemetery entrance of 1849 was made up of two gates flanking a center section that served as a funerary chapel.

The *distyle in antis* and the exorcising battered-pier-cum-church-steeple notwithstanding, it surely recalls an ancient Egyptian kiosque-temple. The memorial or funerary nature of these nineteenth-century structures can be closely related to ideas associated with the Land of the Nile, but there really were no cemetery gates as such, nor any megalomaniacally proportioned single obelisks sprouting from two-storied centralized temples in pharaohnic Egypt. The revival architects adopted a thoroughly creative handling of the form, the function, and even the iconography of the structures they designed, although they were obviously concerned with the archaeological correctness of individual forms and decorative details so that their buildings would unmistakably project a feeling of "Egyptian-ness."

The question of the Gothic Revival inevitably comes to mind. It would be blissfully agreeable if it could neatly parallel the others that have been discussed, but alas, no such Procrustean luck. Gothic forms, no matter how transmuted, simply do not evoke a Romantic Classical, or even Classical, spirit. But certain similarities do emerge. Horace Walpole and Company's Strawberry Hill (1753–c. 1778), as a Georgian house remodeled in a Neo-Gothic style, is certainly as Rococo as Chinese Chippendale and thus could be (and has been) called Pseudo-Gothic. In a sense, Batty Langley's 1742 publication *Gothick Architecture Improved* is of the same ilk.

A. W. N. Pugin carried the banner for the next phase of the style. In this, the desiderata are archaeologically correct forms and decorative details arranged in a relatively nonpicturesque manner. While one could never call his work anti-Picturesque, it is certainly not flamboyantly so either. His *oeuvre* in this mode extends from St. Marie's, Derby (1838–39), to St. Barnabas's, Nottingham (1842–1844), to his own church at Ramsgate (1846–1851). The formal sources for these stem from such publications as his *The True Principles of Gothic Architecture* (1848), which called for archaeological authenticity. But it was Pugin's *Contrasts* (1836) that provided the iconography of this phase of the style. As a convert to Roman Catholicism, he saw English Perpendicular Gothic as symbolic of a Christian Golden Age of peace, justice, morality, and social and aesthetic responsibility. His religious architecture did not copy specific medieval churches but gave original, creative, yet convincing interpretations of the style. In this respect, it is like the second phase of the Classical and Egyptian Revivals.

Similarly, the heavily decorated, ponderous architecture of such mid-Victorian monuments as William Butterfield's All Saints, Margaret Street (1848–1859), and G. G. Scott's Midland Hotel at St. Pancras Station (1865) parallel the third phase of other revivals. The forms and details of these buildings are extremely transmuted Gothic, yet they leave no doubt in the viewer's mind that they are based, however distantly, on "true" Gothic elements. And although the Gothic style of a railroad hotel may be difficult to explain iconographically, the use of the style, with its non-English, Continental Roman Catholic allusions, for a High Anglican church is logical enough. At any rate, it is evident that this revival, too, evolves through a series of phases which are not unlike those of the other two revivals discussed above.[20]

It is to be hoped that some clarification of terms can be gleaned from the above, although attempting definitions is rather like walking a tightrope.

On the one hand, there is the constant danger of oversimplifying a complex problem, and on the other, there is the temptation to hedge. It should emerge, however, that "archaism" ought not to be used interchangeably with "revival." These two related concepts are frequently discussed in current art historical scholarship, and it is all too easy to cross the defining boundaries that give meaningful and effective focus to such discussions.

Neither the archaism nor the revival attempts an exact copy, an effort that belongs only to the history of forgery. But it is also true that the artist who creates an archaism is consciously, or even unconsciously, striving to achieve a work of art that reproduces a past style. Perhaps this concept can be likened to that concerning the creation of styles of costumes, coiffures, furniture, and the like in films with historical settings. Certainly the designers of such elements in the 1908 cinematic version of *Romeo and Juliet* considered they were evoking Shakespearean Verona. Even an audience viewing the film today could be reasonably convinced of the authenticity of the costumes and accouterments. Yet, upon reflection, anyone taking a second look would realize that these were in a very different style than the same elements in equally convincing subsequent versions of the same story. Indeed, the Norma Shearer vehicle of the thirties is different from the Zeffirelli production of the sixties in more ways than the mere absence of color in the former or clothing in the latter. There is something in every historical film that betrays the taste of the time in which it was made. The intent in all of them, however, is to re-create the period in which the drama purportedly occurred.

As for examples in the history of cinema of what we have tried to define as a revival, one need only call forth those innumerable films that recount a modern story but which are set in the past. Thus the meaning of the plot is entirely involved with the here-and-now even though the vehicle for it is clothed in a recognizable historical mode. For instance, the Mae West-W. C. Fields triumph, *My Little Chickadee*, for all its popularity over the past two decades, is a thoroughly late-thirties comedy even though it is apparently set in the 1870s. Thus the visual forms recall the Old Far West, but the iconography concerns the taste and comic routines of the era of the later New Deal. This is not so different from using the forms and trappings of an ancient culture to clothe a nineteenth-century reform prison.

A revival, as we have seen, is not an attempt to re-create a mirror image of the past. With a life force of its own, it evolves in a cycle of stages, each with its own meaning and spirit and each relevant to its own time. Revivalism uses a historical vocabulary within contemporary syntax.

Without wishing to denigrate one of these terms to the profit of the other, a proverb among French chefs might be recalled: "One can imitate, but one cannot always equal." Perhaps an archaism imitates, but a revival attempts to equal.

Notes

I am indebted to my research assistant, Keith C. Simmons, for his diligent aid in numerous matters concerning this paper and for several helpful suggestions and contributions.

1. The source for this essay stems from a paper, "The Origins of the Egyptian Revival," delivered at Professor Seymour Howard's session on Archaisms held at the 1978 Annual Meeting of the College Art Association in New York City.
2. For an introduction to some of the problems of eclecticism, see Richard G. Carrott, *The Egyptian Revival; its Monuments, Sources and Meaning 1808–1858* (Berkeley, Los Angeles, and London, 1978), pp. 1–21.
3. Erwin Panofsky, *Renaissance and Renascences in West-*

ern Art (New York, 1972). Although this book does not really deal with the question at hand here, the author's discussion of the differences between the Renaissance and medieval renascences in the fifth section of chapter 2 provides some interesting parallels, although it would stretch matters to try to imply that the Renaissance was a revival and the medieval renascenses were archaisms.

4. The question of historicism is touched upon in the "catalogue" of the Museum of Modern Art exhibition of Beaux-Arts architecture, Arthur Drexler, editor, *The Architecture of the Ecole des Beaux-Arts* (New York, 1977). See also Peter Collins, *Changing Ideals of Modern Architecture* (Montreal, 1965), pp. 29–41 ("The Influence of Historiography"); and David Van Zanten, "Félix Duban and the Buildings of the Ecole des Beaux-Arts 1832–1840," *Journal of the Society of Architectural Historians*, 37 (October 1978): 161–174. This matter is under further consideration by Christopher C. Mead of the Art Department of the University of New Mexico, Albuquerque, in his doctoral dissertation on Charles Garnier for the University of Pennsylvania.

5. Heinrich Wölfflin, *The Sense of Form in Art* (New York, 1958), p. 13 ff.

6. The whole problem of archaisms in Greek art is a complex one for those of us who are not classical archaeologists. Professor Ridgway in a recent work carefully distinguishes between *archaizing* ("a work of sculpture which belongs clearly and unequivocally to a period later than 480 and which . . . retains a few formal traits of [the] Archaic style, such as coiffures, pattern of folds, gestures and the like"), *archaistic* ("works of art in which archaic traits predominate, and only a few anachronistic details betray the sculptor's knowledge of later styles"), and *lingering archaic* (sculpture "executed after 480 but in a coherent Archaic style [which] seems at first fully archaic"). (Brunhilde Sismundo Ridgway, *The Archaic Style in Greek Art* [Princeton, 1977], p. 303.)

It would appear that our use of the term *archaism* refers to the second of these definitions, while lingering archaic sculpture might be termed *survival*. An archaizing work, one might expect, refers to sculpture exhibiting *retarditaire* elements.

This question has been under consideration for some time now by Christine Mitchell Havelock, who has published two excellent articles which shed considerable light on the problems of Hellenistic archaisms and provide both a clear summary and a nice bibliography of past scholarship in this specialized area. (Christine Mitchell Havelock, "Archaistic Reliefs of the Hellenistic Period," *American Journal of Archaeology* 68 (January 1964): 43–58; "The Archaic as Survival versus the Archaistic as a New Style," *American Journal of Archaeology* 69 (December 1965): 330–341.) In the earlier of the two articles, the author distinguishes between two phases of Hellenistic archaiz-

ing. The earlier one "is not fully governed by a desire to imitate the archaic" and indeed can betray "a formal conception which is far removed from the archaic" (p. 57). In phase II, "The net result is a style in which a relatively successful imitation of the archaic is characteristic" (ibid.). Works from the latter are referred to as "archaisms" in this essay.

More recently, in a paper presented at the *Archaisms in the History of Art* session of the 1978 College Art Association meeting (see n. 1 above), "Ptolemy I and the Rise of the Greek Archaistic Style," Professor Havelock seems to have found an example of early Hellenistic archaizing (i.e., her "phase I") which "reads" as if it were from the later period (phase II). If I have correctly understood the abstract of her paper, this seems to call into question the concept of archaizing as "a continuous and gradually evolving style."

7. This, in spite of the Maison Carrée's having once served as a consulate.

8. See n. 6 above. It would appear that Professor Ridgway's "archaizing," "archaistic," and "lingering archaic" do not logically evolve one to the other. Nor do Professor Havelock's "phase I" and "phase II" seem to lead cyclically from the earlier forms to the later.

9. The term "pseudo-Classicism" was coined by P. F. Schmidt in "Der Pseudoklassizismus des 18 Jahrhunderts," *Monatschefte für Kunstwissenschaft*, VIII, 1915, pp. 372–378, 409–422. See Robert Rosenblum, *Transformations in Late Eighteenth-Century Art* (Princeton, 1967), p. 19. For a clear discussion of the genesis and meaning of the seemingly contradictory term "Romantic Classicism," see H.-R. Hitchcock, *Architecture: Nineteenth and Twentieth Centuries* (Baltimore, 1958), pp. xxi–xxix, 1–19.

10. Whereas one may enthusiastically applaud the fine work currently being undertaken as a *restauration* at the Petit Trianon, the savaging of Ledoux's gem, the Petit Château at Eaubonne, when the building was "remodeled" in 1971 for offices of the Sécurité sociale, can only be deplored. Since the facade alone was *classé*, only this element and one bay in depth behind it were preserved. The rest of that ideal cube and its pyramidal roof was destroyed to make way for the insensitive and tasteless office block that was clumsily attached to the rear of the facade. Thus, French officialdom's comprehension of its national patrimony—in particular, of the Romantic Classical aesthetic of solid geometry. (Hervé Collet, *Eaubonne au XVIIIᵉ siècle* (Paris, 1972), pp. 102–105.)

11. The idea of parallel three-phased cycles expressed in this essay represents a "revisionist" approach to the more general and less elaborately worked-out stylistic development of the Egyptian Revival as set forth in my *Egyptian Revival*, pp. 61–79.

12. This is the same Kléber who as a Napoleonic general was

assassinated—ironically—in Egypt.

13. One thinks of the recent faddish hysteria engendered by King Tut's trappings which have had such a splendiferous peregrination across America and which have produced untold quantities of whiskey bottles, bath towels, tee-shirts and the like. Some of the more kitschy items of this manifestation, many dating from the first wave of Tutamania after the discovery of the tomb in the 1920s, could have been seen at the exhibition held at the Stanford University Art Gallery in 1979 (June 26–August 15) entitled *Tut-tut*.

14. *Egyptian Revival*, pp. 21, 82, 195; Labib Habachi, *The Obelisks of Egypt* (New York, 1977).

15. Hadrian was only following well-established traditions practiced in Egypt over a period of some 2,500 years. See Robert S. Bianchi, "Archaisms in Egyptian Art," *Archaisms in the History of Art* (abstract), Annual Meeting of College Art Association, 1978.

16. Besides the work of Henry-Russell Hitchcock synthesized in his *Architecture: Nineteenth and Twentieth Centuries*, one might cite among other scholars publishing after World War II, Carroll L. V. Meeks, *The Railroad Station* (New Haven, 1956), especially the first two chapters.

17. For a more complete treatment of this point, see *Egyptian Revival*, pp. 4–10.

18. Hitchcock, *Architecture* . . . , p. xxiii.

19. H.-R. Hitchcock, *Early Victorian Architecture in Britain*, 2 vols. (New Haven, 1954), I, p. 194; *Egyptian Revival*, pp. 115, 120–121.

20. Kenneth Clark, *Gothic Revival* (London, 1928; 2d ed., 1950); Hitchcock, *Architecture* . . . , pp. 93–114, 173–190. This discussion, of course, has only dealt with the English Gothic Revival. Indeed, the formula may be uniquely applicable to the movement there. The iconography of the mode on the Continent is a tantalizing subject, be it the legitimacy of restored Bourbons (the 1839 remodeling of the Dreux chapel by P.-B. Lefranc; cf. P.-F.-L. Fontaine's designs for the temporary décor of Rheims Cathedral for the coronation—never held—of Louis XVIII) or the nationalistic aspirations of Germany (completion of Cologne Cathedral 1824–1880). See the excellent work by Georg Germann, *Gothic Revival in Europe and Britain* (Cambridge, 1973), especially for the association of the style with the national heritages of England, France, and Germany.

LODOLI ARCHITETTO*

Edgar Kaufmann, jr.

La retta funzione e la rappresentazione sono i due soli oggetti finali scientifici dell'architettura civile. Che cosa debbasi intendere per l'una e per l'altra, e come convenga immedesimarle a segno che non sieno che una cosa sola.[1]

G RADUALLY A MORE AUTHENTIC picture is becoming available of the once mysterious, yet influential, eighteenth-century rationalist, Fra Carlo Lodoli. In 1964, due to the research of a young Venetian student, Antonio Foscari, it was possible to present a reevaluation of Lodoli's thought.[2] Foscari drew attention to books published at Zara in the nineteenth century from manuscripts of Andrea Memmo, a rather grand Venetian diplomat and a staunch advocate of Lodoli. The Zara texts begin (vol. 1, 1833) with a corrected edition of Memmo's book of 1786 and then add (Tomo 2, 1834) the essential but hitherto unpublished continuation of that work.[3] This gives an account of Lodoli's architectural principles considerably more trenchant and consistent than those, however flawed, that had established the friar among the prophets of modern architecture.[4] The Zara books include two draft outlines for a treatise on architecture probably written by Lodoli himself, possibly the only remaining examples of his writing.[5] Lodoli preached that architecture owed allegiance to the needs and aims of human beings rather than to elaborate formal systems. Furthermore, he argued that "the laws of nature do not permit the division of beauty from use."[6] These ideas were clear, but how were they translated into design?

Here again Foscari has presented evidence on which to base an answer. The recent growth of Italian eighteenth-century studies spurred his interest in descriptions of improvements made by Lodoli in the cloisters of San Francesco della Vigna in Venice, in lodgings assigned to pilgrims to the Holy Land.[7] Lodoli, among his various religious and civic duties, was commissioner in charge of these pilgrims from 1739 to 1748. The rooms available were mean and inconvenient, and as soon as possible Lodoli tried to ameliorate them although funds were limited. Subsequently this area fell into disrepair, and was patched and rearranged so haphazardly that for a long while no one believed Lodoli's improvements survived. Yet parts did, especially masonry and sculptured elements, some of them moved from their original locations.

It was only recently that Foscari—now an internationally recognized architect and professor at the University of Venice—was able to persuade the monks at the Vigna to allow him to have photographs taken of Lodoli's work as a practicing designer. Hitherto only one engraving of a doorway was known (Fig. 10),[8] in fact, Lodoli had been loath to publish either his designs or his writings, so conscious was he of the opposition aroused by his independent concepts and blunt arguments.[9] Foscari's evidence, paired with comments from Memmo's books, gives body to Lodoli's ideas and helps one to trace the gestation of a rationalizing approach to architectural design.

Figure 1. Longhi's telling portrait is inscribed in Latin. A translation reads "Brother Lodoli,/ in the devising of Parables, and in Architectonics,/

*I heartily thank Professor Antonio Foscari of Venice for material basic to this essay, and permission to use it, as well as for critical discussion and guidance. Professor Foscari documented exact dates for Lodoli: born 28 November 1690, died 25 October 1761. Dottoressa Barbara Del Vicario, Professor Foscari's wife and co-worker, generously oversaw corrections to my 1964 article in *The Art Bulletin* (see n. 2 and the corrections, which follow the notes).

in no way to be numbered among the supreme ones./ Alessandro Longhi painted it." One can easily imagine Lodoli adding the "in no way" (*haud*) to the laudatory phrases.[9]

Figure 2. This carefully composed inscription of 1743, moved from its original site, may once have marked the start of Lodoli's work. His manner is revealed in the elegant spacing and erudite letter forms, especially the M and D. After Lodoli's tenure another inscription of 1750 acknowledged repairs paid for by the Doge Pietro Grimani; it is less well lettered but repeats the distinctive M and D in the date.

Figure 3. The Vitruvian maxim again shows fastidious calligraphy, and Lodoli's cast of mind is evident in the playful reduction of *ratiocination* to *reason*.[10] A variation on this paraphrase, "devonsi unir e fabrica e ragione," is inscribed

in an engraving by E. Vitali after a painting by "Ant."—surely Alessandro—Longhi, perhaps the very portrait shown in Figure 1.[11] The chief interest of the engraving lies in its inscriptions; the one just mentioned continues, "e sia funzion la rapresentazione." This colloquial Italian rhyme may be translated "structure and reason must be as one, and let form be function." Two further labels read "ut eruas et destruas, ut plantes et aedifices"; these are taken from Jeremiah, Chapter I, verse 10 (authorized).

Figure 4. This corridor floor evokes the once widely discussed irregular pavement of the Via Appia, an example of Roman engineering. In late engravings by G. B. Piranesi, who as a youth had known Lodoli, the rationale of that irregularity is made clear: economy of material and stability in use.[12]

Figure 5. A small, dead-end courtyard keeps some of its aspect from Lodoli's time. A short span of wall rests on two arches; two windows in the wall have remarkable trim of which details appear in the following photographs.

Figure 6. The left-hand window still conforms, as does its neighbor, to Memmo's description: "First, let us talk of sills. Everyone made

4. *Pavement in corridor, cloisters, San Francesco della Vigna.*

5. *Courtyard wall, cloisters, San Francesco della Vigna.*

them, and still makes them, in one piece so that the jambs bear on the ends thereof; jamb and sill weigh on the wall mass below. The portion of wall not compressed stays in place, creating a kind of fulcrum. This forces the sill upward, usually in the center, as can be seen everywhere. [Lodoli] divided the sill into three parts, the first as wide as the opening of the door or window, so that it bore no weight from the jambs. Shorter than usual and load-free, anyone can see that it would endure better. Nevertheless he wanted to make it stronger and curved it down in a catenary so that

6. *Window frame, courtyard in cloisters, San Francesco della Vigna.*

7. *Window sill, courtyard in cloisters, San Francesco della Vigna. (Photo: Foscari.)*

8. *Window trim, courtyard in cloisters, San Francesco della Vigna. (Photo: Foscari.)*

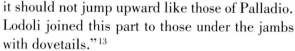

it should not jump upward like those of Palladio. Lodoli joined this part to those under the jambs with dovetails."[13]

Figure 7. A close view of the sill of the right-hand window shows it detailed not only to shed water by being tilted but, also, by means of a central channel and by recessed areas, to contain water wind-driven toward the interior. The two window sills have different lower profiles.

Figure 8. The top molding of the right-hand window, and that of its neighbor, resembles neither traditional pediments nor the drip moldings

9. *Bas-relief, former door lintel, cloisters, San Francesco della Vigna.*

found on medieval structures. The arrangement here tries to avoid carrying all the overhead load to the window jambs, and the topmost point is left slightly open, unlike the joined cornices of pediments which often gaped at the crown in unsightly manner due to wall movement. This design was nicknamed by Lodoli the "tuppé un poco storto"; he found it awkward looking.[14]

Figure 9. This carved stone now set in a corridor wall was the lintel of the doorway to the pilgrims' quarters. It is the only clue we have to Lodoli's idea of architectural sculpture, and as such is surprisingly informal. Memmo wrote, "[Lodoli] had a bas-relief carved which represents the saintly protector of the friars of Jerusalem. One can note that he added four carved screwheads [as if they were] attaching it like a tablet or plaque. Here you see a proper application of ornament."[15] The friars of Jerusalem were those helping the pilgrims; their patron saint, canonized in 1726, was Jacob Picenus, shown among casually disposed emblems of religion,

facing forward eagerly with a refulgent monstrance in his right hand while his left rests on Holy Writ. Below, inscriptions recall his stay as a guest at the Vigna in 1440 and his guardianship over pilgrim traffic as of 1743, the date also shown in Figure 2. Jacob Picenus was a Franciscan, a formidable combatant of Hussite heresy in Austria, Bohemia, Bosnia, and Hungary, where he labored for sixteen years before a well-earned rest at the Vigna. Later in a long and active life he stayed there again, from 1467 to 1470, fomenting a crusade against the Turk. Like Lodoli, when not fasting Picenus ate only vegetables and bread.[16]

Figure 10. This engraving was published in *The Art Bulletin*, June 1964, but without Memmo's description which reads: "Regarding jambs [Lodoli] noticed that many of them fractured, having little resistance at the midpoint when they were made too high and, pressed by the wall mass yet unable to sink, the jambs burst sideways. Therefore he made them in several parts, joining

10. *Frontispiece, second part*, L'architettura di Jacopo Barozzi da Vignola, *Giambattista Pasquali, Venice, 1748.*

ex
Fabrica
et
Ratiocinatione

Vitruvius

TOMO
SECONDO

them to the wall mass itself by means of suitably dimensioned cross members which were linked to the other parts by dovetailing. Thus no part of the jamb could move out of place."[17] The lower edge of the sill is notable. Lodoli's door frame closely resembles ancient but undated peasant structure of the Montefeltro district, some thirty miles south of Forlì, where Lodoli had taught as a young cleric. See illustration, *Abitare* N. 200, December 1981, page 19.

Lodoli's preoccupations at the cloisters of the Vigna were mocked by his adversaries, who thought architecture had higher duties than the correction of structural errors and inconveniences; the exaltation of art above practical considerations was taken for granted in those times.[18] But Venetians also enjoyed a tradition of practicality, and they remained immensely proud of their Arsenal, long the standard setter of military and naval engineering in Europe.[19] It is pertinent that Lodoli's father was a legal expert on the staff of the Arsenal, and Lodoli's mother, an Alberghetti. This family had been chief metallurgists at the Arsenal for generations and their skills were so allied to art that two massive bronze wellheads in the courtyard of the Ducal Palace, their work, are still reckoned among the glories of Venice. Lodoli grew up in an atmosphere of sophisticated practicality.

Rooted in the Venetian past, Lodoli was powerfully drawn toward the future as forecast by the Enlightenment. His principles of architecture were only part, if an important one, of the unorthodox, rational education he directed to benefit the sons of several leading Venetian families.[20] These families saw that Venice must be prepared for the world that was shaping up around them, but there were more who saw in Lodoli's thinking a threat to the Venetian establishment. Dubbed "forse il Socrate architetto," although he did not have to drink hemlock, in his lifetime he had to forego open publication of his ideas and their use in architectural practice.[21] He was condemned to remain a shadowy influence, appreciated only after others had fought for the insights he achieved. Within these limitations Lodoli thought and even acted without precedent and according to principles as he conceived them. More farseeing than his contemporaries, in the mid-eighteenth century he dared to envisage an architecture fully consistent with the rising modern world.

Notes

1. Andrea Memmo, *Elementi d'architettura lodoliana*, etc. (Zara, 1834; hereafter cited as Zara '34), p. 59, lines 10–14. Under this same title all of Memmo's writings on Lodoli have been reproduced sans comment by Gabriele Mazzotta (Milan, 1973). A free translation of the passage quoted reads: "Correct function and significant form are the only two ultimate, scientific objectives of civil architecture. What is meant by each of these elements, and how it is desirable to amalgamate them into one indivisible thing." A strict translation will be found under "Corollaries" on p. 165 of the article cited in note 2, below.
2. Edgar Kaufmann, jr., "Memmo's Lodoli," *The Art Bulletin* 46 (June 1964): 159–175. See corrections, below.
3. "Memmo's Lodoli," p. 161, lines 7–10 and p. 162, lines 2–3. It is believed that Memmo's daughter, Lucia Mocenigo, supplied his manuscripts to the Battara brothers in Zara. She presented both volumes of her father's works to John Ruskin in 1850, as M. Brusatin repeats in *Venezia Nel Settecento* (Turin, 1980). This is one of many peripheral items diligently reported in a tasteless text which cloaks Lodoli's seminal ideas in generalities.
4. Henry-Russell Hitchcock, *Architecture: Nineteenth and Twentieth Centuries*, (Baltimore, 1958), p. xxii. Reliable information on Lodoli is found in "Memmo's Lodoli"; Angelo Comolli's *Bibliografia Storico-Critica dell'Architettura Civile ed Arti Subalterne* (Rome, 1792), Vol. IV, pp. 50–84; and Gianfranco Torcellan, *Una figura della Venezia settecentesca: Andrea Memmo*, Istituto per la collaborazione culturale, Fondazione Cini (Venezia-Roma, 1963).
5. The outlines are printed in "Memmo's Lodoli," pp. 173–175, Italian; pp. 162–166, English (see corrections below).
6. The phraseology is borrowed from Emerson's essay, "Art." Emerson was in Italy just as Memmo's books were issued by the Battara, but I found no direct evidence that he knew of them.
7. Zara '34, pp. 152 ff.
8. Memmo's biographical pages (39–128) in the Zara book of 1833 are explicit but not circumstantial about antagonisms aroused by Lodoli.
9. For further portraits of Lodoli see *The Art Bulletin* 60 (December 1978): 743. The picture reproduced there I wrongly ascribed to Alessandro Longhi; it was painted by his father, Pietro Longhi.
10. Marcus Vitruvius Pollio, *On Architecture*, Book I, chapter 1, section 1.
11. Vitali's engraving serves as frontispiece to [Andrea Memmo], *Elementi dell'architettura lodoliana*, etc. (Rome, 1786).
12. Giovanni Battista Piranesi, *Le Antichità romane*, Tomo III, pl. 7, and idem, *Antichità d'Albano*, pl. 24.
13. This passage is excerpted piecemeal from Zara '34, pp. 155 to 161 inclusive. Palladio had trouble with sills divided at the midpoint in the Ionic cloister with paired columns at San Giorgio Maggiore.
14. Ibid., p. 161, line 24. "A toupee somewhat awry" translates the sally.
15. Ibid., p. 158, last paragraph.
16. Professor Foscari elucidated this carving and supplied an outline life of Saint Jacob Picenus.
17. Zara '34, p. 159, line 8 to end of page.
18. For criticisms of Lodoli see Zara '34, p. 152, lines 14–28.
19. Research in the organization and impact of the Arsenal is being conducted by several scholars at present, particularly Professor Ennio Concina of the University of Venice.
20. Zara 1833, pp. 49–58.
21. See inscription in the engraving cited in note 11.

CORRECTIONS TO "MEMMO'S LODOLI," *THE ART BULLETIN*, JUNE 1964

Page 161, line 20: Angelo Comolli was born in 1760 and died in 1794. See Augusto Cavallari-Murat, "Schedula sulla bibliografia architettonica di Angelo Comolli," in the *Bollettino della Società piemontese di archeologia e belle arti*, n.s. XVIII, 1964, pp. 173–177. I wish to thank Prof. Franco Bernabei of the University of Padua and Dr. Giorgio Tagliacozzo of the Institute of Vico Studies, New York, for assistance in tracing this information. The publishing house of Labor in Milan in 1964–1965 issued a three-volume photo reproduction of Comolli's *Bibliografia*, without comments of any kind.

Page 163, line 9, should begin:
or on buildings already built.

Page 164, under Book VIII, 1, the end of the sentence should read:
just as every product of nature has a fixed character, by dint of which it is what it is, so too a building should have its own character in order to be what it must be, that is, essentially differentiated while in accord with the archetype of its intended purpose.

Page 165, under Book II, the last clause of the first paragraph should read:
whenever a material is demonstratively employed according to its nature and appropriate purpose, the result always is harmony of solidity, proportion, and convenience.

Page 168, lines 12 and 21; and page 169, lines 9 and 20: the office to which Lodoli was appointed, *Revisore*, should not be translated "Censor," which at that time in Venice had a different meaning.

Page 170, lines 9 and 11: the name of an important Venetian family, Soranzo, is misspelled.

SIR JOHN SOANE AND THE REBUILDING OF PITZHANGER MANOR

Dorothy Stroud

N THE TEN YEARS OF HIS OWNER-
ship, Pitzhanger Manor came to represent for
Sir John Soane (Fig. 1) a strange mixture of
fact and fantasy: a retreat from London but at
the same time a showplace in which to entertain his friends, a repository for works of art, and
an object of instruction as well as an intended
legacy for his sons. Time and money were lavished on it, and for some years his energy and
enthusiasm were justified. Like most dreams,
however, this one eventually was to fade. After
1808 Soane was beset with increased responsi-
bilities and personal worries. The sons failed to
respond to his hopes, Mrs. Soane began to suffer
from ill health, and his appointment as Surveyor
to Chelsea Hospital brought him yet another residence. In the end he decided to sell the property,
but at least the house survives, though in a sadly
altered form, and the story behind its creation
and its heyday as a place known for its excellent
hospitality seems worth telling.

That Soane, by 1800, should have wanted a
country villa as well as a town house is not in
itself remarkable. Architects had done so for a
century or more. Sir Christopher Wren had a
house on the Green at Hampton Court; Sir John
Vanbrugh rebuilt a farmhouse for himself at
Esher; Henry Flitcroft bought an estate in then
rural Hampstead; while Sir William Chambers
had a place at Whitton; and James Wyatt acquired a farm at Hanworth. Soane had lived in
the country until he was fifteen and throughout
his long life he was a prodigious walker and a
keen fisherman. The attraction for him of the
countryside between Berkshire and London is
also easy to understand. It had been familiar to
him since boyhood. He had attended school at
Reading and still owned a cottage there; his widowed mother and brother lived at Chertsey; and

by the end of the 1790s he had several close
friends living in and around the villages of Acton
and Ealing (Fig. 2). Moreover, it was on a house
at the latter place that he had first been set to
work as an architectural student when, in 1768,
he entered the office of George Dance.

Dance was then adding two fine reception
rooms to an earlier eighteenth-century house for
a wealthy Quaker and City merchant, Thomas
Gurnell, whose daughter Mary he would soon
marry. As Soane wrote in his *Memoirs* many
years later, "I was naturally attached to this part
of the building, it being the first whose progress
and construction I had attended at the commencement of my architectural studies in Mr.
Dance's office." In the thirty years that had
passed since then, Soane had climbed to the front

1. William Owen, portrait of Sir John Soane, exhibited at the Royal Academy in 1805. (Photo: Sir John Soane's Museum.)

2. Map of Middlesex, showing Ealing and vicinity.

3. Sir John Soane, project for "A House at Acton," 1800. Wooden models. (Photo: Sir John Soane's Museum.)

rank of his profession. After two years with Dance he had, with the latter's agreement, completed his training with another prominent architect, Henry Holland, and had won both the Royal Academy's Gold Medal and King George III's traveling studentship which enabled him to study in Italy. On his return in 1780 he set up a practice which, after two precarious years, met with success and enabled him to marry in 1784. In 1788, with the support of the Prime Minister William Pitt, for whom he had altered a country house, he was appointed Architect to the Bank of England. From 1790, when Soane and his wife received a handsome legacy at the death of her uncle George Wyatt, he became financially independent and two years later built No. 12 Lincoln's Inn Fields as his town house. Here he began to assemble paintings, sculpture, and a library.

By the spring of 1800 the idea of a country villa had taken root in Soane's mind. It appears that at first he contemplated building at Acton where he had recently completed Heathfield Lodge for John Winter, solicitor to the Bank of England. On 25 May he went there to look at a piece of land belonging to a Mr. Selby, which he

subsequently purchased for £500. On 27 May the Office Day Book shows that two of his draftsmen, Thomas Sword and Henry Seward, were drawing out his designs. Although these drawings have not survived, there are at Lincoln's Inn Fields two wooden models which are labeled as "a House at Acton" (Fig. 3). Both are for two-story buildings three bays wide. One of the models has a facade with four giant pilasters. There are roundheaded windows on either side of the entrance, and roundels in place of the outer windows on the floor above. Over the center bay of this facade rises an attic with incised pilaster strips at the extremities topped by acroteria. This model, in fact, shows a composition closely related to the house which Soane eventually built. However, just as the Acton project was about to materialize, Soane heard—probably from George Dance—that Pitzhanger Manor at Ealing (Fig. 4) was about to come on the market.

Dance was one of the three trustees appointed under the will of Thomas Gurnell, who had died in 1785, and although the owner's family continued to occupy the house for some years, the decision to sell had been made by the early summer

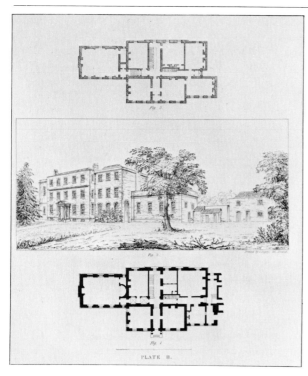

PLATE II.

of 1800. It is evident that by the end of July Soane had transferred his interest from Acton to the house which he knew so well at Ealing. On 2 August Seward was sent to take plans, and on 19 August Soane noted that he had been "at home all day about plans for another house for Ealing." Meanwhile the obliging John Winter of Heathfield Lodge agreed to take over the Acton piece of ground which Soane no longer wanted.

In a short account of Pitzhanger which he compiled in 1802, Soane stated,

> My object in purchasing these premises was to have a residence for myself and family, and afterwards for my eldest son, who at an early age had made very considerable progress in mathematics and mechanics; he had also shewn a decided passion for the Fine Arts, particularly Architecture, which he wished to pursue as a profession; this determination was most gratifying to my feelings and I enjoyed by anticipation the honours he would receive in the practice of an art to which, as it then seemed, he had been led by a natural inclination. With these delightful prospects in view, I wished to make Pitzhanger Manor-house as complete as possible for the future residence of the young Architect, whose classical education, and the facilities and advantages he possessed, would enable him to distinguish himself above his fellows in the practice of a profession calculated to increase domestic comforts and the refinements of civilised society.

It seems, however, that this fatherly forethought for his then sixteen-year-old son was not Soane's only consideration. His London house was restricted by its narrow site and by the requirements of the Building Act. One of the obvious attractions of a country property was that he would be free to design there something expressing those imaginative ideas that had already become apparent in his work of the 1790s, notably in the additions to Wimpole and Buckingham House, at Tyringham, and preeminently at the Bank of England. In short, he wanted a place where he could display the treasures which he was then collecting and impress both friends and potential clients.

Soane was, of course, acquainted with Thomas Hope and William Beckford, both of whom were at the turn of the century building remarkable repositories for their respective collections. He had built a picture gallery for the latter at the old Fonthill Splendens in 1787, and several years later was to buy a number of pictures from Beckford. By 1800, however, neither the new Fonthill nor Hope's house in Duchess Street was complete, and Soane does not yet appear to have been inside either one. However, there can be no doubt that he was influenced by another and slightly earlier house and collection—that of Henry Holland, the architect in whose office he had completed his training. In about 1789 Holland had built for himself Sloane Place in London, where Cadogan Square now stands. Its elegant interior, with an enfilade of reception rooms overlooking a landscaped garden, was in due course embellished with a collection of antique marbles for which Holland commissioned Charles Heathcote Tatham (see below, .pp. 52–63) to go to Rome in 1794. These purchases were duly shipped to London and arranged in Sloane Place where, early in 1796, they were admired by the expert Charles Townley who subsequently, with Sir Henry Englefield, proposed Holland as a Fellow of the Society of Antiquaries. That Soane was immensely impressed by the pieces and their arrangement is confirmed by the strenuous and finally successful efforts he made to acquire the marbles some years later after Holland's death, when Sloane Place was sold. In fact, they now form an important part of the collection at 13 Lincoln's Inn Fields.

Soane's surviving papers give few details as to the course of the Pitzhanger negotiations, but on 8 August 1800 he took Mrs. Soane and her cousin Miss Levick to look over the place, and on Sunday the 11th he went there with his lawyer, Mr. Whetton. On 5 September the purchase price of £4,500 was paid over to the Gurnell trustees and two days later he took his Clerk of the Works, Walter Payne, to inspect the old house and grounds. Payne, who remained in Soane's employment throughout the latter's life and eventually became Clerk of the Works at the Bank of England, had already supervised work at Ryston, Betchworth, and other houses which Soane had altered. He was now to take charge at Pitzhanger

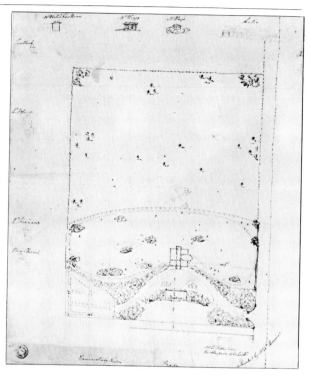

until the new house was completed.

Meanwhile Soane had been in consultation with the landscape gardener, John Haverfield of Kew, as to a plan for the grounds, and on 17 September the latter submitted his first design for a miniature landscape with plantations and a serpentine lake (Fig. 5). This was embellished with thumbnail sketches of houses in the vicinity that belonged to Soane's particular cronies, who included Samuel Wegg of the Bank House at Acton, John Raymond Way whose residence—also at Acton—was described in Lysons's *Environs* as a "commodious and respectable brick villa," and John Winter, already mentioned. Lord Kinnaird, for whom Soane had designed a dairy in 1791, owned Elm Grove, a house which lay immediately to the south of Pitzhanger Manor. A second drawing dated 17 September shows Haverfield's design as put into execution in the

6. *Pitzhanger Manor. Soane, 1801. The new house and entrance gateway. (Watercolor: Sir John Soane's Museum.)*

zarre classical essays of roughly oval outline, and a version in the brick and flint "primitive" style that he was currently adopting for the Cumberland lodges in Hyde Park and for the stables at Betchworth Castle. By the end of the year, however, his fondness for the two rooms added by George Dance prevailed, these being retained while the rest of the old manor was replaced by a new building (Figs. 6, 7) very much on the lines of the Acton models we have already seen. On 7 March 1801 the first courses were laid for a house which, as it took shape, must have caused the inhabitants of Ealing to rub their eyes.

Built of pale stock brick and Portland stone, it was given a dramatic frontispiece of four freestanding, fluted Ionic columns over whose entablatures were placed Coade stone figures modeled from the Erechtheum at Athens. Although the handling is entirely different, the composition of this frontispiece owes something to the entrance front at Kedleston by Robert Adam, which Soane admired and which was similarly reflected in his Lothbury Court gateway at the Bank of England of 1798/99 (Fig. 8). Below the roundheaded windows on either side of the front door are horizontal panels with an eagle within a wreath of oak leaves, copied from an antique relief in the Church of the Holy Apostles near the Palazzo Colonna in Rome. Roundels in the end bays of the upper story also contain copies of antique reliefs, and a stone balustrade encircles the roof line.

While the north (now obscured) and west fronts of Pitzhanger are less ornate in their treatment, they are embellished with incised pilaster strips rising the full height of the house and with carved rosettes replacing the conventional capital. The windows of the principal floor overlooking the garden (Fig. 9) have elliptical heads and

course of the next two years, with two cedar trees flanking the west lawn, both of which survive and are now of immense size.

On 6 October Soane noted that "Payne began pulling down at Ealing," and he went there himself the next day to see what had been done. During the following months a variety of designs for the new house emerged, and Soane clearly had difficulty deciding which he should adopt. At one time he toyed with the idea of retaining the whole of the old house, building on corner turrets for more space. Then there were schemes for an entirely new building, including some bi-

7. *Pitzhanger Manor. Ealing facade. At right, figures representing the architect, his wife, and their two sons. (Watercolor: Sir John Soane's Museum.)*
8. *Bank of England, London. Soane, 1797. Archway to Lothbury Court. (Photo: Sir John Soane's Museum.)*

are unusually wide, originally opening into a long, glazed gallery with a fountain at either end. This, usually referred to in the accounts as the "greenhouse," was described by Soane as "enriched with antique cinerary urns, sepulchral vases, statues, and other sculptures, vines and odoriferous plants, the whole producing a succession of beautiful effects, particularly when seen by moonlight, or when illuminated, and the lawn enriched with company enjoying the delights of cheerful society."

On the decoration of the rooms on the principal floor of the new house Soane lavished particular care, making endless sketches for his draftsmen to draw out, only to scribble over them as fresh ideas took shape, which must have driven the young men to distraction.

From the front door, in the fanlight of which some colored glass still remains, the narrow entrance hall (Figs. 10–12) with rusticated walls leads up a short flight of steps to the inner hall on the *piano nobile*. This inner hall runs the full height of the house and in its treatment has affinities with that at Tyringham (Fig. 13). Across the hall a door on the axis of the entrance opens into what was originally the drawing room, now mutilated with partitions. This room, with two windows overlooking the garden, was apparently decorated in the simplest manner with plain walls and a reeded border to the ceiling. It no doubt relied for color on the pictures that would have been hung here and on the heavily draped curtains to the windows, of which a glimpse shows in an engraving of the entrance hall. Its simplicity would have made all the more striking the elaborate treatment of the two rooms on the north, which in their original form were unique examples of Soane's imaginative approach to decoration.

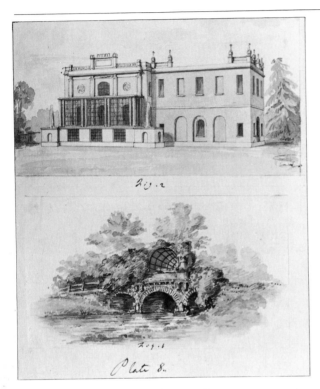

The first door in the north wall of the hall opened into the front parlor or breakfast room (Figs. 14, 15). Here the ceiling took the form of a shallow dome resting on four piers against which were set Egyptian-type caryatids, supplied by Coade and Seeley and painted in copper bronze. The center of the dome was painted to represent cloud effects while the border, with incised fret, was painted pale blue. The four pendentives were filled by winged figures made in plaster by Benjamin Grant and painted in silver bronze. The accounts show that the deep plinth of this room was painted to imitate porphyry, and that the south and west walls were hung with mirrors set within painted panels of decoration which derived from a set of colored engravings based on wall paintings in the Villa Negroni in Rome (Fig. 16). These engravings were published late in the 1770s and Soane sometime later acquired two sets. A similar mirrored panel was placed over the chimneypiece, on either side of which were deep, shelved recesses emulating catacomb niches and housing antique cinerary urns. Against the opposite wall was a pedestal supporting the large fourth-century Greek krater that Soane purchased, together with other vases, from Lord Cawdor's sale in 1800. From this room double doors led to the back parlor or library (Fig. 17).

The ceiling of this room took the form of a shallow groined vault painted with trellis and flowers, almost identical with that of Soane's breakfast room at 12 Lincoln's Inn Fields, decorated in about 1793/94. Indeed his instructions to the decorator at Pitzhanger were to copy "the trellis at 6 inch squares and sunk panels with the same plants" as those in the London house. The painter was almost certainly John Crace, who was responsible for the decorative painting elsewhere

11. *Pitzhanger Manor. Sketch, entrance hall. Reliefs of* Morning *and* Evening *by Thomas Banks, based on the Arch of Constantine, Rome. (Sketches: Sir John Soane's Museum.)*

12. *Pitzhanger Manor. Entrance hall, north wall, view toward front parlor. (Photo: Sir John Soane's Museum.)*

13. *Praed house, Tyringham. Soane, 1793–1796. Design for front hall. (Drawing: Sir John Soane's Museum.)*

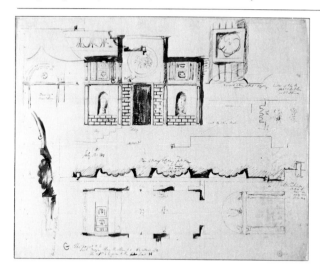

in the house and who carried out similar work at a number of Soane's other buildings. In the Ealing library were displayed more cinerary urns and a selection of the antique vases bought from the James Clerk sale at Christie's in 1802 and from Lord Mendip's sale in the same year. A watercolor drawing of this room, exhibited at the Royal Academy in 1803, shows that among the pictures hung high up on the walls were Soane's rejected designs for the House of Lords, made in 1794. The Academy exhibit also shows a plan of the Bank of England lying on the table, displaying prominently the Lothbury Court, while overlying a corner of the plan is a detail of the Lothbury archway of which the Pitzhanger frontispiece is a reflection. As in the drawing room, an unusually wide and full-length window led from the library to the external glazed gallery or "greenhouse."

14. *Pitzhanger Manor. Front parlor or breakfast room.*
(Drawing: Sir John Soane's Museum.)
15. *Pitzhanger Manor. Front parlor, view as it is today.*
(Photo: Sir John Soane's Museum.)

The main staircase of the new house lay to the south of the hall. Here half-landings connected with the two earlier rooms by George Dance, the lower of which served as the principal dining room while that above was a repository for books, manuscripts, and drawings. Stone stairs led down to the basement hall where the walls were painted to represent gold-veined black marble. Although in his first sketches Soane intended having a kitchen in the basement, he later decided to have a separate two-story block of domestic offices across a small courtyard to the north of the house—a surprisingly old-fashioned arrangement for this date. Only a housekeeper's room and butler's pantry were retained in the basement, the two westward rooms overlooking the garden being used for displaying many of Soane's acquisitions. The room on the north was

16. Angelo Campanella, engraving of Villa Negroni, Rome. (Hand-colored engraving: Sir John Soane's Museum.)
17. Pitzhanger Manor. Back parlor or library. (Drawing: Sir John Soane's Museum.)

to contain statues, architectural fragments, and what Soane called "various ornaments from Egyptian, Grecian and Roman edifices." To the south of this, in the space originally proposed for a kitchen, Soane contrived the strange apartment which, on a plan of 21 July 1801, he called the "Monk's Dining Room."

Soane's attitude to Gothic architecture was something of a paradox. He was never happy when called on to design in that style, nor had he much to say in favor of the Gothic productions of his contemporaries. At the same time, he had a profound respect for medieval buildings, associating them with those sublime, romantic, and picturesque qualities essential to what he called "the Poetry of Architecture." That he should have attempted to catch the spirit of so grand a theme and imprison it in a basement chamber less than 16 feet square seems at least naive, as does his introduction of a hypothetical monk to be the custodian of this dark and heavily beamed apartment.

Soane was, of course, familiar with current romantic literature, of which several examples were on his library shelves. His monk, however, has nothing in common with the character in Matthew Gregory Lewis's novel of that name, nor with the roistering brethren in Ann Radcliffe's *Sicilian Romance*. The gentle recluse of Pitzhanger is more in the tradition of Charles Hamilton's hermit at Pain's Hill, or Sir Richard Hill's mechanical anchorite at Hawkstone. As for his setting, the idea may well have stemmed from Strawberry Hill where, by 1790, the Gothic accretions of Horace Walpole included what Walpole himself called "a small gloomy hall," a cloister, an oratory, and a cabinet lit from above by a star of yellow glass. Walpole's chief Gothic adviser was, it must be remembered, Thomas Pitt Lord Camelford, the earliest and most helpful of Soane's patrons and one whom he continued to hold in the highest esteem. Compared to the scale and richness of Walpole's treasure house, Soane's version seems modest indeed, but it is significant that when his Gothic collection was reinstated at 13 Lincoln's Inn Fields in 1812, his monk was equipped not only with a parlor but a cell, a cloister, and an oratory.

Soane's next problem at Pitzhanger was how best to display his collections of casts, the first of which he had acquired from James Playfair's

widow in 1795. More had come from Benjamin Grant in 1801 and from the Willy Reveley sale in the same year, the latter including casts made from originals in the Museo Clementino, medallions from the Pantheon, and details from the Temples of Neptune and Jupiter Tonans. Two plans of 1801 propose a gallery for these objects on the far side of the domestic offices; the plan adopted called for a narrow gallery on the north with one window and two circular top lights.

It was on this plan that Soane gave the first hint of yet another project then forming in his mind. The plaster-gallery window, as he noted on the drawing, was to overlook "the Ruins of a Temple." Two months later an entry in his notebook recorded that on 7 December he had been to Ealing "about [the] Ruins" (Figs. 18, 19), and it is evident that they were in course of construction on a plot to the north of the house by the end of 1801, and that what materialized was in fact a miniature forum, a cluster of seemingly half-buried classical remains reminiscent of what he had seen in the Campo Vaccino during his student days in Rome.

What put the idea into his head is not re-

vealed. Perhaps it came to him when reading those lines in Richard Payne Knight's *The Landscape* (1794):

> *Bless'd is he who midst his tufted trees*
> *Some ruin'd castle's lofty towers sees*
>
> . . .
>
> *Still happier he (if conscious of his prize)*
> *Who sees some Temple's broken columns rise*
> *Midst sculptured fragments broken by their fall*
> *And tottering remnants of its marble wall.*

The source of the materials from which the ruins were constructed is puzzling. Although Soane kept a meticulous account of expenditure for the house and garden, even down to vegetables, and food for the dogs and poultry, about the ruins he is strangely reticent. Certainly they did not come from the old house which could boast only a modest Doric porch, probably the one that now frames a garden gateway. But two complete pairs of fluted Corinthian columns, three incomplete pairs of the same order with matching responds, a pair of fluted Doric columns, and several detached capitals and broken shafts, add up to a considerable load of which there is no mention. They cannot be tied up with current demolition at the Bank of England, and one can only hazard a guess that they may have been built up from secondhand or rejected pieces found in various masons' yards. For some reason of his own Soane chose to keep these details to himself, and he proceeded to weave an elaborate fantasy whereby the remains had been discovered half-buried among the Pitzhanger plantations. He even went to the length of having drawings prepared with conjectural outlines of what might have been

19. Pitzhanger Manor. View towards end of Soane's own-
ership. Far right, "ruins." (Drawing: Sir John Soane's Mu-
seum.)

their original appearance, and what might still lie below ground level. Unfortunately, we have only Soane's word as to the reactions of the visitors to Ealing when greeted by their host's mixture of hospitality and intellectual exercise; to him they appeared delighted.

To a generation reared in the latter half of the eighteenth century, when landscape gardens often were littered with classical temples and Gothic follies, the Pitzhanger ruins may not have seemed entirely eccentric, although the idea of a miniature forum, and the accompanying account of how much still awaited excavation, was

something that they would not have encountered previously. Most of the shrewder friends no doubt saw through the charade but observed the spirit of the game with amusement. Certainly there was no lack of visitors after 1804, when the family were able to take up residence, although it was 29 April of that year before Mrs. Soane was able to note that they had eaten their first hot dinner in the house.

From this time the entertaining increased, usually on the weekend when Soane felt free to escape from London. Most of the visitors came for dinner, although several stayed for a night or

more, in particular J.M.W. Turner, who was a constant and welcome guest. Others whose names are recorded included the singer Madam Anna Storace, the tenor John Braham, the duc d'Orleans, then living in exile at Twickenham, the duchess of Leeds, Lord Sidney, Lord and Lady Bridport, Sir Francis Bourgeois, Sir William and Lady Beechey, the Flaxmans, de Loutherburgs, Hardwicks, Maltons, Wheatleys, as well as James Peacock, Henry Howard, Augustus Callcott, and other of Soane's Royal Academy friends and such clients as the Praeds of Tyringham, the Peterses from Betchworth, and the Thorntons from Albury. Occasionally, Mrs. Soane noted, they held a dance, and whenever possible Soane would snatch the odd hour or so to go fishing. It was probably the happiest period of his life, but it was not to last.

The year 1806 saw Soane's election as Professor of Architecture at the Royal Academy following which he felt bound to devote much of his time to preparing his lectures. It was also in 1806 that his elder son John, who had been at Pembroke College, Cambridge, came down without taking a degree. After some months in his father's office the young man was placed as an architectural student with Joseph Michael Gandy, but he appears to have shown neither aptitude nor interest, eventually announcing, to the mortification of his father, that he wished to give up further study. The second son having proved even less satisfactory, Soane could no longer see any future for Pitzhanger, and in the summer of 1810 he decided to sell the property to General Cameron. During July, when the agreement was being drawn up, he spent three Sundays there, fishing or entertaining old friends, but by December the last loads of treasures and furniture had been dispatched to Lincoln's Inn Fields. Soane remained on friendly terms with the General and made occasional visits to dine at Pitzhanger or fish in his old haunts, but in 1815 the house changed hands again and there was no longer any cordiality with the new owner, by whom, in Soane's words, "many of the venerable and lofty trees were cut down and sold, a large portion of the columns and other architectural relics which formed the ruins were moved, and the site thereof metamorphosed . . . to a depot for coal, wood and ashes. By these changes the character of the place has been destroyed and the former Gothic scenes and intellectual banquets of Pitzhanger are no more." This was what he had found when, after driving to Brentford with John Robins and Charles Rossi on 20 March 1820, he had gone on by himself to dine at The Old Hats at Ealing and to take a look at the Manor House. Returning to Lincoln's Inn Fields in low spirits, he ended his notebook entry for the day with the bitter comment, ". . . walked round poor Ealing. O John, John: what has idleness cost you."

On that sad note the story of Pitzhanger might have ended but for a cheering little episode which happened some twelve years later. Soane had recently produced a new edition of his book, *Designs for Public and Private Buildings*, of which he had sent a copy to King Louis Philippe who, as the duc d'Orleans, had been one of his Ealing visitors and was now restored to the throne of France. Acknowledging the book through his secretary, the King expressed regret that he had been unable to find any designs "pour le jolie villa d'Ealing" which he remembered visiting so many years before. Although Soane was now almost eighty, his interest was at once rekindled. Old drawings were unearthed, draftsmen were put on to making new ones, engravings were prepared, and a short account of the house was specially printed so that a copy might be dispatched to France. Louis Philippe's kindly acceptance of this, in which he said that he had spent an evening going through the volume with his family, gave Soane much pleasure, as he recounted when he wrote his *Professional Memoirs* in 1835.

In these *Memoirs* Soane at last disclosed that his creation of the ruins at Pitzhanger had been a *jeu d'esprit*. They had, he wrote, provided sources of amusement to the numerous persons visiting this place, particularly on the three days of the annual Ealing fair, held on the Green in front of the Manor House, "on which days our friends were accustomed to visit us by a general invitation, when it was not unusual to entertain from one to two hundred persons to a déjeuner a la fourchette." After this they were shown the ruins and relevant drawings while Soane, tongue in cheek, watched their varied reactions. Confessing to this deception in his *Memoirs*, he explained that "one of my objects was to ridicule those fanciful architects and antiquaries who, finding a few pieces of columns, and sometimes only a few single stones, proceeded from these slender data to imagine magnificent buildings; and by whom small fragments of tesselated pavements were magnified into splendid remains of Roman grandeur, which were given to the world in the most pompous and expensive style."

One can scarcely blame later occupants of Pitzhanger for failing to appreciate Soane's idea of a joke, and the ruins disappeared without trace. The house, however, has survived and is graded as a building of national importance (Fig. 20). Robbed of its furnishings and with its delicate internal detailing obscured by book stacks and office furniture, it continues in municipal use, awaiting the day when enlightenment may lead the authorities to put it to a better use.

PRECEDENTS AND VARIOUS DESIGNS COLLECTED BY C.H. TATHAM[1]

John Harris

THE RECENT DISCOVERY IN A PRIvate collection of two volumes of drawings by C. H. Tatham[2] has prompted the topic of this contribution in honor of my long-time friend, Henry-Russell Hitchcock. As an architect of great promise and significant professional connections, and as the author of a number of influential architectural publications,[3] Tatham deserves a book, and the available material is now considerable. It includes the well-known letters written to Henry Holland from Italy; a fragment of an autobiography that makes us regret that it either was not finished or was destroyed, with his other remaining papers, by his descendants; and now the newly recovered drawings, which go far toward documenting Tatham's early life. They comprise a few designs made in Holland's office before 1794, a few hundred surviving drawings out of some 1,500 made or collected in Italy, a scattering of designs made for Holland after 1796, and a more interesting group of designs made by Tatham as an architect in his own right after 1800. The Italian drawings bring Tatham in line with Robert Adam and Sir William Chambers, whose Italian travels are documented by a large corpus of drawings. It is not, however, the purpose of this article to discuss the Italian items but to provide a list of those drawings representing actual designs by Tatham and others, together with topographical drawings made of buildings that interested him on his English travels; this list appears at the end of this essay.

Tatham was certainly fitted out for achievement. His tenure in Italy from July, 1794 until 1797, when the Napoleonic invasion forced him to leave, brought him into friendly contact with the *haut ton* of the architectural and artistic worlds of Rome and Naples. He was entertained by the William Hamiltons; Antonio Canova was a friend

and so was Angelica Kauffmann, to whom he dedicated a temple design. There were also friendships with an internationally flavored coterie of young architects, among them Don Isodoro Gonzales Velasquez and Prince Borghese's architect, Mario Asprucci, who was to die tragically barely six years after Tatham left Italy. In the 1790s architecture in Italy, as in England, was in an indecisive state, as the mass of theoretical designs surviving from this period demonstrates.

The circumstances of Tatham's visit to Italy are related in his "Autobiographical Fragment." He had saved 70 guineas, John Linnell gave him an additional 100 and Holland 40 plus the promise of 60 a year for two years. There is no doubt that Tatham acted as an agent for Holland, preparing drawings for him of antiquities so as to form a corpus of "Ornamental Architecture." These were intended as exemplars, and they were backed up with a small collection of actual fragments of marbles. After Holland died in 1806 the fragments passed to Sir John Soane (see above, pp. 38–51), who installed them in his museum. While in Italy Tatham must have seen a main chance in a role serving architects, decorators, and designers with a collection of decorative models that had been culled from the detritus and excavations of imperial Roman villas. G. B. Piranesi had done likewise, but his fiery and polemic etchings were presented romantically in chiaroscuro, whereas Tatham adopted the coldly Neoclassic linear style of J. H. W. Tischbein, who was engraving Lord Hamilton's Greek vases from 1791, and John Flaxman, whose pure outline drawings proliferated after 1794.

Despite Tatham's employment by the nobility and early portents of a rise to dizzying prominence in his profession, he never attained the

success of contemporaries like Soane or C. R. Cockerell, or even someone like Lewis William Wyatt, whose Willey Hall of 1813 is the sort of house Tatham would have liked to design had he ever had the chance. The lack of attainment may have been due to the temperamental difficulties—hinted at in the portrait of 1826 by Benjamin Haydon (Fig. 1)—which plagued him for most of his life. Tatham was always nervously strained, perhaps because he felt himself the intellectual superior of many far more renowned colleagues. He may not have been able to marry theoretical with practical endeavor, and here he may be compared to George Dance, a genius who struggled to release architecture in England from the shackles of academicism and yet, in his eclectic

work after 1803, remained unfulfilled. Perhaps only Soane possessed the manic drive that enabled him to break through the stylistic barrier. Tatham tried to do the same in a more traditional manner, using tried sources.

Although there are not many original designs in this collection of drawings, it elucidates much about Tatham's early career and helps fill in our knowledge of what he did when he returned from Italy to London. Holland seemed to have employed him upon concerns of offices, outbuildings, garden works, and cottages. Conveniently, Tatham makes the specific point that the drawing room at Stoke Edith was his first work in an independent capacity after Italy. A few drawings such as those for Clandon and Sloane Place may have been made when Tatham first entered Holland's office in the 1780s. On the basis of the Italian drawings we may infer that in 1794 and 1795 Tatham principally was drawing antique remains and that his real design training did not begin until 1796, when he submitted designs to the Academy of St. Luke in Rome. The drawings or designs he collected or copied throw some light upon Italian architecture in the 1790s, notably Asprucci's contributions to the Villa Borghese and to Lord Bristol's Ickworth.

It is perhaps not surprising that Tatham shows himself to be interested in cottages and *cottage orné*, for after all this was the age of the Picturesque. Apart from the work of Nash and Repton, cottage building, however, is an inadequately discussed category at this time. It is interesting to see that as early as 1797 Holland built a cottage for Southill. In the topographical drawings, Tatham records cottages at Hollycombe, Maidenhead, Stevenson, and Woburn; among his own designs are a "Shepherd's Cottage" at Stoke Edith and houses for Dr. Dicksee. It has not been

2. *C. H. Tatham, Castle Howard, Yorkshire. Partial section of window wall of gallery.*
3. *Tatham, Castle Howard. Partial section of chimney wall of gallery.*
4. *Tatham, Castle Howard. Two transverse sections of gallery.*

possible to trace the location—if it was ever built—of Lord Torrington's seaside cottage in thatch and pisé made in 1799, presumably a Holland commission.

Tatham occupies an honorable place in the history of the Egyptian Revival for his tremendous Mausoleum at Trentham. The Trentham designs show that he employed an Egyptian vocabulary for the fountains and greenhouse there as well as for the remarkable Egyptian desk, whose drawing is inscribed as "executed" for Lord Carlisle at Castle Howard. His drawings for the galleries at Brocklesby and Castle Howard, as well as the attractive laid-out plan for the drawing room at Stoke Park, emphasize Tatham's role as a decorator with a flair for elegance. He clearly took great pains with the arrangement of furniture, and in this he was aided by his brother Thomas and by John Linnell, his relation, both eminent cabinetmakers and upholsterers. In this regard, Holland's influence on Tatham must also have been considerable. As illustrated by Carlton House, which has never received its due as a major, if short-lived force in decoration around 1800, Holland carefully considered the furnishings of his rooms.

Tatham has fared badly with the depredations of time. Cowdray Lodge, Sussex; Stoke Edith, Herefordshire; Alpha Road House in London; Cheshunt Nunnery, Hertfordshire; Wilton Park, Buckinghamshire; Cleveland House, London; 12 Grosvenor Place, London; the gallery at Brocklesby: all the works—except the mausoleum at Trentham; Lynedoch Lodge, Perthshire; Broxmore House, Hampshire; Cowsfield House, Wiltshire; Paultons, Hampshire; Hennerton House, Berkshire—all have been demolished. It is quite a fate for an architect whose output was in any case limited in scope, if not in imagination.

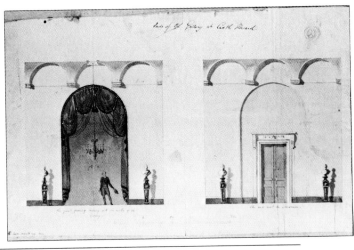

TOPOGRAPHICAL LIST OF DRAWINGS

Numbers in parentheses refer to the album known as "Precedents and Various Designs. . ." with the exception of those preceded by "Vol. II," which refer to the album titled "Collection of Drawings from various antique . . . Models . . ."

BIRMINGHAM, *Warwickshire*: THEATRE ROYAL
Roof section and detailed measure (10) of theater as rebuilt by George Saunders, 1793.

BISHOPSTOKE, *Hampshire*
Rough sketches of a conservatory of an unknown house.

BRIGHTON, *Sussex*: POSSIBLY ROYAL PAVILION
"Blinds applied to outside Windows at Brighton," dated 1822 (102).

BROCKLESBY PARK, *Lincolnshire*
6 drawings prepared for engraving of the Gallery and the drawing for the title page of publication, dated 1811 (1–6); sketch of cast-iron chimney pot, dated December 1806 (73).

Tatham built the Picture Gallery for Lord Yarborough in 1807. It has been destroyed in rebuilding.

CASTLE HOWARD, *Yorkshire* (Figs. 2–6)
10 elevations and wall sections of the Sculpture Gallery and Museum as prepared for engraving, dated August 1801 (122–124, 223, 225, 226, 230, 233); design for "A Table executed for the Earl of Carlisle at Castle Howard 1800" (141).

The fifth earl commissioned the Gallery in 1800.

CLANDON PARK, *Surrey* (Figs. 7–8)
"South Front & Ground Plan for the Fruiting Stove for the Right Honble The Lord Onslow at Clandon" (79); and "Lord Onslow's Fruiting Stove for Clandon" (80).

Work possibly carried out by Tatham for Henry Holland in the early 1790s.

COPPED (or COPT) HALL, *Essex*
"The Gate in the Park at Copped Hall in Essex (J Wyatt)" (88).

Copped Hall was built 1753–1758 by John Sanderson and altered internally in 1775–1777 by James Wyatt.

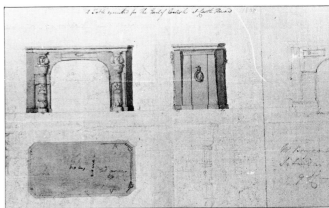

DEE, *Kirkudbrightshire*
"Plan and Elevation of a Bridge for the River Dee at Dee Village in the Stewartry of Kirkudbright," w/m 1796 (44).

DITCHLEY HOUSE, *Oxfordshire*
"Design for decorating the cove in the Hall at Ditchley to be painted in chiaroscuro & gilt,' dated December 1802 (49).

7. *Henry Holland* invenit, *Tatham* delin. *Clandon, Surrey.*
Fruiting stove, plan and elevation.

8. *Holland and Tatham. Fruiting stove, section and elevation of east front.*

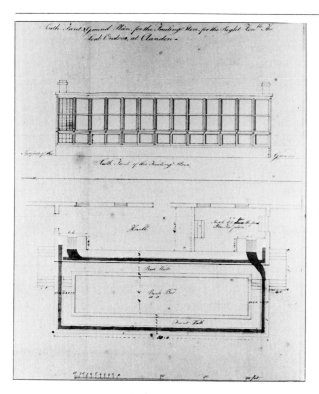

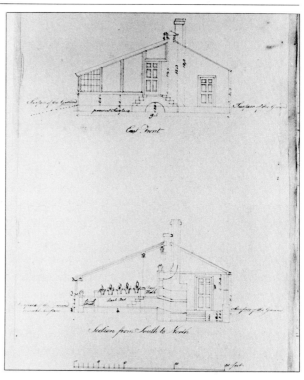

Proposed for the twelfth viscount Dillon, but like Tatham's designs for a library and a shooting box in the park, not executed. The house, c. 1720–1731, is by James Gibbs and the cove remains today undecorated.

GOODWOOD HOUSE, *Sussex*

Plan, elevation, and two sections of the Tennis Court (60).

D. Jacques in his *A Visit to Goodwood*, 1822, mentions the tennis court, a freestanding structure, near the kitchen gardens southeast of the house. It is not known if this was built by Sir William Chambers, who had built the tennis court at Wilton in 1772 and also was patronized by the third duke of Richmond at Goodwood.

HITCHIN, *Hertfordshire:* CHURCH OF ST. MARY

Plan and two elevations of the porch, signed and dated "Henry Baddock delt Feby 12th 1811" (21).

HOLLYCOMBE, *Sussex*

Rough plan, dated May 1815 and note that "The whole buildings are thatched. The fronts are roughcast" (121).

This house was designed by John Nash for Sir Charles Taylor c.

1805 as an example of his Picturesque *cottage orné*. Replaced by a Tudor-style house c. 1900.

ICKWORTH HOUSE, *Suffolk* (Figs. 9–11)

"Lord Bristol's Stable Building" (33): "Plan of a Library for Lord Bristol" (34); "Pier Table designed for Lord Bristol at Rome (M.A. fec^t) Bronze gilt," signed and dated "CHT Rome 1796" (II: 108).

Mario Asprucci had provided the first designs for the fourth earl of Bristol's new house at Ickworth, and it was these that Francis Sandys used as the basis for his design of the present house. Sandys was in Italy at Lord Bristol's expense from 1791 to 1796 and he belongs therefore to the Tatham-Asprucci clique. Tatham's two designs were not executed, but refer to the commission extended to him by Lord Bristol to have a try, for which he was paid five guineas in November 1794.

KINGSTON HOUSE (Dorset?)

Plan and section of an ice house, *w/m* 1796 (50).

LONDON

ALMACK'S CLUB OR ROOMS, KING STREET
Half section of room (9).

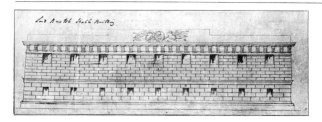

In the 1760s William Almack had contracted with Holland senior for various building works, but Robert Mylne designed the Club in 1764. Tatham and the younger Holland may have carried out minor works in the 1790s.

CARLTON HOUSE, PALL MALL
"Therm of a french Chimney piece statuary marble with gilt or-molu ornaments at Carlton House, Pall Mall" (36); plan of the floor "under" the Riding House, dated December 1788 (59).

This Louis XVI-style chimney piece has not been located, but belongs to the decorations carried out by Holland for George, Prince of Wales, from 1783 to 1796. The drawing is not in the hand of the R.I.B.A. Carlton House sketchbooks. The Riding House or "Ride" was not demolished until 1862, whereas Carlton House went in 1826.

COVENT GARDEN: ST. PAUL'S CHURCH
Roof section and detailed measures (11).

This is of the church by Inigo Jones before its gutting by fire in 1795.

DRURY LANE THEATRE
Roof section and detailed measures (12) of theater built by Holland 1791–1794.

FOLEY HOUSE, PORTLAND PLACE (Fig. 12)
"Sketch of the Plan of Foley House Cavendish Square before it was taken down in 1811" (47).

This is the house built for the second Lord Foley by Stiff Lead-better, 1753–1758, but as the plan clearly shows, added to and altered later in the century.

GREENWICH HOSPITAL
"A Sketch of the New Boy's & girl's Establishment at Greenwich Hospital," dated September 1811 (119).

Correctly ascribed to D. A. Alexander, who built these flanking blocks from 1810, which were connected to the Queen's House by colonnades.

HAYMARKET
Plan and section of the tennis court (57).

MAYFAIR CHAPEL, CURZON STREET
Rough plan for the "Curzon Street Chapel," built 1730, demolished 1898.

SLOANE PLACE, HOLLAND'S HOUSE (Fig. 13)
Plan, section, and details of greenhouse (81); plan, elevation, and section for a "design for addition" to the Grape House (82); and elevation of a gate (84).

Sloane Place was built by Holland for himself as part of the Hans Town development from 1777, demolished in the 1870s.

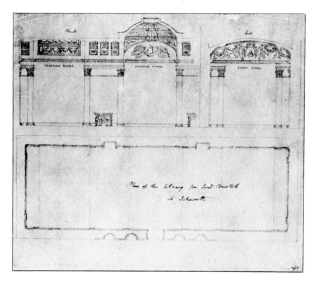

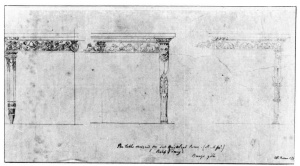

12. *Tatham, Foley House, London. Measured plan.*
13. *Holland invenit, Tatham delin. Sloane Place, London. Plan, elevation, sections, and details of Greenhouse.*
14. *Holland invenit, Tatham delin., Plan, elevation, and sections of Greenhouse and Conservatory for John Stockwell.*

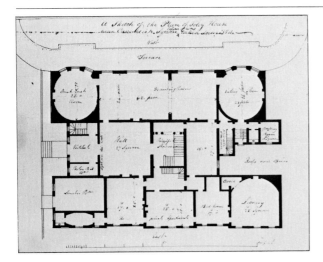

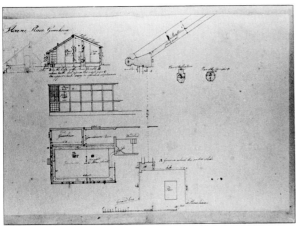

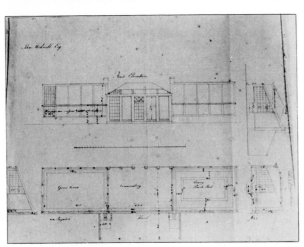

JOHN STOCKWELL'S HOUSE (Fig. 14)

Plan, elevation, and two sections of a greenhouse, conservatory, and pinery (77).

Unlocated, but perhaps in London and on the Hans Town development. The drawings conform to those for Sloane Place and Clandon—i.e., Holland commissions.

MAIDENHEAD, Berkshire
"Sketch of a double Cottage at Maidenhead" (92).

MAIDSTONE, Kent: Goal and Bridewell
Rough plan dated 1817 of D. A. Alexander's 1811 building.

OATLANDS PARK, Surrey
"Wire fence to the Private Garden" (54), referring to Holland's work for Frederick, Duke of York, from 1794.

SALTRAM, Devonshire
"Lord Boringdon's stable at Saltram" (94).

SANDON HALL, Staffordshire
Rough plan and elevation of house and greenhouse (74).

SARK, Dumfriesshire
"Plan and Elevation of a Bridge for the River Sark which is the boundary between the Counties of Cumberland and Dumfries" (44).

The river Sark flows into the head of the Solway Firth.

SCONE PALACE, Perthshire
Rough plan of William Atkinson's house as reconstructed for the third earl of Mansfield, 1803 (120).

SHOBDON COURT, Herefordshire
"The Vinery at Shobdon Court Hereford Wm Hanbury Esq" (78).

SOUTHILL HOUSE, Bedfordshire
Plans and elevation of a "Pise Cottage built by Holland at Southill 1797" (91).

Holland was remodeling Southill for Samuel Whitbread from 1796.

STEVENSON HOUSE, East Lothian
"Sr J. Sinclair's circular domed cottage maybe 2 floors" (18).

Possibly a pisé cottage.

STOKE PARK, Herefordshire (Figs. 15, 16)
"Mr Foley's Boat Shed" (93); "Vine & Peach House 158 long by

15. Tatham, Stoke Edith, Herefordshire. Design for West Drawing Room, 1800.

16. Tatham, Stoke Edith. Design for Entrance Gates.

14 wide in the clear . . . by R. Aird" (96); "Shepherds Cottage" (129); Plans, elevations, and sections of a cottage (130–131); "A Design for fitting up and furnishing the West Drawing Room—shewing the several sides of the Room—and a Plan of the furniture . . . This is the first work in which I was engaged after my return from Rome CHT Sept 1800" (132); "3 cottages to be built of stone & tyles designed for The Hon Ed. Foley Sepr 1802 6 Bed Rooms over C. H. Tatham" (133); "Gates designed for the Entrance of Stoke Park in Herefordshire The Seat of The Honble Edward Foley MP" (134).

Stoke, or Stoke Edith as it is sometimes called, was a great late-seventeenth-century house, now demolished. Tatham certainly carried out the drawing-room design and at least one cottage. His park gate was not executed to this design, which is based upon the entrance gates of the Villa Borghese in Rome. The death of Foley in 1803 ended any further hopes of patronage.

SUDBOROUGH, *Northamptonshire*
Plan and two elevations of a house designed for Sir James Pulteney, *w/m* 1796 (100–101).

It is not known if this was built, or indeed if it is a Holland design.

TRENTHAM PARK, *Staffordshire* (Figs. 17, 18)
"Trentham Hall A Design for a Egyptian Temple proposed to be used as a greenhouse CHT Nov 1805" (142); "Sketches of Fountains for Trentham" (143); uninscribed design for a mausoleum, possibly a project for the Trentham mausoleum as it is partly in the Egyptian taste (121).

Tatham worked for the second marquess of Stafford. It is known that he designed a fountain, greenhouse, park bridges, new lodge, and the celebrated mausoleum, but the above designs may not have been executed in the Egyptian manner.

WANSTEAD HOUSE, *Essex*
Plans, elevations, and sections of the grotto, with detailed description, "sketched on the Spot June 1822" (48) when Tatham visited Wanstead for the celebrated contents sale of 10 June.

WILTON HOUSE, *Wiltshire*
Rough sketches of the grotto by Isaac de Caus (46).

WOBURN ABBEY, *Bedfordshire*
"Plan of the Piggeries" dated December 1798 (22); Plan and sections of the tennis court (58, 62–64); sections of the Riding House (61); "Pise Cottages Extracts from Salmon's Particulars of pise walling & Building at Woburn Abbey 1797" (90).

These drawings relate to the extensive works carried out by Hol-

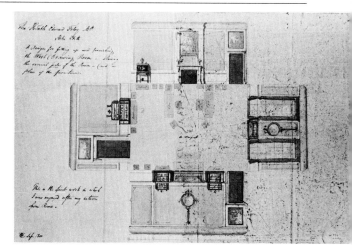

land for the fifth duke of Bedford from 1787 to 1802. The tennis court may have been the reason for Tatham's being sent to the Haymarket and Goodwood to make drawings of the courts there.

DESIGNS FOR UNLOCATED PLACES
"Design for Corn Farm, houses and offices for Dr. Dicksee," *w/m* 1898 (18).

"Dairy Farm House & Offices," *w/m* 1898 (20), possibly for Dr. Dicksee.

Various designs for barns and farm offices, *w/m* 1806 (19).

Plans, elevations, and sections, and "Ground Plan of a Design for a Sea Cottage to be built of Pise and covered with Thatch

17. Tatham, Trentham Park, Staffordshire. Design for Egyptian Greenhouse.

18. Tatham, perhaps Trentham Park. Egyptian Mausoleum.

19. Tatham, Design for a Wall Monument to a "young French architect who died while on his studies in Rome, 1795."

20. Tatham. House designed by the earl of Carisle in 1810. Plan.

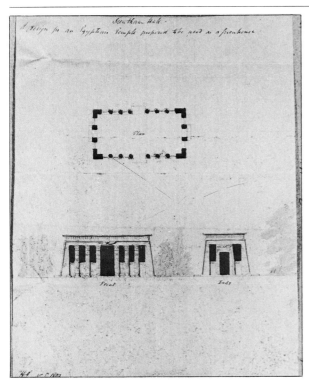

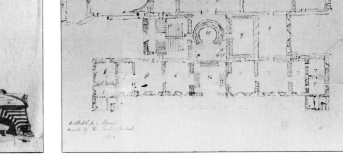

made for The Lord Viscount Torrington," signed and dated May 1799 (38–39).

"Egyptian Sepulchre" and "Egyptian Temple Dedicated to the God Anubus," signed and dated "CHT Rome 1796" (32).

Design for a tomb of "Modern Invention," signed and dated "CHT Rome 1796" (42).

Copy of a plan of Tatham's Casino or Hunting Pavilion submitted to the Academy of Saint Luke in Rome in 1796 (40).

Plan and section of an Ice House by "Wilkins Norwich" (51).

"A Monument designed for a young french Architect who died while on his studies at Rome CHT 1795" (Vol. II: 175) (Fig. 19).

21. *Mario Asprucci. Villa Borghese, Rome. Design for a temple for sculpture for Prince Borghese, 1792. Copy by Tatham, 1796. Plan.*
22. *Asprucci. Temple for sculpture for Prince Borghese. Section.*

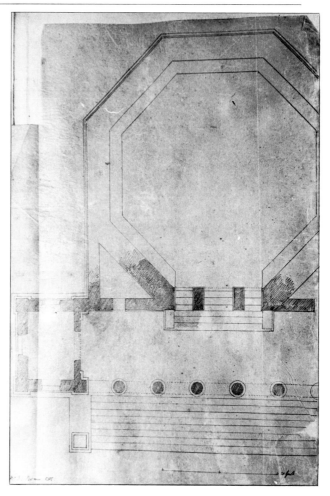

"A Sketch for a House made by the Earl of Carlisle 1810" (71) (Fig. 20).

This was Tatham's patron at Castle Howard. Why Lord Carlisle should make a design for a house is not clear, unless it had something to do with a new house at Naworth Castle, Cumberland, or a whim for a house near London.

"Hotel in Paris Sketched by Lady Grenville" (72).

Unidentified, but Lady Grenville employed Tatham extensively at Dropmore, Buckinghamshire, 1806 to 1809.

DRAWINGS OR DESIGNS BY ARCHITECTS AND OTHERS COPIED OR COLLECTED BY TATHAM IN ITALY

"Antique mosaic pavement bought by the Earl of Bristol at Rome—the whole of very rich colouring. November 1795" (Vol. II: 13).

"Cieling (sic) executed after the Design of Mario Asprucci in the Palais Borghese in Rome 1796" (Vol. II: 1).

Plan, section, and elevation of portico, designed by M. Asprucci in 1792, drawn by Tatham, of "A Design made for Prince Borghese at Rome for a Temple to be built in the Gardens of his villa, to receive the collection of Antique Statues found at Gabie by Gavin Hamilton—1796. Mario Asprucchi Architect" (25–27) (Figs. 21–23).

Letter from Asprucci to Tatham, 29 August 1800, sending him as requested a plan and elevation of the "Eremitorio" near the Villa Aldobrandini at Frascati (loose in Vol. II).

Plan of a garden by a French architect with "Elevation de la Redoute," "Elevation du Temple pres du Casin," and "Façade dessus la Jardin Hollandois" (30–31).

"Design for a observatory and habitable House by a french Architect at Rome" (28) (Fig. 24).

Copy of the mausoleum designed by Mr. Vien for the French Academy in Rome in 1788, "for which he obtained his medal," dated 1795 (41).

"Antique Pilaster found in the Ruins of Adrian's Villa near Tivoli used in a chimney piece belonging to Thomas Jenkins Esq at Rome. Copied from the Original Novr 1794" (Vol. II:6).

Copies of a plan and two elevations and court elevation of a house designed by Charles Percier for Thomas Graham, later Lord Lyn-

23. Asprucci. Temple for sculpture for Prince Borghese. Copy by Tatham. Elevation of portico.

24. Tatham. Design for an Observatory "by a young French architect at Rome." Plan and elevation.

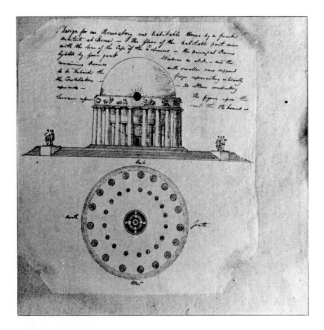

returned to London. Holland seems to have employed him upon concerns of offices, outbuildings, garden works, and cottages. Conveniently, Tatham makes the specific point that the drawing room at Stoke Edith was his first work (in an independent capacity) after Italy. A few drawings such as those for Clandon and Sloane Place may have been made when Tatham first entered Holland's office in the 1780s. The Italian drawings seem to imply that in 1794 and 1795 Tatham was principally drawing antique remains, and his real design training does not begin until 1796 when he submitted designs to the Academy of St. Luke in Rome. The drawings or designs he collected or copied throw some light upon Italian architecture in the 1790s, notably Asprucci's contributions to the Villa Borghese and to Lord Bristol's Ickworth.

doch, for Lyndoch Lodge, Perthshire, together with an "Explication du projet de la maison du Colonel Graham," signed and dated January 1805, together with a copy of a letter from Percier to Graham dated 10 August 1802 (97–99) (Figs. 25, 26).

The job of building a new house at Lyndoch Lodge was eventually given to Tatham in 1807. Perhaps these copies of Percier's designs were made by Tatham at Lyndoch, unless Tatham met Percier if he traveled from Italy to London via Paris in 1796.

SUMMARY

Surprisingly, although there are not many actual design drawings in this collection, it elucidates much about Tatham's early career and helps to fill in our knowledge of what he did when he

Notes

1. This account is based also upon printed sources, notably H. M. Colvin's entry under Tatham in *A Biographical Dictionary of British Architects 1600–1840*, 1978; and C. Proudfoot and D. Watkin, "A Pioneer of English Neo-Classicism," *Country Life*, April 13/20, 1972, and "The Furniture of C. H. Tatham," *Country Life*, June 8, 1972.

2. The volumes measure 520 × 320 mm. One is inscribed "This Collection of Drawings from/various antique & other Models/were made by me at Rome & elsewhere on the Continent/ in the Years 1794.95 & 96/ C. H. Tatham Architect/ Member of the Academy of St Luke at Rome/ and of the Institute Bologna/ & Member of the Soc: of Architects in London/ CHT Warden of Trinity Hospital East Greenwich/ June 1 1840," and in a later hand "Given to John Richmond grandson of C. H. Tatham/ by his father George Richmond March 28 1891/ in due of GR's 82nd birthday."

   The other volume is inscribed "Precedents & Various/ Designs/collected/ C. H. Tatham," to distinguish it as to content from the album of drawings copied from the antique. Both volumes have pasted on the cover a sale catalogue entry as "Lot 728 (TATHAM, C. H.) A Collection of Manuscript Drawings from various antique and other models made at Rome in 1794, 95 and 96, about 150 drawings mounted in an album; Designs for Interiors, Plans for Mansions, Theatres etc. Plans for Mr Holland's Grape House at

Sloane Place etc. about 140 drawings a few coloured, mounted in an album, half calf c. 1800 (2)."

3. Tatham's first book was published in 1800 and titled *Etchings Representing The Best Examples of Ancient Ornamental Architecture drawn from the Originals in Rome and Other Parts of Italy during the years 1794, 1795 and 1796.* There was a second edition in 1803 and a third in 1810. In 1806 the companion volume appeared, titled *Etchings representing fragments of antique Grecian and Roman architectural ornament.* In 1826, both works were combined in a single volume titled *Etchings representing the best Examples of Grecian and Roman architectural ornament drawn from the originals, and chiefly collected in Italy, before the late Revolutions in that Country.* All Tatham's other works are in his linear style: *Three Designs for the Naval Monument* of 1802, *Designs for Ornamental Plate* of 1806, *The Gallery of Castle Howard* of 1810, *The Gallery at Brocklesby*, also of 1810, the *Greek Vase* of 1811, and the *Mausoleum at Castle Howard* of 1812. His technique was emulated and his published works plagiarized by Thomas Hope in *Household Furniture* of 1807, and knowing of Tatham's possible association with Charles Percier, the *Recueil de décorations intérieures* by Percier and Fontaine in 1812 may well owe much to Tatham's examples.

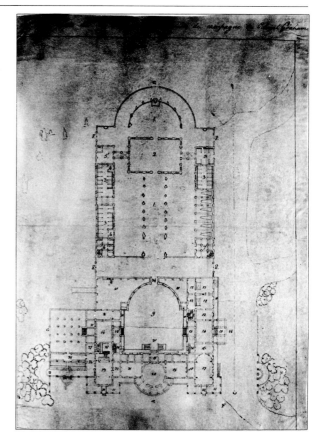

THE BEGINNINGS OF FRENCH ROMANTIC ARCHITECTURE AND FELIX DUBAN'S TEMPLE PROTESTANT

David Van Zanten

I

IN SEPTEMBER 1829, FIVE SETS OF ARchitectural drawings on display at the Académie des Beaux-Arts in Paris caused a great stir, since they demonstrated the penetration of the new Romantic movement into the realm of architecture. Their authors were five students who, having won the Grand Prix de Rome, were then enjoying five-year *pensions* and studying at the French Academy in Rome. The drawings were their *envois* of the previous year, annual projects sent back to Paris to show the progress of their work. They comprised four archaeological studies and—by the most advanced student—a design for a modern building, "Conforme aux usages de la France."[1]

The controversy aroused by those *envois* centered on those of the two most senior *pensionnaires*, the fourth-year project by Henri Labrouste reconstructing the three Greek buildings at Paestum, and the fifth-year project by Félix Duban for a Protestant church, or *temple protestant*. Labrouste's *envoi* started a serious archaeological dispute, but at the time Duban's was regarded as the more inflammatory. Already in 1829, at the time of the display, the academician A.-L.-T. Vaudoyer, Labrouste's *patron*, had written his son Léon, one of the *pensionnaires* in Rome, in reference to Duban's project: "On dit . . . ici que c'est le type de tous les projets qui vont maintenant arriver de Rome."[2] Shortly afterward, in 1833, Petrus Borel—a student architect and Romantic writer who had organized part of the claque at Hugo's *Hernani* from among students of Labrouste and Duban[3]—wrote in *L'Artiste*: "Ce temple parfaitement composé, soigneusement pensé, d'un bel et inaccoutumé aspect, fit jeter les hauts cris à MM les académiciens. . . ."[4] Borel ended by declaring that Duban, "Le premier osait braver face à face l'inviolable section des beaux-arts." As the 1830s passed, Duban's name became synonymous with Romanticism in architecture,[5] and in 1842 the critic Hippolyte Fortoul wrote in overview:

> Une génération s'élève qui a l'ambition de mettre au niveau de tous les autres arts celui qu'elle cultive avec un dévouement modeste et opiniâtre. Je vous ai parlé souvent de ces esprits délicats qui ont rapporté de Rome, avec un sentiment vrai et nouveau des monuments antiques, le besoin de reprendre la tradition architecturale au point où elle était en France au commencement du XVIIe siècle. Vous savez qu'ils ont déjà fait leurs preuves; serrés étroitement et choisissant leur aîné pour leur maître, ils se sont rangés autour de M. Duban, . . . [6]

Labrouste's original project survives; Duban's does not. Labrouste's later career, when his resolute adherence to principle caused him to emerge as the precursor of the unrelenting E. E. Viollet-le-Duc, has tended to satisfy historians that knowledge of his *envoi* alone is sufficient in order to comprehend what was at issue in 1828/29.[7] Yet Duban was the older of the two by four years, his project the more advanced in the pedagogical system, and its subject better adapted to making a statement. And it was of great immediate impact, as we have just seen. It obviously must be considered. Fortunately, some evidence of it is preserved: two sets of pencil sketches, one by Labrouste himself, the other by the architect Joseph Lecointe (Figs. 1, 2).[8] Lecointe's sketches are extraordinarily precise, including dimensions and the arrangement of liturgical furniture, and they are confirmed by Labrouste's. We cannot say anything about the decorative touch Duban displayed in this design, but we can analyze

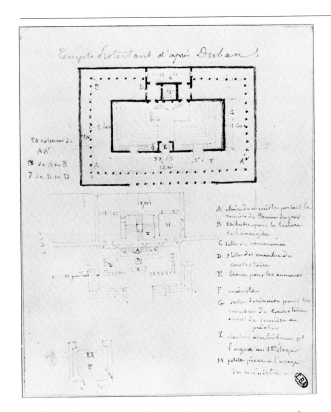

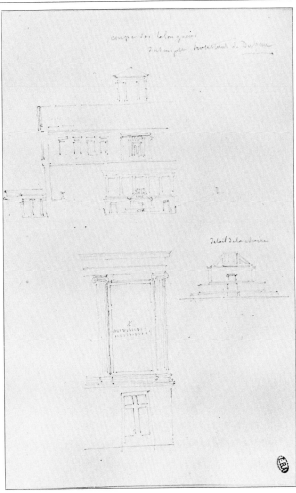

its basic layout—and that, I hope to show, is what matters.

II

Duban's *temple protestant* (Figs. 1–3) consists of a rectangular volume, roughly a double cube, with gables at its short sides. A bell tower at the back and a monumental doorway at the front (*E* in Lecointe's sketch) establish the main axis across the long sides, and the whole mass is surrounded by a low colonnaded space (marked "enceinte," surely the churchyard in the form of a *campo santo*) which echoes its form. Inside, the communion table (*C*), lectern (*B*), pulpit (*A*), and organ loft (*I*) are all set on a vertical axis against the back wall, with the pews for the congregation banked up on three sides facing them. Twelve separate seats for the consistory are set in front (*D*). The pews are reached by four short stairways leading from two secondary entrances flanking the main doorway on the facade. A room for the minister (*H*) and a chamber for the deliberations of the consistory (*G*) abut the tower at the back. A recess (*E*) inside the main doorway enframes a freestanding poorbox, marked "tronc pour les aumônes."

In the analysis of Duban's project two questions immediately present themselves: (1) how could a French Catholic conceive a *temple protestant* in Papal Rome? and, (2) why would he

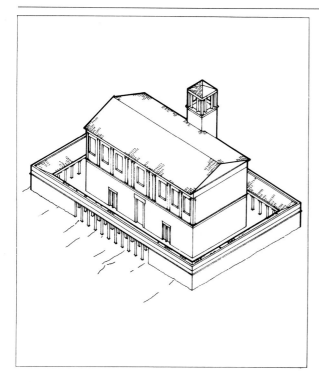

offer such a design in 1828/29 as an *envoi*, that is, a "Projet d'un monument public de sa composition . . . conforme aux usages de la France"?[9]

The second question is more easily answered than the first. The Huguenot church—the French Calvinist Eglise Reformée—had been recognized by the government since 1787 and had been administered by it since 1802. On January 11, 1828, just when Duban would have been turning his mind to the selection of a subject for his fifth-year *envoi*, this administration was reorganized and upgraded by the ministry of the Vicomte de Martignac, installed a few days before, on January 5. The scientist Baron Georges Cuvier (a Lutheran from Montbéliard with strong ties to the influential Huguenots of Paris) was appointed *conseiller d'état* for Cultes Protestants et Israélites, one of eight division heads (equal to those of Ponts et Chaussées or Bâtiments Civils) re-

porting directly to the Minister of the Interior.[10] Previously, the Protestant church had been merely a bureau headed by a certain unsympathetic M. de Lavédine in the Division des Cultes Non-Catholics, des Sciences, Lettres et Beaux-Arts, des Journaux et Théâtres.

The simplicity and small size of Duban's project suggest that it was a model parish church. Likewise the precise and detailed manner in which Lecointe recorded it, especially its liturgical furniture, implies that it set a pattern which an architect might have opportunity to utilize. One would thus suppose that Duban was responding to this reorganization by putting forward a type to guide the more orderly administration of Protestant church-building.

The answer to the first question, however, is more involved. Duban's project is different from any current French type. During the forty years since the recognition of the Huguenot church no consistent architectural paradigm had emerged among the sect's buildings. Indeed, with few exceptions, these buildings were of the crudest sort, being erected by local builders if new. Most frequently, they were churches, barns, or storehouses appropriated from the Catholics.[11] The vast majority were rectangular boxes with a pulpit on the short side facing the door—the ubiquitous provincial church type so familiar in the United States. Behind these meager precedents, of course, loomed the profound tradition of Huguenot church-building of the sixteenth and seventeenth centuries, but the destruction and mayhem following the revocation of the Edict of Nantes left very few physical vestiges of that.

So there was Duban in January 1828—a Catholic in the capital of Catholicism, where Protestantism could not yet be practiced publicly, and from a country where the Protestant architectural

4. *Wilhelm Stier, project for a Protestant church, 1827. Plan. (Illustration,* Der Kirchenbau des Protestantismus, *1893, p. 193.)*

5. *Stier, project for a Protestant church. Section. (Illustration:* Der Kirchenbau des Protestantismus, *p. 192.)*

tradition was only a distant memory—sitting down to design a model French Protestant church. Where would he start? There is one obvious answer: he would address himself to Baron Christian Carl Josias von Bunsen, the Prussian ambassador to the Holy See since 1824 and a leading Protestant layman. Bunsen wrote hymns, worked out a new Protestant liturgy, established the first regular Protestant services in Rome following his liturgy at the embassy in 1819, and, most significantly for us, in 1827 commissioned a design for an ideal Protestant church from the young Prussian architect then in Rome, Wilhelm Stier (Figs. 4, 5).[12] All this was surely accessible to Duban; Bunsen's projects were always open to public perusal. In 1828, while Duban was working on his project, Karl Friedrich Schinkel visited Rome and examined Stier's project; he was so impressed by it that he immediately arranged for Stier's appointment as professor at the newly reorganized Berlin Bauschule, a post he occupied with great distinction until his death in 1856.[13] Stier himself had studied with Lecointe in Paris in 1822/23 and after reaching Rome in the latter year had accompanied Jacques-Ignace Hittorff on his trip to Sicily. He moved on the edge of the French circle in Rome.

Thus one turns eagerly to Stier's project to see what Duban might have copied, and finds that he seems pointedly to have copied nothing. Stier's church consists of a nave of horseshoe shape surrounded by a tier of balcony boxes with a projecting entrance and stairhall at the front and a platform with three chapels—for the altar, the baptismal font, and the funeral service—rising massively at the back. Stier's, however, is a unique monument, a project for the vast Protestant cathedral which throughout the 1820s had been contemplated facing the royal Schloss in Berlin

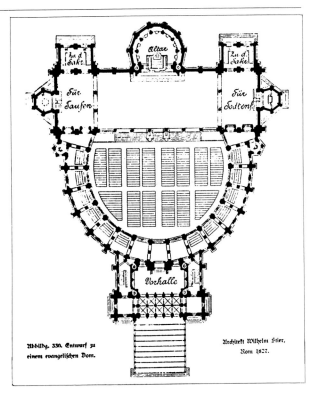

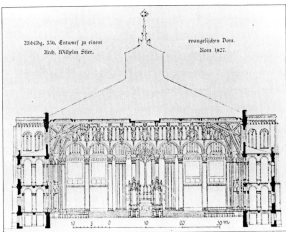

at the base of Unter den Linden.[14] It is a ceremonial building representing the Protestant state, a public symbol. Setting it beside Duban's *temple* reemphasizes that the latter is only a middle-sized parish church, one whose relation to the community, represented by the consistory, is of basic importance. (There is no space provided for the consistory in Stier's project.) Duban's discrete shielding of his building from urban emphasis by setting it within a *campo santo* responds to the fact that in France Protestantism was a dissenting faith whose buildings could not be treated as state monuments.

This distinction in public image, however, is no greater than the distinction in liturgical layout. Bunsen commissioned Stier's design as the embodiment of his new Prussian liturgy. This liturgy was a solution to a unique problem: the unification of the Lutheran rite of the Prussian population and the Calvinist liturgy of the royal house of Brandenburg to produce a unified state Protestantism.[15] Since 1817 such a *Unierte Kirche* had functioned administratively, but it had yet to exist in actual liturgy and faith. A number of differences between the modified Catholicism of Lutheranism and the radical Protestantism of Calvinism had to be resolved, most particularly the divergent views of the significance of communion and its relation to the preaching of the Word. The Lutherans held communion to be a sacramental event, Christ becoming present "under the appearances" of the bread and wine.[16] The Calvinists saw it as a memorial, a reminder. The Lutherans celebrated communion on a static ceremonial stone altar and proclaimed it the center of the service; the Calvinists held the sermon to be central and provided only a light movable wooden table for communion. Bunsen's liturgy was essentially ceremonial and Lutheran (if not actually Catholicizing): he made communion the primary element of the service and emphasized its mystical character.[17] It is this concept that is embodied in Stier's project. The congregation is arranged precisely as if in a contemporary the-

ater, facing a stage where the clergy move before an altar mounted on a tier of steps which is theatrically lighted. Searching for an analogy for Bunsen's vision of a communion-oriented service, Stier hit upon the idea that it would resemble a piece of theater, and so he contained it in the volume of the Neoclassical theater deriving from the Roman Theater of Marcellus. There is only one detail of Stier's scheme that is not literally theatrical: in place of the proscenium arch is an arcade which divides the spaces like a Catholic rood screen, emphasizing that they are nave and chancel, not auditorium and stage.

On the two centermost columns of the screen in Stier's project a pulpit and a lectern are cantilevered forward. The preaching of the Word is thus accomplished in the mundane, not the mystical, space. These pulpits are all that is left of Calvinism in that plan, but they are the essence of Duban's Huguenot, French Calvinist *temple*. Here there is no separate mystical space at all; everything takes place in the auditorium itself, the pulpit being elevated over and dominating the communion table. Duban's scheme, in contrast to Stier's, is emphatically committed to the preaching of the Word. And for this reason Stier's design could provide no model for Duban, although its existence in Rome in 1828 must have clarified the issues, and Stier's broad knowledge of Protestant church design might have been helpful.[18]

Did Duban, then, simply make up his project in his head, counterbalancing Stier's? Not only did he reject that model, close at hand in Rome, but he also seems to have refused all the other monumental paradigms which he might have known about: Vor Frue Kirke in Copenhagen of 1811 to 1829 by C. F. Hansen; the Stadtkirche in Karlsruhe of 1807 to 1816 by Friedrich Wein-

6. *Parish church, Heiden (near St. Gallen), Switzerland, before the fire of 1939. Félix-Wilhelm Kubly, 1836–1840. Exterior. (Photo: Courtesy of Benno Schubiger, Archives Denkmalpflege, Berne.)*

brenner; and Schinkel's and Friedrich Wilhelm IV's projects for the Protestant cathedral of Berlin (1815 ff.).[19] Once again, however, it must be emphasized that Duban's is a typical, not a monumental, structure. And as such it is very much part of a broader, humbler architectural family— that of the Calvinist parish church, especially as the type appears in Switzerland. Significantly, on his way back from Rome in the spring of 1829 Duban visited Geneva and perhaps other cities in Switzerland and Germany,[20] and his observations led him to redraw his *envoi*. In a letter dated August 22, 1829, he petitioned the Académie des Beaux-Arts to let him submit this modified project: "Passant à Genève, à mon retour d'Italie, j'ai eu occasion de mieux connaître les données du Projet . . . et je n'ai pu résister au désir de modifier mon travail."[21] Geneva was the capital of French Calvinism, the city Calvin himself had ruled from 1541 to 1564, where Calvinism remained the state church, where during the years of persecution aid for the Calvinists of France was clandestinely gathered, and where French pastors were trained.[22]

Professor Georg Germann has traced the evolution in Switzerland of the type represented in Duban's project—a simple rectangular volume with the pulpit on the long wall and the bell tower behind. First appearing in the seventeenth century, it received definitive expression in the parish church of Hans Conrad Stadler at Uster, built between 1823 and 1826, and that of Félix-Wilhelm Kubly at Heiden, built between 1836 and 1840 (Fig. 6).[23] These were for Zwinglite congregations around Zurich, but a similar evolution is seen in the Huguenot churches around Geneva, culminating in that at Colombier of 1828/29.[24] Humbler examples of this type could also be seen in

Germany; most importantly, it was recommended and illustrated by Leonhard Christoph Sturm in his *Architektonisches Bedenken von protestantischer kleiner Kirchen Figur und Einrichtung* of 1712 and his *Vollständige Anweisung alle Arten von Kirchen wohl anszugeben* of 1718.

Duban, however, visited Switzerland only after completing his *envoi* (although he modified it as a result);[25] what did he know about this church type before that? Surely a great deal. In his circle of friends in Rome were two Swiss Calvinist architects, Kubly, just mentioned, and Melchior Berri. The former had been a colleague of Labrouste and Vaudoyer in A.-L.-T. Vaudoyer's *atelier* in Paris; the latter a student there of Jean-Nicolas Huyot and the son and son-in-law of Zwinglite pastors in Basel (as well as the brother-in-law of Jacob Burckhardt).[26] It is surely no coincidence that Kubly at Heiden, in the first of a series of churches he was to build, reproduced the basic layout of Duban's *temple protestant* almost exactly. (The roof was originally gabled, the ridge at right angles to the major axis. The building, with its cemetery a hundred yards behind it, dominates the town square, opposite the city hall.)[27]

III

Duban's *temple protestant*, then, was not an original creation, like Stier's, but instead a variation on a specific traditional type, that of the Calvinist parish church. As an *envoi* by a *pensionnaire* at the French Academy at Rome, what might such a choice imply?

The second part of this essay commenced with the proposition that the selection of this subject by Duban in 1828 might be appropriate because of the contemporaneous reorganization of the Cultes Protestants et Israélites. There is a complication, however: this reorganization had been forced on the Bourbon government after two decades of agitation by the powerful Protestants of Paris and more immediately by the fall of the reactionary ministry of Comte J.-B.-S. Joseph de Villèle on January 5, 1828. It was accompanied with neither joy nor fanfare on the part of the royalists. It played no part in the Restoration's reassertion of divine right and was, instead, one of the small concessions offered by the compromising ministry of Martignac before the Revolution of 1830. During the Villèle ministry the reestablishment of Catholicism as the exclusive state church had been discussed seriously. As F.-R. de Lamennais had proclaimed in 1825:

> La réligion catholique doit être tenue pour vraie et les autres pour fausses; elle doit faire partie de la constitution de l'Etat et de là répondre dans les institutions politiques et civiles; autrement l'Etat professe l'indifférence des réligions, il exile Dieu de ses lois, il est athée.[28]

The freedom enjoyed by the Protestant church was a resented vestige of the Revolution. In practice, during the Restoration Protestant churches were denied prominent sites and bell towers. Indeed, during most of the period there were no appropriations for Protestant church-building at all.[29]

The bell tower of Duban's project immediately asserts that it was not simply an embodiment of governmental policy. And indeed during the 1820s "Protestantism" was a catch-phrase indicating resistance to the royalist establishment and the Académie it supported. In a celebrated article in the *Globe* of 1825 the young writer Ludovic Vitet (soon to be influential in the government of 1830 and a close friend of Duban and Labrouste) declared that Romanticism "C'est, en deux mots, le Protestantisme dans les lettres et les arts."[30] Borel, in the article of 1833 already cited, applied this metaphor to Duban's project:

> . . . Cette composition, pour le moins aussi hérétique que les réligionnaires à l'usage desquels elle était destinée, fut traitée comme on traitait les huguenots, et peu s'en fallut qu'on en fît un auto-da-fé, ou, pour parler un langage plus enharmonique, un holocauste au *Dieu du bon goût*. . . . car il est aussi des légitimités et des droits divins à l'Académie; car il est un art légitime et un art illégitime, car il est un art révélé et un art apocryphe non reconnus tels par le concile de Nicée ou de Trente, mais par le concile Fontaine and Guénepin.[31]

Duban's *temple protestant* challenged the academic system in architecture, and all the more boldly for challenging that system's governmental underpinning in its subject. It undermined the whole idea of the *pensionnaires' envois* and set an example that was followed by the seven subsequent fifth-year projects submitted by the younger Romantics at the Academy in Rome—Labrouste, Louis Duc, Vaudoyer, Théodore Labrouste, Marie-Antoine Delannoy, Simon-Claude Constant-Dufeux, and Pierre-Joseph Garrez.[32]

What the Académie wanted for a fifth-year *envoi* was, to quote the regulations of 1821 again, "Le projet d'un monument public de sa composition, et conforme aux usages de la France." In application, this *envoi* was to be based clearly on the archaeological studies made for the four previous *envois*. The fifth-year projects of 1822 and 1826 by L.-N.-M. Destouches and François-Alexandre Villain, respectively, gratified the academicians, and their comments at the *séance publique annuelle* made clear what they sought.

The project by Destouches for a race course was appropriate, the Académie declared, because the Restoration government had been supporting the breeding of fine horses, and furthermore because his previous, fourth-year archaeological *envoi* had been a reconstruction of an ancient Roman race course, the Circus of Caracalla.[33] The latter *envoi* is a parish church (understood to be Catholic).[34] What pleased the Académie here was the variety of ancient and Renaissance models Villain cited in his design—even including drawings of the originals on his sheets. They noted his reference to the Portico of Octavius in his entrance colonnade and continued, "Au milieu de cet enceinte [the surrounding *campo santo*], il élève, pour servir de baptistère, un petit édifice circulaire, qui rappèle le petit temple de Bramante à San-Pietro-in-Montorio; fort bonne réminiscence encore d'anciens usages. . . ."

Clearly the Académie intended that the material of the preceding years' *envois* should be used directly and literally in the fifth-year project, to the point that Villain was praised for making a compendium of the historical precedents he used. It understood the "usages de la France" to be aristocratic and Catholic (horse-racing and Catholic churches). And by "composition" it clearly intended something large with a complex spatial layout, a more sophisticated version of the Grand Prix designs with which the students had won their five-year pensions in Rome. Fifth-year *envois* that the Académie praised after the Romantic interlude included the *Cour de Cassation* of Jean-Amand Léveil, of 1838, the *Conservatoire de Musique* of Victor Baltard, of 1839, and the *Hôtel des Invalides de la Marine* by Guénepin, of 1843, all common Grand Prix subjects.

Duban's *temple protestant*, in contrast, reflected no apparent Roman precedents, served an

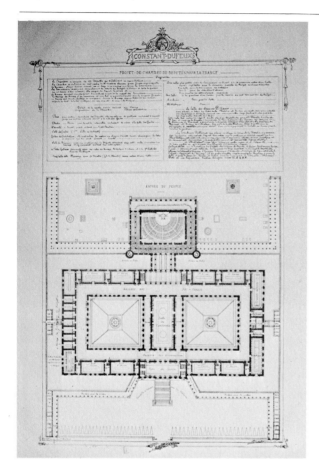

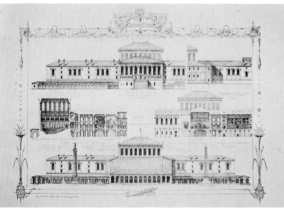

heretical sect, and was without compositional complexity or display. The Académie shrugged off Duban's effort with the comment, "Cet édifice n'admettant ni sculpture, ni peinture, ni richesse d'ornement, on regrette que M. Duban . . . n'a pas pu trouver, dans la simplicité obligée du sujet qu'il a choisi pour sa composition, les moyens d'y faire l'application de ses précédentes études."[35] But that body grew increasingly impatient as small compositions of uncanonical style and unusual subject followed: Labrouste's *Pont frontière* of 1830; Duc's *Monument aux victimes de la révolution de 1830* of 1830 (a line drawing on a single sheet); Vaudoyer's *Beffroi* of 1831; Théodore Labrouste's *Baptistère* of 1832; Delannoy's *Monument triomphal à élever à Teulon en l'honneur de l'armée d'Afrique* of 1833; Constant-Dufeux's *Chambre des Députés* of 1834 (Figs. 7, 8); and finally Garrez's *Halle aux Grains* of 1835, seen by the Académie as Gothic and bizarre and by the utopian socialists as revolutionary.[36] Four of these were not buildings—that is, spatial compositions—at all, but monuments, and the other four were spatially simple, made more so in execution.

In the case of one of these *envois*, documents exist which permit us to glimpse more vividly the mood of this conflict between the Neoclassical academicians and the Romantic *pensionnaires*. During his stay in Rome (1826–1832) Léon Vaudoyer corresponded regularly with his father, the academician, and when in 1831/32 his selection of a belfry as his fifth-year project was disputed,[37] he made the announcement in a letter of August 27, 1831. Vaudoyer *père*, surprised, responded on September 20:

Est-ce que là, me suis-je dit, un motif de faire l'application (suivant le but, l'institution de ce dernier envoi) de toutes les hautes et bonnes études que tu as fait pendant tes quatres premières années? Y'a-t-il là aucune invention de plan? Une occasion de disposition et proportions architecturales et monumentales? N'est-ce pas une simple composition d'esquisse de seconde classe et peu digne d'occuper un Pensionnaire de Rome qui a déjà eu sur les bancs de l'Ecole une médaille d'esquisse sur le même sujet? . . .

Ne crains-tu pas qu'on ne dire de ton Beffroi ce qu'on a dit . . . de la prêche de M. Duban, du pont de M. Labrouste, et enfin du petit monument de Juillet de cette année en une demie feuille du simple trait sans plan ni coupe par M. Duc. . . ?

He went on to cite a list of proper subjects he had suggested in a letter of February 8, 1828—a *Chambre des Pairs avec Salle de Trône*, a *Bibliothèque publique*, a *Campo Santo comme à Pise*, etc. But, a loving father, he devoted the rest of his letter to advice about how Léon might make his belfry a good one. "Voilà ton coup de tonerre," he ended, "tache qu'il soit éclatant!" Receiving in response only a few remarks about details, interspersed with fierce declarations of adherence to Romanticism, Vaudoyer *père* wrote again on October 15 to suggest that Léon emphasize the decorative rather than the functional in his project. What came back from the son, dated November 17, was this:

. . . Je ne transige jamais avec mes doctrines et . . . je ne sacrifie aucune de mes idées à l'avance de plaire un moment. Je ne ferai point de pétard. Je n'en ai ni le temps ni les moyens ni le désir. Si on me demande demain un projet comme j'entends un projet vaste doit être fait je réponderais, je ne suis pas architecte, mes études ne sont pas terminées, et cela parce que les arts

ne sont pas enseignés en France comme ils devraient être.

In ending, Léon mentioned that he was examining the campaniles at Venice, Cremona, Modena, and Valencia for his *envoi*.

Vaudoyer *père* responded on December 10:

Quant au campanile de Venise, il n'a pour bon que son élévation. Ceux de Pise et de Florence du même temps, sont un peu mieux, mais j'espère que tu ne prendras pas leur architecture pour modèle, et qu'au lieu de retomber dans l'enfance de l'art, tu recueilleras dans les siècles des lumières les monuments qui datent des beaux siècles de l'architecture.

Le Romantisme ne peut s'aveugler au point de faire rétrograder au lieu de faire avancer la marche de l'intelligence humaine.

His *envoi* finished and his departure from Rome approaching, Léon made his last declaration on this subject on January 4, 1832.

Comment peut-on faire de l'architecture comme [the temple of] Vénus et Roma [the subject of his fourth-year *envoi*] avec les idées, les besoins, les matériaux d'aujourd'hui? Voilà bien la vieille école de l'antique quand même . . . et cela produit la Madeleine, monument sans caractère local, puis en face la Chambre des Députés, qui est un autre temple antique, puis la Bourse, puis enfin le portique du Panthéon avec ses infames plates-bandes. Voilà comment depuis longtemps notre architecture; voilà pour mieux dire nous n'avons pas d'architecture. . . . Pauvre France!!! Ce que je désire le plus c'est d'avoir un mauvais rapport sur mon projet parce qu'alors je pourrais croire qu'il n'est pas mal. . . . Voilà au commencement du succes puis qu'on désapprouve le choix.

The Académie duly reported that Vaudoyer *fils*,

"S'étant renfermé dans un sujet si peu considérable, il s'est lui-même privé de tous ses moyens," and went on to attack all the fifth-year *envois* that had recently been executed.

Duban's *temple protestant* of 1828/29 flouted the Académie's prescriptions in much the same ways as Vaudoyer's was to do. It was based on post-antique models and was inartistically simple in plan and decoration. Its architectural heresy was, however, more categorical, insistent, and inevitable than any belfry's could be. Catholicism traced its origins to the Roman Empire, Protestantism to the sixteenth century; Catholicism was still centered in the Eternal City, Protestantism existed only north of the Alps. A Catholic church, like Villain's *envoi*, could be Neoclassical; a *temple protestant* could only be modern and Northern. In executing his project, Duban in no way softened these implications. He made his design a practical Huguenot parish church—a rectangular box in a rectangular churchyard—with no shaped rooms, long enfilades, or other complications of spatial planning. He refused to offer the conventional displays of compositional *virtu* and Greco-Roman borrowing, and instead busied himself with the study of modern types and functional forms. His project thus seems to be addressed to a building committee, not to the Académie des Beaux-Arts. That body, accustomed to designs like Destouches's *Cirque* and Villain's *Eglise paroissiale*, anticipating with A.-L.-T. Vaudoyer a senate building, a public library, or a *campo santo*, must indeed have been at a loss to judge what Duban had set before them.

IV

One is compelled to wonder whether Duban's heresy was merely architectural. Since the *pen-* sionnaires were being trained for careers as government architects, their projects had unavoidable political implications. And Duban had pointedly raised a religious issue as well. His *temple protestant* was an expression of support for the government of Martignac and a helpful model for the furtherance of Protestant churchbuilding that might be presumed to follow upon Cuvier's consequent appointment to head the Cultes Protesants et Israélites.

What did support of Martignac imply? First of all, it implied hostility toward Charles X, who had been forced to ask for Villèle's resignation though continuing to consult him and praise him as the man whom he would like to lead his parliament. Secondly, support of Martignac implied support of his government's accomplishments of 1828: reform of the electoral lists; loosening of the control of the press; restriction of the teaching activities of the Jesuits. Lastly, support of Martignac was a desperate gesture, for he was assailed throughout the nineteen months of his tenure and was replaced in August 1829 with the reactionary Jules-Armand de Polignac, whose policies finally brought on the revolution of July 1830.[38] (Thus, Duban's project, though executed under Martignac, was judged by the Académie during the ministry of Polignac.)

But one might question whether a *temple protestant* was simply an expression of support for the compromising Martignac, or whether it was a gesture to the party that had forced these liberalizations into being—the Liberal party in the Chamber of Deputies and most particularly its Protestant leaders, Benjamin Constant and François Guizot. In the public mind Protestants and Liberals were much the same thing; Bourbon police reports evince equal suspicion of both.[39] Nor had the royalist vigilantes during the Terreur

Blanche of 1814/15 discriminated between them in their burning and murdering. And this prejudice had considerable foundation. The great Protestants of Paris were Liberals almost to a man, leading the opposition in the Chamber. Mme. de Staël in the generation before and Edgar Quinet in the generation just emerging formulated Liberal philosophies influenced by their Calvinist faith. De Laborde, Delessert, Cuvier, and Stapfer were prominent Liberal Protestants. In Alsace the progressivism of the Protestant manufacturers Köchlin and Dollfuss shaded into socialism.[40]

Furthermore, republicanism was a fundamental part of French Protestantism. Calvin's *Institutes* (1536) outlined the democratic governance of the church as well as its reformed doctrine and implied an all-encompassing politico-religious entity which Calvin actually succeeded in creating at Geneva in 1541. In 1828/29 that Genevan republic was still there, although since 1814 a canton of Switzerland, and for some time previously its French-speaking citizens had reached out to disturb the monarchic complacency of France, most particularly in the person of Jean Jacques Rousseau.

Thus it was indeed bold for Duban to use the king's stipend to go to Geneva in order to propose a way to spend the king's funds to nurture the piety of such subjects. And Duban seems to have emphasized the political message in his project. There are in his design several small departures from the typical Swiss Huguenot type that underline the Liberal nature of Calvinism. The members of the consistory are provided with twelve seats on three sides of the pulpit, isolated in front of the congregation. There is also a space inside the central doorway formed by two short walls, and in the center of this is a large, freestanding

poor box: the congregation, having entered by the side doors, would leave through this space and publicly contribute to their community's welfare.

The Huguenot consistory was a very powerful body with two primary functions: the determination of religious doctrine, in conference with the pastor, and the visitation of the congregation to distribute charity and to survey conduct.[41] In spite of this, the consistory and its charitable function had not received architectural emphasis in contemporary Huguenot churches: its members sat with the rest of the congregation and the poor box was a mere box on the wall.[42] Typically, there were several doors, and worshipers used whichever one was most convenient. Duban, however, sets off the consistory as a body mediating between the congregation and God and lays out a path by which the parishioners pass through the church, making the poor box into something like a tax office.

This political configuration—a board of elders or representatives as the seat of power, dominating both head of state and citizens—was that which the Liberals, particularly Guizot, had been articulating during the late 1820s.[43] Describing both the absolute power of the king and the absolute power of the people as tyrannies—the latter the tyranny of any majority over the minority—Guizot proposed the rule of moral principles which were self-evidentially reasonable. These principles he envisioned being worked out in discussion by representatives who were the ablest citizens and who simultaneously embodied a multiplicity of interests and the ability to reason among themselves and to find common ground. The basis of his system was clearly Calvinist,[44] and the function of his representatives came close to that of a consistory. (The Liberals of 1829 were distinct from those of 1789 in perceiving the people as a force and in being concerned to control them at the same time they curbed the king and the church.) After Guizot and the Liberals took power in 1830 a younger Romantic *pensionnaire*, Simon-Claude Constant-Dufeux, offered as his fifth-year *envoi* a *Chambre des Députés* embodying this idea of government (Figs. 7, 8).[45] The building is divided into two volumes, a large one for offices and committee rooms, walled off from the public, and a smaller, boxlike space for the deliberations of the representatives, with a public gallery and surrounded by a public square filled with commemorative monuments. Constant-Dufeux's design, with its rectangular hall set crosswise to the axis amid a monument-filled *enceinte*, parallels Duban's, but the wing at the back—merely for the deliberations of the consistory in the case of the *temple protestant*—here has grown into a separate and larger mass. Liberal representative government was oligarchic, the projects of Duban and Constant-Dufeux state in their separate ways.

To attribute anti-Bourbon sentiments to Duban is not to suggest much: the younger intelligentsia of 1828/29 felt no sympathy for the dying regime. To attribute specifically Liberal, as opposed to republican, political ideas to Duban is to say more, but with the confidence that such inclinations were general among his immediate friends in Rome[46] and were to be typical of his circle during the 1830s.[47] (Architects have always been firmly middle-class: of all the arts, architecture imposes the smallest social risk and requires the most intimate cooperation with the establishment.) What is remarkable is that Duban's Liberalism was sufficiently important to him that he would make of his *envoi* a political as well as an aesthetic statement.

V

If Duban's intention was in part political, why did he not simply submit a project for a Liberal *Chambre des Députés*, as Constant-Dufeux was to do soon afterward? The buildings of the Chamber of Deputies in Paris were under reconstruction in 1828/29, giving him at least as good an excuse for such a project as Cuvier's appointment to the Cultes Protestants et Israélites gave him for choosing a church. The design of a *temple protestant*, however, had two important advantages over that for any theoretical legislative hall of the future. First, in the microcosm of a congregation brought together under one roof, Duban could show the whole political organism—parishioners, consistory, pastor—in hierarchic relation, while in a legislative hall all that could be shown were the representatives. Second, as a building that was—or rather, should have been—a part of the French architectural tradition, Duban could underline that the Liberal future was already present in French culture and needed only to be recognized and drawn out. Duban's way of thinking, in a word, was an historical one that envisioned the future as an extension of the past.

The last observation is the crux of this essay and must be explained carefully.

The only direct statements surviving of the Romantic *pensionnaires'* intentions, aside from their *envois*, are Vaudoyer's letters.[48] As we have seen, while these express passionate contempt for academic platitudes, they do not lay down the principles of a new architecture, although they contain hints.[49] As we have seen, he insisted, ". . . je ne suis pas architecte; mes études ne sont pas terminées . . ." During the 1830s, however, Vaudoyer and Duban became part of a small circle of writers who did work out and publicize principles that accorded with the hints in Vaudoyer's letters and with much of what appears in his *envois*.

Duban was the artist of the group, and it was his work, especially his rebuilding of the Ecole des Beaux-Arts of 1832–1840, that they cited as the model for modern architecture. The writer Hippolyte Fortoul was their most prolific propagandist, publishing a mass of critical articles on architecture during the 1830s and capping that work with his two-volume *De l'Art en Allemagne* of 1842. The engineer and architect Léonce Reynaud, appointed professor of architecture at the Ecole Polytechnique in 1837, likewise spread the doctrine, providing the architectural entries for his brother Jean's *Encyclopédie nouvelle*, beginning in 1834, and later producing his own massive *Traité d'architecture* of 1850–1856. Vaudoyer, without significant architectural work down to the mid-1840s, also wrote, first for the *Encyclopédie nouvelle* and then, beginning in 1839, a history of French architecture for the *Magasin pittoresque*, which in 1846 he rewrote in summary form for the short nationalist encyclopedia *Patria*.[50] These four men met socially during the 1830s and made common critical cause. Among the letters from Vaudoyer in Fortoul's papers, for example, is a note of May 19, 1839 announcing a "pique-nique" arranged for the next day by Duban, Reynaud, Vaudoyer, and Duc, to which Fortoul together with the editor of the *Magasin pittoresque*, Edouard Charton, were invited.[51]

Although they all joined in attacking the existing Greco-Roman academicism, this group's conception did not offer a recipe for the architecture of the future, to the frustration of some utopian critics like Théophile Thoré.[52] This was in part because they held that architecture was a "posterior art," generated from social institutions and thus evolving after them. Fortoul confided to a notebook in the late 1830s:

L'architecture est de tous les arts celui qu'on peut le moins deviner, parce que c'est un art postérieur, qui présuppose l'existence de quelque chose à satisfaire et à envelopper. Or si pareille chose existait de nos jours, nul doute que l'architecture ne lui prêtât son vêtement. Si on peut prévoir l'esprit de cette chose, on saurait en prévoir la forme.[53]

Toward the end of his *De l'Art en Allemagne* of 1842, Fortoul restated this:

Autant de fois que vous verrez l'architecture changer ses formes, autant de fois vous pourrez dire que la civilization sera renouvelée; et si vous assistez à une époque où les constructions manquent d'originalité, dites aussi sans crainte que ses idées n'en ont aucune: les monuments sont la vraie écriture des peuples.[54]

In 1846 Vaudoyer chose to quote these words to end his history of French architecture in *Patria*. This *apercu*, which seems to have operated as a basic truism in this circle, implied two things: first, that architecture is but the shell of the social institutions that call it into being, so that the former is dependent upon the latter;[55] second, that at a moment of social transition like 1830, when institutions have lost their meaning, architectural forms also become meaningless.

What does an architect do in this situation? He cannot act, but he can study. And he studies institutions and architectural types of the past in order to perceive the historical currents which will eventually broaden to produce the art of the future. Léon Vaudoyer, in the one lengthy statement of principles in his letters from Rome, wrote thus to his cousin, the architect Hippolyte Lebas, on November 28, 1832:

Les idées ont changées; est arrivé le système constitutionnel qui nous a apporté l'esprit d'examen, de raisonnement et d'économie. On a commencé dès lors à penser qu'il ne suffisait pas d'avoir un excellent goût d'arrangement, d'ajuster parfaitement des ornements, de les dessiner dans la perfection, de surcharger les monuments de figures, de bas reliefs, etc. pour faire de l'architecture. . . . On est arrivé à comprendre que nos institutions politiques et sociales veulent une architecture sage, raisonnée, d'une exécution facile, simple et économique. . . . Je crois donc que pour arriver à satisfaire aux besoins de notre époque, il faut de préference étudier l'architecture radicale des anciens, c'est-à-dire celle qui eut à satisfaire des usages primitifs et non encore corrompus par le Luxe. C'est dans cette architecture première qu'on retrouve davantage la raison des formes, le squelette enfin, qui, plus tard, se dérobe sous les habits bordés. . . . N'est-il pas naturel pour connaître le véritable sens d'un mot de remonter a son étymologie?[56]

Reynaud, in the *Encyclopédie nouvelle* in 1834, restated this more broadly.

Les sociétés modernes, avant de se créer un nouveau système d'architecture, avaient dû examiner ceux qu'avaient suivis nos pères pour en vérifier la valeur et en étudier les lois. Elles ne pouvaient, ignorantes de ce qui s'était fait jusqu'à elles, s'élancer vers de nouvelles destinées, et produire instantanément une organisation complète.[57]

Among the young architects of that moment, Reynaud continues, some are studying science and industrial processes ("ils essaient d'appliquer artistement à nos construction les nouveaux matériaux que les progrès de cette industrie mettent à leur disposition"), while others are studying the history of architecture ("en mettant en évidence aux yeux de tous la marche qu'il a suivie dans son développement"). He ends: "Les principes de notre foi dans l'architecture sont religieusement liés à notre foi dans l'humanité; et si l'humanité doit continuer à s'élever, l'architecture, ce grand art où elle se reflète sans cesse, lui sera fidèle et saura s'élever avec elle."

Thus, in this group's view, the occupation of an architect in 1830 must be the study of history, society, and technique, to grasp the laws of evolution. Indeed, this accounted for most of their time and writings: Fortoul's, Reynaud's, and Vaudoyer's publications are all essentially histories, while Duban's accomplishment at the Ecole des Beaux-Arts was to make it an historical museum of architectural fragments.[58]

Let us return to Duban's *temple protestant* and address two final questions: (1) what was perceived to be the significance in historicist circles of Protestantism during the late 1820s? and (2) what historical "architecture radicale" might lie at the origin of the specific configuration Duban chose to give his building?

1). During the 1820s French Protestantism was viewed from two complementary standpoints: as a traumatic historical episode during the sixteenth century and as an element in the evolving national philosophical experience. The historical view is represented in the novels of Ludovic Vitet, whose 1825 declaration that Romanticism "C'est . . . le Protestantisme dans les lettres et les arts" we noted earlier. A Catholic and the nephew of Casimir Périer (soon to become Louis Philippe's second prime minister), Vitet had been of great help to Guizot at the *Globe* and in organizing the Liberal network *Aide-toi, le ciel t'aidera*. In 1826, 1827, and 1829 he published three historical novels, called collectively *La Ligue*, which dramatized the events of the Wars of Religion during 1587/88. Vitet's friend, almost protégé, Prosper Mérimée (a Protestant at death), in 1829 published his *Chronique du règne de Charles IX*, depicting Saint Bartholomew's Night in 1572. Their stated aim was the evocation of a specific moment in the past,[59] and Mérimée's novel in particular avoids judging the events depicted, but the moments they chose to bring into such sharp relief were precisely those when Protestantism demonstrated itself to be an elemental part of French culture. Their enterprise was parallel to that of Victor Hugo in his *Cromwell* of 1827, studying the conflicting loyalties of the English Calvinist revolution, only theirs was more pointed for being specifically Gallic.

Contemporaneously several philosophers were insisting upon Protestantism's value for the evolution of French civilization. Mme. de Staël during the Napoleonic era, then, during the 1820s, Benjamin Constant and Edgar Quinet—all themselves Calvinists—refined the idea that a new religion must emerge in France which would subsume Protestantism, yet go beyond it.[60] The concept that historical progress required a new, modern religion was a commonplace since the Revolution; in 1825, for example, it had engendered *Nouveau Christianisme*, the modified Catholicism of Comte de Saint-Simon. De Staël's, Constant's, and Quinet's proposals were more influential, however, because of the historical sanction provided by the Reformation.

These two movements in literature and philosophy during the 1820s should be seen in the light of the declaration by Fortoul cited at the beginning of this essay: "Je vous ai parlé souvent de ces esprits délicats qui ont rapportés de Rome, avec un sentiment vrai et nouveau des monuments antiques, le besoin de reprendre la tradition architecturale au point ou elle étoit en France *au commencement du XVIIe siècle*" (my italics). What he meant by this in 1842 had been made abundantly clear in Reynaud's article "Architecture" in the *Encyclopédie nouvelle* and in Vaudoyer's pieces in the *Magasin pittoresque*, where the late seventeenth and early eighteenth centuries are described as infertile periods of academicism, the reflection of Louis XIV's centralization of government and culture, prematurely terminating the creative promise of the Renaissance. The latter they described in architecture as the delicate and appropriate application of the principles, proportions, and ornament of antiquity to modern types and modern construction. "Ses édifices rappelaient encore les édifices gothiques," wrote Reynaud of the Renaissance:

> ils avaient les mêmes dispositions et les mêmes proportions générales; toutes les exigences qui les avaient commandés étaient franchement exprimées, toutes les convenances sagement satisfaites. C'étaient encore des édifices gothiques, mais avec des formes plus harmonieuses, des contours plus purs et plus gracieux, et recouverts, en quelque sorte, d'un voile étranger, voile riche et diaphane qui décorait sans rien dissimuler.[61]

The historical fragments which Duban gathered in the courtyards of the Ecole des Beaux-Arts were all late Gothic or early Renaissance.

The Renaissance had a very special place in these men's minds: it was the moment when antiquity and the present were fruitfully related.

The modern architect's task was to penetrate back to this wonderful historical moment through the academicism of the age of Louis XIV and to start a new, natural evolution out of it. Did the Romantic *pensionnaires* in 1828/29 understand this only in the architectural sense? Might we not assume, in the light of the literary movement represented by Vitet, Mérimée, and Hugo, as well as the philosophical movement represented by de Staël, Constant, and Quinet, that these architects were interested in Renaissance culture as a whole, including the most extraordinary of its elements, the Reformation? In this case the design of a *temple protestant* would be the logical place to start in the study of the French Renaissance and its heritage.

2). Was there a root form, an *architecture radicale*, embodied in Duban's project? We have observed that he went to Switzerland to study Huguenot architecture because of the destruction of French Protestant churches following the revocation of the Edict of Nantes. One might rephrase this to say that he went to Switzerland to study the modern descendants of the lost Huguenot type, because the model he chose to copy there was, in fact, the continuation of that French form. Professor Germann has traced the evolution of the rectangular church set crosswise to its axis from Heiden and Colombier to Embrach, and thence to the great Huguenot temple at Charenton erected by Salomon de Brosse in 1621 to 1623.[62] (Indeed the memory of this paradigm survived in France as well and reemerged at least once after the recognition of Protestantism in 1787 in the design by one Joffroy of Orange for the large church at Dieulefit [Drome] executed in 1803.[63])

But if this model led back to Charenton, that building in turn disclosed an idea. It has been periodically pointed out—at least twice as an original discovery—that de Brosse's building is an adaptation of Vitruvius's paradigmatic basilica at Fano.[64] Did Duban note and judge significant this derivation? (It was his friend Vaudoyer who first mentioned Fano as Charenton's model, albeit in 1845.)[65] Fano was certainly on the *pensionnaires'* minds in 1828: Labrouste had decided to make his fourth-year *envoi* a reconstruction of that building and had visited the site with Vaudoyer in July and August of 1828 to see whether there were any remains.[66] For some reason—perhaps the lack of vestiges at Fano—he subsequently changed his mind and submitted his celebrated reconstruction of the buildings at Paestum instead.

The idea that sprang from the linking of Charenton and Fano was that the Republican Roman administrative hall was similar to the Huguenot church, being a place for reasoned discourse rather than for ritual mysteries; to quote Vaudoyer: "Cette disposition [at Fano] se prêtait parfaitement au programme qu'il [de Brosse] devait suivre." It was this kind of realization that constituted the "sentiment vrai et nouveau des monuments antiques" with which the *pensionnaires* returned from Rome determined "reprendre la tradition architecturale au point ou elle étoit en France au commencement du XVIIᵉ siècle."

The form Duban chose for his *temple protestant* was not necessarily the most practical; a hemicycle of the sort used for lecture and legislative halls during the previous half-century would have been more functional. (There is evidence Duban experimented with this shape, but decided against it.)[67] It was, instead, an historical form, recalling a chain of ideas. Indeed, one element in Duban's design, foreign to the German and Swiss Calvinist church model, seems a clear development of the idea of historical memory: the colonnaded *enceinte* around the building, which must have been a *campo santo* filled with grave monuments. As the congregation gathered before the service they would have stood amid these markers which signified for them the story of their culture. This *campo santo*—this history in stone surrounding a building—became henceforth a leitmotif of French Romantic architecture, reappearing in the courtyards of the Ecole des Beaux-Arts, the monument-filled plaza of Constant-Dufeux's *Chambre des 'Députés*, and, subtly transformed, in the lines of names on Duc's Colonne de Juillet (1830–1840) and Labrouste's Bibliothèque Ste.-Geneviève (1838–1851). The building amid these mementos was itself a memento, in the case of Duban's *temple protestant*, a memento of Charenton and Fano, a reminder of the deliberative Huguenot faith.

VI

The revolution signaled by Duban's and Labrouste's *envois* in 1828/29 was called "Romantic" then and, no better label being presented since, is still called that today. This borrowed label, however, tells us little of what was specifically at stake in these *envois*. The revolution of 1828/29 might have been merely stylistic, the replacement of the Greco-Roman by the Gothic. It might have been a change in architectural conceptualization, from the anthropomorphism of Quatremère de Quincy to the structural rationalism of Viollet-le-Duc. It might have been political, the architectural reflection of absolutism transformed into Liberalism. Or it might have been a religious and philosophical revolution of the broadest sort.

I have studied Duban's *temple protestant* because its very subject suggests that it may hold

the answer to whether the Romantic revolution in architecture was indeed a revolution of this last sort—the most interesting and profound change in style.

In their writings, as in their architecture, the men of Duban's circle phrased things historically. What they depict as the moment of greatest interest is the period around 1600 in France. Why France? Because they themselves were Frenchmen and could not hope to grasp the evolution of world history except as it manifested itself upon their soil. Why the period around 1600? Because this was the moment of the appearance of the seeds of modern culture: Renaissance art, humanism, individualism, capitalism, and Protestantism.

Still, the question remains as to just which aspects of French history around 1600 the Romantics held to be important, and Duban's *temple protestant* presents itself as the place to seek the answer. The *subject* of Duban's project is its most important element. It is about Protestantism, not about architecture. Duban clearly did not choose this subject in order to demonstrate new ideas in planning and decoration. Nor did he go to the convenient German models offered by Stier and Schinkel, Hansen and Weinbrenner to find a ready-made type. Instead he worked hard on his liturgical plan, keeping close to the French Protestant tradition and showing consciousness of its social as well as its ritual nature. It is a dense and subtly inflected design, somewhat like a contemporaneous historical painting or novel, which evokes Huguenot culture in France around 1600 and its subsequent evolution in Switzerland.

What did Duban imagine he might accomplish with his *envoi*? The dramatization, I think, of the Protestant strand woven into the fabric of French culture, valuable because ready to be picked out to make the warp of a new culture for a new epoch. The *temple protestant*, in the particular form chosen by Duban—the basilica transformed into a preaching box at Charenton and preserved in the parish churches of Switzerland—was an element of the French architectural landscape which should have existed in 1828/29, but which did not exist because of Louis XIV's act of violence against the natural evolution of society. Duban was trying to right that wrong with his *envoi*, to rewrite the history of French architecture by reintroducing this missing element, so that things might thereafter proceed naturally.

Notes

The research for this essay was accomplished during a half-year in Paris, Switzerland, and Germany made possible by a grant from the Graham Foundation for Advanced Studies in the Fine Arts, to which organization and its director, Carter Manny, I owe the sincerest thanks. Warmest thanks are due also to Professor Georg Germann of Zurich for help of many sorts, including reading and criticizing the manuscript. Further aid on specific points I gladly acknowledge from Professor Max Vogt and Benno Schubiger of Zurich, Livio Fornara of Geneva, Rev. Gary Satler of the Phillips Universität, Marburg, and Dieter Radika of the Plansammlung at the Technische Universität, Berlin. In Paris, Mlle. Annie Jacques, librarian of the Ecole des Beaux-Arts, was kind in helping me examine the Lecointe sketches of Duban's project, as was M. Gérard Rousset-Charnys in aiding my study of the Labrouste sketches of it. I also am immensely indebted to the various members of the Vaudoyer family who, some years ago, permitted me to examine their ancestor's papers. Here in the United States, as many times before, I owe profoundest thanks for their advice and aid to Professor Frank Bowman of the University of Pennsylvania, to Professor Neil Levine of Harvard, and to my wife, Ann Lorenz Van Zanten.

1. Quoted from the "Reglements pour les travaux des pensionnaires à l'Académie de France à Rome" of 1821 (kindly provided to me by Neil Levine). The *envois* of the first three years were to be analytical studies of ancient remains, that of the fourth year a reconstruction of a single ancient building. The five *pensionnaires* at the Academy in 1829, in order of seniority, were Félix Duban, Henri Labrouste, Louis Duc, Léon Vaudoyer, and Théodore Labrouste.

2. Letter of October 9, 1829 in a private collection, Paris.

3. *Victor Hugo raconté par un temoin de sa vie* (Paris, 1868), Ch. LIII; T. Gautier, *Histoire du romantisme* (Paris, 1872), Ch. IX.

4. P. B[orel], "Du Mouvement en architecture," *l'Artiste*, 1833, II, p. 75.

5. For example, *l'Artiste*, 1834, no. 2, p. 82; 1835, no. 1, p. 148.

6. H. Fortoul, *De l'Art en Allemagne*, 2 vols. (Paris, 1842), 1:170.

7. Neil Levine is chiefly responsible for this conception today ("The Romantic Idea of Architectural Legibility: Henri Labrouste and the Bibliothèque Ste.-Geneviève," in A. Drexler, ed., *The Architecture of the Ecole des Beaux-Arts* [Cambridge, Mass., and London, 1977], pp. 325–416).

8. The Labrouste sketches are two pages of a sketchbook now in the Académie d'Architecture, Paris; the Lecointe drawings are two small sheets in the so-called "Carnets Hittorff" in the library of the Ecole des Beaux-Arts.

9. "Reglements pour les travaux des pensionnaires à l'Académie de France à Rome."

10. *Moniteur universel*, January 13, 1828. Cf. the *Almanach royal pour l'an 1827* . . . to that of 1828. See also D. Robert, *Les Eglises Réformées en France (1800–1830)* (Paris, 1961), pp. 317–343.

11. There is a very illuminating *carton* in the Archives Nationales (F^{19}10621) containing drawings of more than sixty Protestant churches built or repaired between 1798 and 1860. It is not all-inclusive, but it provides a good cross section. See also Archives Nationales F^{19}10616, a circular of 1822 surveying the construction of Protestant churches in France. Daniel Robert summarizes this material in the appendices of his book cited in note 10 above.

12. Stier's project today is lost, although a number of draft descriptions of it, together with diagrammatic sketches, survive in the Plansammlung at the Technische Universität, Berlin. It was redrawn for publication in 1893 in *Der Kirchenbau des Protestantismus von der Reformation bis zum Gegenwart* (Berlin, 1893), pp. 192–193, by the Vereinigung berliner Architekten. On Bunsen see F. Bunsen, *A Memoir of Baron Bunsen*, 2 vols. (London, 1868).

13. "Wilhelm Stier," *Kunstblatt* (Berlin) VII (1856); 371–374, especially p. 371.

14. L. Dehio, *Friedrich Wilhelm IV von Preussen: ein Baukunstler der Romantik* (Munich, 1961), pp. 34–42, 104–121.

15. L. von Ranke, *Aus dem Briefwechsel Friedrich Wilhelm IV mit Bunsen* (Leipzig, 1873).

16. *Der kleine Katechismus Doktor Martin Luthers* (1977 ed., Kassel), p. 24. I owe this reference to Rev. Gary Satler.

17. Von Ranke, op. cit.

18. Stier's papers in the Plansammlung of the Technische Universität, Berlin, include several illustrated essays, evidently of 1827, reviewing all the forms a Protestant church might take. He had obviously made himself an authority on the

general topic.

19. Dehio, op. cit.; K. F. von Schinkel, *Sammlung architek-tonischer Entwürfe* (Berlin, 1819–1840), pls. 31–34, 93–106.

20. A.-L.-T. Vaudoyer, in a letter of August 4, 1829, refers to Duban's "voyage en Suisse." In 1833 Borel stated: "Duban avait fait en Suisse et en Allemagne une étude sérieuse et minutieuse des temples protestans . . . " (*l'Artiste*, 1833, no. 2, p. 75).

21. Institut de France, Archives de l'Académie des Beaux-Arts, *carton* 5.E.19.

22. D. Robert, *Genève et les Eglises Réformées de France, de la 'Réunion' (1798) aux environs de 1830* (Geneva, 1961).

23. G. Germann, *Der protestantischer Kirchenbau in der Schweiz,* (Zurich, 1973), especially pp. 124–135. Kubly joined the *pensionnaires* in many of their activities, Vaudoyer's letters show.

24. Ibid., p. 144.

25. Labrouste's sketches of Duban's project, presumably done in Rome from the original *envoi,* accord with Lecointe's, done in Paris from the modified version. Labrouste's sketch, however, does not show the liturgical furniture, which would thus seem to be the thing Duban modified.

26. G. Germann, "Melchior Berris Rathausentwurf für Bern (1833)," *Baseler Zeitschrift für Geschichte und Alter-thumskunde* LXIX (1969): 239–309. Benno Schubiger, *Der Kirchenbau im Werk von Felix Wilhelm Kubly (1802–1872)* (thesis, University of Zurich, 1979).

27. E. Steinmann, *Die reformierten Kirchen beider Appen-zell: ein kunstgeschichtlicher Führer* (Herisan, 1979); Schubiger, op. cit., pp. 26–34.

28. G. de Bertier de Sauvigny, *La Restauration* (Paris, 1955), pp. 375–376.

29. The announcement in the *Moniteur universel* (January 13, 1828) could not have been briefer. Cf. D. Robert, *Les Eglises Réformées en France,* pp. 316–413, especially pp. 327–329.

30. L. Vitèt, "De l'Independence en matière de gout," *le Globe,* no. 89 (April 2, 1825), p. 443.

31. *l'Artiste*, 1833, no. 2. p. 75.

32. See Neil Levine, op. cit., and my own essay in that volume, "Architectural Composition from Charles Percier to Charles Garnier," especially pp. 196–231.

33. From the 1822 publication of the reports read at the *séance publique annuelle* of the Académie des Beaux-Arts.

34. Ibid., 1826.

35. Ibid., 1829.

36. Cf. T. Thoré, *le Siècle,* August 25, 1836.

37. Preserved in a private collection in Paris.

38. Bertier de Sauvigny, op. cit., pt. 4, ch. 3.

39. C.-H. Pouthas, *Guizot pendant la Restauration: pré-paration de l'homme d'état (1814–1830)* (Paris, 1923), p. 362.

40. Ibid., especially ch. 11; F. B. Artz, *France under the Bourbon Restoration, 1814–1830* (Cambridge, Mass., 1931), pp. 122–124.

41. Robert, *Les Eglises Réformées en France,* p. 80: the duties of the consistory as stated in the Organic Acts of 1802.

42. There was a contemporaneous revival movement in French Protestantism, "le Reveil," but it does not seem to explain the changes Duban has made. See ibid., pt. 2, ch. 13.

43. Pouthas, op. cit., chs. 9 and 10.

44. Ibid., p. 321.

45. The original drawings are lost, but upon Constant-Dufeux's death in 1871 they were reproduced lithographically by the printer A. Joilly for distribution among his students and friends.

46. Vaudoyer's letters show him to have been both anti-Bourbon and anti-Republican. Constant-Dufeux, the only one of the *pensionnaires* to display his political inclinations, during the *Jours de Juin,* 1848, and at the time of Napoleon III's *coup d'état* in 1851, was firmly for the *juste milieu.*

47. Which included Hippolyte Fortoul and Ludovic Vitet, both later Liberal members of the Chamber of Deputies (although Fortoul later showed himself to be a Bonapartist and became a cabinet minister of Napoleon III).

48. There also exist a number of letters by Henri Labrouste, some excerpted in *Souvenirs d'Henri Labrouste: notes recueillées et classées par ses enfants* (Paris, 1928).

49. He compares his and the *pensionnaires'* intention to those of Victor Hugo, Lamartine, and the painter Gros, at different times.

50. I have discussed this group's ideas in my essay in *The Architecture of the Ecole des Beaux-Arts,* cited above, especially pp. 223–231, and in my article "Félix Duban and the Buildings of the Ecole des Beaux-Arts, 1832–1840," *Journal of the Society of Architectural Historians,* 37 (October 1978): 161–174.

51. Archives Nationales, 246.A.P.14. The note bears the post-script, "J'oublie de vous dire que demain nous devons aller visiter la colonne de Duc—le rendez vous est à 2 hrs. 2½ hrs. chez lui . . ."

52. See specifically his critique of Duban's Ecole des Beaux-Arts: *l'Artiste,* 1839, no. 2, pp. 220–222, 305–307.

53. Archives Nationales, 246.A.P.2.

54. Fortoul, op. cit., 1: 177.

55. Reynaud uses the specific analogy of the shell ("Architec-ture," *Encyclopédie nouvelle,* I [1834], p. 773), and his brother, Jean, elaborates it wonderfully in his later article "Villes" in that publication (VIII [1839], especially p. 682).

56. In a private collection, Paris, and published in part in G. Davioud, *Notice sur la vie et les ouvrages de Léon Vau-doyer* (Paris, 1873).

57. "Architecture," *Encyclopédie nouvelle,* I (1834), p. 778.

58. See my article "Félix Duban . . . " cited in note 50, above.

59. See especially the preface to Mérimée's *Chronique.* Also

P. Trahard, *La Jeunesse de Prosper Mérimée (1803–1834)*, 2 vols. (Paris, 1925), vol. 2, ch. 1.

60. De Staël sketches these ideas briefly if assertively in chapter 2 of the fourth part of *De l'Allemagne*, "Du Protestantisme":

> . . . La reformation a introduit dans le monde l'examen en fait de religion. . . . l'esprit humain étoit arrivé à une époque où il devoit nécessairement examiner pour croire. La découverte de l'imprimerie, la multiplicité des connaissances, et l'investigation philosophique de la verité, ne permettoient plus cette foi aveugle dont on s'étoit jadis si bien trouvé. . . .

> Il est très-probable que le genre humain est susceptible d'education, aussi-bien que chaque homme, et qu'il y a des époques marquées pour les progrès de la pensée dans la route éternelle du temps. La reformation fût l'ère de l'examen et de la conviction éclairée, qui lui succède. Le christianisme a d'abord été fondé, puis altéré, puis examiné, puis compris, et ces diverses periodes étoient nécessaires a son développement; elles ont duré quelquefois cent ans, quelquefois mille ans.

By the time Quinet began to write, twelve years later, these suggestions of what might be "très probable" had become part of a neat scientific doctrine. (E. Quinet, *Introduction à la philosophie de l'histoire de l'humanité*, written in 1825 and published in three volumes, 1827/28; *Le Génie des religions*, 1842; *Le Christianisme et la Révolution française*, 1845.)

61. "Architecture," *Encyclopédie nouvelle*, I, 1834, p. 777.

62. Germann, op. cit., pp. 35–39.

63. Archives Nationales, F^{19}10621: drawings of the plan, elevation, and section.

64. *Magasin pittoresque*, 1845, pp. 77–78; L. Hautecoeur, *Histoire de l'architecture classique en France*, Vol. I, pt. 2, p. 714; Germann, op. cit., pp. 38–39.

65. Duban's friend, Vaudoyer, the author of the *Magasin pittoresque* article cited in note 64 above, considered the derivation to be self-evident; he presents it as no stunning discovery.

66. Letters from Léon Vaudoyer to his father of June 27 and August 3, 1828 document the trip.

67. Beside Labrouste's sketches of Duban's project in his notebook are three alternative plans, presumably also after Duban, two of which show a semicircular auditorium.

G.E. STREET AND
THE CHURCH OF ST. PAUL'S IN ROME

Henry A. Millon

ARTHUR STREET'S BIOGRAPHY OF his father, the architect George Edmund Street, includes an anecdote which illustrates Street's measuring and drafting skill and the speed with which he worked. The anecdote follows a passage that cites a not often equaled "quickness of conception."[1] Street is portrayed as a gifted designer, draftsman, and sketcher who could conceive an entire design in a moment of inspiration, or "conceptual flash." Committing it to paper was then only a matter of hours due to his prodigious skill in drafting.[2]

That these conceptual flashes were common to Street is underlined by another account in Street's biography of the design of the Church of the Holy Trinity in Paris. Once the church site had been approved, Street "returned with the rector to his house, and there and then made the sketch . . . following which the church was built and which church today . . . corresponds in all its essential elements . . . with the first idea."[3]

Street's design of the American Church of St. Paul's Within the Walls in Rome was also immediate and on the spot. Robert J. Nevin, in his account of the early history of the church, says Street "made his first sketch on the ground after careful study of the situation of the church-lot and of its surrounding buildings."[4]

Street's conceptual flashes were not confined to the overall massing and plan but apparently extended to details as well. His obituary in *The Times* of London, in a paragraph devoted to his decorative iron and stone work, includes the following observation (obviously by someone who had seen him at work): "His fancy seemed absolutely to run riot. The most delicate curves and figures grew under his hand as if by magic, and so rapidly did he draw that it was hard to believe that the hand was not moving mechanically. It seemed scarcely possible that the imagination should have been able to picture to itself the thing required so instantaneously."[5]

Arthur Street states that when a drawing left Street's office, it usually meant he was satisfied he could not better it; if, however, an improvement later suggested itself, Street "never hesitated to sacrifice what he had done."[6] The individual that emerges, therefore, is complex: Street was a gifted architect with "spontaneous ideas" that he trusted and committed to paper; he was also a practitioner who learned from experience of the building under construction and altered designs as he saw fit in order to improve the initial concept.

The recent reappearance of a large signed and dated watercolor perspective and plan by George Street of the American Church of St. Paul's Within the Walls (Fig. 1)[7] prompts an examina-

1. (previous page) St. Paul's Within the Walls, Rome. G. E. Street, 1872–1876. Street's watercolor perspective and plan, signed and dated 1875. (Private collection, Rome.)

tion of the design, dating from 1872, and of the construction of the building, which is thought to be one of Street's better efforts.[8] New nuggets of information have been gathered by Richard Dorment for his dissertation on the decoration of the church in the 1880s and 1890s by Sir Edward Coley Burne-Jones.[9] The "first sketch on the ground" has been lost, but still extant are seven of the working drawings for the church and rectory (all that remains from nearly a hundred sheets prepared for the commission), of which only two have been reproduced.[10] To these can be added a woodcut perspective, probably made from the watercolor but with alterations, which appeared in *The Architect* in 1875,[11] while the church was under construction. Further, the Minutes of the meetings of the Vestry of the Church, which contain information about the development of the design, have never been fully mined.[12]

The Vestry Minutes enable a reconstruction of the steps leading to the commission. On 30 January 1872, after returning on 23 December 1871 from a fund-raising tour in the United States,[13] the rector was authorized to arrange for G. E. Street to visit Rome as soon as a building lot was secured.[14] Street was to come "for the purpose of preparing plans for [the] new building." On 13 February the rector was authorized to purchase a site on the corner of the Via Nazionale and Via Napoli.[15] Richard Dorment quotes from a letter of Street's written to F. G. Stephens on 25 February stating that he intended to leave for Rome the next day.[16] Street must have arrived in Rome the first week in March (the letter also says that he will stop on the way to look at the new church he had built for the English at Geneva) and, as his son tells us, he stayed only six days in Rome.[17] During this period negotiations for the property were concluded and Street made his

first sketch on the ground, described earlier.[18]

The Vestry Minutes record that on 8 March the rector reported that the lot had been purchased with a frontage on the Via Nazionale of 29.6 meters and 55 meters on the Via Napoli (a total of 1,485 square meters) for a suitable price under $19,000.[19] The same minutes also record that designs for the church prepared by Street and two other architects (Thomas J. Smith of London and Luigi Eynard of Rome) were exhibited. The meeting adjourned "without coming to decisions on the subject of a plan."

Four days later the vestry met again and adopted Street's design for a new church, noting the dimensions and specifications: a width of 64 feet in front, a depth of 132 feet, a facade height of 70 feet, a campanile, and a capacity to seat 800 persons; they noted also Street's declaration that he could build the church for $60,000.[20]

Nevin records that Street's "original plan" showed the campanile "advanced beyond the rest of the facade about a foot and a half."[21] Rome's Municipal Commissioner in charge of the new district objected to a broken facade on the Via Nazionale. Street was forced to pull the tower back into the plane of the facade.[22] Nevin's account does not state when the local authorities rejected the salient tower but, in any case, it would have been before ground was broken on 5 November 1872,[23] and presumably earlier rather than later in the year.

The rector and vestry had hoped to break ground in the spring. The Vestry Minutes of 2 April 1872, however, note the rector's view that "at the present period of the season it would be impossible to get the foundations advanced to the ground level until sometime in June and that going forward with them now would prevent his visiting the United States this summer to raise

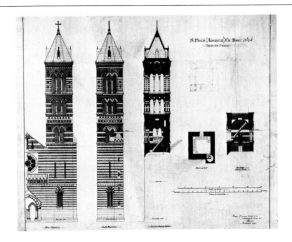

money." The vestry postponed the laying of the foundations until late in the autumn.[24] The rector departed for the United States on 9 April and returned 8 October[25] to prepare for the initiatory ceremony on 5 November.

Plans, sections, and working drawings for the body of the church were probably prepared in Street's office after he returned to London. All the drawings may have been traced and sent to Rome, as noted on the four extant sheets from 1874 for the last portions of the building to be finished.[26] If this be so, the originals as well as the copies have disappeared.

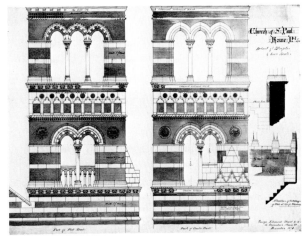

In Rome, Rudolf Lanciani, as local supervisory architect (and one of Italy's outstanding archaeologists), saw to the foundations. Work above ground was supervised by a Swiss architect in Rome, Heinrich Kleffler.[27] Nevin translated the feet/inch system to the metric and fought to insure that the building methods and materials employed by the Italian contractors would conform to the standards important to Gothic Revivalists, both architects and churchmen, in Britain and America.[28]

With the ground broken in November 1872, the excavations, although deeply dug to find undisturbed clay, were sufficiently advanced in two and a half months to allow the laying of the cornerstone on 25 January, the feast day of the Conversion of St. Paul.[29]

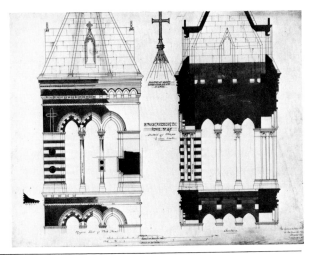

Street visited the church at least four times while it was under construction, but the precise dates are unknown.[30] (According to his son,[31] he was in Rome on his wedding trip after his marriage to Jessie Holland on 11 January 1876, perhaps intending to be present at the consecration of the church, originally scheduled for 25 January but postponed until 25 March.)[32] By December of 1874, almost two years after the laying of

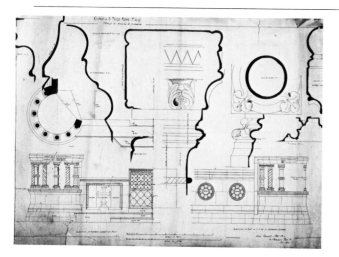

the cornerstone, Street prepared three sheets of details for the campanile (Figs. 2, 3, 4). They were traced, presumably for sending to Rome. The tower was not completed until the summer of 1876.[33] Shortly after the campanile drawings, a fourth sheet of details, dated 17 December 1874, for the marble choir rail and ambone (Fig. 5) was also traced and sent to Rome.

Nevin notes that in July 1875 the walls were "quite finished," with the roof and the floor still to be done.[34] A brief notice, published with an engraved perspective in *The Architect* on 20 November 1875 (Fig. 6), states that the church was fast approaching completion, with the nave roofed, the aisles vaulted, the brick semidome roofed, and the marble screens surrounding the choir in place.[35] Not yet built or installed at that date, according to the notice, were the campanile with its bells, the two ambones, the stained-glass windows, mosaic in the apse semidome, and the pavement.

In December 1875, Street prepared a pair of drawings (Nos. 82 and 83) with ink-and-wash full-size details for the wrought-iron churchyard railing (Figs. 7, 8) that was to enclose the site

along Via Napoli and the Via Nazionale.[36] The railing was fashioned in Britain by Thomas Potter and Sons and shipped on completion to Rome. The contract was signed, however, only on 28 July 1879,[37] and it is therefore unlikely the railing arrived before 1880. The design of the railing differs from the more elaborate version shown in the watercolor perspective.

The church was finished nearly enough to be consecrated on 25 March 1876, only due, apparently, to the frenzied supervision, encouragement, and probable harassment of the workers by Nevin, who said it took more than five months to recover from the strain of this effort.[38] An engraving that appeared in the 16 April 1876 edition of *Illustrazione Italiana* (Fig. 9) documents the incomplete state of the interior at the time of the consecration. (An accompanying perspective of the church from the southwest appears to derive

7. Street, drawing No. 82 for churchyard railing, December 1875.
8. Street, drawing No. 83 for churchyard railing, December 1875.

9. D. Paolosci, engraved perspective of the interior of St. Paul's Within the Walls during the consecration ceremony of 25 March 1876. (Illustrazione Italiana, *16 April 1876.*)

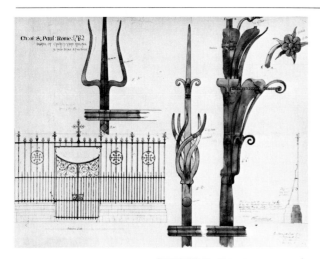

with an entrance from the churchyard, but not extending the full depth of the site along its eastern boundary. On 15 October, Street prepared a handsome section/elevation (Fig. 12) for the upper two and one half levels of the south facade with full-size ink-and-wash details of its two superimposed levels of Venetian Gothic windows. The drawing bears a pencil notation "traced and sent," and the number 18 (or possibly 8)[42] (the sheets previous to this drawing and subsequent sheets have been lost). The design differs from that shown in the watercolor perspective of March 1875. The earlier perspective omits the present entrance from the Via Napoli and shows three levels of elaborate, paired Venetian windows of descending height on the Via Napoli elevation, rather than the mezzanine, *piano nobile*, and *secondo piano* of the drawing and of the rectory as it is today.

Lowrie notes that the western portion of the rectory "soon had to be lengthened by one room . . . to wedge [brace or buttress longitudinally] the side wall of the church between the rectory and the campanile thus preventing the enlargement of a crack which seriously threatened the

from that published in *The Architect* four months earlier.)[39] By 4 July 1876 the campanile was completed and dedicated. The carving of capitals and moldings carried on for many years (Fig. 10). Even after the first of the Burne-Jones mosaics (the apse semidome) was installed in 1885 most of the capitals of the piers and moldings of the arches remained uncarved.[40]

With the body of the church, the campanile, and the churchyard railing complete by 1880, work could begin on the rectory.[41] In an early state (Fig. 11), a design for the rectory showed it abutting the lot line on the Via Napoli to the south

church."[43] The crack appeared in the exterior wall of the south aisle of the church to the west of the campanile, the result, most likely, of the differential loading of the foundations under the campanile compared to that of the nave and the south aisle walls.[44] The three-story buttress made it impossible to "carry out the original design of a cloister connecting the rectory to the church" (Figs. 11, 13). Only in 1924 was a cantilevered wooden roof covered with tile built to protect the passage between the entrance in the easternmost bay of the south aisle and the vestibule of the new three-story buttress.[45]

With neither a precise date for the new buttress nor a drawing for it by Street or his office, the authorship of the design of the buttress must remain open. Street's health had begun to fail in 1881 and after suffering two strokes he died on 18 December, perhaps before the crack in the south wall was noticed.

For purely stylistic reasons, the addition does not appear to be Street's. The windows of the buttress, for example, resemble more those of the church than of the rectory (Figs. 14, 15). Street had been careful to distinguish church from rectory, assigning the more elaborate three-dimensional Venetian tracery to the rectory, in keeping with its secular functions. The windows of the main circular stair, which are trabeated at the lower two levels, have cross mullions and a Venetian profile at the upper level. The buttress addition, with its simple single Gothic-arch windows, and paired windows with a tondo and quatrefoil above pointed arches, appears to be an attempt to conform to the character of the church,[46] negating thereby Street's formal, associative, distinction between a secular appurtenance and the sacred vessel that gave meaning to the site.[47]

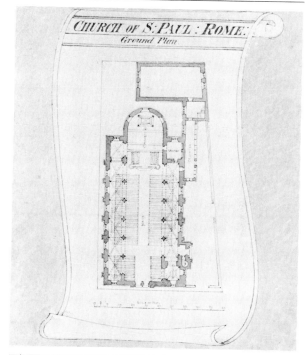

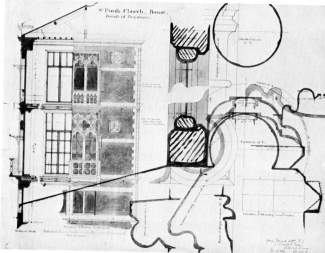

The remainder of the rectory, up to the lot line on the north (Figs. 13, 16), containing five rooms on each of the four floors, "was not begun," according to Lowrie, "till 1892 and therefore it was barely finished" by 1895.[48] Lowrie attended to the work during the first seven years of his rec-

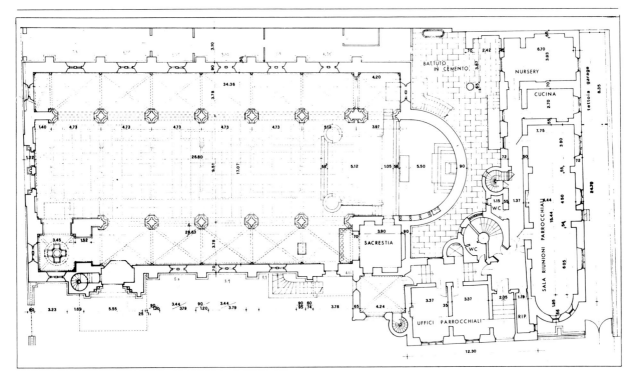

torship, completing the rectory only in 1914. The elevations and details suggest that the design came from the same hand as the three-story buttress addition. Are the two sections perhaps by Arthur Street, who inherited the office and continued his father's work?

STREET'S WORKING METHOD

Although Street's initial design and most of his working drawings are lost, as are the detailed building records that, by 1877, already filled over 1,200 foolscap pages[49] according to Nevin, enough remains to limn a picture of Street at work on a project.

After the initial "conceptual flash" that resulted in his first sketch on the ground in Rome, Street turned out presentation drawings during his short stay there. Unlike the case of the Amer-

ican Church in Paris, the record in Rome suggests continued modification and alteration whenever the opportunity arose or was necessitated, as, for instance, in the altered placement of the tower to satisfy municipal aesthetic considerations.

Without the original scheme and working drawing it would be difficult to propose what the changes might have been were it not for the watercolor perspective and plan dated March 1875 (Fig. 1). Although tagged with a date three years after the initial design of the church, there are elements in the plan that suggest it portrays an earlier state of the design (Fig. 11). One need only look, for example, at the equal spacing of the buttresses along the north wall. In the building (Fig. 13) the spacing between buttresses varies from 3.75 meters to 4.35 meters between the easternmost pair. The wider spacing in that bay

14. St. Paul's Within the Walls. Section/elevation showing west wall of buttress of the rectory in 1977. (Drawing: P. Marconi.)

15. St. Paul's Within the Walls. Elevation of south wall of the rectory in 1977. (Drawing: P. Marconi.)

enables the east buttress to receive the thrust from the ribs of the vault of the north aisle. In the watercolor plan, the easternmost buttress lies to the west of the point where the ribs intersect the wall. The foundations for the buttresses would, of course, have been laid out in the fall or winter of 1872/73 and have rendered the plan obsolete in this respect.[50]

Even more telling is the depth of the elongated apse in the watercolor plan; it extends 6 feet or so beyond a semicircle. When constructed, the overall length of the church and apse was kept to about the same dimension but the aisles were lengthened to the east, reducing the apse to a semicircle. Again, the watercolor plan must antedate the foundations.

Still further, the plan does not show the set-back west-facade wall of the north aisle (recessed at the level of the window where the horizontal section is taken.) That, too, would have been built by March 1875, the date inscribed on the watercolor.

In December 1874, three months before the dated watercolor, Street prepared detail drawings for the marble choir screen and ambones. That sheet (Fig. 5) shows three steps up to choir level while the watercolor plan shows only two.[51] The six steps in three pairs as shown in the watercolor plan are, as constructed, bunched at the entrance to the chancel.[52]

Yet other details in the watercolor plan—for example, colonnettes to receive the ribs on the north and south aisle walls, a double window on the facade at the west end of the north side aisle, an altar with baldachino, and the absence of a bishop's chair on axis—signal an early state of the design. Indeed, if the tower were projecting from the plane of the facade, it would be tempting to think of this plan as that presented to the vestry

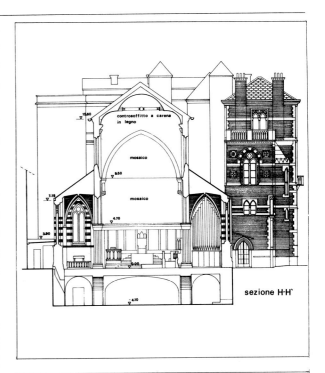

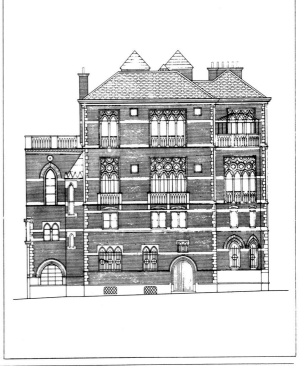

16. St. Paul's Within the Walls. Elevation of west wall of the rectory and section through the rectory on Via Napoli in 1977. (Drawing: P. Marconi.)

on 8 March 1872.[53] In any case, it cannot represent a stage very much later; it was obsolete by the time working drawings were prepared.

A more precise date may be implied from the content of the Vestry Minutes of 2 April 1872, in which the rector requested postponement of the ground-breaking ceremony. The original intention was, apparently, to initiate excavation as soon as practicable, and, if possible, to bring the foundations to ground level before the rector was to leave on a summer fund-raising tour.[54] Had work begun on the foundation in April, according to a revised final plan, our watercolor plan would represent the second stage, drawn in March and obsolete before April; had the final design changes not yet been made, the plan of St. Paul's today would be that of the watercolor plan. The design, therefore, went through at least three distinct stages:

St. Paul's I—with salient tower—early March 1872
St. Paul's II—the watercolor plan—March–August (?) 1872
St. Paul's III—the plan as constructed—prior to 5 November 1872

The change from St. Paul's I to II was necessitated by municipal authority, the change from II to III by improvements Street himself wished to make to both the church and the rectory (the changes to the rectory were major). The watercolor perspective, while agreeing with the plan in many respects, includes elements that speak for a date later than the plan, perhaps as late as the date it bears, March 1875.

One of the drawings for the campanile (Fig. 2), dated December 1874, includes an obsolete version of the main pediment with only three instead of the nine blind lancets found in the watercolor perspective and on the building today. The campanile drawing was also obsolete in the coursing of the lower level, showing ten courses (instead of nine as constructed) of light-colored travertine (including the base course) in the first level of the facade. In this respect the watercolor perspective is, however, also obsolete in showing only eight courses in the same area.

All three sheets of elevations and details dated December 1874 (Figs. 2, 3, 4) were prepared for construction of the campanile, which was to be begun as funds became available after the walls were completed in July 1875. That Street used an obsolete version of the section of the facade below the point at which the campanile stands free is not surprising, but its inclusion is further evidence of the freedom Street exercised in altering designs during construction.

The watercolor perspective is, nonetheless, faithful in many details and may help to indicate the state of construction at that date.[55] The travertine course at the top of the square reveal that encloses the rose window is depicted as it is on the building, breaking upward to act as a molding at the head of the square. The nine blind lancets in the pediment above, however, are shown in the perspective to be formed completely of travertine, while as built only the base course and arches from spring height to raking cornice are of travertine, with the remainder in brick. Was the building height of the facade in March 1875 at the level of the top of the rose window and cornice?[56]

On the other hand, below the rose window in the perspective the horizontal molding (above the eleven-bay blind colonnade) is shown with a sculpted boss at its north end. At its southern end the molding turns downward perpendicularly and runs to the string course marking the cornice height of the side aisles. In this case, the perspective is obsolete, depicting a state already superseded, for the building has neither boss nor vertical molding.

The churchyard railing, as shown in the watercolor perspective, underwent redesign to that drawn up in December 1875, nine months later (Figs. 7, 8).

The plan (Fig. 11) shows an opening in the wall and railing along the Via Napoli opposite the fourth bay (from the facade) of the south flank of the church. The opening is omitted in the perspective (Fig. 1), which might indicate it was an early idea, later discarded, were it not that the wall was built with the opening.

The engraved perspective that appeared in *The Architect* on 20 November 1875 (Fig. 6), eight months later, appears to be drawn from the watercolor perspective (or from a preparatory sketch or copy of it), since it adheres to most of the details found in the watercolor.[57] While the design of the churchyard railing from the watercolor is preserved in the wood engraving, the south flank of the railing on the Via Napoli is shown with an opening and gateway farther to the west than in the watercolor plan. To the north of the church on the Via Nazionale the railing is continued northward, as if the church's property extended a good deal farther along the Via Nazionale than is shown on the watercolor plan.[58]

The parentage of the engraved perspective is confirmed by comparing the treatment of the string course on the facade and campanile at the level of the cornice of the walls of the side aisles and of the third stage of the campanile. In both cases, errors in the watercolor are repeated in the engraving. The watercolor shows the decorated string course continuing, albeit with changes, around the salient of the circular stair at the southeast corner of the campanile. The engraved perspective shows that the upper molding (but not the brackets) of the string course continued around the salient. On the building the string course (brackets and molding) terminates at the salient for the stair.[59] For the third stage of the campanile, the watercolor and the engraved perspective show, incorrectly, seven horizontal courses of travertine (including the base). The elevation drawing of December 1874, no. 47, (Fig. 4) shows eight courses, as there are on the building today.

The watercolor perspective and the plan show, therefore, different stages of the design. The plan is close to the original, perhaps as early as March/April 1872, certainly no later than November 1872, by which time it would have been obsolete. The perspective, on the other hand, while including some details that were already superseded (horizontal molding above the eleven blind windows of the colonnade on the facade, and the churchyard railing without an opening on the via Napoli), shows, in the main, the church as it had been constructed up to that point (north aisle facade setback and single window, entrance portal, coursing, top molding of square around the rose window)[60] and, with some variations, as it was to be completed (nine blind lancet windows in pediment, campanile, etc.); it represents therefore, with varying degrees of accuracy, the design as of the date inscribed on the watercolor, March 1875.[61]

This somewhat extended examination of the development of Street's designs for St. Paul's confirms the dictum that he often conceived a scheme in an instant and committed it to paper. Yet the examination may also modify our view of his working method by demonstrating that Street, rather than adhering to an initial design, often (perhaps always) took the opportunity to modify and improve his designs.

The designs for St. Paul's depict an architect redesigning portions of an initial design as the moment of construction of that section approached. St. Paul's II and III—with attendant sections, perspective, and details for foundations and walls—were designed in 1872/73 and constructed in 1872 to 1875. Designs for the campanile and interior choir and ambones were done in 1874 and constructed in 1876. Also in 1874/75 portions of the facade and vestry roof were redesigned; they were executed in 1875/76. The churchyard railing was redesigned in 1875 and constructed in 1879. The rectory, programmed for construction after the church, was thoroughly redesigned, probably in 1879, and constructed from 1880 on.

Many architects have worked in this manner; many certainly wish they could do so.[62] That Street should have done so is perhaps to be expected, even though this has not been discussed in the literature. Further study of Street's work is likely to reveal a consistent working method that admitted revision and exploited opportunity. He is, after all, reported to have "prepared by his own hand" some three thousand drawings for the Law Courts in the Strand.[63] Once enough material describing Street's modifications of designs throughout his career is assembled, it may be possible to penetrate more deeply into his mind and ponder the urbanistic, architectural, formal, associative, and perhaps, iconographic, goals that caused him to seek alternatives.

To develop a balanced view of Street as an architect, the image of Street as an inspired designer who turned out, in record time, completed finished designs ready for inking, should be modified to include the view presented here.

Notes

The scholar to whom this volume is dedicated first introduced me to the architecture of George Edmund Street in an article published in the *Journal of the Society of Architectural Historians* in 1960. It is a pleasure to be able to offer him a piece that, without his essay, might never have been written.

Acknowledgment is due for the assistance of Alison Luchs and the counsel of Judith Millon in the preparation of this paper. Elizabeth Jones and C. Ron Ostberg secured and transported material about the church across the ocean; Philipp Fehl, Margaret De Popolo, and Karin Einaudi helped with illustrations. The Rector of St. Paul's, Wilbur Woodhams, did all he could to make study of the church fruitful and enjoyable.

1. A. E. Street, "George Edmund Street by his son Arthur E. Street, M.A.," *Architecture* 1 (February–December 1896) (hereafter cited as *Street by his son*); and A. E. Street, *Memoir of George Edmund Street, R.A. 1824–1881* (London, 1888), p. 284 (hereafter cited as *Memoir*).

2. The anecdote included by Arthur Street was the often repeated one told by Richard Norman Shaw, who worked in Street's office from 1859 to 1861 (Andrew Saint, *Richard Norman Shaw* [New Haven/London, 1976], pp. 15–23). Shaw marveled at the "rapidity and precision with which [Street] drew," and told of a day in which Street went to

measure an old church, took a ten o'clock train, and returned to the office about half-past four. Street then, in the privacy of his office, drew in about an hour the "whole church carefully . . . to scale," including the "proposed additions . . . ready to ink in and finish" (*Memoir*, p. 284; *Street by his son*, p. 39).

3. *Memoir*, pp. 133–134; *Street by his son*, p. 39. A. E. Street knew that his father altered designs after the initial sketch. His account of the American Church in Paris in *Memoir* shows what correspondence "in all its essential elements" meant to A. E. Street. "It [the initial sketch] practically represents the church as it stands there now. It is true that one large window has taken the place of two smaller ones in the west front, and that the tower and spire have been shifted from the south side to the north, but these are the only important modifications. Every proportion is exactly similar . . . the great point is the wonderful power of imagination . . . and the immense self-reliance which could enable a man to bind himself, definitely, once and for all and at a moment's notice, to a design for . . . about the most costly parish church which he had ever had to build."

4. R. J. Nevin, *St. Paul's Within the Walls* (New York, 1878), p. 257 (hereafter cited as *Nevin*).

5. *The Times*, 29 December 1881, p. 8. There are other similar accounts. "He had no first thoughts and second thoughts about a thing, but decided rapidly and once for all what would be suitable . . . " (*Memoir*, p. 131). "His rapidity was astonishing, and his command of hand for large curves for metalwork and the like, equally so; as, however quickly done, they could generally be followed with the pen implicitly" (*The Builder* 41 [24 December 1881]: 779). "A clergyman whose church he was restoring having written for details that did not arrive, called at Cavendish Place and came down from Mr. Street's room in an hour or so with a large roll of papers under his arm, and a triumphant smile, saying 'I have got them all!'" (ibid., p. 779).

6. *Street by his son*, p. 39.

7. St. Paul's Within the Walls, Rome. Perspective from the southwest and, in upper right, on a drawn inset scroll, a labeled plan with a scale of 100 feet. Inscribed: "Church of S. Paul, Rome." Watercolor with pencil underdrawing (554 × 505 mm.). Signed and dated, lower right: "George Edmund Street, March 1875."

This watercolor drawing is probably that exhibited in April 1875 at the 107th exhibition of the Royal Academy, discussed in a review published in *The Builder* 33 (1 November 1875): 382: "'The South-west View of the Church of St. Paul in the via Nazionale, Rome,' for the use of the American Church, by Mr. Street (963), exhibits a return to the Italian particoloured Gothic style, which the architect had for a long time deserted; there is hardly much to remark in it; we should be curious to know on what grounds the Americans in Rome are given an Italian design, when the English residents were given a distinctly *Street-ish* one."

8. For Street see the obituaries in *The Building News* 41 (23 December 1881): 813; *The Architect* 26 (24 December 1881): 406; *The Builder* 41 (24 December 1881): 777; *The Times*, 29 December 1881, p. 8; *The Morning Post*, 30 December 1881, p. 5; and the following: *Memoir* and *Street by his son* (see n. 1); *Dictionary of National Biography*, ed. Sidney Lee, Vol. LV (London, 1898), pp. 42–45 (entry by Paul Waterhouse, not Philip Webb); Hermann Muthesius, *Di Neuere Kirchliche Baukunst in England* (Berlin, 1901), pp. 29–31; G. G. King, *George Edmund Street: unpublished notes and reprinted papers with an essay* (New York, 1916); Walter Millard, "George Edmund Street's sketches at home and abroad," *Journal of the Royal Institute of British Architects* 25 (March 1918): 97–103; B.F.L. Clarke, *Church Builders of the Nineteenth Century* (London/New York, 1938), pp. 146–152; H. S. Goodhart-Rendel, "George Edmund Street," *The Builder* 184 (3 April 1953): 519–20; Henry-Russell Hitchcock, *Early Victorian Architecture in Britain*, 2 vols. (New Haven, 1954): pp. 601–605; *Architecture: Nineteenth and Twentieth Centuries* (Baltimore, 1958), pp. 174, 175, 178, 180, 186, 200–201; and "G. E. Street in the 1850s," *Journal of the Society of Architectural Historians* 19 (December 1960): 145–171; Peter Howell, *Victorian Churches* (London, 1968), pls. 11, 24 and p. 39; B.F.L. Clarke and John Piper, "Street's Yorkshire Churches and Contemporary Criticism," *Concerning Architecture, Essays on Architectural Writers and Writing presented to N. Pevsner*, ed. John Summerson (London, 1968), pp. 209–225; *Catalogue of the Drawings Collection of the Royal Institute of British Architects*, ed. M. Richardson (Farnborough, 1976), pp. 117–122; John Summerson, *Victorian Architecture—Four Studies in Evaluation* (New York/London, 1970), pp. 47–76; Stefan Muthesius, *The High Victorian Movement in Architecture 1850–1870* (London/Boston, 1972), pp. 39–53, 93–114, 134. See also Judith Rice Millon, *St. Paul's Within the Walls, Rome: A Building History and Guide* (Dublin, N.H., 1982).

For Street's major secular structure, The Law Courts, see Joseph Kinnard, "G. E. Street, The Law Courts and the Seventies," *Victorian Architecture*, ed. Peter Ferriday (London, 1963), pp. 221–234; M. H. Port, "The New Law Courts Competition, 1866–67," *Architectural History* 11 (1968): 75–120; J. Summerson, *Victorian Architecture*, pp. 77–117; S. Muthesius, *The High Victorian Movement*, pp. 183–188; and David Brownlee, *George Edmund Street and the Royal Courts of Justice* (diss., Harvard University, 1980).

Hitchcock, "G. E. Street in the 1850s," p. 145, n. 5, says that as his article neared completion "I learned that

J. R. Lambert . . . had in hand a book on *George Edmund Street and the Gothic Revival*." If what Professor Hitchcock learned is true, then Lambert apparently still has the book in hand.

Street's obituary in *The Building News* lists, on p. 815, Street's published works, lectures delivered, and notes that he drew the illustrations for J. Baron, *Scudamore organs* . . . (London, 1858). For Street's publications up to 1860 see H.-R. Hitchcock, "G. E. Street in the 1850s."

9. Richard Dorment, *Burne-Jones and the Decoration of St. Paul's American Church, Rome* (diss., Columbia University, 1975 [hereafter cited as *Dorment*]).

10. All seven drawings are listed in *Catalogue of the Drawings Collection of the Royal Institute of British Architects*, Vol. S, ed. Margaret Richardson (Farnborough, 1970), p. 122. Paul Joyce wrote the entry on Street. The drawings are numbered as follows:

R.I.B.A. CATALOGUE		INSCRIBED NOS.
[14]	1	46
	2	43
	3	47
	4	49
	5	82
	6	83
	7	*

*Not noted in the Catalogue but either 8 or 18.

R.I.B.A. nos. [14] 1 and 5 are reproduced among the plates of the volume; [14] 5 has also been reproduced in P. Howell, *Victorian Churches* (London, 1968), pl. 24 on pp. 34–35.

11. "American Church of St. Paul, Rome," *The Architect* 14 (20 November 1875): 288.

12. St. Paul's Parish Archive. The Minutes of Vestry Meetings (hereafter cited as *Minutes*) are entered in sequential ledgers. The first volume covers the period up to 15 January 1873. Specific treatment of the architecture of St. Paul's (prior to the reference in Dorment's dissertation) was made by C.L.V. Meeks in an article in 1953 on the two churches by Street in Rome (the other is All Saints, built a few years later for the British congregation) and summarized again in 1966 in his book on Italian architecture (Meeks, "Churches by Street on the via Nazionale and the via del Babuino," *Art Quarterly*, 16 [1953]: 215–227; *Italian Architecture 1750–1914* [New Haven, 1966], pp. 275–284). Meeks discussed the building and the circumstances of its commission utilizing documentary information contained in the two histories of the church written by Robert J. Nevin, rector when the church was commissioned and built (see n. 4) and Walter Lowrie, who succeeded Nevin in 1906 and guided the church until 1930 (see *Fifty Years of St. Paul's American Church, Rome*, [Rome, 1926; hereafter cited as *Lowrie*]).

13. St. Paul's Parish Archive, ms. "St. Paul's American Protestant Episcopal Church, Service Records of Rev. R. J. Nevin, July 1867 to March 5th, 1876," quoted in *Dorment*, p. 2, n. 1.

14. *Minutes*, 30 January 1872.

15. *Minutes*, 13 February 1872.

16. *Dorment*, p. 3.

17. *Memoir*, p. 209.

18. *Nevin*, p. 257.

19. *Minutes*, 8 March 1872. *Nevin* p. 54 records the dimensions in feet as 101 × 182, different from the dimensions (97.09 × 180.4 feet) recorded in the Minutes. The site is trapezoidal in shape, narrower on the east.

20. *Minutes*, 12 March 1872. The design approved by the vestry has not survived. The dimensions in plan are similar to those of the church today, although the facade as constructed is 64 feet 7 inches, 5 feet 5 inches lower than specified (measurements used here are taken from the measured drawings prepared by the architect Paolo Marconi before restoration of the church in 1979/80).

21. *Nevin*, p. 257.

22. It may have been at this juncture, when the vertical salient of the campanile was scotched, that Street slightly recessed the plane of the facade of the north aisle above the base course, reinforcing the verticality of the facade.

23. The date is recorded in *Nevin*, p. 56.

24. *Minutes*, 2 April 1872.

25. *Dorment*, p. 2, note 1.

26. There are four extant sheets in the collections of the British Architectural Library (R.I.B.A.) for portions of the building constructed in 1876 as it neared completion. Three sheets (carrying numbers 43, 46, and 47) are for the campanile. Two of the sheets (43 and 46) bear the notation in pencil "traced Dec '74," not found on the third. All three are dated in ink "December 1874." The fourth sheet (no. 49) for the choir screen and ambone, also dated in ink "Dec. 1874," bears the pencil notation "Traced and sent 17. 12. 1874."

27. *Nevin*, p. 258. As Meeks, *Italian Architecture 1750–1914*, p. 275, n. 81, points out, Kleffler is best known in Rome for his design of the Villa Savoia outside the Porta Pia.

28. *Nevin*, pp. 77–78.

29. The ceremony is the subject of the third chapter in *Nevin*, pp. 58–80.

30. *Nevin*, p. 80, says Street visited Rome three times. The *Memoir* lists five certain visits to Rome: March 1872 (p. 209); Christmas holidays, 1873 (p. 223); winter 1874/75 (p. 227); January/February 1876 (p. 230); and spring 1880 (pp. 251, 259). Street may also have been in Rome a sixth time in May 1877 or 1878 (*Memoir*, p. 255).

C.L.V. Meeks, "Churches by Street . . . ," *Art Quarterly* 16 (1953): 220, says Street was in Rome four times in 1872, 1874, 1878, and 1880, adding that the "earlier trips were . . . in connection with building the American Church." The English Church was begun in February 1880 (Meeks, "Churches by Street. . . ," p. 225, n. 12), although it was apparently already designed in the spring of 1875; see n. 7.

31. *Memoir*, p. 230.

32. When his wife contracted her fatal illness, Street hurried back to London (*Memoir*, p. 230).

33. *Nevin*, p. 97.

34. *Nevin*, p. 81.

35. The description is probably not completely accurate. A representation of the interior (the earliest known) during the consecration service published in *Illustrazione Italiana*, 16 April 1876, p. 388, (Fig. 9) shows the north choir marble screen in place but not yet that to the south. Only the base for the north ambone was complete, but for the ceremony a temporary wooden pulpit apparently was built atop it.

36. Sir Gilbert Scott admired Street's metalwork; see P. Howell, *Victorian Churches* (London, 1968), p. 35.

37. Figs. 7 and 8 bear the inscription, "This is one of the three contract drawings referred to in the contract signed by me the twenty-eighth day of July in the year of our Lord one thousand eight hundred and seventy nine."

38. *Nevin* speaks of the strain of completion on pages 82 and 83. With the exception of the appendix (pp. 257–280), which discusses the construction and characteristics of the church, the remainder of Nevin's book from page 81 to page 255 is devoted to the consecration of the church, accompanying speeches, and sermons of the octave.

39. Portions of the Italian text by Cesare Donati accompanying the article appeared in English in *The Builder* 34 (11 November 1876): 1094.

40. As late as January 1893 capitals were still being carved (*Minutes*, 13 January 1893). Some of the moldings on the arches remain uncarved and incomplete today.

    A photograph showing the interior of the church after the semidome mosaic was in place (25 December 1885) and before the mosaics of the transverse arches were installed (begun 1894) is in the archive of the Gabinetto Fotografico Nazionale in Rome (Series D-1945). Uncarved capitals and moldings can be seen in the photograph.

41. The Vestry Minutes of 9 November 1880 record Nevin's report of $9,500 in hand for the construction of the rectory that according to Street would cost $17,000. Nevin states the designs prepared by Street would contain two vestry rooms, a library or schoolrooms, an apartment for the sacristan, and two large apartments for the use of clergy or for rental (see Fig. 13). Work probably began shortly after this date. Street had been in Rome the preceding spring (*Memoir*, pp. 251, 259).

42. Of interest are the structural details that show Street using iron I-beams as joists with arched masonry (or tile or concrete) spanning between the joists, square wood sleepers and wood flooring above the wood furring strips, lath and plaster for the ceiling below, all color-coded in section and elevation as follows:

MATERIAL	ELEVATION	SECTION
wood	yellow	brown
iron	blue	blue
stone		red
masonry (?) arches	pink*	pink*

*stippled

43. *Lowrie*, p. 39.

44. Such initial settlement before stabilization could perhaps have been predicted. In any case, once arrested it caused no further problem.

45. There exists today, in the otherwise largely completed building, a rough stucco wall surface below an exposed large relieving arch on the interior of the easternmost bay of the south aisle, above the doorway leading to the churchyard. The Alinari photograph of the interior from about 1910/11 (Fig. 12) shows in this bay an unfinished rough masonry surface. The interior perspective of 1875 from *Illustrazione Italiana* (Fig. 9) shows the south wall of the bay complete with a door and uniform horizontal stripes in light and dark.

    Lacking any obvious prior reason, it may be that the arch and unusual treatment in this bay are a result of efforts made (at the time the buttress between south aisle and rectory was added) to absorb imagined longitudinal thrusts in the plane of the wall or to resist vertical fractures in the wall. Vertical fissures appeared in the clerestory wall of the bay adjacent to the campanile and caused the three-story buttress bay to be added to the rectory. *Lowrie*, in Figure 3, shows that during his tenure the interior wall was completed but without obliterating the anomaly.

    The three-story buttress resulted in the opening of an entrance into the vestry space from the new vestibule. The doorway from the south aisle was closed and the organ was placed above the vestry room.

46. The balustrade of the terrace of the roof is, however, modeled on that by Street for the balconies and terraces on the south elevation of the rectory.

47. With regard to hierarchical distinctions and stylistic differentiations between sacred and secular, S. Muthesius (*The High Victorian Movement in Architecture 1850–1870*, [London/Boston, 1972], pp. 47–48), when speaking of Street's domestic architecture, notes, "The range, that is the degrees of importance accorded to domestic and collegiate buildings, is very marked. This difference may be found even within one building, as at Cuddesdon College, between the domestic wing and the chapel wing. For smaller country buildings, Street made use of 'cottage' features." Muthesius also notes (p. 47) in the caption to Figure 10 (All Saints, Boyne Hill, Maidenhead), "A typical group of church (its western parts were not executed as shown

here), vicarage, school rooms, school-master's cottage, with the hierarchy of decoration clearly shown."

48. *Lowrie*, p. 40. The Vestry Minutes of 7 December 1891 authorize the rector to proceed with the building of the second section of the rectory after $37,111 had been received or pledged. Work was soon suspended temporarily in January because the plans violated a new municipal requirement that limited the height of a building to three times the width of space left between neighboring buildings (*Minutes*, 16 January 1892). The new section of the rectory was roofed in the fall of 1892. (*Minutes*, 13 January 1893).

49. *Nevin*, p. 76.

50. As suggested by Professor William Loerke in November 1980, it would have been possible to alter the final plan of the Church after the foundations had been begun or laid, but to do so would have necessitated changes in the masonry of the foundations as they approached pavement level or lower. Even though there is no evidence visible (as far as I know from examining the walls in the undercroft) of changes in the foundation during construction, the possibility cannot be ruled out.

51. *Nevin*, p. 260, mentions the three steps up to the choir.

52. In 1969 the chancel was lowered by one step during the rectorship of Wilbur Woodhams. Physical evidence of the lowering is, however, lacking. The altar was moved forward to accommodate the new (old) liturgy.

    Nevin, however, pp. 260–261, says "the apse will be separated from the choir by the communion rail—not yet given—and is raised two steps above the floor of the choir."

    In the building today there are six steps between the nave and the apse: three at the entrance to the choir, one at the end of the choir, and two at the apse. The watercolor plan shows eight steps. Have there been other, unchronicled changes?

    Incidentally, the interior perspective reproduced in *Illustrazione Italiana* (16 April 1876) shows, probably incorrectly, only two steps up from the nave to the choir.

53. Nevin states only that Street was "forced to abandon . . . the original design," but he does not say at what date the municipal commissioner objected. If Nevin acted with his customary expeditiousness, and if the municipal commissioner acted quickly (unusual in such offices), Street may have known of the objections before leaving Rome. It is more likely he heard of the ruling after his return to London. The drawing would date, therefore, from the period between c. 15 March and late summer of 1872.

54. The pertinent portion of the Minutes reads as follows: "The Rector having stated that at the present period of the season it would be impossible to get the foundations advanced to the ground level until sometime in June, and that going forward with them now would prevent his visiting the United States this summer, to raise money . . . "

55. The facade of the north aisle, for instance, is shown correctly set back above the base coursing with a single win-

dow rather than the double one shown in plan, and the column and pier clusters in the jambs of the main entrance portal are indicated as they are on the building rather than freestanding without a cluster as indicated on the plan on the same sheet.

56. Further support for a height of construction approaching the top of the rose window in March 1875 may be found in comparing the series of narrow windows that light the circular stair of the campanile in drawings and on the building. The south elevation of the campanile in drawing no. 46 (Fig. 2) of December 1874 includes four windows in the salient for the stair as does the watercolor perspective dated three months later. The building, however, omits the uppermost window planned for a level somewhat above the middle of the rose window on the west facade. The engraving in *The Architect*, 20 November 1875, includes all four windows. The windows are omitted entirely in the engraving by Bonamore reproduced in *Illustrazione Italiana*, 6 April 1876, p. 389, and in *The Builder* 34 (11 November 1876): 1094. The engraved frontispiece in Nevin includes all four windows.

57. At least three other engraved representations depend from the engraving first reproduced in *The Architect* (itself unsigned, printed by W. W. Sprague and Co., London, E.C.). See *Illustrazione Italiana*, 16 April 1876, p. 389 (by A. Bonamore); *The Builder* 34 (11 November 1876): 1094 (reengraved but with Bonamore's signature rather than taken from the earlier English publication); and the frontispiece to Nevin's book, 1878 (unsigned).

58. In the plan, the dimension of the site on the Via Nazionale scales 97 feet, the same dimension as that recorded in the Minutes of 8 March 1872 [29.6 m.] (see n. 19).

    It was not until 29 April 1879, three years later, that the Minutes record authorization given the rector to purchase "a sufficient number of metres of land to preserve a line of three metres clear from the base of the church throughout the whole length of the property on the northeast side of the church, at 81 Italian lire the metre." On 28 November the Minutes recorded a further purchase "to preserve and continue our line of three metres . . . "

    In return for supplying flowers for the church on Christmas, festivals, and other occasions, and for keeping the yard to the south of the church in proper order, a florist, in 1893, sought and secured permission to occupy the three-meter space to the north of the church (*Minutes*, 24 February 1893).

59. In this regard it may be worth noting that the sheet with elevations and section of the campanile, no. 46 (Fig. 2), shows on the west elevation only the molding continuing around the salient for the stair. The south elevation, on the other hand, eliminates the molding and bears traces of the erasure of brackets on the salient stair. At that spot there is an inscribed notation "37 steps" indicating the number of steps in the stair to that level.

60. The ceiling above the vestry room may not yet have been constructed. The interior view from *Illustrazione Italiana* (Fig. 9) shows a half barrel vault covering the vestry room bay rather than a ribbed groin vault as in the other bays of the south side. In this respect the view agrees with the plan found on the watercolor perspective, which omits any indication of vaulting in the vestry space. The wood rafters and sheathing of a shed roof can be seen today above the organ pipes.

61. Changes yet to come after March 1875 include redesign of the churchyard railing (December 1875) and the rectory (c. 1879/80).

62. H. H. Richardson, a younger contemporary of Street, is reported by F. L. Olmstead to have believed that an architect's revisions "should never end until his building is 'in stone, beyond recovery'; and he [Richardson] exemplified this belief by altering much and often after construction had actually been begun" (M. G. Van Rennselaer, *Henry Hobson Richardson and His Works* [New York, 1888], p. 119).

63. *Dictionary of National Biography*, ed. Sidney Lee, Vol. LV (London, 1898), p. 44.

T.G. JACKSON AND
THE CULT OF ECLECTICISM

J. Mordaunt Crook

NOT MANY NAMES ARE MISSING FROM Hitchcock's *opus magnum*, *Architecture: Nineteenth and Twentieth Centuries* (1958). One strange lacuna, however—at least in an English context—is Thomas Graham Jackson. Jackson's architecture—indeed his whole life-style—was peculiarly English. Yet his career has broader implications; it tells us much about the strengths and weaknesses of the late-nineteenth-century cult of eclecticism.

Jackson was a scholar and a gentleman[1] (he even looked like Philibert de l'Orme).[2] And he achieved a curious distinction: so far he is the only English architect to have received an hereditary title, being made a baronet in 1913. Born in 1835, the son of a Hampstead solicitor, he read classics at Wadham College, Oxford (between bouts of rowing) and was elected in 1864 to one of the last unreformed, nonresident Fellowships.[3] Meanwhile, in 1858—"steeped in Ruskin and mad about Hunt and Millais"—he had entered the office of Sir Gilbert Scott.[4] At Wadham, Jackson had been taught to paint by Turner of Oxford.[5] Now he learned architectural drawing from the most successful Gothicist of his generation. In 1862 he set up practice independently. Those were the years when younger architects had begun to flirt with the Queen Anne Revival, "that vexatious disturber of the Gothic movement," as Scott called it.[6] And in 1873 young Jackson electrified the architectural world with *Modern Gothic Architecture*, a lucid and forceful exposition of the deficiencies of unmitigated Neo-Gothic.

"Some sentences and paragraphs," wrote *The Architect*, "are worthy of Ruskin or Reynolds."[7] Not bad for a book written in fragments on the train between London and Sevenoaks.[8] Certainly, *Modern Gothic* still reads well, and its themes can be stated simply: Gothic was the natural expression of British architectural genius; unlike Classicism it did not fetter creativity; its revival was therefore a valid artistic exercise; but its future lay not in reproduction but in adaptation and absorption, in the assimilation of collateral styles, and in the integration along Ruskinian lines of architecture, painting, and sculpture. In other words, although its details are never spelled out, the future of architecture lay in eclecticism. The Gothic Revival alone—and this came as something of a thunderbolt from one of G. G. Scott's ablest pupils—was not enough.[9] "I asked myself," Jackson recalled in 1904, "what was the τελos—the end of the movement. Clearly the τελos proposed to themselves by the prime movers had been to make Gothic architecture become once more a living vernacular style, to the exclusion of any other, and they had failed. They had got the old dead style on its legs and propped it up, but they could not make it walk."[10] Jackson, therefore, became an eclectic.

> My early love was English Gothic [Jackson wrote in later years], and I have been faithful to her all my life. But I do not consider that those who reproduce the forms of ancient Gothic deserve to be called her lovers. I regard all buildings which conform to the conditions of English climate, material and habit, as Gothic. The English Renaissance, as it appears in such buildings as Audley End, and Kirby . . . Knole, [Burghley] and others . . . , is from my point of view, a Gothic style; and when the Gothic element drops out of it, as in pure Palladian, it becomes, to my taste, uninteresting.[11]

Moving on from Decorated to Perpendicular, and so, via Elizabethan, Jacobean, and Caroline to Queen Anne, Jackson throughout his career con-

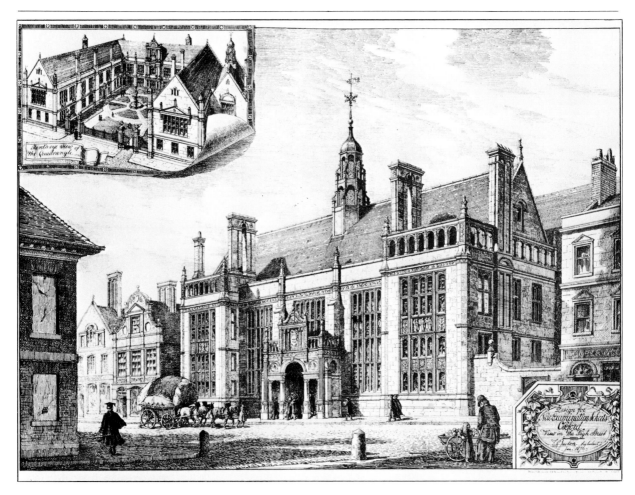

tinued to discover Gothic in the most unlikely places. In fact, he ended as an apostle of "Wren-naissance." "We are inclined," wrote the *Architectural Review* in its very first volume, "to utter a gentle remonstrance to Mr. Jackson: his work seems varied to the point of eclecticism."[12] And of course an eclectic is exactly what he was, despite all his sophistry about the continuity of the Gothic tradition. Happily for his intellectual standing, however—and it turned out to be doubly fortunate for his career—Jackson made his mark in one of the few places where Gothic Survival, Gothic Revival, and Renaissance not only

had cohabited but had given birth to a viable architectural vernacular: Oxford University.

Jackson graduated at Wadham, the same college where Sir Christopher Wren had studied. Its seventeenth-century mixture of styles must have intrigued him. Close at hand was another building which surely influenced him greatly, Thomas Holt's multiple Tower of the Orders (1619) in the Old Schools building, now part of the Bodleian Library.[13] And just across Radcliffe Square was another structure in which Jackson must have taken secret delight, that insouciant mixture of Gothic and Classic—Brasenose College chapel.

It was at Wadham in 1871 that he received his first college commission, the redecoration of the warden's lodgings.[14] But his real Oxford debut took place in 1874 at Christ Church, where he competed against Scott, Bodley, Hussey and Basil Champneys for the honor of completing Cardinal Wolsey's staircase tower. He failed. But Dr. Acland called his soaring design "the finest thing ever rejected."[15] And in the following year he triumphed over Sir Thomas Newenham Deane, Champneys, Bodley, and Oldrid Scott in the competition for the new Examination Schools.

At the Examination Schools (1876–1882) (Fig. 1), Jackson established the style for which he became famous. He began the design in Gothic. But, he recalled,

the more I did the less I liked it. . . . Before my eyes seemed to come the haunting vision of Elizabethan and Jacobean work, and especially of those long mullioned and transomed windows at Kirby Hall in Northamptonshire. . . . Jacobean work . . . seemed to me eminently suitable to modern usage, more elastic than either Gothic or free Classic. To my mind it is

3. *Examination Schools. View of sculpture above entrance. (Photo: National Monuments Record, London; courtesy of Oxfordshire County Libraries.)*
4. *Examination Schools. View of sculpture above entrance. (Photo: National Monuments Record, London; courtesy of Oxfordshire County Libraries.)*

really Classic, though it made use of the Classic orders in a way of its own. . . . The defect of the work seemed to me to be the rudeness of the ornament. . . . It seemed to me that it was possible to refine English Renaissance by avoiding its eccentricities, retaining that Gothic feeling which gave it life and instead of imitating the gross ornamentation to which it was prone, looking rather for example to the lovely decorative work of the early or Bramantesque Renaissance in Italy.[16]

And so the "Anglo-Jackson" style was born: a bold rejection of High Victorian Gothic, an act of faith in the elasticity of the classical tradition, a vote of confidence in the endless viability of the eclectic process. "The odd phantasies of Jacobean workmen," wrote Beresford Pite, "were extended by the solemn exercise of his scholarship."[17] Windows in the manner of Kirby Hall, a silhouette with memories of Burghley House, patterned marbling reminiscent of San Miniato in Florence, columns with Byzantine details, antique marble fragments from the Baths of Caracalla, a Tudor-style hammer-beamed roof, sculptured corbels worthy of François Premier: by 1882 Jackson's Examination Schools had cost nearly £100,000. And this sum—as well as the building's stylistic range—was much increased in 1887/88 by an additional mixed-Gothic wing (Fig. 2) for the use of noncollegiate students (now the Ruskin School).[18] Jackson had found his métier: during the next half-century he remained an historicist to his fingertips, consistently refusing to "substitute rolled iron joists for brains."[19]

John Ruskin, at that time Oxford's Slade Professor, disapproved. He was horrified by these costly "ball-rooms," built "in a style as inherently corrupt as it is un-English."[20] But the Anglo-Jackson mode—a mixture of Hardwick and

Brereton, of Charlton and Hatfield, of John Thorpe and Joseph Nash, seasoned with a dash of François Premier—caught the imagination of late Victorian academia. Those mixed-Renaissance prototypes seemed scholarly without being pedantic, free without being licentious. As Halsey Ricardo put it, "learning sits easy on them and, like the speech of their owners, the main fabric is English (and the English too, of the Bible)."[21] And what building could be more appropriate for such a display of learning than a set of Examination Schools (Figs. 3, 4) in the Oxford of Benjamin Jowett? Pevsner notes, "What an image of examination such a building creates: the puny candidates and the Moloch of the testing machinery." One professor, Goldwin Smith, likened the whole operation to "gilding a treadmill."[22] But no one could deny the bravado of the style. "Wherever," Pevsner asks dubiously, "has one seen such impudence or such courage?"[23] Here, for those who care to look, Jackson has shown generations of undergraduates how to sidestep the academic traces; how to scale the alpha barrier by bending the rules of grammar and logic in pursuit of originality. Jackson's Examination Schools are a temple dedicated to the goddess Mimesis: the art of creative imitation. But this is painter's architecture rather than architect's architecture: functional criteria—accessibility, acoustics, structural intelligibility—are sacrificed to symbol and silhouette. The qualities involved are essentially pictorial. H. S.

Goodhart-Rendel christened this "the vicious picturesque," or "the general public's idea of a work of architecture."[24] As Dickens's Joe Gargery might have put it in *Great Expectations*, it is all very "architectooralooral."

Understandably, Oxford commissions came flooding in: the Grove Building at Lincoln, 1880–1883;[25] the President's Lodgings and new buildings at Trinity, 1883–1887 (Fig. 5);[26] the annex at Corpus, 1884/85 (Fig. 6);[27] the new quadrangle and High Street front at Brasenose, 1886–1889 and 1909–1911 (Fig. 7);[28] the chapel and new buildings at Hertford, 1887–1890 and 1903–1913 (Fig. 8);[29] the restoration of Merton and Oriel chapels, Carfax Tower,[30] and St. Mary's spire, 1893–1896;[31] the refitting of St. Peter's-in-the-East[32] and All Saints, 1896; the Acland Nursing Home, 1897;[33] the restoration of Wadham, 1900–1908; the Schools of Rural

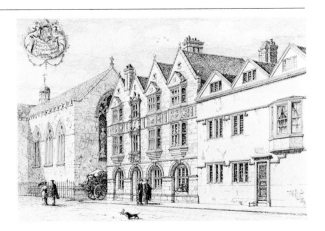

Economy and Forestry, 1907/8; the Electrical Laboratory, 1908–10;[34] restoration at the Clarendon Press, Frewen Hall, and the Bodleian; the circular tower in the grounds of the Radcliffe Observatory; a small block at Somerville; work on the Radcliffe Infirmary and Radcliffe Camera; the new Radcliffe Science Library, 1901;[35] the organs at Wadham, Oriel, Brasenose (Fig. 9), and the Sheldonian; library fittings at All Souls;[36] the Balliol house known as King's Mound;[37] the Cricket Pavilion in the Parks, 1881; the timber bridge in Christ Church Meadows;[38] even the Oriel Barge, 1892.[39] Indeed, the appearance of Oxford in modern times owes more to Jackson than to any one man. His "Bridge of Sighs" at Hertford (Fig. 10) has become a favorite university landmark;[40] and his multigabled, richly Gothic front at Brasenose—the graveyard of abortive schemes by Nicholas Hawksmoor, Thomas Hardwick, and Sir John Soane—exploits to the full the complicated perspectives of the High Street. At Brasenose, Jackson had hoped to add another dreaming spire to the Oxford skyline: an open-crowned steeple with echoes of Edinburgh or Newcastle.[41] That was not to be. But he did absorb and recycle the college's peculiarly mixed inheritance; in effect, Jackson's Gothic is Gothic Survival revived.

Jackson's contribution to Oxford caught exactly the traditional eclecticism of collegiate building, caught it, then magnified its components into compositions of real originality. He managed to translate the eclecticism of the sixteenth and seventeenth centuries—Gothic, Elizabethan, Jacobean, Baroque, and Palladian—into a new eclecticism of the nineteenth century. "Anglo-Jackson" is sometimes hard to swallow; Pevsner calls it "elephantine" and "impudent," but he admits that its creator displayed "tremen-

8. New Buildings, Hertford College, Oxford. Jackson, 1887–
1890 and 1903–1913. (Photo: National Monuments Record,
London; courtesy of Oxfordshire County Libraries.)

dous panache . . . no fear of over-ornateness, no fear of noise." It is also a chameleon style that is hard to classify: Jacobean, Caroline, Baroque, Palladian. "That Jackson left Oxford a grosser place than it had ever been," Pevsner remarks, "nobody should deny, but he left it as a place with a potential for architectural adventure, and for that we should be grateful to him."[42] At the very least, Jackson's Oxford had supplied an eclectic alternative to the otherwise omnipresent "Queen Anne Revival."

Jackson's work at Cambridge was quieter and less conspicuous, but equally eclectic. Refitting the Senate House and enlarging King's College Hall were no more than minor works.[43] But the Sidgwick Geological Museum, the Squire Law Library and Schools, the Archaeological Museum, and the Physiological and Psychological Laboratories—all built between 1904 and 1911—were all large-scale vehicles for Jackson's rep-

ertoire of Jacobethan and Caroline motifs.[44] Like seventeenth-century Oxford, seventeenth-century Cambridge could boast an eclecticism of its own, and Jackson's buildings live up to this mongrel inheritance. Long may they delight the eclectic soul of Jackson's seventeenth-century predecessor, Bishop Cosin of Peterhouse.

A prolific school-building practice followed naturally from Jackson's work at Oxford and Cambridge. In Oxford itself there were his Jacobean High School for Boys (Fig. 11)[45] and his Caroline High School for Girls.[46] Just outside Oxford he was responsible for a Jacobean Military School at Cowley.[47] Not far away, at Radley in 1891 to 1895 and 1910, he designed the chapel, cloister, and hall in Northern French Flamboyant Gothic, as well as a South African War Memorial.[48] He was also active at schools in the Midlands. In 1889 to 1897, at Uppingham, he placed a Jacobean library and science block

next to Street's Gothic chapel;[49] and at Rugby he added aisles to Butterfield's chapel in 1897, plus a Tudor-Baroque speech room, 1908/9 (Fig. 12).[50] Farther south he worked at Westminster School and Aldenham School, Hertfordshire.[51] In Kent he designed the bricky Big School at Cranbrook, 1883/84;[52] the anonymous block at Otford, 1872;[53] and a set of Dutch-gabled buildings for the Manwood School at Sandwich, 1894/95.[54] In Sussex, in 1883 to 1887, at his own school—Brighton College—he added Gothic additions to the work Scott had been designing when Jackson himself was a schoolboy.[55] Then there are Jackson's Queen Anne additions at Harrow,[56] and a characteristic list of works at Eton: the Cricket Pavilion, 1901, on Agar's Plough, the Club House on Queen's Eyot, the racquet courts, the science and music schools, and Lawson's Museum.[57] Finally, he was responsible for Lampeter College chapel and improvements to the principal's house.[58]

In the field of church restoration Jackson was prolific and usually sensitive. But out of a list of nearly fifty items[59] only a handful merit particular mention. One early work—Dursley church, Gloucestershire, of 1866—must have been of special interest to him: Dursley tower is a Gothic Survival landmark of national significance.[60] His restoration of Slindon church, Sussex, 1866/67, was not a success.[61] But he took particular care at All Saints, Stamford, Lincolnshire, 1870–1873;[62] its spire possessed such majesty that Sir Walter Scott would doff his hat whenever he passed it on the Great North Road. And in his adopted county of Kent, Jackson scored some striking successes: five medieval parish churches restored with skill and restraint.[63] His restoration of Holy Trinity, Coventry, was a late work in which he completed Scott's efforts with rather

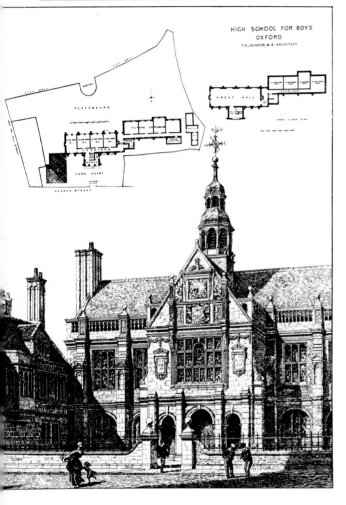

more caution than his master usually achieved. Among a whole clutch of cathedral restorations,[64] Jackson's work at Bath Abbey, 1895–1901 and 1925–26,[65] and Winchester Cathedral, 1905–1912[66] was outstanding. Appropriately, at the conclusion of his Winchester operations—which involved formidable underpinning and buttressing—Prime Minister Asquith awarded him that baronetcy.

Jackson's own churches were fairly few in number. Two early works were both in Somerset: at Lottisham, 1876,[67] and Hornblotton, 1872–1874,[68]—the latter a suave piece of Surrey vernacular in the vein of Richard Norman Shaw, happily transplanted to the West Country. Then came a trio of flint-faced churches in Hampshire: at Curbridge, 1887/88;[69] at East Stratton, 1885–1890, (Fig. 13);[70] and at Northington, 1887–1890.[71] Both the latter were in Baring territory; Thomas Baring had been his patron at Hertford College, Oxford. At St. Nicholas, Pepper Harrow in Surrey, 1876/77,[72] Jackson successfully enlarged an earlier church by A. W. Pugin. All Saints, New Annesley, Nottinghamshire, 1908, really counts as a new project; Jackson rebuilt it in Early Decorated after a fire.[73] So does St. James, Bourton-on-the-Water, Gloucestershire, 1875 and 1890/91, where he incorporated an eighteenth-century tower and medieval aisle with striking success. Such commissions appealed to

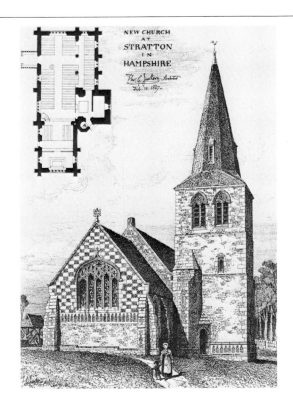

Jackson. Another enlargement of a stylistically mixed inheritance was the eighteenth-century church at Billinge in Lancashire of 1908.[74] Some of his happiest designs consist merely of interior fittings in mixed Renaissance style: at St. John, Hampstead, c. 1878,[75] for example; or at St. Mary, East Bergholt, Suffolk;[76] or at St. Peter's, 1906, and St. Michael's, 1920, in Bournemouth.[77] Jackson's Patteson Memorial Chapel, 1875, on Norfolk Island, New Zealand, was of course a special case; particular regard had to be paid to local considerations of style and material. Much more typical were his church commissions at Wimbledon[78] and Aldershot.[79]

There were other churches,[80] but they are neither numerous nor outstanding. Jackson was never in the top flight of late Victorian church architects. His interior at Farnham Castle chapel[81] is a virtuoso decorative performance. But only one of his ecclesiastical designs is really memorable: the chapel at Giggleswick School, Yorkshire, of 1897 to 1901 (Figs. 14, 15). In this extraordinary synthesis of Gothic and Romanesque, polychrome brick, stone, and marble, Jackson's eclecticism at last attained full maturity. "I was determined to show that domes and Gothic architecture are not incompatible," he recalled, "and though I shocked all the purists, I am not dissatisfied with the result." Local Yorkshiremen were much puzzled by this "heathen temple," but Goodhart-Rendel was delighted.[82]

Jackson was never a prominent town- or country-house architect. Send vicarage, 1861–1863,[83] near Ripley, was his first commission; enlarging Thornaugh rectory, in 1878, was a later one.[84] Three houses at Sevenoaks were designed in 1873.[85] Then there is a house in Wimbledon,[86] and another in Bromley.[87] A set of artisans' cottages in Hampstead, and the New Cottages and old Coffee House in Lime Tree Walk, Sevenoaks, 1878/79,[88] were primarily philanthropic gestures on Jackson's part. But their oriels and dormers were designed with grace and executed with characteristic competence.[89] Then there are a few additions to older mansions: Cheam House in Surrey; Evercreech House and Thorne House in Somerset;[90] Water Eaton House on the Cherwell near Oxford;[91] Rothampstead Manor House, Hertfordshire;[92] and Stamford House and Eagle House—his own home—in Wimbledon.[93] He even executed minor improvements at several major country seats, among others, Castle Ashby,[94] Montacute,[95] and Blenheim.[96] He was, after all, well equipped to modernize medieval and Renaissance monuments.[97] Still, he never built up a fashionable domestic practice.

Similarly, Jackson's buildings in London are

14. *Chapel, Giggleswick School, Yorkshire. Jackson, 1897–1901. Exterior. (Photo: National Monuments Record, London.)*

15. *Chapel, Giggleswick School. Interior. (Photo: National Monuments Record, London.)*

few and mostly unmemorable.[98] Paradoxically, some of his best metropolitan work is hardly ever noticed, precisely because it is so good: his refurbishment of the Royal Academy's entrance hall in Burlington House, Piccadilly, for example—a discreet and elegant setting for Angelica Kauffmann's painted panels.[99] But Jackson will probably be remembered by Londoners for his Franco-Flemish-Gothic mansion at Kensington Court, overlooking Kensington Gardens.[100] Here he also designed for the owner, Athelstan Riley, a famous Broadwood piano. Painted by Burne-Jones, it was built of green-stained mahogany, inlaid with boxwood and mother-of-pearl, and decorated with Jacksonian Jacobean patterns in red and gold gesso.[101] Not for nothing did he later become President of the Art Workers Guild.

If it lacked anything, the "Anglo-Jackson" style lacked monumentality. Not surprisingly, prizes in the greater public competitions consistently went elsewhere: to rival architects with a greater sense of mass and a greater capacity for large-scale planning. Leeming & Leeming beat him at the Admiralty and War Office, 1883/84;[102] Sir Aston Webb at the South Kensington Museum, 1891 and the Queen Victoria Memorial;[103] Thomas Collcutt at the Imperial Institute, 1887;[104] Ralph Knott at County Hall, 1908. Aston Webb even beat him to a school commission: Christ's Hospital, Horsham. Most of Jackson's public buildings outside Oxford and Cambridge are small, almost trivial in scale.[105] Only Tipperary Town Hall (Fig. 16)[106] escapes such a generalization. Certainly, it is small in scale, but it is conceived with the eye of a miniaturist. Nevertheless, it has to be admitted that monumentality was never Jackson's strong card.

But then Jackson hoped to be judged not just

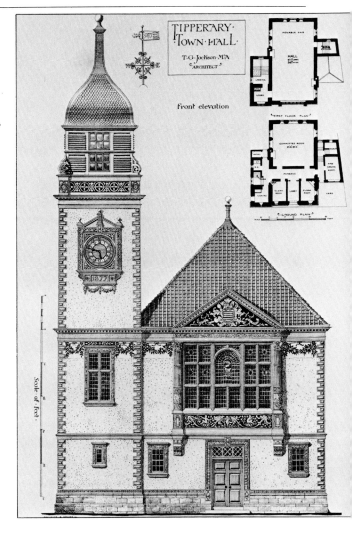

as an architect, but also as a scholar. His writings, indeed, were as prolific as his buildings—and just as eclectic. After *Modern Gothic*, his major literary works were not polemical but archaeological and topographical: *Dalmatia, the Quarnero and Istria* (3 vols., 1887);[107] *Wadham College* (Oxford, 1893); *The Church of St. Mary the Virgin* (Oxford, 1897); *Byzantine and Romanesque Architecture* (Cambridge, 2 vols., 1915); *Gothic Architecture in France, England and Italy* (Cambridge, 2 vols., 1915);[108] *A Holiday in Umbria* (1917); *South Slav Monuments* (1918); *The Renaissance of Roman Architecture* (Cambridge, 3 vols., 1921–1923); *Memories of Travel* (Cambridge, 1923);[109] and "French Architecture" in *Medieval France*, ed. A. Tilley (Cambridge, 1892). Jackson was an inveterate traveler. His books were illustrated with sketches made in a dozen countries over more than half a century.[110] And it was his rare knowledge of architecture in Southern and Eastern Europe which brought him one particularly exotic commission: the campanile of the Romanesque cathedral at Zara in Dalmatia, 1889–1891,[111] plus one tantalizingly missed chance—his Russian Byzantine design for a church at Saint Petersburg in memory of an assassinated Czar.[112]

Jackson's later theoretical writings are a disappointment. *Reason in Architecture* (1906) and *Architecture* (1925) merely repeat his earlier ideas at greater length and with rather less force. Having made his mark with *Modern Gothic* as early as 1873, he seems as a critic to have been quite unequal to the problems confronting architects in the twentieth century.[113] His opponents must have thought him better occupied in writing ghost stories.[114] He could still turn a good phrase: "Ornament is the last resource of the incompetent architect";[115] "Architecture [is] more than . . . a page from a dictionary of quotations";[116] "Architecture is the poetry of construction";[117] "Art is the poetry of craftsmanship."[118] And such was his standing that even his enemies at the Royal Institute of British Architects agreed to his nomination as Royal Gold Medallist in 1910.[119] But the future was to him a blank. Jackson's brand of eclecticism was no longer "progressive" in the High Victorian sense; that is, eclecticism as the matrix of a new nineteenth-century style, incorporating new material and old motifs in pursuit of novelty through synthesis and abstraction. Jackson's eclecticism had emerged as eclecticism for its own sake; he had drifted into just the sort of historicist cul-de-sac he had so brilliantly attacked as a young man. And he was well aware of the paradox. Like many of his generation—Norman Shaw for one—he reveals between the moldings, as it were, a nagging doubt as to the validity of the historicist process. The passage of time merely confirmed his early conclusion that the Gothic Revival had "failed."[120] He still believed in architecture as craft, but in old age he also came to suspect that this craft-based eclecticism had failed too: ". . . who can foresee what, if anything, will come of it?"[121] Toward the end of his life, however, Jackson could take comfort in the success of at least one rearguard action: with Norman Shaw he edited a volume of essays, entitled *Architecture: A Profession or an Art?* (1892), that managed to delay the emergence of the British architectural profession for the better part of a half-century.[122]

Jackson's attitude to the architectural profession was very much bound up with his concept of architectural style. For him, the architect was first and foremost an artist; professional and stylistic restrictions were equally anathema to him. Professional freedom and artistic freedom were one and the same; the autonomy of the artist was indivisible. Hence his hostility to the growth of a "closed-shop" mentality among architects.

The foundations of an architectural profession had been laid during the early nineteenth century, after preliminary maneuvers dating back to the 1790s.[123] The Institute of British Architects was established in 1834, gained its first charter in 1837, became Royal in 1866, gained a new charter in 1887, and set guards to maintain the purity of its standards by instituting voluntary tests in 1863 and compulsory examinations in 1882. Logically, the next step was the statutory closure of the profession—the elimination of architectural freebooters—along the lines practiced in medicine and law. And it was at this point that the crisis erupted. Many of the most talented architects in the country had no faith whatsoever in the measurement of genius by statute. *Architecture: A Profession or an Art?* is a monument to their professional agnosticism.

Hostilities opened in 1888 with the introduction to Parliament of a private member's bill enforcing the registration of architects. Jackson wrote at once to Norman Shaw and received a soothing reply: "the Bill . . . has such a very slender chance of becoming law that it is hardly worth troubling about. . . . Of course one sees perfectly well what these people are aiming at. They look on Architecture as a trade, or perhaps to put it more politely as a profession. . . . To me it is an art—or nothing."[124] Shaw guessed correctly: the R.I.B.A. ignored the scheme,[125] and the bill was quickly withdrawn. But in 1891 the Society of Architects, a younger rival of the R.I.B.A. founded in 1884, "anxious to justify its existence by a show of energy," put up an M.P. named Wilson Noble to introduce a second Registration Bill. "This time," Jackson recalled, "Norman Shaw took it up hot."[126] He called a meeting at Mervyn Macartney's house at the corner of Berkeley Square. And the famous Protest[127] against professionalism was drawn up, sent around for more than seventy signatures, and dispatched to *The Times* and the Council of the R.I.B.A. "I remember drafting the protest," Jackson tells us, "writing on my knee."[128]

On the R.I.B.A.'s behalf Aston Webb and William H. White denied that they were party to

Noble's bill.[129] But the Protesters knew better. The leading members of the Institute, Alfred Waterhouse for example, were merely biding their time and undermining the Society of Architects. The R.I.B.A. refused even to confer with the Protesters, unless their premises for discussion were accepted—principally that compulsory examination be regarded as a sine qua non.[130] The Architectural Association, officially at any rate, felt much the same way.[131] "No compromise was possible", Sir Reginald Blomfield concluded; "the only thing to do was to fight it out. Shaw and Jackson were the leaders. I acted as their aide-de-camp and general liaison officer."[132] Blomfield and a number of leading architects resigned from the R.I.B.A. *en bloc*.[133] "I have no doubt you feel happier and more independent," wrote Shaw—himself a notable nonmember. "It must be war now and no quarter."[134]

The Protesters comprised the elite of British architects. And they were supported by at least part of the architectural press: *The Architect* and *British Architect* defended them against attacks in *The Builder* and *Building News*.[135] But it was not for the great men that the Registration program was designed. It set out to regulate and elevate what the *Building News* called "the rank and file of the profession."[136] Hence the ambivalence of the Architectural Association.[137] Complained Blomfield, "By the admission of its own supporters the Institute examination has been framed with careful reference to a dead level of mediocrity. . . . [Whereas] the ideal architect is not merely a tradesman, a man of business, or even an honest dull man, but necessarily a man of strong individuality, a creator and something of a poet."[138] That was the nub of the debate: liberty for the Royal Academy prizewinner, or security for the slowest surveyor? And in thrash-

ing out this problem the debate touched on several related topics: state action *versus* artistic autonomy; the division of labor *versus* cooperation; industrialization *versus* craftsmanship; collective training *versus* pupilage; and—by implication at least—stylistic uniformity *versus* the cult of eclecticism.

Architecture: A Profession or an Art? had mixed reviews.[139] By committing themselves to eclecticism in style and pupilage in practice, Jackson and his allies were turning their backs on the Beaux-Arts programs of Continental Europe. "A German or a Frenchman would be incredulous," noted *The Architect*, "if he were told that in a volume which in great measure treats of the education of architects, mathematics, physics, chemistry, history, law and aesthetics are ignored. . . . But we have followed insular ways for three centuries since England emancipated herself from Continental influence."[140]

Inevitably, perhaps, the professionals eventually won the day. The Beaux-Arts triumphed over the Art Workers Guild. The *Zeitgeist* was on the side of the big battalions. Many of the leading secessionists drifted back to the R.I.B.A. The examination system was maintained and developed. Pupilage was replaced by the architectural school and the university. And statutory registration of architects was reintroduced in 1927, passed in 1931, and finally achieved in 1938. But the great debate was not entirely wasted. Jackson had dismissed the registration policy as merely a series of "stupid and vulgar arguments" designed to turn architects into lawyers and doctors, to make them "gentlemen by Act of Parliament," so that "their wives might go down to dinner before the attorney and apothecary."[141] That was an exaggeration. Both sides had something important to say. The professionals spoke a new language, the language of industry and class. The Protesters cherished a set of values based on a single premise of eternal validity: the autonomy of the creative artist.

In Jackson's case that autonomy resulted in an eclecticism peculiar to himself but by no means uncharacteristic of Late-Victorian England. From Oxford to Dalmatia, from Giggleswick to Tipperary, Jackson's hand is evident. And Jackson's epigoni—Henry T. Hare and Basil Champneys, for instance—were equally eclectic and equally prolific. As a style "Anglo-Jackson" has suffered from excessive blame and excessive praise. Sir Albert Richardson thought its author impressive as a scholar, but "no good as an architect—no grandeur of effect, too much detail—Plateresque."[142] But Goodhart-Rendel's judgment of 1924 gets the balance about right:

Rickman's Gothic Revival was the taming of a wild and superstitious architecture to fit it for the service of evangelical religion. Pugin's Gothic Revival was an attempted escape from reality, and flight from an age that found him a fanatic to a dream-come-true in which Christian art was rewarded by God and honoured by man. Butterfield's Gothic Revival was a mission, a gospel of Gothic mortification preached to those who found sinful ease in the aesthetic doctrines of the Great Exhibition. Scott's Gothic Revival was a reconciliation of piety and five-per-cent blessed by Bishops and promoted by Deans. Sir T. Jackson's Gothic Revival was the procedure of a competent and scholarly architect, who on appropriate occasions recreated and varied without prejudice the forms of an architecture which he knew and loved well. . . . Sir Thomas was an individualist, and dreaded alike the rules of guilds and the dogmas of academies. . . . Though still confined in the prison of the past,

[his generation] had broken into forbidden chambers, exploring which they felt themselves to be free. . . . Queen Anne . . . was the chosen patron of the party of youth, the protector of the rebel from Gothic, the Faerie Queen of the new Renaissance. In so far as this movement was a renaissance of the Renaissance it is as indigestable by most of us as twice-cooked meat. If Ernest George, Thomas Collcutt, George Devey, and Sir Thomas Jackson's other like-minded contemporaries had achieved nothing save the elaborate reproduction of miniature architectural detail . . . , if they had innovated in no way save that of deliberately contrived accidental-looking compositions, there would be little to recommend their work. . . . However . . . these men . . . were true architects, masters from whom we can learn a great deal. Forget the haphazard planning . . . forget the no longer admired confusion of their elevations, forget the terra-cotta they loved [Jackson in fact rarely used it], forget the crowded ornament of their room decoration, and you will find plenty to respect in their individuality, in the abundance and the unassuming intimacy of their conceptions; in the modest easy opportunism that, if it has been the bane of our monumental architecture, has obtained for our house-building a supremacy in Europe that is . . . unchallenged. In Sir Thomas Jackson's design you will find, besides these qualities, a careful refinement upon . . . Renaissance models. . . . Unlike Ernest George, he could not tolerate the coarseness of Low German motifs; unlike Devey, he never mimicked those motifs in their Elizabethan form. The small orders that he applied lavishly to his façades, though typically Renaissance in their arbitrary placing, are invariably graceful and pure in themselves. The sculptured foliage in which he delighted is free from the clumsiness which disfigures so much of the sixteenth and early seventeenth centuries. He was, as it was right that a nineteenth-century architect should be, sophisticated and urbane where the English Renaissance pioneers were ignorant and rustic. His details are those of an artist who knew his Bramante and his Philibert de l'Orme. Indeed, as a designer of ornament in the Renaissance and late Gothic style Sir Thomas Jackson displayed exceptional accomplishment."[143]

So it is as an artist and archaeologist, a scholar-architect of school and college, a doughty opponent of professional uniformity, above all as a committed eclectic, that Jackson must ultimately be judged. Generations of undergraduates and schoolboys have grown up in the shadow of Anglo-Jackson. Cambridge he adorned and a dozen public schools. But Oxford made him, and he remade the face of Oxford. How he must have smiled when, sitting in the Sheldonian Theatre (Wren's auditorium and Jackson's fittings), his old university bestowed on him an Honorary Doctorate of Civil Law: Sir Thomas Graham Jackson, Bart., R.A., F.S.A., who, in the words of the public orator, "created a new form of beauty . . . by combining all styles of architecture . . . *Artifex Oxoniensissime*."[144]

Notes

1. "Fundamentally an English gentleman" (Beresford Pite, *The Builder* 127 [1924]: 753). "A gentleman, a scholar and a very able architect" (Sir R. Blomfield, *Memories of an Architect* [1932], p. 66). "A deeply religious man," with "a strong family feeling. . . . His vitality was extraordinary" (*The Times*, 8 November 1924, p. 7; 10 November 1924, p. 8; 18 November 1924, p. 20). He left £37,174 (*Times*, 9 January 1925, p. 15).

2. Blomfield, *Memories of an Architect*, p. 66. Photograph from *Building News* 58 (1890): 221. Portraits by Hugh Rivere (1900) at Wadham College, Oxford, and by S. J. Solomon (1903) at the Art Workers Guild, London.

3. This gave him an assured income (T. G. Jackson, *Recollections*, ed. B. H. Jackson, 1950, p. 100).

4. When Jackson told Scott of his Pre-Raphaelite enthusiasms, the great man replied, "Well, bring your Pre-Raphaelitism into architecture: that is exactly what architecture needs at the present time" (ibid., p. 50). Jackson's first duty was to draw Tintern Abbey (ibid., p. 53).

5. In 1857/58 (L. Herrmann, "William Turner of Oxford," *Oxoniensia* 26/27 [1961/62]: 312–318).

6. G. G. Scott, *Recollections* (1879).

7. *The Architect* 9 (1873): 294. See also *Builder* 31 (1873): 597–598.

8. Jackson, *Recollections*, p. 119.

9. "I was at this time already beginning to feel a revulsion from the fanatical medievalism with which I was surrounded"; Scott's classical Foreign Office seemed "the finest thing he ever did" (Jackson, *Recollections*, p. 73).

10. Ibid., p. 123.

11. Quoted by C. E. Mallows, *Architectural Review* 1 (1896): 136–162.

12. Ibid.

13. Catherine Cole, "The Building of the Tower of Five Orders in the Schools' Quadrangle at Oxford," *Oxoniensia* 33 (1968): 92–107.

14. Jackson, *Recollections*, p. 125. Jackson left his drawings to Wadham College.

15. Ibid.; *The Architect* 14 (1875): 160.

16. Jackson, *Recollections*, pp. 133–142. Jackson's drawings are in the Bodleian Library (Mss. Top. Oxon, a 19), and the British Architectural Library (R.I.B.A.), W 15/30.

17. *Builder* 127 (1924): 753.

18. *Builder* 42 (1882): 719–720; 51 (1886): 535; and 59 (1890): 108; also, *The British Architect* 25 (1886): 466 J; *Architectural Review* 3 (1898): supp. While the Schools were being built, Jackson organized lectures on political economy at Wadham for the two hundred workmen (Jackson, *Recollections*, p. 163).

19. A. T. Bolton, in *Architect's Journal* 60 (1924): 758–763.

20. Ruskin, *Works*, ed. Cook and Wedderburn, vol. 33, pp. 363, 476.

21. *Architectural Review* 2 (1897): 42.

22. *Oxford Magazine*, 2 June 1886.

23. N. Pevsner and J. Sherwood, *Oxfordshire* (1974), p. 266.

24. "That the . . . style [is] sixteenth century is . . . unimportant. . . . What is of great importance is that the style is . . . plastered over a building in which all traditional honesty and good sense have been ignored—in which haphazard has taken the place of order, in which accident is simulated in a work of art deliberately planned" (H. S. Goodhart-Rendel, "Oxford Buildings Criticised," *Oxoniensia* 17/18 [1952/53]: 205–206).

25. *Building News* 42 (1882): 790.

26. *Building News* 49 (1885): 488; 53 (1887): 258.

27. *Builder* 46 (1884): 672; 49 (1890): 490; also, *Building News* 50 (1886): 245.

28. *Builder* 55 (1888): 84; 58 (1890): 416–417; also, *Build-*

ing News 54 (1888): 252. The New Quad was finished in 1911 and was criticized in *The Times* of 23 June 1911. See also *The Brazen Nose* 1 (1909–1914): 198–199. For Jackson's drawings see the British Architectural Library (R.I.B.A.), W 15/29 and Brasenose archives.

29. Ill. by H. S. Goodhart-Rendel, in the *Journal of the Royal Institute of British Architects* 33 (1926): 467–478 (hereafter cited as *R.I.B.A. Journal*); Pevsner and Sherwood, *Oxfordshire*, pp. 139–141; *Building News* 58 (1890): 262.

30. Jackson, *Recollections*, p. 252.

31. For controversy, see *Builder* 63 (1892): 516; 64 (1893): 346; and 70 (1896): 493; also, Jackson, *Recollections*, pp. 235–236. Jackson's drawings are in the Bodleian (MS. Top. Oxon, a 34, R and G. A. Oxon. 8°540).

32. Jackson, *Recollections*, p. 179.

33. Ill. in *Architecture* 2 (1897): 2–24, 84–96.

34. Jackson, *Recollections*, p. 185. Jackson left his drawings to Wadham College.

35. *Building News* 72 (1897): 860; *Builder* 77 (1899); 200; also, ill. in *Architecture*, loc. cit. Jackson left his drawings to Wadham College.

36. Jackson, *Recollections*, p. 185.

37. Ibid., p. 198; ill. by Mallows in *Architectural Review* 1 (1896): 136–162.

38. Jackson, *Recollections*, p. 185.

39. Ibid., p. 233; *Country Life* 141 (1967): 6–8, 659; *Architectural Review* 120 (1956): 39. Broken up 1954. Jackson probably also designed Wadham barge (1897).

40. For details see *Times Higher Education Supplement*, 14 July 1978, p. 9. It was opened in 1914, when Jackson was working in a London wartime munitions factory (Jackson, *Recollections*, p. 255).

41. See Jackson, in *Magazine of Art* 8 (1889): 332–340. He was determined to design something "worthy of the most important site in the most beautiful street in Europe" (Jackson, *Recollections*, pp. 69, 186). For details, see E. W. Allfrey in *Brasenose Quatercentenary Monographs* vol. 1 (Oxford, 1909), pp. 56–62.

42. Pevsner and Sherwood, *Oxfordshire*, pp. 59–60.

43. Jackson, *Recollections*, p. 259.

44. N. Pevsner, *Cambridgeshire* (1970 ed.), p. 208. Jackson left his Cambridge drawings to Cambridge University Library.

45. *Building News* 38 (1880): 190, 340. He defeated a Gothic design by F. Codd. Now the College of Further Education.

46. *Architect's Journal* 60 (1924): 758–763; now the Department of Metallurgy.

47. 1877; now part of the Morris Motor Works (British Leyland).

48. *Builder* 62 (1892): 340; 66 (1894): 352; and 68 (1895): 332; also N. Pevsner, *Berkshire* (1966), p. 197. For the memorial gateway, see British Architectural Library (R.I.B.A.), W 15/26 and *Builder* 121 (1921), p. 285.

49. *Builder* 58 (1890): 12; 61 (1892): 189; 74 (1898): 419; also, N. Pevsner, *Leicestershire and Rutland* (1960), pp. 330–331.

50. N. Pevsner and A. Wedgwood, *Warwickshire* (1966), pp. 388–390.

51. Jackson, *Recollections*, p. 190.

52. J. Newman, *West Kent and the Weald* (1969), p. 236.

53. Ibid., p. 429.

54. J. Newman, *North East and East Kent* (1969), p. 433.

55. *Builder* 48 (1885): 794; I. Nairn and N. Pevsner, *Sussex* (1965), p. 443; drawings and correspondence, Brighton College archives.

56. Ill., *Architecture* 2 (1897): 84–96.

57. *R.I.B.A. Journal* 31 (1924): 49; N. Pevsner, *Buckinghamshire* (1960), p. 129.

58. *Builder* 37 (1879): 504; Jackson, *Recollections*, p. 162.

59. E.g., St. Mary, Ketton (1863) and St. Martin, Lyndon (1866), both in Rutland; St. John Baptist, Old Malden, Surrey (1863; 1873–1875); St. Mary Magdalen, Madehurst (1864), St. Mary, Binsted (1867), and St. Mary, Burpham (1869), all in Sussex; St. James, Iron Acton, Gloucestershire 1878/79); St. Peter and St. Clare, Fenny Compton, Warwickshire (1879); St. Mary, Chessington (1870), St. Mary, Ripley (1869), St. Nicholas, Pyrford (1869), St. Thomas, East Clandon (1900), and St. Peter and St. Paul, West Clandon (1913), all in Surrey; St. Lawrence, Hatfield, Yorkshire (1873); St. Mary and St. Helen, Elstow, Bedfordshire (1881); St. Caradoc, Llawrenny, Pembrokeshire; St. Peter, Bishop's Waltham (1894–1897), St. Mary, Ellingham (1869–1885), and Holy Trinity, Wonston, all in Hampshire; plus lesser work at Hagley, Laverstoke, Stapleford, Whitchurch, Mold, Wrexham, Duddington, and Ashbourne. See lists in Jackson, *Recollections*, passim; and *R.I.B.A. Journal* 31 (1924): 49.

60. D. Verey, *Gloucestershire: the Cotswolds* (1970), pp. 225–226.

61. *Ecclesiologist* 27 (1866): 127; I. Nairn and N. Pevsner, *Sussex* (1965), pp. 326–327.

62. Jackson, *Recollections*, p. 114.

63. St. Nicholas, Sevenoaks (1909); St. George, Sevenoaks Weald (1873); St. Mary, Kemsing (1890/91); and the churches of St. Peter and St. Paul at Ash (1901–1903) and Bramley (1883/84).

64. Worcester, Ripon, and Hereford cathedrals; and Christ Church and Malvern priories.

65. N. Pevsner, *North Somerset and Bristol* (1958), pp. 99–105.

66. *Builder* 98 (1910): 524; N. Pevsner and D. Lloyd, *Hampshire* (1967), pp. 661, 672. For controversy, see *Builder* 94 (1908): 36, and Jackson, *Recollections*, pp. 264–266.

67. N. Pevsner, *South and West Somerset* (1958), p. 222.

68. N. Pevsner, *North Somerset and Bristol* (1958), p. 101.

69. *Builder* 54 (1888): 396.

70. *Builder* 53 (1887): 362 British Architectural Library

(R.I.B.A.) Ran. 9 EI, 59.74.

71. *Builder* 53 (1887): 362, and 58 (1890): 453.

72. I. Nairn, N. Pevsner, and B. Cherry, *Surrey* (1971), pp. 407, 599.

73. *Builder* 32 (1874): 339.

74. N. Pevsner, *South Lancashire* (1969), 75–76, pl. 27.

75. N. Pevsner, *London*, vol. 2 (1952), p. 185.

76. N. Pevsner, *Suffolk* (1961), p. 177.

77. N. Pevsner and D. Lloyd, *Hampshire* (1967), p. 119.

78. St. John (1865); St. Luke (1909).

79. St. Augustine (1907); St. Michael (1910/11).

80. E.g., St. Augustine, Brighton (1913); St. Mary, Basing-stoke (1912); All Saints, Botley (1892–1895); St. John, Caterham (c. 1890); St. Mary, Hellesdon, Norfolk (1903); and churches at Narbeth and Robeston-Wathen in Pembrokeshire (1881).

81. The Bishop's Chapel, restored by Jackson: I. Nairn, N. Pevsner, and B. Cherry, *Surrey* (1971), p. 235.

82. Jackson, *Recollections*, pp. 253–254, pl. 22; N. Pevsner, *Yorkshire: West Riding* (1967), pp. 218, 625; *R.I.B.A. Journal* 33 (1926), pp. 467–478. The donor of the chapel, Walter Morrison, seems to have insisted on a dome. The mosaics are by Powells of Whitefriars; the stained glass by Burlison and Grylls (*Giggleswick School*, Oxford, 1901). Jackson also designed the gate lodge and cricket pavilion.

83. Jackson, *Recollections*, p. 85.

84. N. Pevsner, *Northamptonshire* (1961), p. 424.

85. "Woodlands," "Maywood," and "St. Julians"; See *Architecture* 2 (1897): 84–96; *The Architect* 12 (1874): 30.

86. 54, The Ridgeway.

87. "Plank's Hill," for Prebendary Thring of Hornblotton.

88. Jackson, *Recollections*, pp. 153–154, pl. 13.

89. For his theories of urban design, see "Street Architecture," *Builder* 87 (1904): 661–663.

90. *Builder* 54 (1888): 396; N. Pevsner, *South and West Somerset* (1958), p. 168.

91. Jackson, *Recollections*, p. 179.

92. N. Pevsner, *Hertfordshire* (1953), pp. 194–195.

93. *Builder* 58 (1890): 450. The architect ended as "Jackson of Wimbledon" in *Burke's Peerage and Baronetage*.

94. N. Pevsner, *Northamptonshire*, p. 142.

95. Library ceiling, ill, anonymously in N. Pevsner, *South and West Somerset*, pl. 50A.

96. Chapel interior, removing the work of S. Sanders Teulon, ill. *Academy Architecture* (1889), p. 61.

97. E.g., Longleat, Wiltshire; Catton Hall, Norfolk; Rushton Hall, Northamptonshire; Danby Hall, Yorkshire; Laverstoke, Hampshire; Nottingham and Durham Castles; Eltham Palace, Kent; and St. Cross Hospital, Winchester.

98. Wrennaissance additions to Drapers' Hall and Grocers' Hall; 2–3 Hare Court in Inner Temple, *à la* Norman Shaw; Powells' stained-glass works in Whitefriars; a Jacobean insertion for Westminster School in Little Dean's Yard; and minor alterations fon John Murray Ltd. in Albermarle Street

and Dover Street.

99. N. Pevsner, *London* vol. 1. (1962), p. 569.

100. N. Pevsner, *London* vol. 2 (1952), p. 265.

101. *The Builder* much admired its Tuscan legs: "supports . . . which ought to make a revolution in piano legs" (64 [1893]: 15). It was equally admired by Goodhart-Rendel (*R.I.B.A. Journal* 33 [1926]: 467–468). See also Jackson's essay on "Intarsia and Inlaid Woodwork," in *Arts and Crafts Essays* (1893), p. 330.

102. *Builder* 47 (1884): 383.

103. Jackson's drawings, British Architectural Library (R.I.B.A.) W 15/31 (1–3).

104. *Builder* 53 (1887): 94, 168.

105. E.g., Wimbledon Hospital, Barnet Public Library, Cheam Village Hall, Sevenoaks Hospital for Children, Castle Avenue Offices in Winchester, Dorking Cottage Hospital, and the Jackson Hospital at Sevenoaks. See *Architectural Review* 1 (1896): 136–162; *Architecture* 2 (1897), 2–24, 84–96.

106. *Building News* 35 (1878): 400–401.

107. See also "Ragusa: il palazzo rettorale, il duomo, il reliquario del teschio di S. Biago," *Annuario Dalmatico*, 1885; reprinted Zara, 1885); also "The Architecture of Dalmatia," *R.I.B.A. Trans.*, N.S. 3 (1887): 161–178.

108. See P. B. Wright, "Jackson's Gothic Architecture," *Architectural Record* 40 (1916): 282–284.

109. E.g., Dauphinée, Venice, Assisi, Salonica, Constantinople.

110. A collection of Jackson's topographical sketches is now in the possession of Nicholas Jackson Esq. The manuscript "Journal of his Travels in Dalmatia" was recently sold (Marlborough Rare Books, catalogue 1979, lot 141).

111. *Builder* 56 (1889): 394, and 60 (1891): 392.

112. *Building News* 42 (1882): 794; Jackson, *Recollections*, pp. 191–192.

113. E.g., his dismissal of Art Nouveau and his assumption that the collapse of part of the roof at Charing Cross Station implied the end of iron as an agent in the revolution of architectural style (*Reason in Architecture*, 1906, pp. 171, 183). His views on the function of ornament remained Puginian: "ornament [should] express . . . the anatomy of structure" (ibid., p. 176).

114. *Six Ghost Stories* (1919): "written in idle hours for the amusement of the home circle."

115. *Some thoughts on the Training of Architects* (1895), p. 6.

116. *Reason in Architecture*, p. 185.

117. *Architecture* (1925), p. xxi.

118. *Address to the Students of the Durham School of Art* (Durham, 1898), p. 8.

119. See speech by Ernest George, *R.I.B.A. Journal* 17 (1910): 620–629.

120. *Gothic Architecture in France, England and Italy* vol. 2, pp. 316–318; *Magazine of Art* 8 (1889): 332–340.

121. *Renaissance of Roman Architecture* vol. 3, p. 210; *Reason in Architecture* (1906), pp. 176–177, 185; *Some Thoughts on the Training of Architects* (1895), pp. 6–7; "Architecture in Relation to the Crafts," *Builder* 72 (1897): 334–339.

122. "It postponed the evil day for forty years" (R. Blomfield, *Memories of an Architect*, p. 65). The other contributors were J. T. Micklethwaite (1843–1906), Sir Mervyn Macartney (d. 1932), Sir Reginald Blomfield (1856–1942), G. F. Bodley (1827–1907), Ernest Newton (1856–1922), E. S. Prior (1852–1932), J. R. Clayton, Basil Champneys (1842–1935), W. R. Lethaby (1857–1931), Sir William Richmond (1845–1921), and G. C. Horsley (1865–1917). The volume took its title from a saying of Gilbert Scott: "Architecture has too generally become a profession rather than an art" (Scott to Jackson's father, 12 August 1858). See Jackson, *Recollections*, p. 5.

123. See J. Mordaunt Crook, "The Pre-Victorian Architect: Professionalism and Patronage," *Architectural History* 12 (1969): 62–78.

124. Jackson, *Recollections*, p. 223.

125. *Times*, 12 February 1888.

126. Jackson, *Recollections*, p. 224.

127. *Architecture: A Profession or an Art?* pp. xxxiii—xxxv; *Times*, 3 March 1891.

128. Jackson, *Recollections*, pp. 224, 227.

129. *Times*, 10 March 1891; presidential address, *R.I.B.A. Proceedings* (1891/92), pp. 21–27; *Architecture: A Profession or an Art?*, pp. xvii, xxxi.

130. *R.I.B.A. Proceedings* (1892/93), pp. 24, 179.

131. J. Summerson, *The Architectural Association, 1847–1947* (1947), pp. 18–22.

132. Blomfield, *Memories*, p. 62.

133. For details, see *Architecture: A Profession or an Art?*, p. xxxv; *Builder* 60 (1891): 192.

134. Blomfield, *Memories*, p. 63.

135. E.g., *Building News* 60 (1891): 348, 354, 358, 863; *Builder* 60 (1891): 184, 203, 273; *Architect* 45 (1891): 153, 156–157, 163–165; *British Architect* 35 (1891): 174, 211–212.

136. *Building News* 63 (1892), 554–555.

137. *Architectural Association Notes* 5 (1891): 97–101, 115–117; 6 (1892): 161–163, 186–188, 189–191.

138. *Architecture: A Profession or an Art?*, p. 37.

139. E.g., *British Architect* 38 (1892): 311; *Spectator* 19 November 1892; Blomfield, *Memories*, pp. 64–65. One vigorous supporter was J. T. Emmett in *Quarterly Review* 176 (1893): 40–72. For his violent attacks on the profession see J. T. Emmett, *Six Essays* (1891), ed. J. Mordaunt Crook (1973).

140. *Architect* 48 (1892): 258–260, 274–276.

141. Jackson, *Recollections*, p. 212. "To the typical Institute man—like Charles Barry [Jr.] . . . it was gall and wormwood to see men practising prosperously outside their gates" (ibid., p. 213). For more measured arguments by Jackson, see *Builder* 53 (1887): 869, 873–876, 894–897; 54 (1888): 260; 56 (1889): 47–49; 61 (1891): 460–463, 468–471, 488; 68 (1895): 375–376.

142. Quoted by Nicholas Taylor in A. Service, ed., *Edwardian Architecture and its Origins* (1975), p. 449.

143. *R.I.B.A. Journal* 33 (1926): 467–478.

144. Jackson, *Recollections*, 272. Jackson's drawings for the Sheldonian organ case, British Architectural Library (R.I.B.A.), W 15/27.

ACROBATIC ARCHITECTURE: WILLIAM SHARP OGDEN AND OTHERS

Mark Girouard

WILLIAM SHARP OGDEN HAS BEEN entirely, and some may think deservedly, forgotten. Little is known about his career, and his few identifiable buildings are completely without interest. If he has any right to fame it must lie in his books.[1] Of these, *Manchester a hundred years ago* (1875), *Sketches of Antique Furniture* (1888), and *Shakespeare's Portraiture* (1912) have little except curiosity value. But the designs in *Christian Gravestones* (1877) are at least original; and in *Mercantile Architecture* (1876; enlarged eds. 1885 and 1892) oddity and originality are carried to lengths which deserve to be called inspired. What, one may wonder as one turns the pages, lay behind these extraordinary designs? What influence, if any, did they exert?

Ogden was born in 1844, practiced in Manchester from the 1870s to the 1890s, and died in London in 1926.[2] It is not known where he studied architecture or under what architect or architects he worked before setting up on his own. Unless further evidence comes to light, surmise as to what influenced him must depend on his designs. These suggest that he should be placed as one of a little group of Victorian architects, scarcely cohesive or consistent enough to be called a school, that experimented with new ways of creating movement in architecture.

Most architecture does not, or at least should not, move. But the technique of giving an illusion of movement to essentially static buildings is one that from time to time has interested architects. It seems to lie behind the very curious and clever design by Thomas Harris for a proposed terrace in Harrow, Middlesex, published in *The Builder* of October 20, 1860 (Fig. 1). The approach behind this had already been foreshadowed by the same architect's much less ambitious design for a shop building in South Audley Street, published in the *Building News* of February 18, 1859 (Fig. 2). The shop, unlike the terrace, was actually built but has been demolished.

The Builder linked the Harrow design to a pamphlet published by Harris in the same year, *Victorian Architecture. A few Words to show that a National Architecture adapted to the wants of the Nineteenth Century is obtainable.* In spite of its intriguing title the pamphlet itself is of little interest; nothing in it would lead one to expect the terrace. Admittedly, the latter

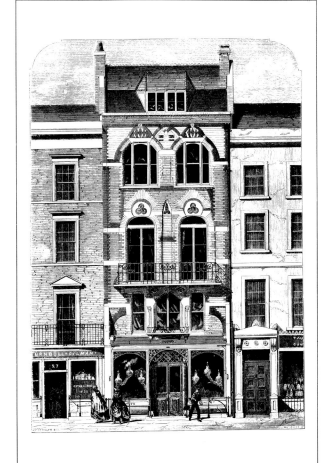

can perhaps be related to Harris's statement that "*Brickwork* from the variety of good coloured bricks available, presents a larger scope for originality of design than any other material," and to his suggestion that red brick, as "implying strength," should be used for constructive bands and relieving arches. But the statement gives no idea either of Harris's peculiar form of originality, or of the use to which he put his brick relieving arches in both the terrace and the shop.

The shop building was a remodeling of an earlier house, but in spite of the constraints of a limited brief and little money Harris did everything he could to get away from the conventional rectangular grid, typical of London terraces and to be found in the houses to either side. The facade was kept on the move by shallow but complex recessions in the brickwork, by differences in the size and rhythm of the windows, and above all by its elaborate variety of shaped window heads and relieving arches—the latter used far in excess of any structural need. Brick of three different colors was combined with blocks, courses, and voussoirs of stone to give an impression of continuous but also continuously interrupted movement. In looking at the engraving, the eye jumps from opening to opening and arch to arch. The line of the brick arches is broken by the interposition of windows or of blocks of stone; in one place the arches give the illusion of interlacing, in another, the bricks have jagged heads so that the arches seem almost to be bursting through the surrounding brickwork.

In his Harrow design, Harris set out, as Sir George Gilbert Scott had done in Broad Sanctuary, Westminster, to reinterpret the conventional early nineteenth-century formula not just for an individual terrace house, but for an entire terrace. Harris's reinterpretation was, by the standards of the time, outrageous, but it was also a great deal cleverer and more entertaining than Scott's, and it is sad that it was never built. All the devices of his North Audley Street design were reused and amplified on a much larger scale. The main material seems to have been intended to be stone, but pierced by an extraordinary variety of openings and threaded through by an equally extraordinary variety of courses and relieving arches of brick. The lines of the arches are constantly interrupted by voussoirs of stone; the central archway is framed in a counterpoint of reversed arches and arches of different section; jagged brick edges proliferate as at North Audley Street. Three-dimensional modeling is provided by porches, bay and oriel windows, buttresses, balconies, turrets, the central tower, and ten different varieties of dormer windows. The cumulative effect is of a restless and flickering movement that is almost, but not quite, chaotic. In fact, the line of the main balconies and the ridge line of the roofs provide just enough of a framework to prevent the composition from dissolving entirely; and the apparently wild diversity of elements is subtly orchestrated so that it gradually builds up to the central tower.

Stripes, diapers, and arches of different-colored brick or stone, curves overlaid on or opposed to other curves, and a profusion of faceted and splayed surfaces are to be found in many buildings of the later 1850s and the 1860s (Fig. 3). The intention behind them often seems to be to produce strength, variety, or at times perhaps just originality, rather than movement. They are commonest in Gothic Revival buildings, but also appear in Classical, or more or less Classical ones. They are by no means absent from, and indeed often were pioneered by, architects such as William Butterfield, G. E. Street, J. L. Pearson and George F. Bodley—the architects backed by *The Ecclesiologist*. But such architects usually kept them subordinated to strong and relatively simple compositions, and to a much closer approximation to medieval Gothic architecture. It was the architects Goodhart-Rendel classified as "rogues" who used them in the most profusion. The rogues make up a curious and by no means unified group, the best description of which would be a negative one. They were the architects of whom *The Ecclesiologist* disapproved. Besides Thomas Harris, they included E. B. Lamb, S. S. Teulon, Bassett Keeling, Joseph Peacock and, in Scotland, F. B. Pilkington.

In 1864, *Building News* pilloried Bassett Keeling's Strand Music Hall in an article by J. P. Seddon entitled "Acrobatic Gothic."[3] The adjective was applied both to the activities for which

4. Vinegar Warehouse, 33–35 Eastcheap, London. R. L. Roumieu, 1868. (Illustration: The Builder, *10 October 1868.)*

the Music Hall was built, and to the "high jinks and comic capers" of its architecture. This, admittedly, was eccentric rather than interesting; but "acrobatic" is a suggestive way of describing those varieties of rogue architecture in which the eye is stimulated to move or jump to such an extent that the building becomes the architectural equivalent of a complicated trapeze act.

Harris's two buildings have a strong acrobatic element. The vinegar warehouse by R. L. Roumieu in Eastcheap, of 1868 (Fig. 4), uses somewhat different means to develop the technique even further. There are hints of its approach in other buildings by Roumieu,[4] but the Eastcheap warehouse is his masterpiece. *The Builder* commented at the time that "the design, if a little overdone, may be considered picturesque and original."[5] Reactions to it and to his other buildings have always been mixed. Hitchcock calls them "wild fantasies . . . hardly worth considering."[6] Pevsner describes the Eastcheap warehouse as "utterly undisciplined and crazy."[7] Both descriptions seem unfair to a dazzling piece of architectural juggling in which Roumieu, as the juggler, appears to know exactly what he is about.

The design is worked out in terms of diagonals and receding planes. The three main planes are those of the principal building face, the recessed face at the back of the arched openings, and the face of the six projecting canopies. The main diagonals are provided by the gables over the canopies and main entrance and on the skyline, by the crisscross of the brickwork diapers and by a wide variety of arched openings. The facade reads like a succession of overlays, each cut away to reveal the layer behind it and kept on the move by the main diagonals and by a bewildering series of chamfers, corbels, and setbacks. These make the eye slide in and out and to and fro, or leap from point to point as diagonals are interrupted and then taken up again. Yet, as in Harris's Harrow terrace, the composition as a whole is strong enough to keep the facade from dissolving into chaos.

William Sharp Ogden almost certainly knew of the Eastcheap warehouse, for it was illustrated in *The Builder* in 1868, when he was twenty-six and must have been well started on his professional career. At any rate, in his *Studies in Mercantile Architecture* (1876) he plays a rather similar game with unflagging zest through fifty different designs.

Studies in Mercantile Architecture was published jointly in London and Manchester. It contained, as the title page announced, "fifty suggestive designs for warehouse, shop and office buildings, suitable for the commercial districts of large cities." Each design carries a date, running from 1869 to 1875. The plates follow a short introduction. The latter—as curiously tended to be the case with the more outrageous productions of Victorian rogues—gave no hint that the contents are in any way unusual, or other than down-to-earth commercial designs, economically tailored to their function. They are described as "eclectic in character; the author preferring to select and combine features of beauty or utility from any available source, all picturesqueness of grouping or detail save that springing from evident and natural requirements being avoided."

The book received a short but appreciative notice in *The British Architect*[8] (which at that date was published in Manchester) and a much longer, but also much more critical one, in *The Builder*.[9] In the latter the anonymous reviewer's reactions were mixed but on the whole scathing. The book showed, he wrote, a

desire for something clever and out of the way, an almost total absence of real taste and refinement in style and detail, combined with a considerable degree of cleverness and originality. . . . The vulgarity of some of these designs is astounding. . . . The author seems to have a great fancy for playing clever, or at least odd tricks with string-courses and window labels, especially of making the latter interpenetrate and cross each other, in a manner which is essentially unarchitectural. . . . No designer possessed of a particle of what may be called architectural morality would perpetrate such a thing. . . . Entire want of repose is a quality which no cleverness can atone for. There are a good many designs in it for which the author will probably condemn himself before very long [the book was presumed to be written by a young man]. But there is a certain spirit, cleverness and originality about even some of the more objectionable ones, which is, perhaps, more promising than merely dull good taste running in a well known groove.

This was at least the kind of review calculated to make readers curious to look at the book; and

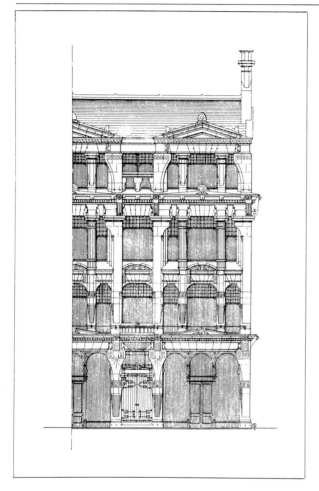

a look at it shows what the reviewer was getting at. "Clever, or at least odd tricks" and "entire want of repose" are abundantly in evidence; stylistic consistency and correct use of the grammar of Classicism or even the accepted Victorian conventions of Gothicism are entirely absent.

What is interesting and at times fascinating about the designs is the way in which they experiment with ways of obtaining "entire want of repose," or to put it in positive terms, the maximum of movement (Figs. 5–11). They do this by numerous variations and combinations of a number of devices, the main ones of which can be classified as intersection, interruption, opposition, continuation, and explosion. Moldings and arches intersect one another, arches and gables cut through horizontal or vertical moldings, the line of a roof reappears underneath the cornice in the form of a molding. Arches start off from their two springing points but change into some other shape and fail to come to a peak; horseshoe arches carry the eye round two-thirds of an interrupted circle; moldings are unexpectedly discontinued. Curves are broken into by triangles; some are set in opposition to other curves of a different radius; convex curves are opposed to concave

ones; large-scale motifs are violently contrasted to similar small-scale ones. A line is carried across or down a facade, changing direction as it goes, so that it sweeps, snakes, or seesaws. Voussoirs, glazing bars, or incised ornament are treated so as to give the impression of radiating lines exploding from a central point through the surrounding elements.

In nearly all the designs, several of these devices are combined in one facade; any one element can often form part of several different and unexpected sequences. There are almost no closed shapes or conventional rhythms. The eye, as a result, is constantly surprised or bewildered and kept continuously on the move. It is encouraged to behave in much the same way it does when watching a tennis match, a fireworks show, or a display of acrobatics; in this way an illusion of architectural movement is obtained.

The plates in *Studies in Mercantile Architecture* are all elevations; there are no plans, no perspectives, and only an occasional section, added as a detail on the elevations. These sections show that on occasion the glazing was intended to take the form of curved or polygonal bays, recessed or projecting between the ma-

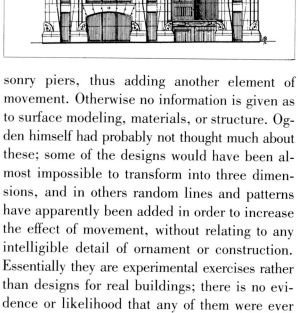

sonry piers, thus adding another element of movement. Otherwise no information is given as to surface modeling, materials, or structure. Ogden himself had probably not thought much about these; some of the designs would have been almost impossible to transform into three dimensions, and in others random lines and patterns have apparently been added in order to increase the effect of movement, without relating to any intelligible detail of ornament or construction. Essentially they are experimental exercises rather than designs for real buildings; there is no evidence or likelihood that any of them were ever built.

Clearly, however, many of them were conceived as relying heavily on iron or steel, which, of course, was common practice for mercantile buildings by the 1870s. Without an element of metal construction, the high proportion of window to wall found in some of the designs would have been impossible; so would one of the most distinctive features of the shops and offices—the filling of the ground floor with sheets of plate glass, above which the masonry piers of the upper floor appear to be suspended. The balancing effect produced by this device gives these particular designs an extra degree of surprise and insecurity, which Ogden clearly enjoyed.

Stylistically, Ogden's claim that his designs were eclectic was all too justified. Like other architects of the time, he seems to have been experimenting with an outrageous eclecticism as a route toward a modern "Victorian" style. Facades start off and end vaguely Classical but in between are wildly Gothic or Rundbogenstil. Corinthian columns support piers of Gothic section. Flemish gables are combined with Greek anthemions, Georgian arched window heads merge into Gothic arches, Rococo cartouches are mixed with Lombardic tracery. Even when whole buildings are more or less Classical, the accepted grammar of the orders is mercilessly disregarded: columns are truncated or distorted, pediments perch on top of voussoirs or arches. Some designs are fairly consistently Gothic; their stylistic treatment is often equally wild, but less distressing than in the Classical designs, because the acrobatic effects that Ogden aimed at relate to an element that is actually to be found in Gothic architecture. Much of the detail derives from contemporary buildings, especially from those by the more offbeat or outrageous architects; apart from the possible influence of Roumieu and Thomas Harris, there are what appear to be echoes of Bassett Keeling's churches, "Greek" Thomson's warehouses, and E. L. Paraire's public houses. But the character of the final mixture is unique to Ogden.

In 1877 Ogden produced another book of designs, *Christian Gravestones; illustrated by 150 examples*. In the introduction, he wrote:

In issuing this little volume the Author has endeavoured to work out certain fixed principles, the observance of which he thinks is of the first importance, viz., simplicity of outline, severity of detail, and a general motive of design in which the Cross or other Christian emblem, monogram, or text are leading features. 'Style', as generally understood and as the expression of various systems of thought is intentionally avoided, the object being to obtain an elastic and harmonious combination of workable detail, at once effective, inexpensive and durable. . . .

"Some of the best of these designs," the introduction concludes, "were prepared as studies for my Father's grave stone and these suggesting the others I dedicate them to his memory. Dear old Father; warmest, truest friend. Peace to thee."[10]

As in *Mercantile Architecture*, the unexceptionable sentiments of the introduction give little idea of the nature of the plates that follow—unless, perhaps, there is a forecast in the adjective "elastic." The designs, although by no means as stimulating as those in *Studies in Mercantile Architecture*, are clearly related to them. They are based on various interactions and contrasts of curved and straight lines, some obtained by the outlines of the stones, others by incision (Fig. 12). A few of the monuments are decorated with interleafing foliage made up of distinctively stiff and curling fronds, as though cast in metal. Most of the shapes and motifs relate to conventional gravestones of the period, but they are combined and distorted by Ogden in a way that makes *Christian Gravestones* a curious and rather disturbing little book.

Second and third editions of *Mercantile Architecture* (as the title was now abbreviated) were published in 1885 and 1892. The second edition had five additional designs, and another five followed in the third edition, which also contained an appendix on hydraulic lifts. The additional designs could be described stylistically as commercial "Queen Anne" (Ogden called them "free classic"), fairly crude in the second edition and

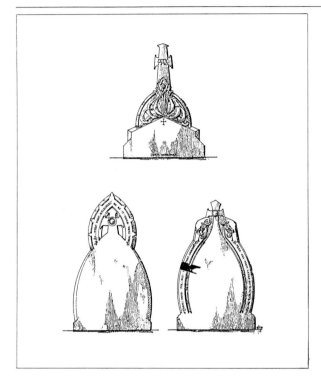

latter draws attention to the combination of piers and glazing in the new designs,

> an arrangement at once satisfactory to the eye and of vast importance as yielding almost uninterrupted light. It will be seen that considerable prominence is with this intention given to the Bay or Bow Window, forms which readily lend themselves to any detail; are picturesque, agreeable and profitable, as giving additional floor space, allowing more glass and facing the light at several angles, are superior to any other kind of window.

The Builder had already, in its review of the 1876 edition, pointed out that bow windows give less rather than more light than ordinary ones. This fact is a commonplace to anyone who has experience of lighting calculations, and if Ogden did not know of it, he ought to have. But one suspects that in spite of his protestations that "Convenience and Utility must ever be of the first importance," what really attracted him was the aesthetic excitement of devising delicate multistoried lanterns of curved and faceted glass. The idea almost certainly derived from earlier "Queen Anne" buildings by better-known architects—such as the New Zealand Chambers by Richard Norman Shaw, of 1871 to 1873, and Belcher and Son's Queen Anne Chambers, Poultry, of 1875—but Ogden carried it considerably further.

rather more restrained in the third. They have little of the wild movement of the 1877 designs; much their most interesting feature is their glazing. All the buildings appear to be designed to have a metal frame, and as a result they are lit by almost continuous glazing; roofs and gables as well as the main wall surfaces are sometimes filled with glass. The space between the piers is invariably given over to bow or bay windows; on the first and second floor of one design, elaborately shaped glazing is carried in front and well clear of the iron columns of the main structure, to produce a genuine and very early example of curtain walling (Fig. 13).

Ogden was clearly proud of his glazed metalframe structures, which are referred to both in the subtitle ("specially prepared to combine Lightness with Constructional Design") and in the new introduction of his second edition. The

The known executed buildings by Ogden, all in Manchester, are Read's Buildings, on the corner of Peter Street and Deansgate (1878); York Street Synagogue, Cheetham (c. 1889); Sunday Schools, Broughton Congregational Church (c. 1889); and the Talmud Torah School, Best Street, Cheetham (c. 1894).[11] Some of these were built in partnership with E. W. Charleston. None is of the slightest architectural interest; the contrast between them and the designs in Ogden's books is almost ludicrous in its completeness. Although *The Builder*, reviewing *Studies in Mercantile Architecture* in 1876, described the designs in it as "typical of a certain type of Manchester architecture" and labeled them "Manchester goods," they appear to bear little resemblance to any known Manchester building by Ogden or any other architect. It would seem that Ogden's own taste was so completely out of step with Manchester's that he made no attempt to sell it to the few clients that came his way.

Ogden's other published works, and what little is known of his life, suggest a character mildly out of gear with his contemporaries and reacting to the situation by slight eccentricity. He was the grandson of that "revered but ruptured Ogden" (as Canning is said to have described him) who called the famous meeting at Peterloo,[12] and the great-grandson of Peter Ogden, a Manchester antiquarian whose sketches of the city, made in the 1770s, he reproduced or professed to reproduce in *Manchester a hundred years ago* (1875). Although W. S. Ogden declared that the contents were "not . . . mere fancy pictures but genuine representations,"[13] the sketches look so much like buildings in the style of Norman Shaw and other contemporary architects as to suggest that they were either substantial redrawings, or complete fabrications.

His *Sketches of Antique Furniture* (1888) is chiefly remarkable for the crudity with which the various examples are drawn. Ogden himself was something of a collector and antiquarian; in his will he distributed his collections of engravings, topographical drawings, prehistoric and classical pottery, and other antiquities to the Manchester Museum, the Whitworth Gallery, and the Society of Antiquaries.[14] He owned a supposed portrait of Shakespeare, which was reproduced in his *Shakespeare's Portraiture* (1912). It seems likely that he had some kind of private income. There is no evidence that he practiced as an architect after the 1890s. He died in London in 1926.

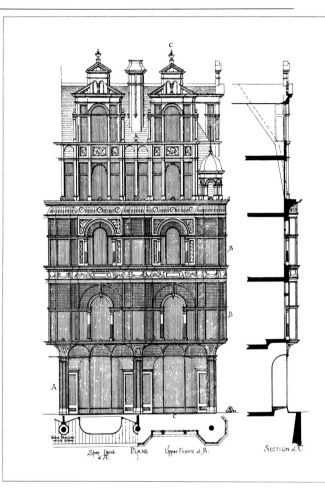

In the second edition of *Mercantile Architecture*, Ogden complained of the "complacent obtuseness" with which the first edition had been reviewed by "one or two of the professional papers," as opposed to "that admirable and unprejudiced paper *The British Architect*." He was presumably referring to the review in *The*

Builder. But, apart from an on-the-whole friendly notice in *The British Architect*,[15] the second and third editions were ignored in the professional press. The fact that the book ran to three editions suggests that it enjoyed some popularity; perhaps it had an influence on late-nineteenth-century commercial and public-house architecture, but it is hard to point to specific examples. By the time of Ogden's death, what little reputation he had enjoyed as an architect had been completely forgotten; the only (short) obituaries were in the *North Western Naturalist* and the *Manchester City News*.[16]

In 1904, however, his old ally *The British Architect* gave him one last piece of publicity. On October 14 of that year it published a leader on "L'Art Nouveau," together with two pages of illustrations by Raffles Davison, showing new buildings in Brussels. One passage mentions Ogden as providing possible prototypes for the style.

> It is a good many years since there was published in Manchester a book entitled "*Mercantile Design*", by Mr Ogden, which contained the germ of a good deal that was inventive and good about the methods of *l'art nouveau*; and though, when it was published the energy and restlessness of much of it was over the heads of current ideas, it deserves some recognition as an attempt to break loose from the bonds of academic formality and servile tradition. . . . When we saw the latest erection of *l'art nouveau* in Brussels the other day, we felt that the whole *motif* of the design had a most remarkable parallel in more than one of Mr Ogden's designs published now some twenty years ago.

These comments have some point. However outrageous as a designer, Ogden was by no means despicable. If he had been one of a group, rather than out on a limb in Manchester, he might have produced some remarkable buildings. Even if his designs lack Art Nouveau's sinuous line, total asymmetry, and freedom from historicism, in some ways they do point suggestively toward it: in the flickering detail, experiments with movement, and attempts to escape from style of the 1876 designs; in the undulating glass walls and turrets of the later ones. The building in Brussels which struck *The British Architect* (and which was illustrated by Raffles Davison) was a nearly completed office block near the General Post Office, but perhaps the parallels with buildings such as Saintenoy's Old England Store in Brussels, or Guimard's Maison Coilliot in Liège (Fig. 14) are even more suggestive. Was this pure coincidence? Or did copies of *Mercantile Architecture*, by some chance, find their way to Brussels or to Paris?

Notes

Biographical information, references in periodicals, and extracts from Ogden's books were generously communicated to me by Stuart Hodgson and were of the greatest help in providing material for this article.

1. There are copies of all editions of Ogden's books of designs in the Manchester Public Library, but elsewhere they are hard to find. All the British Library copies, except for the 1885 edition of *Mercantile Architecture*, were destroyed in the war. The R.I.B.A. library owns only the 1885 edition of *Mercantile Architecture*, and has no copy of *Christian Gravestones*.
2. In 1876 he was living at 162, Rydal Mount, Waterloo Road, Manchester; in 1885 and 1892 his office was at Read's Buildings, Peter Street (Prefaces, *Mercantile Architecture*).
3. *Building News* 11 (1864): 780. The title was reused by the author for an article on the architecture of S. S. Teulon *Country Life*, December 31, 1970, pp. 1282–1286.
4. For biographical information and a description of the R.I.B.A.'s interesting group of drawings by Roumieu, see his entry in *Catalogue of the Drawings Collection of the Royal Institute of British Architects* O–R.
5. *The Builder* 26 (October 10, 1868): 748–749.
6. *Early Victorian Architecture in Britain* (1954), I, p. 158.
7. *The Buildings of England, London I* (1962 ed.), p. 99.

8. *The British Architect* 6 (September 1, 1876): 136 (reproducing 2 designs).
9. *The Builder* 34 (August 5, 1876): 753.
10. Ogden's design for his father's gravestone was presumably executed, and may still be identifiable in a Manchester cemetery.
11. *The Builder* 38 (May 1, 1880): 538; *The British Architect*, October 4, 1889, p. 4 (with 2 illustrations); *The Builder* 56 (1889,1): 11; *The Builder* 67 (1894,2) p. 119. Read's Buildings (where he had his own office) survives; I have not tried to trace the others.
12. The relationship is referred to in Ms. comments written in the front of the Manchester Public Library copy of *Manchester a hundred years ago*. The Peterloo meeting was for the purpose of petitioning Parliament for reform of suffrage; it resulted in the "Manchester Massacre" of 1819.
13. So he assured the writer of the Ms. comments referred to above.
14. See the report of his will in *The Times*, April 24, 1926.
15. *British Architect* 25 (January 1, 1886): 1–2. The review criticizes him for "some eccentricity (and here and there some bad taste)," but is otherwise favorable, and reproduces two designs.
16. *North Western Naturalist* 1 (1926): 150–151; *Manchester City News* May 1, 1926, p. 12. He died at his home in Finchley and was cremated in Golders Green Crematorium.

AMERICAN ARCHITECTURE TO 1900: ROMANTICISM AND REINTEGRATION

THE TALL OFFICE BUILDING ARTISTICALLY RECONSIDERED: ARCADED BUILDINGS OF THE NEW YORK SCHOOL, c. 1870-1890

Sarah Bradford Landau

NEW YORK'S LATER NINETEENTH-century commercial buildings have always been ranked a poor second to Chicago's. Yet New York has been credited with the first buildings meriting the designation "skyscraper," and lately scholars have been increasingly attracted to the work of the Beaux-Arts-trained easterners. Despite all this attention, the long outmoded judgment that New York's commercial architecture is antirational, excessively historicizing, and unprogressive still prevails. Chicago's superiority in the commercial field, in respect to design as well as technical achievement, is taken for granted, in part because some of New York's most significant buildings have been overlooked.

Louis Sullivan, of course, is widely credited with the development and dissemination of a highly successful design method for expressing the height as well as the use and structure of the tall office building. As exemplified by his well-known Wainwright (1890/91) and Guaranty buildings (1894/95), he prescribed a three-part division in which the lower one or two stories are unified as the first layer, "tiers of typical offices" are combined as the second, and attic story and cornice represent the terminating third part.[1] The scheme supports his famous dictum, "form follows function." However, well before Sullivan published his prescription other architects had used the Renaissance-inspired tripartite scheme, and the critics had already recommended the Classical order, or more specifically the column, as the most suitable model for the tall building.[2] Sullivan himself reviewed the column analogy, if only to dismiss it as superficial. The three parts of the building were to represent proportionately the base, shaft, and capital, and the shaft could be

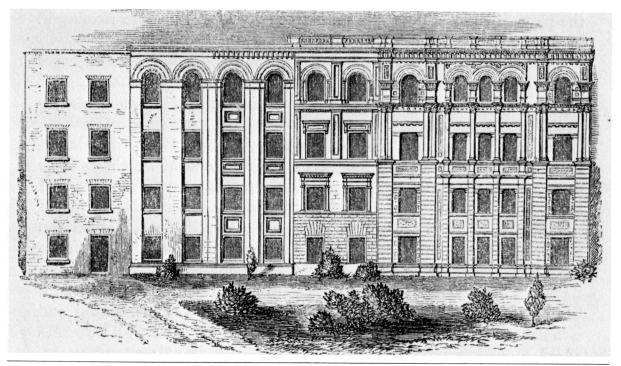

either "plain" or "fluted." Indeed, the Guaranty Building in Buffalo, with its soaring arcades— that is, the series of continuous piers uniting the windows in vertical rows and joined at the top by arches—might be considered the paradigmatic fluted-column skyscraper. "Thus the fact that the edifice is a hollow cage is very strongly suggested," observes Henry-Russell Hitchcock, who also notes that the building "should probably be considered Sullivan's masterpiece."[3] Few would disagree.

So closely has Sullivan been identified with the arcaded, tripartite commercial building that a "Sullivanesque" style, said to have been prevalent from 1890 into the 1920s, has been discerned by several writers attempting to define the succession of American architectural styles.[4] So-called Sullivanesque buildings often barely resemble the master's work, yet the designation has persisted, and Sullivan continues to receive the lion's share of the credit for their appearance. The contribution of Henry Hobson Richardson to the design of the tall building and to Sullivan's style, specifically the legacy of his Cheney Block (1875/76) and Marshall Field Wholesale Store (1885–1887), has long been acknowledged, although recently the preeminence of the Field Store in the line of arcaded buildings has been questioned. Yet, properly, some of the credit for both "Sullivanesque" and "Richardsonian" buildings belongs to New York architects. This essay concentrates on a group of commercial buildings designed for New York City in the 1870s and 1880s. It aims to demonstrate that arcading was utilized in these masonry-walled buildings to unify multiple stories vertically as well as horizontally, to permit larger expanses of glass, and even to express structure—virtues that are usually attributed exclusively to the Chicago School—

and that arcading served these purposes for a decade or more before Sullivan and other Chicago architects recognized its potential. The tripartite scheme also was used frequently in New York in this period, well before Sullivan discovered it.

I

Hitchcock, Winston Weisman, and others have established that neither the arcades of the Guaranty Building nor the related tall piers that articulate the earlier Wainwright Building were Sullivan's invention. Hitchcock has pointed to the trabeated granite skeletons of certain American buildings of the early nineteenth century (the commercial fronts by Alexander Parris built along North and South Market Streets in Boston in 1823 and the Granite Block in Providence of 1824 by John Holden Greene were among the earliest and most conspicuous) as looking forward to the skeletal cast-iron fronts of the 1850s.[5] Greek Revival commercial buildings with unadorned granite piers only at the ground-story level were built in lower Manhattan; several groups have survived in the South Street Seaport and on Stone Street.

As for arcades, Hitchcock has informed us that C. R. Cockerell and other English architects applied them to one and even two stories of commercial buildings in the 1840s. J. W. Wild, E. W. Godwin, and various others, who like Godwin were influenced by John Ruskin, adopted arcading; and the motif flourished from the late 1850s through the 1860s. Sometimes it was combined with iron construction, and arches could be either round or pointed. Of particular interest, especially in respect to later developments in America, was Wild's St. Martin's District Northern School in London of 1849/50, published in *The Builder* in 1849. There the entire length of the

2. Bank of the Republic, northeast corner, Broadway and Wall Street, N.Y.C., demolished. Hurry & Rogers, 1851/52. (Perspective: Courtesy of the New York Public Library, Prints Division, Eno Collection, No. 305n.)

three-story facade was arcaded in two stories for the first time, at the ground and the first stories.[6] The rhythms of the Gothic arcades and top-story colonnettes presaged Richardson's and George B. Post's designs of the 1880s.

In *The Illustrated Handbook of Architecture* published in London in 1855, James Fergusson offered successively more elaborate designs for the embellishment of an ordinary four-story building such as a factory or warehouse (Fig. 1). In two of the designs arcades link all four stories. American architects and builders surely took notice, for the illustration was published in several subsequent editions of Fergusson's book, but well before 1855 they had been grouping windows vertically under arches or using tall abutments joined by arches on four- and five-story buildings. All the same, that illustration may well have specifically motivated the design of arcaded warehouses and factories in America.

In his important article, "Philadelphia Functionalism and Sullivan," Weisman begins by asking, "Have we overemphasized Sullivan's contribution at the expense of other men too long forgotten and still all too obscure?"[7]—a question which might be repeated here in another context. By the end of that article the reader should be persuaded that Sullivan not only noticed the abutted and arcaded buildings of the Philadelphia architects while he was working for Furness & Hewitt in 1873 but that he learned much from those rationally designed structures of the 1850s. Charles Peterson had already stressed the striking resemblance between the pier system of the Wainwright Building and the slender granite arcades of the tripartite Jayne Building in Philadelphia of 1849 to 1851.[8]

At midcentury buildings with tall abutments

or arcades were not limited to Philadelphia but could be found elsewhere. And most of them belonged to a round-arched genre which came into fashion in the later 1840s and included several variations drawing on styles ranging from the Early Christian and the Byzantine to the Renaissance.[9] Some were derived from the German Rundbogenstil, and English sources were also influential, especially for the "Italianate" variety. Frequently, as in the Philadelphia examples cited by Weisman, arcades or abutments embraced several stories, and the design emphasis was usually vertical. This genre was particularly well suited to large utilitarian buildings several stories high, requiring much light and open floor space, for example, mills, warehouses, and hospitals.[10] By 1860 New York was the scene of arcaded buildings of all types.

Several banks in the Wall Street area participated in the midcentury vogue for arcades, among them the peculiarly forward-looking Bank of the Republic designed by Hurry & Rogers and built in 1851/52 (Fig. 2). The exterior combined the verticalism of the "Italianate" with the ornate segmental pediments and consoles of the related Palazzo mode, and the stories were organized in three sections: an arcuated and rusticated base, a vertically articulated midsection, and an attic story above the cornice.[11] Surely the post-Civil War architects noticed this building. Although it was replaced in 1880 by the United Bank Building of Peabody & Stearns, the resemblances between it and the Goelet Building of McKim, Mead & White are too striking to be easily dismissed (cf. Fig. 21). The more imposing and floridly Italianate New York Times Building of 1857/58 by Thomas R. Jackson displayed superposed two-story arcades, perhaps made of cast-iron, on its Park Row front (Fig. 3).[12]

By the mid-1850s New York's cast-iron fronts were simulating the arcaded Venetian palace; and around 1860 two-story arcades, often in double rhythm, as on the Times Building, became popular motifs. Sometimes designated as "sperm-candle buildings," fronts with the double rhythm were exceptionally light and open. Noteworthy examples are 85 Leonard Street of 1860 by James Bogardus, the demolished Tefft, Weller & Company Store of 1859/60 (Fig. 4), and its near twin, 55 White Street, designed by Kellum & Son and built in 1861.[13] Number 63 Nassau Street, of c.

1860, perhaps a Bogardus design, has three-story arcades, and—apparently exceptional for the time—171 Duane Street has a front constructed in 1859 with slender four-story arcades[14] (this can be seen at the right in Fig. 12). Although some architects openly scorned cast-iron fronts, or took on such commissions as a source of easy money,[15] others apparently admired them enough to imitate them in masonry. Whole blocks of masonry-fronted commercial buildings and tenements displaying two-story arcades, some built as late as the 1890s, still exist in New York City. After the Civil War, faced with new and challenging aesthetic problems posed by the arrival of the elevator building, architects would again turn to the familiar device of arcading.

II

During the Civil War building came nearly to a standstill in New York but was enthusiastically resumed soon afterward. Henry Hobson Richardson and Richard Morris Hunt were perhaps the first to recognize the potential of arcades as a means of ordering the stories of the new, taller office buildings that soon began to rise. In Richardson's competition design of 1867 for the Equitable Life Assurance Building in New York (Fig. 5), the first-story windows are topped by segmental arches; the fifth story is shallow and trabeated; and heavily molded, round arches join piers linking the second and third stories. This was the first appearance in Richardson's work of motifs that would later distinguish his mature commercial buildings.[16] Perhaps he was influenced by New York's prewar arcaded buildings. Hunt also experimented with two-story arcades in several alternative proposals for the Equitable competition.[17] As built from 1868 to 1870 to the Second

Empire design of Gilman & Kendall, with the technical assistance of Post, the seven-story Equitable Building had no arcades. However, windows were paired vertically at two levels, giving the illusion of single, tall stories. Its chief importance in the history of the skyscraper is the fact that it was the first office building that incorporated an elevator as part of its design.

Throughout the 1870s arcades were apparently preferred for buildings of six stories or less. Unfortunately, several of the more ambitious projects calling for them remained unbuilt. Perhaps there was some reluctance at first to apply arcades to the new elevator buildings because they had so long been identified with cast-iron fronts. However, the Tribune Building of 1873 to 1875 by Hunt included superposed arcades—with segmental rather than round arches—which

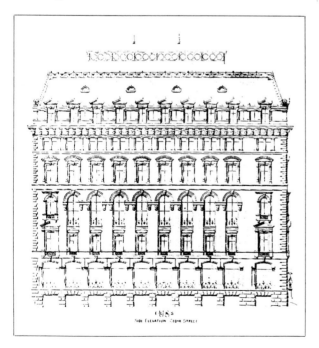

encompassed two and three stories. This building is considered one of the first skyscrapers (the other having been Post's Western Union Building begun late in 1872[18] and also completed in 1875), and it may have inaugurated the triple-window bay as well. Heavy piers, apparently functioning as supports, were visible elements of both, and the Western Union Building included arches strategically placed over the windows of the sixth and eighth floors as well as a rudimentary tripartite organization of its ten stories.[19]

J. Cleveland Cady's competition design for the Tribune Building (Fig. 6) also incorporated three-story arcades, and four tiers of arcades are proposed. And in an early elevation drawing of the building (Fig. 7), perhaps his competition entry, Hunt proposed a quadruple rhythm that anticipates the rhythms of Richardson's much later Field Store. Hunt's and Cady's designs forecast two modes of the future: taller arcades and superposed arcades. Cady's was surely influential for it was published in the *New-York Sketch-Book* in 1874, the year before Richardson was commissioned to design the Cheney Block. Its round arches and bold structural polychromy would have been sympathetic to Richardson at that time.[20]

George B. Post's remarkable Neo-Renaissance project for the Marine National Bank (Fig. 8) is undated but may well be from about 1871 when the bank moved its offices from 90 Wall Street to 78 Wall at the corner of Pearl Street.[21] If so, its three-story arcades precede those of Cady and Hunt. The project belongs to a group of related designs by Post, among them Chickering Hall of 1874/75, where two-story arcades described the concert auditorium within.[22] Piers, evidently constructional elements, rise the full height of the bank's facades demarcating wide bays. This well-proportioned, minimally ornamented design

6. *J. C. Cady, project for the Tribune Building, 1872.* (Perspective: New-York Sketch-Book of Architecture, *Vol. I, July 1874, pl. xxv.*)

7. *R. M. Hunt, project for the Tribune Building, c. 1872.* (Elevation: Courtesy of the A.I.A. Prints and Drawings Collection.)

seems incredibly precocious for its probable early date. The walls are more glass than masonry, and the two-story "base," arcaded "shaft," and sixth-story "capital" augur Sullivan's tripartite formula.

Just as Chickering Hall was being completed an extraordinary building began to rise on the northeast corner of Sixth Avenue and 26th Street. This was the old Racquet Club designed by Alfred H. Thorp and built in 1875/76 (Fig. 9).[23] The building somewhat resembles a fifteenth-century Florentine palace, an indication that it belongs to a developing Neo-Renaissance trend which seems to begin with Post in the early 1870s but is partially rooted in the Italianate and Palazzo modes of the prewar era. Stylistically the club is a very successful hybrid of the High Victorian round-arched mode as practiced by Cady, Hunt's version of the Néo-Grec as represented by his Studio Building of 1857, and the very premature Neo-Renaissance of Post.

Curiously, the building exhibits none of the domesticity usually associated with clubs of the time but instead resembles a commercial block—

probably to accommodate its mixed uses. Its arcades, narrow top story, and wide eaves supported by slender iron brackets were doubtless influenced by Chickering Hall, but these features were said to have resulted from the structure and functions of the building. The buttresses were included for "greater strength and economy"; the roof was designed to shield the racquet courts from the sun and to obviate the need for blinds over the upper windows of the courts.[24] Lighted by a skylight in the roof as well as by side windows, and flanked by a gallery beneath the eaves, the racquet courts extended upward for the full

height of the two top floors. Originally there were no windows on the Sixth Avenue side above the third floor because of the athletic facilities, and there was a balcony on the 26th Street side at the level of the fifth floor. The shingled canopy that shades the ground floor stores was surely a later addition. Although neither the brick walls trimmed in bluestone and granite nor the interesting brick patterns and layered bricks seen below the top story and on the chimneys were unusual for the time—and certainly the cast-iron columns supporting the floors inside were commonplace constructional elements—the building appears to be

later in date than it actually is. Roofs of the time usually were towered like that of Richardson's contemporary Cheney Block in Hartford (Fig. 10), or piled high like the mansards of Post's designs.

Here the tall arcades, now four stories high, are a real surprise. Even the Cheney Block has only three stories under its tallest arcades. And the Racquet Club is distinctly tripartite as well.

The Cheney Block of 1875/76 was of great consequence in the development of arcaded buildings. Superposed arcades articulate its facades in successive single, double, and triple rhythm,[25] introducing an alternative system to the tall arcades of the Racquet Club: the tall building treated as a series of arcuated layers. The method is less "structural" and therefore less suited to the lofty towers of the 1890s than the system of the Racquet Club, but it works extremely well for buildings of blocklike proportions and moderate height.

Proceeding along lines parallel to Richardson, but perhaps influenced by the Cheney Block or by the preliminary design for it in brick, published in the *New-York Sketch-Book* in 1875, Post utilized superposed arcades on his Long Island Historical Society building of 1878 to 1880 (Fig. 11).[26] Again he employed the tall arcade to serve a functional purpose: here it signifies the two-story height of the reading room. The shallow, trabeated top story forms the third layer of a three-part scheme. Stylistically, the fine pressed brick exterior with its intricate terra-cotta relief ornament brings to mind Quattrocento Italy more distinctly than the architect's earlier buildings and also evokes the Néo-Grec style of Henri Labrouste. Post's knowledge of French sources would have come largely if not entirely from Hunt, in whose *atelier* he had studied, and from French publications available in New York. In the Post collection at The New-York Historical Society, with a group labeled "inspirational photographs," there is a view of the Palais de l'Industrie built for the Paris Exposition of 1855.[27] This vast iron-and-glass structure was encased in masonry walls, and its main facade was probably inspired by Labrouste's famous Bibliothèque Ste.-Gene-

vième, which had been completed in 1850. Although there is no way of determining just when
Post acquired the photograph, it is reasonable to
suppose that he knew of the building and others
of its type by this time. The arcading and the
placement of the ceramic decoration in the spandrels of the arches foretell similar features of the
Long Island Historical Society. Post's Produce
Exchange of several years later reflected Labrouste's library more directly.

Large round arches cap only three stories of
the six-story warehouse at 173 Duane Street (Fig.
12) designed by Babb & Cook and built in 1879/

80,[28] but the vertical and rational organization of
the fine brick facade is nonetheless impressive.
Interrupted only by the entablatures of the second and fourth stories, the arch-topped bays project so forcefully that the interior construction
would seem to be accurately represented; however, this is not the case. Although the superposed, deep-cut arcades of varying sizes, the flat
roof, and the cast terra-cotta ornament suggest
the Quattrocento, something of the massiveness
of this front also calls to mind the round-arched,
utilitarian buildings of the 1850s. In respect to
style, the architects were apparently following
Post's lead, but simplifying details to suit a
smaller, more modest building. Mariana Griswold van Rensselaer cited Babb's buildings, especially this one, as exemplary; in fact she recommended them as more suitable models for
ordinary street architecture than Richardson's far
more imposing Bedford Street Ames Building in
Boston of 1882/83.[29]

In 1881 arcades were apparently still being
limited to a height of four stories. The nine-story
United Bank Building of 1880/81 (Fig. 13), designed by the Boston firm of Peabody & Stearns
to occupy a corner at Broadway and Wall Street
in New York, prominently displayed four-story
arcades accommodating piers that were visible
from the ground up. The trabeated attic story recalled Post's buildings, and the corbeled cornice
was probably inspired by the Cheney Block, but
other ornamental details conformed to the commercial style of the previous decade, a mixture
of High Victorian Gothic and "Neo-Grec." The
design scheme approached the tripartite formula.
For the R. H. White Warehouse Store (Fig. 14),
until its recent demolition Boston's most distinguished arcaded building, Peabody & Stearns
adapted the theme of the upper part of their bank

building to blocklike dimensions. The warehouse store was more unified, with careful proportioning, and in three distinct divisions. The McCormick Building by Burnham & Root of 1885/86; Richardson's Marshall Field Store, and especially the latest of his Ames buildings—the one built in 1886/87 on Harrison Avenue in Boston—and probably also Sullivan's Walker Warehouse of 1888/89, may be indebted to the R. H. White Store.[30]

Following the precedent of his own Long Island Historical Society, Post further elaborated the theme of superposed arcades on his mammoth New York Produce Exchange of 1881 to 1885 (Fig. 15) by doubling the rhythm as on the Cheney Block. The Exchange epitomized that peculiar combination of quasi-rational design and technological achievement for which the nineteenth century has so often been unfairly censured. The interior housed offices and an enormous, skylighted exchange room which rose to a height equal to five stories at the center aisle, one story more than the four-story arcades of the facades would lead one to anticipate. And the

15. New York Produce Exchange, intersection of White-
hall, Beaver and Stone Streets, N.Y.C., demolished. Post,
1881–1885. (Photo: Courtesy of The New-York Historical
Society.)

two-story arcades of the exterior described two tiers of offices surrounding the exchange room, not an open space two stories high as might be expected.[31] The interior iron framing is acknowledged as having been close to skeleton, or skyscraper, construction,[32] and it is now generally recognized that the Produce Exchange probably influenced the Marshall Field Store and also the Auditorium Building by Adler & Sullivan.

Arcades reached a height of five stories with the six-story factory (Fig. 16) by William A. Potter of 1882/83 at the corner of Mulberry and Grand streets[33]—hesitantly, however, because the reveals are shallow, and brownstone banding and profiled brick moldings below the fourth story impede the upward motion. Begun the same year and completed in 1884, McKim, Mead &

White's American Safe Deposit Company and Columbia Bank (Fig. 17) presented an alternative design mode: strongly accentuated, wide bays alternately projecting beyond the plane of the wall. The tripartite scheme was fully developed here, with the smoothly rusticated "base" comprising the two stories occupied by the banks. Stylistically, the building is comparable to the firm's Tiffany mansion of 1882 to 1885; both were Stanford White designs.[34] However, the bank had more of a Neo-Renaissance character, especially the attic story with loggias and flaring cornice.

Next in the sequence comes Babb, Cook & Willard's innovative Hanon & Son Building of 1884/85 (Fig. 18), a shoe factory.[35] The arcades were no taller than four stories, but contrary to

16. *186 Mulberry Street, N.Y.C., (ground story and cornice altered). William A. Potter, 1882/83. (Photo: Sarah B. Landau.)*

17. *American Safe Deposit Company and Columbia Bank, southeast corner, Fifth Avenue and 42nd Street, N.Y.C., demolished. McKim, Mead & White, 1882–1884. (Photo:* American Architect and Building News, *January 30, 1886.)*

which we have to consider."[36]

In about 1883 Chicago architects took up the arcade motif. In the 1870s, according to Hitchcock, and demonstrated by the examples discussed above, "Architectural leadership was still centered in Boston and New York. . . . If the Chicago architectural scene had any virtues around 1880 they were largely negative ones: no established traditions, no real professional leaders, and ignorance of all architectural styles past or present."[37] In his Borden Block of 1879/80 and Rothschild Store of 1880/81 Sullivan did not actually use arcading, but instead implied it with lunettes or arches over the windows of the floor just below the attic story. However, structure received considerable emphasis, through the opening up of the wall surface in the Borden Block and by means of strong piers in the Rothschild Store. The vertical is even more strongly accen-

the usual arrangement they began at ground level and articulated the lower half of the building rather than the upper portion. Widely spaced, heavy piers were set well forward of the wall planes, and, despite the presence of projecting stone bands and the termination of the arcades midway up the facades, the bays were stressed for the full height of the building, right through the arcaded parapet. This rather Roman-looking terminal feature also appears on the Duane Street warehouse. Russell Sturgis considered the Centre Street front "one of the most striking . . . and one of the most sincerely designed of all the warehouse buildings

18. *Hanon and Son Building, southeast corner, Centre and White Streets, N.Y.C., demolished. Babb, Cook & Willard, 1884/85. (Photo:* Architectural Record, *January, 1904, p. 9.)*

tuated in Sullivan's plainer Troescher Building of 1884, which was his first clearly tripartite design. The ground story was arcaded, and tall, widely spaced piers link the four stories of the midsection.

In 1884, two Chicago buildings incorporating four-story arcades began to rise: the Chicago Opera House by Cobb & Frost, where the arcade formed the third of four tiers, and the Insurance Exchange by Burnham & Root, also ten stories but layered in five tiers. In neither were the proportions entirely satisfactory or the arcades used to full potential. Three-story arcades capped the continuous piers of the extraordinarily skeletal, and tall, J. B. Mallers Building of 1884/85. This twelve-story masonry building was designed by John J. Flanders.[38] Evident to some degree in all these examples is a certain openness of the wall, in contrast to the heavier walls of contemporary

New York buildings. This difference did not reflect the alleged structural advancement of Chicago buildings—certainly none of those mentioned above had full metal frames—but resulted from the conservative nature of the New York Building Law which required thick walls. Even after skeleton construction was adopted in 1892, nonbearing walls were required to be increased in thickness in proportion to the building's height.[39] A sense of decorum, conditioned by architectural training in Paris and stylistic preferences, may also have played a role in preserving the heavy wall.

Commercial buildings with arcades, sometimes in double rhythm but no taller than four stories, did begin to multiply in Chicago in 1885, a year in which the quality of the Chicago work improved markedly. The famous and much imitated Marshall Field Wholesale Store was begun in 1885. On it Richardson repeated the superposed arcades of his Cheney Block and the early Ames Building of 1882/83 but in newly simplified form and with more assured proportions. He included a trabeated attic story, probably under the influence of the R. H. White Warehouse Store, and at the ground story substituted the segmental arches of his Equitable project for the monumental round arches over the lower stories of his previous commercial buildings. Burnham & Root's Rookery of 1885/86 has two tiers of tall arcades, and the same firm's seven-story McCormick Building, already mentioned, made effective use of a three-story arcade in the well-coordinated scheme of its facades.[40]

Meanwhile, in New York the utilitarian style of warehouse and factory buildings that so impressed Sturgis came to a climax in the handsome De Vinne Press building of 1885/86 by Babb, Cook & Willard (Fig. 19). Although several of the New York buildings discussed above, and perhaps Richardson's work, contributed to the formation of its seemingly elemental but highly sophisticated design, the De Vinne Press is quite original. The building was described by Homer Saint-Gaudens as "so clean-cut and essentially American as to win instant respect"; Sturgis declared that it "shows what this style is capable of" and noted its unexpected monumentality, while Hitchcock has designated it as "not altogether unworthy of comparison with the Field Store"[41]—high praise indeed. Segmental and round arches with deep reveals call attention to the massiveness of the brick walls. The terracotta decoration, spare but well placed and of high quality, consists of interlace-filled roundels with initials and the date of construction at either side of the main entrance, long, narrow quoins at the corners, and thin bands with Quattrocento-inspired designs running between the stories. The rhythms are skillfully varied from front to side, and each facade is individually framed by rows of windows and the quoins. An especially felicitous touch is the arcaded, pedimentlike gable of the main front, a resolution of the Duane Street and Hanon & Son parapets.

In comparison, the contemporary Puck Build-ing, a press building designed by Albert Wagner at 295 Lafayette Street, may seem uncontained and unnecessarily complex. However, the single, double, and triple rhythms of its arcades are har-nessed by heavy piers which divide the long, cagelike facades, greatly extended by Wagner's addition of 1892,[42] into distinct bays. Just a few blocks to the west and south, at 468–472 West Broadway, stands the old Marvin Safe Company Building (Fig. 20) designed by Oscar S. Teale and also constructed in 1885/86.[43] Its arcaded brick front with monumental three-story arches

and fine iron decoration recalls the Produce Ex-change especially, but also the Cheney Block project and the Hanon & Son Building. The iron panels with swag motif were surely inspired by the Produce Exchange. Following close on one another within the same year, the De Vinne, Puck, and Marvin Safe buildings illustrate the spread of a local commercial style best repre-sented by ordinary warehouses and factories and more aptly described as "Postian" than "Ri-chardsonian." A New York School had emerged.

For the Goelet Building of 1886/87 (Fig. 21), McKim, Mead & White repeated the dominant vertical theme of the firm's American Safe De-posit Company and Columbia Bank, using con-trasting colors of brick and terra-cotta to set off the windowed areas from the tan brick walls. Re-sponding to the window bays, a giant arcade forms an impressive two-story base apparently expressive of the structure, and the building rounds the corner smoothly with only the most subtle changes of pattern and color. The attic story (replaced in 1905 by a four-story addition) unified the design horizontally and functioned as the terminating layer of the tripartite scheme. It would be two years before Sullivan, with his ar-caded Walker Warehouse in Chicago, arrived at a comparably successful tripartite formula.

In 1887 arcades again reached a height of five stories, this time with no timidity whatsoever, in the nine-story Aldrich Court, later the Hamburg-American Building, by Youngs & Cable (Fig. 22). Begun in 1886 and extant until 1971,[44] this Lower Broadway building had arcades defining two bays of a section intended to resemble a tower. The Richardsonian treatment of the base, the five-story arcades, and the towerlike aspect may have influenced the design of Bradford Lee Gilbert's better-known Tower Building, which

21. *Goelet Building, 900 Broadway, N.Y.C. McKim, Mead & White, 1886/87. (Photo:* Building, *May 26, 1888, supplement.)*

22. *Aldrich Court (later Hamburg-American Line), 45 Broadway, N.Y.C., demolished. View shows the building with alterations to the top story of the left portion. Youngs & Cable, 1886/87. (Photo:* King's Views: New York, 1908–1909, *p. 17.)*

skeleton construction, the long-demolished Tower Building of 1888/89 (Fig. 24) made the most of its narrow 21.6-foot frontage.[47] The ingeniously designed, masonry-clad "tower" displayed slender, five-story arcades on its midsection reminiscent of fluting; the top two stories and high, tiled roof formed the last segment of a three-part composition that by now could be considered standard in New York. McKim, Mead & White's contemporary Judge Building (Fig. 25), commissioned by Robert and Ogden Goelet and built in 1888 to 1890, and now so altered as to be barely recog-

was constructed almost directly across the street two years later.

In 1887/88 John Jacob Astor built a strikingly skeletal warehouse (Fig. 23), designed by William Schickel & Company, in the SoHo section of New York.[45] The facades comprise broad bays defined by continuous brick piers and capped by thermal windows; effectively, these bays are five-story arcades. Decoration is confined to lush terra-cotta plaques in the spandrels of the arches and brick moldings on the cornice. Sills and lintels counterpoint the strong vertical thrust of the "arcades," and the piers correspond exactly to the rows of cast-iron columns supporting the floors inside. By the late 1880s the tall arcade had begun its ascent in New York but it would take skeleton construction and daring to stretch it higher than five stories.[46]

Credited as the very first example of complete

nizable, was not innovative in either construction or design but carried the style of Babb, Cook & Willard to greater lengths of decoration and detail.[48] Sturgis thought it "the most interesting example which is possible of the warehouse treated in a grandiose way, treated in a way to fit a Fifth Avenue corner."[49]

Post continued to explore the arcade theme sporadically in the late 1880s. His New York Times Building of 1888/89 is arcaded in quadruple rhythm; and the multilayered scheme he had helped to initiate with the Produce Exchange, now applied to a thirteen-story building with

taller proportions, is combined with the popular Richardsonian style. T. R. Jackson's old Times Building, utilized in the new construction,[50] helped determine the character of the first five stories. Post's inconsistency as a designer is readily apparent; for his twenty-six-story World or Pulitzer Building of 1889/90 he employed the layered palazzo scheme—confining the arcades to the individual layers—instead of using tall arcades or some other kind of vertical organization. Perhaps he elected the heavier, horizontal system because the building still had bearing walls. More pleasingly proportioned and organized with

24. Tower Building, 50 Broadway, N.Y.C., demolished. Bradford Lee Gilbert, 1888/89. (Photo: Courtesy of the Museum of the City of New York.)

25. Judge Building, 110–112 Fifth Avenue, N.Y.C. McKim, Mead & White, 1888/89. (Photo: Architectural Record, January 1904, p. 11.)

But it is worth reiterating that Post arrived at the combination long before Sullivan did, in his Marine Bank project of the early 1870s. Perhaps the distinction conferred on Post by Daniel Burnham, "father of the tall building in New York,"[52] ought to be simply "father of the tall building."

After 1890 buildings soared ever higher, and arcades grew incredibly tall, notably so in the work of Sullivan and his Chicago contemporaries. In 1891 Sullivan's tripartite Wainwright Building was completed in Saint Louis; there windows representing seven stories are mounted between tall piers. In the same year his towerlike fewer layers than his Times Building, his Union Trust Company Building of 1889/90 had five-story arcades on the shaft. Montgomery Schuyler cited it as the first example of the three-part or column formula, and Weisman considers it a key monument of "Phase IV," the tripartite phase in the history of the skyscraper.[51] However, the tripartite scheme, if not specifically the column formula, was in use considerably earlier in New York, although not consistently until about 1888. The opportunity to apply it and tall arcades to really tall buildings had to wait for the 1890s and the wide application of skeleton construction.

Schiller Building was begun with fourteen stories under arcades and a tripartite organization. Burnham & Root's Masonic Temple in Chicago, also started in 1891, was tripartite and had twelve stories under arcades. The ten-story arcades of Sullivan's Union Trust Company Building in Saint Louis of 1892/93 are repeated in his Guaranty Building in Buffalo where the Sullivanian formula reached perfection. Meanwhile, in New York, Post designed seven-story arcades— the tallest yet for him—for his fifteen-story Havemeyer Building of 1891/92. Post's arcades continued to grow throughout the 1890s, possibly under Sullivan's influence, reaching at the end of the decade the astonishing height of twenty-nine stories in a project for a tower addition to his Prudential Life Insurance Building in Newark.[53] His preference for the tripartite scheme, if not for arcading, remained fairly constant in keeping with the current fashion.

All through the 1890s, and even after 1900, arcaded buildings continued to flourish in New York. One of the finest is McKim, Mead & White's Cable Building, constructed for the Broadway and Seventh Avenue Railroad Company in 1892 to 1894 (Fig. 26). Its tall, arcuated base, tripartite

27. *U.S. Federal Building, 641 Washington Street, N.Y.C. W. J. Edbrooke et al., 1892–1899. (Photo: Sarah B. Landau.)*

organization, and distinctive corner treatment recall the Goelet Building, but this time the walls are almost skeletal, indicating the steel frame. The Renaissance styling and superposed arcades, well suited to the relatively low height and broad proportions, invoke, once again, the Produce Exchange. In contrast to the Goelet Building, which depends almost entirely on "constructional polychromy" for its decoration, the Cable Building displays a sculptural, "Roman" type of ornament representative of Stanford White's taste[54] and that of the period. When faced with the task of designing a nineteen-story tower in competi-

tion for the American Surety Building in 1893, McKim, Mead & White submitted a heavy-walled, six-layer design with banks of windows concentrated at the centers of the facades rather than one utilizing the skeletal treatment of the Cable Building. The thick walls mandated by the building code perhaps influenced the selection of the heavy French Classical style. For really tall buildings, which the firm does not seem to have built until after the turn of the century, McKim, Mead & White relied on the column metaphor as officially introduced by Post's Union Trust Building and Bruce Price's American Surety Building of 1894/95.[55]

In Henry-Russell Hitchcock's estimation, the U.S. Federal Building (Fig. 27) on Washington Street in New York is, "after the long-demolished Marshall Field Store, the finest arcaded building."[56] Begun in 1892 but not completed until seven years later, and only after four men had successively occupied the post of Supervising Architect of the U.S. Treasury, the building was originally an appraiser's store. Willoughby J. Edbrooke, Supervising Architect from 1891 to 1893, designed the lower two stories and perhaps also the rest of the exterior, but the latter cannot be proved.[57] The rhythms and detailing of the arcades, the battered ground story, and the massiveness of the ten-story block recall the Field Store and also the Harrison Avenue Ames Building. But the influence of the New York buildings—for example, the prototypal Produce Exchange, the De Vinne Press, and even the Judge Building—informs such features as the narrow, arcaded top story and rounded corners, as well as the whole aspect of this impressive building.

In summary: the design essentials associated with some of the best Chicago School work—specifically, arcading, verticality, and the tripartite scheme—were practiced much earlier in New York. By the mid-1880s a distinctive New York commercial style had crystalized and was available for the instruction of the Chicago architects.[58] New York's commercial buildings of the 1870s and 1880s provide the missing link between Philadelphia's of the 1850s and Sullivan's of the 1890s. And the finest New York examples more than rival Chicago's—so long regarded, with some exaggeration, as the major component of the late-nineteenth-century commercial style.

Notes

I am very grateful to Henry-Russell Hitchcock. He not only encouraged me to develop a section of my doctoral dissertation into this larger study but also offered valuable suggestions and criticisms during the preparation of my essay. And I would like to thank the students in his seminar on post-Civil War New York architecture held in the spring of 1979 at the Institute of Fine Arts, especially Leslie Ike and Julie Ann Kodmur. A New York University Faculty Research Grant awarded for the summer of 1978 helped make my researches possible.

1. Louis Sullivan, "The Tall Office Building Artistically Considered," *Lippincott's* 57 (March 1896): 408.
2. Hugh Morrison believed the analogy was prompted by the Wainwright Building, completed in 1891. See Morrison, *Louis Sullivan, Prophet of Modern Architecture* (New York, 1935), p. 155. Montgomery Schuyler applied it to Sullivan's buildings early in 1896: "Architecture in Chicago. Adler & Sullivan," in *Architectural Record*, Great American Architects Series (February 1896), pp. 29, 31, and passim.
3. Henry-Russell Hitchcock, *Architecture: Nineteenth and Twentieth Centuries*, 4th ed. (Harmondsworth, 1977), p. 344.
4. See, for example, Marcus Whiffen, *American Architecture Since 1780: A Guide to the Styles* (Cambridge, Mass., 1969), pp. 191–200; John J.-G. Blumenson, *Identifying American Architecture: A Pictorial Guide to Styles and Terms, 1600–1945* (Nashville, 1977), pp. 64–65; and Frank E. Przybycien, P.E., *Utica: A City Worth Saving* (Utica, n.d.), pp. 119–120.
5. H.-R. Hitchcock, *Architecture: Nineteenth and Twentieth Centuries*, p. 328, and *Rhode Island Architecture* (Providence, 1939; reprint ed., New York, 1968), pl. 38 (Bristol Hotel).
6. H.-R. Hitchcock, *Early Victorian Architecture in Britain* (New Haven, 1954; reprint ed., New York, 1972), 1: 401 and 578. Hitchcock has uncovered many pertinent English examples and has pointed out the similarities of several from the early 1870s to Richardson's Marshall Field Store and to Sullivan's work. See his "Victorian Monuments of Commerce," *Architectural Review* 105 (February 1949): 61–74; and also *Architecture: Nineteenth and Twentieth Centuries*, pp. 328–333; and *Early Victorian Architecture*, vol. 1, chapter 12, especially pp. 388–401.
7. *Journal of the Society of Architectural Historians* 20 (March 1961): 3 (hereafter cited as *JSAH*).
8. Ibid., p. 3.
9. The most frequently cited study of the genre is Carroll L. V. Meeks, "Romanesque Before Richardson in the United States," *Art Bulletin* 25 (March 1953): 17–33.
10. Such as the demolished House of Refuge on Randalls Island designed by Robert Griffith Hatfield and built 1852–1854. For an illustration, see New York City Common

Council, *Manual of the Corporation of the City of New York* (1860), p. 336.

11. Pointed out by Ellen W. Kramer in "Contemporary Descriptions of New York City and Its Public Architecture ca. 1850," *JSAH* 27 (December 1968): 279–280. Other banks with tall (two-story) arcades were Thomas & Son's Chemical Bank of 1849/50 at 270 Broadway and the Bank of New York designed by Vaux & Withers and built from 1856–1858 on the corner of Wall and William streets. See Winston Weisman, "Commercial Palaces of New York: 1845–1875," *Art Bulletin* 36 (December 1954): fig. 2; Kramer, p. 280; and Henry W. Domett, *A History of the Bank of New York, 1784–1884* (New York, 1884), pp. 93–94. The Bowen & McNamee Store of 1849/50 by Joseph C. Wells, formerly at 112–114 Broadway, was as vertically designed and as skeletal as some of the Philadephia examples cited by Weisman as influential for Sullivan; see Weisman, "Commercial Palaces," p. 290, and Kramer, pp. 271–272.

12. According to *Miller's New York As It Is; or Stranger's Guide-Book . . .* (New York, 1863), p. 54, the walls were light olive-colored Nova Scotia stone, and iron was included in the construction. Dates of construction and attribution to Jackson from Weisman, "Commercial Palaces," p. 295, n. 59.

13. The Tefft, Weller, & Co. Store is dated and attributed on good evidence to Kellum & Son by Weisman in "Commercial Palaces," p. 298. For the other examples cited, see Margot Gayle and Edmund V. Gillon, Jr., *Cast-Iron Architecture in New York* (New York, 1974), pp. 21, 28 and 3. No. 62-66 Thomas Street, a rare example in New York of a Gothic cast-iron front, has two tiers of two-story arcades. It has been dated as 1866/67 by Weisman in "Commercial Palaces," p. 310. See also elevation drawings of the I. M. Singer & Co. Building by G. H. Johnson, the Gilsey Building by John W. Ritch, and a design for an Odd Fellows Hall in Architectural Ironworks of New York, *Illustrations of Iron Architecture* (New York, 1865), pls. 4, 9, and 30. On the "sperm-candle style" see New York City Landmarks Preservation Commission, "SoHo–Cast Iron Historic District Designation Report" (New York, 1973), p. 11.

14. This front masks an older, Federal-period house. See Gayle and Gillon, *Cast-Iron Architecture*, p. 16.

15. To design a cast-iron front required little more than selecting components from a pattern book; and parts made from the same pattern could be, and were, repeated again and again. Peter B. Wight doubtless spoke for the many devotees of Ruskin when he denounced cast-iron buildings as "the greatest architectural monstrosities" and observed that "no single attempt has yet been made to adapt the construction and ornamentation of such buildings to the material used, unless we may except some shot towers and some buildings in which iron has been only partially used" (*The New Path*, September 1863, p. 55).

16. H.-R. Hitchcock, *The Architecture of H. H. Richardson and His Times*, rev. ed. (Hamden, Conn., 1961), p. 78. Hitchcock cites Guadet's Prix de Rome design of 1864 for a hospital in the Alps and the tall arcades on English buildings of the 1860s as probable sources for Richardson.

17. These and other Hunt drawings mentioned in this essay are in the Prints and Drawings Collection of the American Institute of Architects Foundation.

18. The building permit for the Western Union Building was filed on April 12, 1873 (NB 259-1873), but the docket states that the date of commencement was January 2, 1873 (New Building Docket Books, N.Y.C. Municipal Archives). The date of January 2 does not agree with the information given in George B. Post's first record book, p. 54 (The New-York Historical Society). There it is recorded that contracts for the foundations were let out in the fall of 1872, and the succession of those contracts indicates that the building actually was begun at that time. The backdating to January 2 was probably an attempt to cover up the fact that the permit was not filed at the proper time. Therefore the commencement date should be given as 1872 rather than 1873, as has been customary.

19. The walls of the Western Union Building were gridlike, representing an altogether different formula from the one under discussion. In his "A New View of Skyscraper History" in *The Rise of an American Architecture*, ed. Edgar Kaufmann, jr. (New York, 1970), Weisman analyzes the system of the Western Union Building (p. 127).

20. Cady's sources were most likely the Ruskinian commercial buildings of the 1850s and 1860s illustrated in the English architectural periodicals; but he may well have known Richardson's Equitable project or his Brattle Square Church, Boston (1870–1872), or even his competition design for Trinity Church in Boston of 1872. Hunt's fascination in these years with tall arcades is also evident in his competition designs of 1872 for the Western Union Building and in his cast-iron-fronted buildings of the early 1870s.

21. According to *Trow's New York City Directory* for 1870/71 and 1871/72, the bank moved in the interim. And at about this time it was designated as Long Island City's bank (*Evening Post*, May 7, 1884), possibly the explanation for its desire to build new, larger quarters. Unfortunately the bank did not build but took over a building already on the site and continued there until the crash of 1884 when it failed.

22. The other related design is the Troy Savings Bank of 1871–1873, where a tall arcade reflects a large music hall in the upper part of the building. Chickering Hall was at Fifth Avenue and 18th· Street. Weisman discusses these and specifies the elements that were influenced by Hunt, with whom Post studied from 1858 to 1860. See Weisman, "The Commercial Architecture of George B. Post," *JSAH* 31 (October 1972): 180–181.

23. According to the building permit, NB 593-1875, filed with

the N.Y.C. Dept. of Buildings, the owner was Andrew Sturges Thorp. Evidence from city directories and the Racquet Club archives indicates that the owner and the architect were brothers. Alfred Huidekoper Thorp was the partner of E. T. Potter for the Mark Twain House commission of 1873; see my *Edward T. and William A. Potter, American Victorian Architects* (New York/London, 1979), pp. 68–70, 317, and 322–324. Thorp's death date given there on page 68 as 1919 is incorrect. I have since determined from his will filed in the Surrogate Courthouse in New York City that he died in 1917. Thorp may have designed only one other significant building in New York, the Orient Mutual Insurance Building of 1877/78, formerly on Wall Street. He was not on the whole very productive. His design for the Union League Club competition of 1879 is another Florentine palazzo, this time with the windows grouped together vertically and a heavy corbeled cornice (*American Architect and Building News*, August 23, 1879).

24. The *Sun* (New York), June 21, 1876, p. 1. Other descriptions can be found in the *New York Times* of June 4, 1876 and the *Sun* of May 7, 1876. Although the club was not illustrated, it won favorable notice in the *American Architect and Building News* (May 12, 1877, p. 150).

25. See Hitchcock, *The Architecture of H. H. Richardson*, pp. 164–167. Richardson's Hayden Building in Boston has only a two-story arcade, but it precedes the Cheney Block commission by several months and is apparently the first of Richardson's buildings with the motif to be realized. See Cynthia Zaitzevsky, "A New Richardson Building," *JSAH* 32 (May 1973): 164–166.

26. Post was the winner of a competition held in 1877. According to the minutes of The Long Island Historical Society for January 8, 1881, he submitted three sets of "elevations and arrangements" before the building committee reached a decision on September 26, 1878. The New-York Historical Society holds preliminary drawings which show colonnettes flanking the windows and other differences from the building as constructed. See also Weisman, "The Commercial Architecture of George B. Post," pp. 184–185.

27. J. M. V. Viel and F. A. Cendrier, with engineer Alexis Barrault, designed the building, which was completed in 1854. See Alexis Barrault and G. Bridel, *Le Palais de L'Industrie et Ses Annexes* (Paris, 1857).

28. According to NB docket 634-1879. Born in New York City, George Fletcher Babb was established as an architect by 1861 and from about 1860 to 1865 was the junior member of the partnership of Foster (Nathaniel G.) & Babb. About 1868 he joined the office of Russell Sturgis as a draftsman and remained in Sturgis's employ for a number of years, probably until the mid-1870s. About 1879 he contracted a partnership with Walter Cook. About 1883 Daniel Wheelock Willard joined the firm which then became Babb, Cook & Willard. For information on the Babb partnerships before 1900, see Dennis Steadman Francis, *Architects in Prac-*

tice, New York City, 1840–1900 (Committee for the Preservation of Architectural Records, 1980), p. 12. And see also Peter B. Wight, "Reminiscences of Russell Sturgis," *Architectural Record* 26 (August, 1909): 124. Babb's birthplace and dates of birth and death were discovered by Mosette Glaser Broderick. According to the *Dictionary of American Biography* 4 (1953), p. 379, Cook "became the dominating factor" in the firm's work. He had studied with Vaudremer in Paris where he was admitted to the Ecole des Beaux-Arts in 1874. Afterward he studied at the Royal Polytechnic School in Munich, and he returned to the United States in 1877. Of interest is the fact that 173 Duane Street was built for Catharine Cook, surely a relative of Walter Cook. On Babb's relationship to the McKim, Mead & White firm, see below, n. 48.

29. "Recent Architecture in America. III. Commercial Buildings," *Century Magazine* 28 (August, 1884): 512–513.

30. Wheaton Holden, "The Peabody Touch: Peabody and Stearns of Boston, 1870–1917," *JSAH* 22 (May 1973): 125–127. See also James F. O'Gorman, "The Marshall Field Wholesale Store: Materials Toward a Monograph," *JSAH* 37 (October 1978): 191–192.

31. Van Rensselaer particularly deplored the incongruity of exterior design and interior arrangement: "Recent Architecture in America," pp. 519–520.

32. Carl W. Condit, *American Building* (Chicago, 1968), p. 116; and Weisman, "The Commercial Architecture of George B. Post," pp. 188–189.

33. Landau, *Edward T. and William A. Potter*, pp. 321–322 and 477.

34. According to Leland M. Roth, *The Architecture of McKim, Mead & White, 1870–1920* (New York, 1978), pp. 21 and 149. Hereafter the dates given for McKim, Mead & White's buildings and, if known, the names of their specific designers are taken from the above-cited source. See also Roth's "The Urban Architecture of McKim, Mead, and White: 1870–1910" (Ph.D. diss., Yale University, 1973), chs. 2, 3, and 5, where most of the firm's buildings discussed in this essay are analyzed in detail; and Roth's essay in *A Monograph of the Works of McKim, Mead & White 1879–1915* (1915; reprint ed., New York, 1977), pp. 33–34. The firm's house for Phillips and Lloyd Phoenix, which was contemporary with the American Safe Deposit Company and Columbia Bank, had its windows grouped similarly, in three's at the center of the facade. Roth observes that McKim, Mead & Bigelow's Benedict Apartment Building in New York of 1879–1882 has the tripartite division "as well as the quickened rhythm in the attic story . . . ", observable in the firm's later work ("Urban Architecture," p. 309).

35. Information from the building permit, NB 1546-1884.

36. "The Warehouse and the Factory in Architecture," *Architectural Record* 15 (January 1904): 8. Chances are the facades were no more expressive of the interior structure

than is that of 173 Duane Street.

37. *Architecture: Nineteenth and Twentieth Centuries*, pp. 336–337.

38. It is illustrated in the *Inland Architect and Builder* (July 1885), and see Carl W. Condit, *The Chicago School of Architecture* (Chicago, 1964), p. 59.

39. The law passed in 1892 prescribed 12-inch-thick curtain walls for the top 50 feet of a building. Thereafter, going downward, these walls had to increase in thickness by 4 inches, cumulatively, for every additional 50 feet. Thus, the walls of the lowest five stories of a twenty-story skeleton building would be approximately two feet thick, the walls of the next five stories would be approximately 20 inches thick, and so forth. Obviously this requirement influenced the size, number, and placement of windows. See William H. Birkmire, *Skeleton Construction in Buildings* (New York, 1894), pp. 13–16; Birkmire considered the 12-inch thickness to be adequate no matter how tall the building (p. 2).

40. The dates are close, but the McCormick Building apparently preceded the Field Store by a few months. See Donald Hoffmann, *The Architecture of John Wellborn Root* (Baltimore/London, 1973), pp. 45–46.

41. Homer Saint-Gaudens, ed., *The Reminiscences of Augustus Saint-Gaudens* (New York, 1913), p. 283; Sturgis, "The Warehouse and the Factory," p. 6; Hitchcock, *Architecture: Nineteenth and Twentieth Centuries*, p. 388.

42. Information from building permits NB 581-1885 and NB 36-1892. Wagner was also the architect of 267–271 Mulberry Street built in 1886/87 for Hawley & Hoops just south of the Puck Building (NB 361-1886). It is similar in appearance to the Puck Building, but has four stories under its principal arcade. The German-born Wagner emigrated to the United States in 1871. Before he opened his own office in New York in about 1880, he worked for A. B. Mullet in the office of the Supervising Architect of the U.S. Treasury and afterward for Leopold Eidlitz in New York. See *New York, the Metropolis* (New York, 1893), pt. I, pp. 255–256.

43. I am grateful to Françoise Bollack and Tom Killian for directing my attention to this remarkable building and also for supplying the information concerning its original owner, architect, and dates of construction (facts from NB docket 911-1885). The building extends through the block from West Broadway to Thompson Street (No. 138), where starkly plain arcades surmounted by rows of segmental-headed windows seem peculiarly modern. However, the Thompson Street facade is the result of later additions. Both Wagner and Teale seem to be totally forgotten, but the quality of their work, especially Teale's, suggests they deserve further study. The late Dennis Steadman Francis found material concerning Teale's extensive practice in New York and New Jersey and kindly informed me that Teale not only was a magician, but the designer of Houdini's tomb (1927) in Machpelah Cemetery in Cypress Hills, Glendale, New York City. Teale died in 1934 at the age of eighty-six.

44. Information from Block and Lot folder, Municipal Archives. The building was completed in December 1887 and sold to the Hamburg-American Line in 1907.

45. N.Y.C. Landmarks Preservation Commission, "SoHo Cast-Iron Report," p. 136. Mentioned in respect to its similarity to Chicago School work by Winston Weisman in his review of Condit's *The Chicago School of Architecture*, *JSAH* 26 (December 1967): 313, and also in his "The Chicago School of Architecture: A Symposium—Part I." The Chicago School Issue, *Prairie School Review* 9, no. 1 (1972): 23 (illus.). In the latter article Weisman argues against the validity of the term "Chicago School," calling instead for "a broader designation capable of embracing all examples" (pp. 22–23).

46. In 1888 the Brooklyn-born and New York-trained Solon S. Beman designed Grand Central Station in Chicago with a 250-foot clock tower articulated by tall arches, two on each face (as on Richardson's Allegheny County Courthouse tower), encompassing thirteen stories. The final design included only one tall arch on each side, and the station opened in 1890. See Folke T. Kihlstedt, "Grand Central Station, Chicago," *Prairie School Review* 11, no. 1 (1974): 5–19. Beman's Pioneer Press in St. Paul, also designed in 1888, had five-story arcades and was tripartite (*American Architect*, May 5, 1888). Minneapolis architect Leroy S. Buffington published a design for a twenty-eight-story skyscraper with eighteen-story arcades in the *Inland Architect and News Record*, July 1888, but it was not constructed. William LeBaron Jenney's proposal for the Hercules Manufacturing Building in Chicago, to have had nine stories under arcades, also remained unbuilt (*Inland Architect*, May 1889).

47. See *A History of Real Estate, Building, and Architecture in New York City* (1898; reprint ed., New York, 1967), pp. 467–471; and Montgomery Schuyler, "The Evolution of the Skyscraper," *Scribner's Magazine* 46 (September 1909): 257–271, and reprinted in William H. Jordy and Ralph Coe, ed., *American Architecture and Other Writings by Montgomery Schuyler* (Cambridge, Mass., 1961), 2: 419–436. According to *A History of Real Estate*, p. 471, the second New York building with skeleton construction was the Lancashire Insurance Company Building of 1889/90 by J. C. Cady & Co.; and the third was Youngs & Cable's Columbia Building of 1890/91. Neither is extant.

48. Babb was very close to the members of the McKim, Mead & White firm and actually worked in the firm's office in January 1880, according to Charles Moore, *The Life and Times of Charles Follen McKim* (1929; reprint ed., New York, 1970), p. 327. According to Charles C. Baldwin, *Stanford White* (New York, 1931), p. 111, Mead worked

directly under Babb's instruction in Sturgis's office. On several occasions Babb worked in close collaboration with the firm, notably in the instance of Babb, Cook & Willard's Turner Building in Newburgh, New York, which was intended to complement McKim, Mead & White's YMCA building of 1882–1884 next door. See Clarence Cook, ed., "Seed in Stony Places," *The Studio*, n.s., no. 3 (September 13, 1884), p. 27, where the Newburgh buildings are compared. I owe the reference to Cook's article to Dennis Steadman Francis, and I am grateful to Mosette Glaser Broderick for sharing with me her knowledge of Babb.

49. "The Warehouse and the Factory," p. 10. This article, which is continued in the February 1904 issue of the *Architectural Record*, includes numerous later examples of related buildings in New York.

50. Alteration docket 102-1888 (Alteration Docket Books, Municipal Archives), and Moses King, ed., *King's Handbook of New York City*, 2d ed. (Boston, 1893), p. 618. Lynn Shapiro, a student in my Spring 1981 seminar, discovered that Post's building is listed as an alteration.

51. Schuyler, "The Skyscraper Up-to-Date," *Architectural Record* 8 (January–March 1899): 233–234; and Weisman, "A New View of Skyscraper History," pp. 119, 136, and 158.

52. Quoted in Francisco Mujica, *History of the Skyscraper* (Paris, 1929), 2: 22.

53. See Weisman, "The Commercial Architecture of George B. Post," p. 198.

54. According to Baldwin, *Stanford White*, p. 320, White designed the building. NB docket 129-1892 specifies steel timbers and steel girders.

55. For photographs of this design and the firm's American Surety project see Roth, *The Architecture of McKim, Mead & White*, figs. 405 and 64.

56. Conversation with the author on January 21, 1980.

57. Marjorie Pearson, memo of June 9, 1977, appended to the N.Y.C. Landmarks Preservation Commission's designation report on the Federal Building (1966), and also reported in her talk on the building presented to the New York Chapter of the Society of Architectural Historians on May 9, 1979. Edbrooke was a Chicago architect.

58. In his autobiography, Sullivan recalls visits to New York in 1873, when he saw Richard Morris Hunt, and again in the summer of 1874 en route to France (*The Autobiography of an Idea* [New York, 1922], pp. 190 and 213). Sullivan surely came again on other occasions after he was established in practice and before the Bayard Building commission of 1897. His failure to mention New York buildings in his autobiography is probably not significant for he mentions very few buildings there; and in later years he developed a marked antipathy toward New York's office buildings, no doubt related to his prejudice against the eclecticism and Beaux-Arts Classicism generated by the Columbian Exposition. See Louis Sullivan, "An Office Building," *Kindergarten Chats and Other Writings* (New York, 1947; reprint ed., 1968), pp. 75–79.

H.H. RICHARDSON'S YOUTH: SOME UNPUBLISHED DOCUMENTS

John Coolidge

THE FRIENDS OF H. H. RICHARDSON enjoyed writing about him. Indeed, his early death occasioned an outpouring of appreciation that culminated in Marianna Griswold van Rensselaer's excellent biography.[1] What she wrote has always seemed so definitive that there has been almost no further research on his personal, as distinct from his professional, life. But the man was singularly uncommunicative about himself, and his contemporaries were restrained by Victorian reticence. So the publication of new documents, even when they solve no major problems, may at least relieve some of our curiosity.

THE APPLICATION TO WEST POINT[2]

Richardson was born September 29, 1838, on the sugar plantation of his maternal grandfather William Priestley. The future architect grew up in New Orleans where his father, Henry Dickenson Richardson, a somewhat shadowy figure, was a cotton broker. Mrs. van Rensselaer writes that Richardson senior was an "intimate friend" of Judah P. Benjamin, a senator from Louisiana in the 1850s, later "the brains of the confederacy," and ultimately a distinguished London barrister.

> *Washington 18th May 1854*
> Honble *Jeff. Davis*
> *Secretary of War*
> *Sir*
> I have the honor to enclose herewith an application in behalf of Henry D. Richardson to the military academy at West Point—& to beg that young Richardson's name may be duly registered on the list of applicants in the Department—
>
> *Resp^t yr obt s^t*
> *J. P. Benjamin*

> *New Orleans. May 10th, 1854*
> Honble *Jefferson Davis*
> *Washington City, D.C.*
>
> *Sir*
> I desire, if possible, to obtain admission to the Military Academy at West Point for my son Henry H. Richardson—He is a permanent resident of the city of New Orleans in the second Congressional district of the State, is five feet high and will be sixteen years old on the 29th of September next (1854)—
> I have before me a printed copy of the regulations relative to the admission of Cadets into the Military Academy and can confidently affirm that he is in every respect qualified to enter that institution should he be fortunate enough to obtain the nomination.
> For the past seven years he has enjoyed all the advantages of one of the best private schools in our city where he has acquired a knowledge of the usual branches of an English education, Algebra, French, Latin, and some little Greek &c.
> His present studies in French and Mathematics are the same as those prescribed for the first years course at the Academy—He has reached the 8th Chapter in Davies' Bourdon and as far as the 6th Book of Davies' Legendre—He has a good knowledge of French and can speak it with tolerable facility.
> I enclose a certificate from his teacher and trust this application will meet with a favorable consideration.
>
> I am, Sir, very respectfully
> Your obt. Sert.
> H. D. Richardson

New Orleans. May 9, 1854.

To the Hon. Jefferson Davis
Secretary of War
D.C.

Sir,

Learning that Master Henry H. Richardson is about to become an applicant for admission into the U.S. Military Academy I beg leave herewith to present the following certificate as to his character and qualifications.

Henry H. Richardson, oldest son of H. D. Richardson Esq. of New Orleans, and admitted as a pupil into my School on the 1st Nov. 1847, at the age of nine years and has continued in regular attendance ever since, with the exception of temporary absences during a portion of the summer months.

During all that time I have found him uniformly correct in his deportment and assiduous in his Studies as evidence of which I have not once had occasion to resort to physical coercion.

He is entirely free from the vices too common among boys in our cities and larger towns, and I have never known him to be guilty of falsehood or equivocation, or the use of profane or indecorous language.

He is a boy of much more than ordinary mental capacity, especially for Mathematical Studies, in which department I consider him the most promising pupil I ever had under my care.

In addition to the required literary qualifications in which I think he will be found well versed, he is, for a boy of his age, a fair Latin scholar, being thoroughly grounded in the forms and principles of construction and having read Cornelius Nepos, Caesar, and Virgil—has commenced the Greek—has finished Emerson's Third Arithmetic, Davies' Elementary Algebra, Davies' Bourdon as far as Chapter 8th—the first six books of Bourdon's Legendre's Geometry—and has a good general knowledge of Geography & History.

To the best of my knowledge he has no physical defect which would in the least impair his qualifications.

He has a sound constitution and has uniformly enjoyed good. Health. He is of the nervous bilious temperament with dark hair and eyes, spirited expression of countenance and finely formed head—of good stature and proportions. I have found him ambitious of distinction, easily enkindled by motives of emulation, steady and persevering in the pursuit of an object. In the qualities of generosity and courage he is surpassed by few boys of his age. And should he have the good fortune to be admitted into the noble Institution provided by our Government for the Military Education & training of our gallant youth, I have no doubt he will do credit to himself and honor to his country.

I have the honor to be, Sir, very respectfully

Your Obedient Servant
G. Blackman
Principal of a Classical Academy, New Orleans.

HARVARD AND RICHARDSON'S ACADEMIC CAREER

The Army turned down Richardson's application; we do not know why. Mrs. van Rensselaer believed "an impediment in his speech rendered him unfit for military service."[3] Richardson senior died in Philadelphia that same summer. His son spent the following year in New Orleans at the University of Louisiana (now familiarly known as Tulane) and in the autumn of 1855 went to Cambridge, Massachusetts, with the intention of entering Harvard. But he was backward in classics and instead had to enter a cramming school run by Reginald Heber Chase and Thomas Chase. Reginald was also a resident tutor in Latin at Harvard. Perhaps because of this happy combination of activities, the Harvard College Faculty voted on February 28, 1855 that Richardson, along with six other students, should be admitted at once into the freshman class.[4]

Nonetheless, six months later, on July 7, 1856, the Faculty "Voted Richardson required to study in vacation at least 500 lines of Agamemmnon, 3 weeks, 4 times a week," and the following September 22, "condition modified: to recite to a tutor thrice a week for six weeks."[5] Almost two-thirds of Richardson's course of study at Harvard was devoted to Greek, Latin, and mathematics.

"These were days of carelessness and plenty," wrote his close friend, the Right Reverend Phillips Brooks. The "seriousness of life" had laid hold upon him less even than it does upon most college men. Some interest in mathematics as a special study seems to be all that is remembered as the slightest prophecy of what was to come later."[6] Even in mathematics Richardson was not among the top sixth of his class. Richardson was "admonished" by formal votes of the Faculty on no less than sixteen occasions, a good many times for recitations missed and a truly astonishing number for cutting obligatory religious services.[7] Students were permitted ten absences a term; between January and June of his senior year Richardson was admonished for being caught absent from prayers forty times! "There was nothing spiritual about him," declared Mrs. van Rensselaer in one of the understatements of all time; Phillips Brooks agreed.[8]

HARVARD AND RICHARDSON'S SOCIAL CAREER

But, as his college mate and close friend Henry Adams wrote later, "A student like H. H. Richardson, who came from far away New Orleans, and had his career before him to chase, rather than to guide might make valuable friendships at college."[9] One opportunity for forming friendships was provided by the handful of clubs, and the innumerable "societies," literary, religious, or scientific. These, and these alone, brought together men of common interests from different college years. Otherwise Harvard strictly segregated its undergraduates, class by college class.

We know that Richardson belonged to three organizations, the Hasty Pudding Club, the Porcellian Club, and the Pierian Sodality. However, the surviving records of the Hasty Pudding and the Porcellian contain no mention of him.[10] Not so the Pierian Sodality, the college musical club. Almost half a century old, it had only a couple of members by the early 1850s. Then the energy of two or three of Richardson's contemporaries revived it. What he was expected to contribute, beyond playing second flute, is suggested by the official description of his initiation:

Owing to the disordered state of our rooms, the Sodality met this evening at the apartment of the Secretary to install Mr. Richardson of the sophmore class.

The exercises were somewhat brief and *decidedly informal* everyone being quite alive to the prospect of a good supper and a jolly time at Parker's.

It would be useless for me to attempt a description of Mr. Richardson's entertainment. Abounding in everything that the most fastidious Pierian could ask and unsparingly moistened with Parker's choicest brand of wine, we do not hesitate to say that the Sodality has never seen a better supper. In fact, how could it be otherwise with so notorious a connoisseur as Mr. R. to do the polite. His generous hospitality has long ago secured him the name of a jolly good fellow among his own classmates, and we venture to say the Pierian will readily acquiesce in that opinion.

The festivities were protracted till quite a late hour and most reluctantly did we leave that pleasant room to catch the last car for Cambridge.[11]

But, dining and wining were only what Richardson liked second best (as Calvin Coolidge said of shaking hands). The Sodality were to give their first public performance in the chapel on May 5, 1857. The day before, after a most successful dress rehearsal, they went back to their rooms for a gala party:

Not a Pierian was there that did not immortalize himself. Last but not least, bro. Richardson signalized himself in a remarkable degree in having on the night of May the 4th 1857 left the rooms of the Pierian Sodality at an early hour, in a state of *perfect sobriety* at once affording a most obvious illustration of *feminine influence* and exhibiting those sterling virtues moral courage & self denial in such glowing colors that Pierians of the next century will look back on the name of Richardson with profound respect and admiration.[12]

Even Richardson's younger brother William declared "he was fond of ladies' society."[13] Of this aspect of Richardson's life at Harvard we know only (as will appear shortly) that by February 1859 he was already engaged or at least deeply attached to his future wife, Julia Hayden. His family were aware of this, and his younger brother William, who was later, and briefly, a Harvard undergraduate, seems to have been acquainted with her brothers David (Richardson's classmate) and John.

Meanwhile, his widowed mother had married John D. Bein, who ran a hardware store in partnership with her brother, William Priestley II. Other sides of Richardson's youthful personality are revealed by a letter his stepfather wrote to Harvard's President Walker:

New Orleans, 5th May 1857

Jas. Walker, Esq.
President
Harvard University
Dear Sir,

My stepson Mr. Henry Hobson Richardson is now and has been for some time a student in the University you preside over, his mother is very anxious to here [sic] of him through you, if it is not asking too much, how he is coming on in his studies, & how his behavior is generally, her reason for wanting me to put these questions are simply these, Henry in the first place has not written his mother since the 31st of last January and has of late been much too lavish with the money that has been remitted him, not that she thinks, for a moment, that he either Gambles or drinks, but that he spends a great deal too much money is certain, how it goes she is at a loss to know, very great extravagance in dress is one of the causes, and I rather think that Horses is another, so, my dear sir, on account of his mother particularly, as well as myself, give him the first opportunity you can get a good lecture which I know you are able and willing to do, shame him a little for neglecting a mother who has always been so kind to him & never yet refused him whatsoever he might ask for, make him write, it is his duty to do so, he certainly is showing a very poor example to his younger Brother who is now at Taunton Mass. In charge of Dr. Wheelwright preparing for the sophmore year at Harvard. [A long encomium on that brother, William Richardson, follows.]

John D. Bein[14]

THE CHOICE OF ARCHITECTURE

When and why did Richardson decide to become an architect? At the time of his death nobody knew; nobody knows today.[15] The first record of that decision is the following letter:

New Orleans 25th Fby 1859

My dear Henry

I have not had this pleasure for some time. I have been so much engaged in business that when I get home, I feel tired enough to go to bed. I for some time past have been thinking seariously regarding your future prospects, & have talked a great deal, with those competant to Judge & all appear to be of one opinion, that a good Architect, if he is industrious, Cannot help but Succeed, & in order before you come out to New Orleans to pursue the Architectural business, I have thought that Six or Nine Months in London & Paris, where you will have full scope for your Instruments(?) in Drawing, will do you more good than three times the time spent in N.O. I have Conversed with many on the Subject, & all are of the same opinion, that it will be of great Serivce to you. I want you to consult with your friends in Boston & Cambridge, & see what their opinion is, After making every inquiry write me fully on the Subject, so that I can make arrangements for your departure, if you go in June next. An other thought, as I am on that subject, is this. You know how I have had to Struggle in business for the last Two Years, & the
very large amt I have lost, & I am still behind hand, with some but hope before next Jany to have all Square again, therefore economy, must be your watch word, if you go, you can live in either London or Paris at a very Moderate expence, or you can spend a Fortune, all I aim at is to give you such an Education, as your Father, would have done had he been spared, & I have too good an opinion of you to think that you would abuse the confidance I put in you. I know your aim will be to study & get to the top of the Ladder, & not to spend money Recklessly (?).

I do not know how Julia will like this step, but I have to good an opinion of her, to Think for a moment that she will through Cold Water on it, on the Contrary I think she will encourage it, give her my warmest regards. Your Mother does not know what to think of your going away; still she thinks that it is all for the best, All send love to you

Your Father (step-father)

John D Bein

P.S. Mr Barney (?) has been here, & spent several days in the City, we all did our best to make his Visit an agreeable one, which I have no doubt he will tell you, he appeared to go away with regret. JDB.[16]

Richardson did leave for Europe upon graduating from Harvard and traveled in England during the summer of 1859. By November he was in Paris where he brashly attempted to enroll at once in the Ecole des Beaux-Arts. Refused admission, he joined the *atelier* of Jules André and was accepted into the Ecole a year later. This suggests that even before leaving America Richardson had made up his mind to get his training in Paris, and was planning to stay there for years rather than months. Presumably he had consulted his friends in Boston and Cambridge.

RICHARDSON AND HIS FAMILY
IN NEW ORLEANS

When Richardson returned to America in October 1865 he settled first in Brooklyn and had difficulty getting started. Although he was devoted to his mother, he never returned to New Orleans. But his relation to his brother William remained cordial, as this letter to him from William testifies:

New Orleans July 5th 1865.

Dear Fez,

It is now 10.30 P.M. The mother & the girls have just Kissed me and gone to bed, and at the same time, knowing of my intention to write to your dear self gave an extra Kiss to be sent to you.

This is my sixth week at home, and O Fez! I have so longed for you to enjoy them with me. While in the army I never allowed my thoughts to dwell on the pleasures I have realized since my return; so many had been taken from my side, that, naturally, I thought my turn too would come.

The most just cause, sword was ever drawn for, has failed, and we have become unwilling subjects of the worst despotism the world ever saw.

Our terms of surrender, under the circumstances, were all we could have asked for, and our treatment since has given us nothing to complain of. All this has been from soldier to soldier; we have not yet been made to feel we are a subjugated people, but one can see all this in the not far distant future, and O! it is a terrible thought. It shames me to confess it, but we have brought this destruction down on our own heads: we live today a self-subjugated people; two thirds of the Southern people deserve even a worse fate if such can be. This is to those who have "stood" to their

colors a proud satisfaction, and one that even our enemies grant us—that had our armies been properly supported our efforts would have met with success.

My whole heart was in our couse [sic] and the result has cost me a sore trial, and blighted my fairest hopes. Hite Hayden has been here, & is still in town. He was received, for your sake, as, cordially, as if we had both served in the same army—he was invited to dinner but on account of sickness could not come. Hite is the same old fellow, and we all feel the same towards him but of course in these times, it may be the couse of some feeling receiving him, at all times as of old, our visitors, at present being numerous, and only of the vilest class of rebels; in consequence I had to have a pretty plain talk with him, all of which he seemed very sensibly to understand the propriety of & act on—i.e. I advised him, on "calling", to select the morning, when there would be less chance of his meeting those with whom any awkwardness might be occasioned. He has been sociable and encouraged to be more so. Although Julia is in debt to Sis, she has not received a letter since my arrival. We are very anxious to hear from her. Through Hite we were glad to hear of John's safety.

Sis has received a letter from and written to you since my return. Your letter, to me, bespoke good spirits, a blessing which I trust you may ever enjoy and one considered by me, of great importance towards success in this life.

My prospects are not very cheerful now, but in that respect I am like a thousand others. I have uninterrupted health and when business sets in that in itself will guarantee a livelyhood; besides I have several openings to hope for in the fall, one, with Hewitt, Norton & Co., another with Uncle Camden, either of which will be all I ask for—a start. That's what is wanting; give me a start, and I'll promise to do the rest, especially with such an incentive as our dear Mother & sisters to support.

We all look to you for grand things[.] I give you five years to stand at the head of your profession. Your friends Harrod & Olivier amongst others make frequent enquiries about you, and wish for your return in our midst. Kittie B (or Duc) & Sarah Dudley send seperate love. I can now add all the rest. Hugh has been down with his wife, (a charming woman), but has returned to Clinton, Miss. taking sister Rosy & Frannie with them. this leaves us quite a small family, only our own—if you, dear Nana & Uncle were here we would be complete. Have you seen G. Norton? I wrote you a letter by him enclosing a photograph . . . [17]

William Priestley Richardson—"Billy Rich"—was a very attractive man. Somewhat restless, he moved from job to job, eventually in 1884 being employed as the agent in New Orleans of the Pacific Guano Company of Boston, representing Glidden & Curtis. It is tempting to suppose that the architect may have had a hand in obtaining this position for him. William's continuing affection for the Boston branch of the family is demonstrated by the fact that he named the ninth of his ten children after the architect's wife, Julia Hayden Richardson. [18]

Notes

I wish to express to the staff of the Harvard Archives my profound gratitude for their unfailing courtesy and imaginative helpfulness. Original spellings in unpublished material have been retained.

1. Marianna Griswold Van Rensselaer (Mrs. Schuyler), *Henry Hobson Richardson and His Works* (Boston, 1888; reduced facsimile, New York, 1969), hereafter cited as V.R.
2. I wish to express my gratitude to Stanley P. Tozzeschi, Chief, U.S.M.A. Archives, West Point, who kindly supplied me with photocopies of Benjamin's, Richardson's, and Blackman's letters to Davis. These documents are from frames 1679–85, roll 196 of the National Archives publication 688, U.S.M.A. Cadet Application papers.
3. I am grateful to Michael P. Musick of the Navy and Old Army Branch of the Military Archives Division of the National Archives and Records Service who, at my request, kindly searched series 206, 234, and 249 of Record Group 94, Records of the Adjutant General's Office. Mr. Musick could find no documents explaining why the Army turned down Richardson's application to West Point. Since Richardson's stammer was conspicuous, I see no easy way of explaining Blackman's statement above—"he has no physical defect." V.R., p. 4.
4. Harvard Faculty Records, p. 34; February 28, 1856.
5. Ibid., p. 63, July 7, 1856, and p. 81, September 22, 1856.
6. Phillips Brooks, "Henry Hobson Richardson," *The Harvard Monthly*, III, no. 1, p. 2.
7. *Faculty Records*. There is an admirable card index of references by the name of the student in the Harvard Archives.
8. Ibid., p. 2., and V.R. p. 37.
9. Henry Adams, *The Education of Henry Adams* (Boston, 1918), p. 64.
10. The records of the Hasty Pudding are in the Harvard Archives. The records of the Porcellian are retained by the club but were searched for me by a member to whom I am most grateful.
11. *Records of the Pierian Sodality*, 1852–1867, in the Harvard Archives, p. 59; the date was March 5, 1857. Parker's is the present day Parker House.
12. Ibid., p. 74.
13. V.R. p. 4.
14. Harvard Corporation Papers, 1857, May 5.
15. Brooks, op. cit., p. 2.
16. Copies of this and the following letter were supplied to me by the late Joseph Richardson, the architect's grandson. I am grateful to him both for the documents and for permission to publish them; I do not know where the originals are. "Julia" was Julia Hayden. I cannot identify Mr. Barney.
17. "Fez" was the family's nickname for the architect. "Hite" was Richardson's classmate and Julia's brother, David Hyslop Hayden. "Sis" is the Richardsons' sister, Mrs. J. W. Labouisse. John is Julia's brother John. The remaining individuals have not been identified. The letter is fragmentary.
18. For William Priestley Richardson, see *Report of the Secretary of the Class of 1863 of Harvard College* (Cambridge, 1888), and *Class of 1863 Memoirs* (Cambridge, 1911).

THE EARLY WORK OF
JOSEPH LYMAN SILSBEE

Thomas J. McCormick

HENRY-RUSSELL HITCHCOCK'S MAjor monograph on Frank Lloyd Wright, *In the Nature of Materials: the Buildings of Frank Lloyd Wright, 1887–1941,* published in 1942, was probably the first study to comment on the importance of the architect Joseph Lyman Silsbee as Wright's first employer in Chicago during the years 1887 and 1888. Hitchcock characterized Silsbee's work as Suburban Richardsonian and Queen Anne and made a preliminary assessment of Silsbee's influence on Wright.[1] Two years later, Hitchcock singled out the Colonial Revival elements in Silsbee's architecture as they appeared in Wright's early designs.[2] Following Hitchcock's lead, every later study of Wright, particularly those by Grant Carpenter Manson and Vincent Scully, has taken Silsbee's work and influence into account.[3] Wright's own comments on Silsbee ("he had style . . . how that man can draw . . . I adored him") appeared in his autobiography, published in 1943, a year after Hitchcock's monograph.[4] Wright was unquestionably the most important architect to have worked with Silsbee, but research in recent years has shown that two other notable architects of the Prairie School, George Maher and George Grant Elmslie, were fellow draftsmen in Silsbee's office with Wright in 1887,[5] further evidence of Silsbee's importance as a teacher and of his influence on midwestern architecture.

There is no doubt that Silsbee's greatest significance in the history of architecture is his relationship to Frank Lloyd Wright, which causes us to look at his buildings from that point of view. Silsbee's career as a whole has been neglected. The only study of his work is one limited to his first fifteen years in Chicago (1882 to 1897, which includes the period of Wright's employ-

ment) by Susan Karr Sorell.[6] This sensitive assessment is the most complete one we have of his mature work. She suggests that Silsbee probably did not introduce the Shingle Style into the Midwest, as tentatively put forth by Hitchcock and followed by others,[7] nor that he was necessarily the pioneer in the use of the Colonial Revival style, which Manson implies.[8] Susan Karr Sorell carefully analyzes the architect's great volume of work published during these years, dividing it into time periods according to their dominant style—Queen Anne, Shingle, Colonial Revival (with an occasional Romanesque detail), and Eclectic. Most important of all is the exhaustive catalogue of Silsbee's work documented by newspaper and periodical references from 1882, when she deduces he arrived in Chicago,[9] until 1897, when his work declined in quality and was no longer published.

Oddly enough, Susan Karr Sorell omits one of Silsbee's favorite works during these years, the Moving Sidewalk at the World's Fair of 1893 (Figs. 1, 2). As far as I know, no writer since the time of the fair has commented on it. In 1894 Silsbee wrote in the Twenty-fifth Anniversary Report of the Harvard Class of 1869:

> My only other hobby (other than my children) that is worthy of mention is the moving sidewalk which was in use at the World's Fair and for which a medal was awarded there. I have since received the Edward Longstreet medal from the Franklin Institute for this as one of the two inventors of the system, which will in all probability be in practical use both in Chicago and New York within a year.[10]

During the early stages of the construction of the fair in Jackson Park, a working model of this unusual structure was placed between the Illinois and Women's buildings. It was intended to provide a means of transportation to the various buildings of the widely spread-out fair. However, the push-chair interests complained and when executed it was relegated to a 2,500-foot pier which jutted into Lake Michigan and was located directly behind the Peristyle opposite the Administration Building (Fig. 1). It consisted of 315 cars, with seats for 5,610 people (at five cents a seat) joined together in a continuous chain shaped with enlarged circles at each end (Fig. 2). This chain of cars was placed on a track whose platform concealed the propelling power of ten streetcar motors with the wires and trolleys beneath, allowing some of the cars to move at three miles per hour and the rest at six.[11] This fascinating structure reveals a more practical side of Silsbee than previously known, but the idea of the sidewalk does not seem to have caught on as he hoped, although it is a forerunner of the moving platforms of today.

Silsbee's later years after 1897 have always been a mystery, but he continued to practice.[12] His son Ralph was associated with him in the office at 115 Dearborn Street from 1907 to 1911,[13] but little is known of his work during these years. The house he designed for his

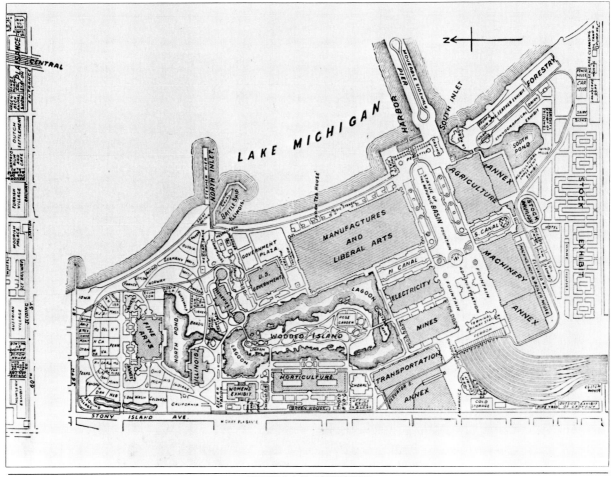

daughter Margaret (Mrs. Frank Wade) of 7 Brattle Road in Syracuse, New York, dates from these years. It is a large symmetrical Georgian house with a hip roof.[14] His last work is the only one we know much about, for it is mentioned in the memorial read after his death by Harvard classmate Gardner Goodrich Willard and repeated in the Fiftieth Anniversary report of his Harvard class.

> At the time of his death he was in charge of the building of a magnificent residence—a king's palace it may properly be called—at Vermejo Park near Trinidad, New Mexico to cost when all completed with its extensive additions and outhouses in the neighborhood of half a million dollars.[15]

While one should make allowances for the hyperbole of this description of a work by a departed classmate, it does indicate that Silsbee

was still practicing when he was sixty-five, presumably in the eclectic style he had adopted in the early 1890s.

The above discussion made no mention of Silsbee's training or earlier achitectural career in the East. Not surprisingly, it was only Hitchcock who briefly discussed Silsbee's pre-Chicago work in New York State, particularly Syracuse, which he characterized as "in no way exceptional . . . a confused Queen Anne like that of his Chicago contemporaries."[16] While it is to be hoped that this article may slightly modify Hitchcock's description, this study would never have been undertaken had it not been for the writings and encouragement of Professor Hitchcock.[17] Such a work seems a most appropriate one for a volume dedicated to the pioneer of Silsbee research—who, incidentally, is distantly related to the architect.[18]

Joseph Lyman Silsbee, a descendant of generations of distinguished New Englanders and member of a well-known Salem family, was born in Salem, Massachusetts, on November 25, 1848, the son of William and Charlotte Lyman Silsbee, the latter from Northampton, Massachusetts.[19] His mother died shortly after his birth, and Joseph spent his early years in Salem; in 1859, he went to live in Northampton where his father had been the minister of the Unitarian church since 1855. Presumably Joseph was looked after by his mother's relatives, the Lymans, a prominent local family. Unitarianism was to play a major role in his life. It may explain his settling in Syracuse in 1873, and Hitchcock suggests that it may also have been the reason for his move to Chicago, where he received the commission to design All Souls Church for Jenkins Lloyd Jones; this in turn led to his hiring Jones's nephew, Frank Lloyd Wright.[20]

In keeping with his New England background, Silsbee was educated at Phillips Exeter Academy and at Harvard, where he rowed on the Charles River in his spare time and graduated in 1869. Even then he is described as a born gentleman, preferring the amenities of life.[21] He spent the year following graduation taking special studies in architecture at the Massachusetts Institute of Technology as a member of the junior class, and during 1870/71 he worked for the Boston firms of Ware & Van Brunt and William Ralph Emerson, then in partnership with Carl Fehmer.[22] At this time he may have been involved in the design and building of Van Brunt's First Church, on Marlborough Street at Berkeley,[23] or possibly in the final revisions of the design for Memorial Hall at Harvard. It is also tempting to think that he first became aware of the possibilities of wooden architecture during his time with Emerson &

Fehmer, who had just built the M. H. Sanford House in Newport in Stick Style with a mansard roof.[24] Silsbee spent much of 1872 and 1873 traveling in Europe and sketching; according to family tradition, he was in the company of John Singer Sargent, but there is no evidence that the two men actually met.[25]

Upon his return from Europe sometime in 1873 he moved to Syracuse and became associated with the local architect Horatio Nelson White,[26] who worked in a variety of midcentury Renaissance-Italianate and Second Empire styles. That same year he was named Professor of Architecture in the College of Fine Arts at Syracuse University, which had been founded in 1870.[27] This position was an unpaid one and cannot be the reason for his moving to Syracuse in the first place. He held his teaching position until 1878 when, presumably, the pressure of his architectural career left him little time for other activities. It is also possible, although there is as yet no evidence to substantiate it, that he may have been attracted to Syracuse by the family of Dr. Samuel May, the distinguished Unitarian minister and abolitionist who had been the assistant to William Ellery Channing before settling in Syracuse and had strong New England connections (his sister was married to Bronson Alcott). May had died in 1871 but his family was still there.

By 1875 Silsbee had set up his own office,[28] and on June 5 of that year he married Anna Baldwin Sedgwick, the daughter of Charles Sedgwick, a prominent local citizen and banker.[29] According to family tradition he did this on the strength of receiving his first major commission, the design of the Syracuse Savings Bank, which he won over such competitors as Archimedes Russell of Syracuse, Frederick Merry of New York, and Cummings & Sears of Boston.[30] This building,

erected in 1876 and still occupied by the original bank, is one of the handsomest and most impressive examples of Victorian Gothic (Fig. 3). The large cubic structure occupies most of a small city block (what is now the street on one side was the Erie Canal at the time the bank was built) with three facades but with two main portals, each crowned by a Gothic porch. The enormous size of the building is relieved by its polychromy: bands of pale red sandstone alternate with pale buff Ohio sandstone to provide a pleasing but not strident contrast, unlike the works of Silsbee's first employer, Ware & Van Brunt. The subtle coloring, restrained Gothic decoration, and vertical accents give the building an almost unique lightness. The mass of the main block is repeated on a smaller scale in a central tower that rises to a height of 140 feet. While the bank occupied the basement vaults and the lower floors, the upper ones were let commercially and, appropriately enough, Silsbee had his office at the top of the tower,[31] reached by the first passenger elevator installed in Syracuse as part of a building's original design. The cost of construction was $280,000. This building not only established Silsbee's local reputation but even today has almost become a paradigm of American Victorian Gothic and literally a textbook illustration of the style.[32]

In 1876 Silsbee designed another more elaborate but somewhat conventional Victorian Gothic commercial building in Syracuse, the White Memorial Building (Figs. 4, 5). This structure was erected by the White brothers, one of whom was president of the Syracuse National Bank, which was located on the second floor. His brother, Andrew Dickson White, was the first president of Cornell University and there is considerable correspondence between Andrew and

Silsbee over the next few years. They became close friends and Andrew tried, unsuccessfully, to persuade Silsbee to become first dean of the new School of Architecture at Cornell. He later wrote letters of reference to possible clients.[33] Silsbee's friendships with influential people is a hallmark of his career and played a role in his obtaining numerous commissions.

In the White Memorial Building, the decorative bands of black and sand-colored brick contrast markedly with the dark red brick of the main structure, and the decoration is much richer than in the Syracuse Savings Bank (Fig. 5). The extreme width of the main facade facing Washington Street is relieved by the insistent verticality of the window strips, sharply pointed gables, and steep roofs. The broad segmental arches of the ground floor commercial space contrast with the elaborate Gothic entrance to the upper floors. Shortly after it was built, the edifice was described as having "unusual artistic feeling."[34]

These two major structures still standing in downtown Syracuse brought Silsbee a wealth of commissions. By 1877 numerous houses, including three for Syracuse University faculty members, were under way although none of these is extant.[35] Pictures of two other houses survive and one, the Westcott House, stood until the 1950s. Oddly enough, one of these residences was *retarditaire* and the other forward-looking. The Theodore Vorhees House, 40 West High Street, Ballston Spa, New York, was a competent essay in a simplified wood mansard style such as Silsbee's first Syracuse employer, Horatio White, might have designed.[36] Perhaps its location or its owner account for its conservative quality. The other, the Edward Noyes Westcott House, which stood on James Street in Syracuse (Fig. 6), shows Silsbee's first attempt at the Queen Anne style

but with remnants of the Stick Style in its simple porch column, decorative gable, and framing. The projecting overhanging gable, L-shaped plan with square entrance porch, and incipient tower at the entrance junction will reappear in one of Silsbee's best-known Chicago works, the J. L. Cochrane House of 1888 in Edgewater, shown here in a rendering signed by Frank Lloyd Wright (Fig. 7). While this Syracuse work has long been called the first Queen Anne style house in that city, it is better known as the residence of Edward Noyes Westcott, who wrote part of his best-seller *David Harum* in this house.[37] I suspect that Silsbee's father-in-law had something to do with this commission, since Westcott was a fellow banker and the house was only a short distance east of the Sedgwick residence on James Street. Undoubtedly Silsbee did numerous other houses and buildings during this period which will come to light.

Susan Karr Sorell has shown the evolution of Silsbee's architectural style in Chicago in the mid-1880s and 1890s. Not surprisingly his earlier work followed a similar pattern. The Victorian Gothic of 1876 gave way to the Queen Anne of 1877, and a third style can be seen beginning in 1878—the Richardsonian Romanesque in which Silsbee was to continue to work during his remaining years in Syracuse and in Chicago as late as 1891. The first example of his use of the style was the Reformed (Dutch) Church designed in 1878,[38] dedicated on February 10, 1881; it stood until its demolition in 1968.[39] It was reminiscent of various works of Richardson and showed Silsbee's interest for the first time in massive rough-cut stone—in this case Onondaga limestone, with a minimum of decoration. As in so many of his works, the flatness of the wall was emphasized, being opened up only by a rose win-

6. *Edward Noyes Westcott House, Syracuse. Silsbee, 1877.*
(Photo: Onondaga Historical Association, Syracuse, N.Y.)
7. *J. L. Cochrane House, Edgewater, Chicago. Silsbee,*
1878–1881. Rendering by F. L. Wright. (Illustration: The
Inland Architect, *March 1888.)*

dow and tall, narrow windows and a Romanesque arcade which unified the disparate towers. The color and quality of the stone work made up for the lack of originality of design and composition. More interesting in its details is the Oakwood Cemetery Chapel, designed in 1879 and dedicated November 24, 1880,[40] where Romanesque and Gothic elements are combined in the Richardsonian tradition (Fig. 8, 9). The massive projecting stones are impressive but the whole lacks coherence as a composition. However, the details of the juxtaposed elements in the gable (Fig. 9) and those of the wooden vaults of the porch help to compensate for this.

During these years Silsbee, according to various accounts, worked throughout New York State. Emmerton's genealogy of the Silsbee family, published in 1880, specifically mentions Albany among other places[41] and it is possible he was involved, like so many others, in the work on the

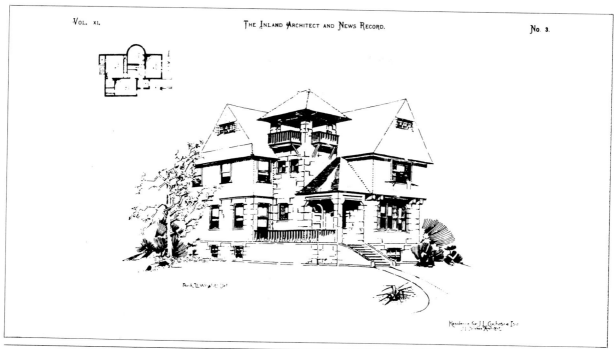

8. *Oakwood Cemetery Chapel, Syracuse. Silsbee, 1879/80.*

Henry Ives Cobb.[44] The memorial read after Silsbee's death gives the date of his move as 1883.[45] As mentioned earlier, Hitchcock suggested a date of 1885 when All Souls was designed,[46] but Susan Karr Sorell says it is prior to May–June 1882 as he is listed in the Lakeside Directory for that year.[47] The matter is confused by the fact that *Boyd's Syracuse Directory* continues to list him until 1884/1885, when his firm is called Silsbee & Hall;[48] by 1885/1886 it is just Hall.[49] This seeming to be in two places at once can be explained by the fact that he maintained offices in both Chicago and Syracuse as well as one in Buffalo as late as May 14, 1883, when he wrote Andrew Dickson White on a letterhead listing all three offices.[50] In any case, by the mid-1880s, Syracuse had lost "the most notable architect to practice [there]."[51]

However, Silsbee's ties with Syracuse did not break with his move.[52] His wife's family continued to live there and later one of his daughters, Margaret, married and settled there. As already mentioned, he later designed a house for this daughter as well as several other houses for friends of hers. The most important of these later Syracuse works was the F. R. Hazard Residence. Designed for the president of the Solvay Process Company, it was erected in 1892 and demolished in 1939.[53] It was vaguely half-timbered Tudor but combined with heavy Richardsonian stone arches. The picturesque composition was reminiscent of Silsbee's earlier Chicago houses in the Shingle Style. Most appropriately, certain elements recall his earlier Syracuse work: the half-timbering is reminiscent of the Stick Style detail of the Westcott House of 1877 (Fig. 6) and the Richardsonian stonework recalls that of his Reformed (Dutch) Church of 1878 to 1881.

This study does not reveal a great or original

Albany capitol, but there is no evidence of this. In one of his letters to President Andrew Dickson White of Cornell, dated February 26, 1879, he mentions that he is designing an Albany church,[42] and a newspaper account of 1878 states that he has designed furniture for the new Peekskill house of the famous clergyman, Henry Ward Beecher.[43]

In the early 1880s Silsbee moved to Chicago. The exact date and reason have been matters of debate. Family tradition said he was called to Chicago by Potter Palmer in 1884 to do the interiors of his new house, erected in 1882 by

architect. While the Syracuse Savings Bank can hold its own with nearly any example of American Victorian Gothic, Silsbee's other early works, as Hitchcock suggests, are often awkward. Nevertheless, they reveal a sensitivity to material, detail, and surface. These characteristics became developed in his mature Chicago work and were carried further by his talented draftsman, Frank Lloyd Wright. But an evaluation of Silsbee cannot be limited to his architecture alone. Throughout his career, it was his aristocratic heritage, personality, ability to get along with people, whether they were talented draftsmen or social and literary figures, which made him a successful architect and teacher.[54] While not an innovator,

he was open to new artistic ideas which he adapted, often with great sensitivity, and he passed this ability on to others. Joseph Lyman Silsbee's office, with Frank Lloyd Wright, George Maher, and George Grant Elmslie all working there at the same time in Chicago in 1887, has been compared with that of Peter Behrens of 1910 in Berlin, where Ludwig Mies van der Rohe, Walter Gropius, and Le Corbusier were all employed.[55] Although it may be stretching a point to make this comparison, the very fact that the parallel has been suggested is significant.

Perhaps Frank Lloyd Wright summed up Silsbee best of all when he said "Silsbee was a born artist."[56]

Notes

1. Henry-Russell Hitchcock, *In the Nature of Materials; the Buildings of Frank Lloyd Wright, 1887–1941* (New York: Duell, Sloan and Pearce, 1942), pp. 4–7.

2. Henry-Russell Hitchcock, "Frank Lloyd Wright and the 'Academic Tradition' of the Early Eighteen-Nineties," *Journal of the Warburg and Courtauld Institutes* 7 (January–June 1944): 47, 57–58. This volume did not actually appear until 1947. This little-known but important article has recently been reprinted in *The Garland Library of the History of Art*, vol. 11, *Nineteenth and Twentieth Century Architecture* (New York: Garland Publishing Co., 1978), p. 11.

3. Grant Carpenter Manson, *Frank Lloyd Wright to 1910: the First Golden Age* (New York: Reinhold Publishing Co., 1958), pp. 15–22; Vincent Scully, *Frank Lloyd Wright* (New York: George Braziller, 1960), p. 15. Scully showed a similar concern in his earlier, and brilliant, *The Shingle Style: Architectural Theory and Design from Richardson to the Origins of Wright* (New Haven: Yale University Press, 1955), pp. 158–159.

4. Frank Lloyd Wright, *An Autobiography* (New York: Duell, Sloan and Pearce, 1943), pp. 67–71, 93.

5. H. Allen Brooks, *The Prairie School, Frank Lloyd Wright and his Midwest Contemporaries* (Toronto: University of Toronto Press, 1972), pp. 29, 34.

6. Susan Karr Sorell, "Silsbee: the Evolution of a Personal Architectural Style," *Prairie School Review* 7, no. 4 (1970): 5–21. Much of the biographical material cited was provided by the present writer. I am citing Susan Karr Sorell by her full name each time since she began her scholarly career as Susan Karr and has now resumed that name professionally.

7. Susan Karr Sorell, ibid., p. 3.

8. Manson, op. cit., p. 14.

9. Susan Karr Sorell, op. cit., p. 5, n. 1.

10. *Report of the Secretary of the Class of 1869 of Harvard College, December 31, 1887–August 1, 1894, Eighth Report, Twenty-Fifth Anniversary* (Boston: Press of Rockwell and Churchill, 1894), p. 78. I am indebted to the late David McKibben of the Boston Atheneum for suggesting that the Harvard Class Reports contained a wealth of information.

11. N. D. Thompson, *The Dream City, A Portfolio of Photographic Views of the World's Columbian Exposition*, Educational Series I (St. Louis: N. D. Thompson, 1894), unpaginated; James W. Shepp and Daniel B. Shepp, *Shepp's World's Fair Photographed* (Chicago: Globe Publishing Co., 1893), p. 322.

12. *Harvard University Directory* (Cambridge: Harvard University Press, 1910), p. 613. I am indebted to Professor H. Allen Brooks of the University of Toronto for first raising this question.

13. *Princeton University, Class of 1903, Statistics for Decennial Record* (Princeton: Princeton University Press, 1913), unpaginated; *Twenty Year Record of the Class of 1903, Princeton University* (Princeton: Princeton University Press, 1923), unpaginated. Ralph Silsbee died in 1950, a week before I wrote him for information about his father.

14. Letter from Margaret Silsbee (Mrs. Frank Wade) to the present writer, February 10, 1950, p. 2 verso (hereafter cited as Wade). The late Major Harry Durston, Secretary of the Onondaga Historical Association, confirmed this information. I remember the Wade house from my youth in Syracuse. Donald Pulfer of Syracuse University kindly provided me with a photograph of the house.

15. Gardner Goodrich Willard, "Memorial," *Eleventh Report of the Class of 1869 of Harvard College, June 1919: Fiftieth Anniversary* (Cambridge: Riverside Press, 1919), p. 252.

16. Hitchcock, *In the Nature of Materials*, p. 4.

17. From its very beginnings, this study was intended to be one emphasizing Silsbee's career in New York State, but it was also my intention to study his entire career, and I began collecting material with this aim in view. The Library of the Art Institute of Chicago provided me with a short list of Silsbee's works for which I am much indebted. I later sent them a more complete one with references based on my findings.

The late E. Baldwin Smith very generously read an early version of this study. When Susan Karr Sorell began her work on Silsbee's Chicago career I abandoned my more extensive project and cooperated with her. I hope my comments on her article express my admiration for what she has done. And, in turn, she has recently encouraged me to publish my material on early Silsbee.

18. On a more personal level, it was over thirty years ago that the present writer, living in his native city of Syracuse, became aware of Silsbee's early work there, first through Hitchcock's writings and later in conversation. This resulted in a scholarly friendship which has continued to this day, and it is a pleasure to pay tribute to a great and generous scholar who has played a major role in my life and professional career.

19. James A. Emmerton, *A Genealogical Account of Henry Silsbee and Some of his Descendants* (Salem, Mass.: Essex Institute, 1880), p. 52. I wish to thank the staff of the Essex Institute for helping me with various genealogical problems; Mrs. Wade's letter provided the information about Charlotte Lyman Silsbee (p. 1 recto).

20. Hitchcock, *In the Nature of Materials*, p. 4.

21. Willard, op. cit., p. 251.

22. Willard, idem.

23. I owe this suggestion to the late David McKibben.

24. Cynthia Zaitzevsky, *The Architecture of William Ralph Emerson, an exhibition presented by the Fogg Art Mu-*

seum in collaboration with the Carpenter Center for the Visual Arts, Harvard University, May 30 through June 20, 1969 (Cambridge: Fogg Art Museum, 1969), pp. 4–5, pls. 1 and 2. However, there is no mention of Silsbee working for the firm. The late David McKibben was unable to find any mention of Silsbee in the manuscript history of the Boston Society of Architects written by William Austin and based on the minutes of the meetings beginning in 1867 (letter to the present writer, January 31, 1950).

25. Wade letter, p. 1 verso. I have been unable to find any mention of this in any of the literature on Sargent. Richard Ormond of the National Portrait Gallery, London, a leading Sargent authority, confirms this. However, the painter did do a portrait drawing of Edward Silsbee, a first cousin of Joseph's, which is now in the Bodleian Library, Oxford (William Howe Downes, John S. Sargent, His Life and Work, [Boston: Little, Brown & Co., 1925], p. 302), but according to Evan Charteris, John Sargent (New York: Charles Scribner's Sons, 1927), p. 13, this was done in 1900.

26. Boyd's Syracuse Directory 1874–75 (New York: Directory Publishing Co., 1875), "with H.M. White, 12 Wieting Block, home 152 Lodi St."
   Mrs. Wade wrote the present writer that Silsbee first went to Buffalo from Boston and worked for the firm of Kent and Miller before moving to Syracuse (Wade letter, p. 1 verso). I suspect that she is mistaken as Silsbee never referred to his having been in Buffalo before Syracuse. There is no record in the Buffalo city directories of such a firm between 1871 and 1874. Much later, Silsbee's early Chicago partner, Edward Kent, moved to Buffalo and seems to have run a branch office there, and I think Mrs. Wade may have been thinking of this. See note 50 below.

27. The Syracuse University catalogue of 1873 lists him as "Joseph Lyman Silsbee, A.M. Professor of Architecture." There is no record of his ever receiving a master's degree at either Harvard or M.I.T. Perhaps the degree was given to him by Syracuse University when he was appointed. The Syracuse University Alumni Record 1872–1910 lists him as "John Lyman Silsbee, Professor of Architecture, College of Fine Arts, 1873–78." I am grateful to the Syracuse University Library Archives Collection for providing this information from their publications.

28. Boyd's Syracuse Directory 1875–76 (New York: Directory Publishing Co., 1876), gives Silsbee's business address as "16 & 17 Granger block, home 217 James."

29. Emmerton, op. cit., p. 52; repeated in Wade letter, p. 1 recto. The Sedgwicks, incidentally, lived in a lovely Gothic cottage on James Street designed by Alexander J. Davis in 1845; it is now gone.

30. Wade letter, p. 1 verso; New York State Council on the Arts and Syracuse University School of Architecture, Architecture Worth Saving in Onondaga County (Syracuse: Syracuse University School of Architecture, 1964), p. 71. This excellent publication provides the best factual summary of the building and includes as its frontispiece a color photograph of the Syracuse Savings Bank. Cited hereafter as Architecture Worth Saving. I am indebted to Donald Pulfer for confirming the date of the competition as 1875.

31. Boyd's Syracuse Directory 1876–77 (New York: Directory Publishing Co., 1877), gives Silsbee's business address as 42 and 41 Syracuse Savings Bank Building.

32. Photographs of it are included in Architecture Worth Saving, p. 70 and frontispiece; Wayne Andrews, Architecture in New York, a Photographic Survey (New York: Harper & Row, 1969), p. 65; Marcus Whiffen, American Architecture Since 1780, A Guide to the Styles (Cambridge, Mass.: M.I.T. Press, 1969), p. 93; and in Leland Roth, A Concise History of American Architecture (New York, Harper & Row, 1979), p. 134, fig. 121. Roth also illustrates and discusses Silsbee's Chicago work, pp. 151–152 and fig. 132. Alas, he calls him James Lyman Silsbee.

33. Architecture Worth Saving, pp. 73–75 provides the best recent summary of the building; Lawrence Wodehouse has found in the Andrew Dickson White Collection of the Cornell University Archives several letters between Silsbee and White dating from 1876 to 1883. One of these, dated June 30, 1876 and written by Silsbee, says he was having trouble with a builder named Moore "over your building," ("Letters to the Editor," Prairie School Review 8, no. 2, [1971]: 30). This building is undoubtedly the White Memorial Building.
   The choice of Victorian Gothic for the building may have been due to Andrew Dickson White, who was a follower of Ruskin. Earlier, in 1864, White was a professor at Yale and a member of the Building Committee for the Yale School of Fine Arts and it has been suggested he may have influenced the committee's choice of Peter Wight (whose brilliant National Academy of Design building in the Ruskinian Gothic style was going up in New York) as architect of the school's new building. (Michael Thomas Klare, "The Life and Architecture of Peter Bonnett Wight" [master's thesis, Columbia University, 1968], p. 54 as quoted in Sarah Bradford Landau, P.B. Wight: Architect, Contractor and Critic, 1838–1925 [Chicago: Art Institute of Chicago, 1980], p. 21, n. 34.)

34. Goodspeed Publishing Co., Industrial Chicago, the Building Interests (Chicago: Goodspeed Publishing Co., 1891), 1:629. The late Hugh Morrison of Dartmouth College suggested that I look at this work.

35. Syracuse University Herald, 1877, mentioned the following three houses designed by Silsbee for Syracuse University professors as being under way that year: residence of Dr. John J. French, 728 Chestnut St.; residence of Professor Durston, University Avenue, at Harrison Street; and the residence of Rev. Dr. Charles W. Bennett, 729 Irving Avenue. The late Lester G. Wells of the Syracuse Univer-

sity Library first told me of these houses. Later the late Harley McKee of the School of Architecture at Syracuse University wrote me about them as he was assembling information on all the architects who had worked in Syracuse in the nineteenth century. Professor McKee and I exchanged information and photographs over the years and all of his material is now in the Arents Library (Special Collections) of the Syracuse University Library. I was delighted to hear recently that Donald Pulfer, a graduate student at Syracuse, has undertaken a master's thesis on Silsbee's New York State work. I have provided him with some information and he very kindly confirmed a date for me (see note 30). I feel sure that Mr. Pulfer will discover many new buildings and information as well as solving many of the problems I have raised.

36. I owe this reference and illustration to the late Harley McKee. See preceding note.

37. Franklin Chase, *Syracuse and its Environs, a History* (New York: Lewis Historical Publishing Co., 1924), p. 345.

38. The church's first permanent building designed by Minard Lafever burned February 3, 1878; see Thomas J. McCormick, Jr., "A Study of Church Architecture in Syracuse, New York, 1820–1875, Based on Lost Examples" (master's thesis, Syracuse University, 1949), pp. 75–79 and Appendix V-K; statement of N. F. Graves, Chairman of Building Committee, *Dedication of the Reformed Protestant Dutch Church, February 10, 1881* (Syracuse, 1881), unpaginated.

39. *Syracuse Herald-American*, November 17, 1968.

40. The late Major Harry Durston of the Onondaga County Historical Association kindly provided the dates of this work. They are also given in the account in *The Syracuse Daily Journal* of 1878 according to information given to me by the late Harley McKee.

41. Emmerton, op. cit., p. 52.

42. Wodehouse, op. cit., p. 30, cites a letter from Silsbee to White of February 26, 1879: "As after your kindness on my behalf, you will be glad to learn that I have been fortunate enough to secure the Albany Church."

43. *Syracuse Daily Journal*, 1878. Prof. Harley McKee kindly gave me this reference.

44. Wade letter, p. 2 recto. Mrs. Wade also said that every time they went past the house, her father made clear that he had only been involved with *the interior* (p. 2 recto).

45. Willard, op. cit., p. 252.

46. Hitchcock, *In the Nature of Materials*, p. 4.

47. Susan Karr Sorell, op. cit., p. 5, n. 1; 1882 is also the date given in Goodspeed, op. cit., 1: 628.

48. *Boyd's Syracuse Directory 1884–85* (New York: Directory Publishing Co., 1885) lists Silsbee and Hall, 42 and 43 Syracuse Savings Bank Building.

49. *Boyd's Syracuse Directory 1885–86* (New York: Directory Publishing Co., 1886) lists just Hall at the same address as the year before.

50. Wodehouse, op. cit., p. 30. The Buffalo Office presents another complication. Susan Karr Sorell, op. cit., p. 5, n. 2, says he formed a partnership in Chicago in 1882 with Edward Kent, a former draftsman in his Syracuse office, which lasted from 1882 until 1884. She informed me in a letter dated May 9, 1969 that Kent left to practice in Buffalo. Taken in conjunction with the Andrew Dixon White letter, this might suggest that Kent was associated with Silsbee in Buffalo as well. Susan Karr Sorell reproduces and discusses a house by Silsbee for a Buffalo client in 1884 (op. cit., pp. 6, 7, and 17, n. 13).

The *Buffalo City Directory* for 1882 lists Silsbee for the first time (but misspells his name "Silsber"), gives his office address as 112 White Building and residence as Syracuse, while the 1883 *Directory* lists him as Joseph L. Silsbee (Silsbee and Marling) still with his residence in Syracuse. Edward A. Kent appears for the first time in the *Directory* of 1885. I am indebted to the Buffalo and Erie County Historical Society for their help.

This Kent may be the Kent of Kent & Miller which Mrs. Wade said her father first worked for in Buffalo before moving to Syracuse (if indeed he did). See note 26.

51. *Architecture Worth Saving*, Introduction by Harley McKee, p. 14.

52. His continued correspondence with President Andrew Dixon White is also evidence of this; see Wodehouse, op. cit., p. 30.

53. *Inland Architect* 19 (March 1892); also listed, but not discussed, in Susan Karr Sorell, op. cit., p. 21, n. 95.

54. As far as I know, no one has commented on the fact that Silsbee was one of the corporators of the Illinois Chapter of the American Institute of Architects on February 8, 1890. Among the other corporators was Dankmar Adler (Goodspeed, op. cit., p. 305).

55. H. Allen Brooks, op. cit., p. 34 and n. 27.

56. Conversation with the present writer, New York, early 1950s.

A PLACE WHERE NOBODY GOES:

THE EARLY WORK OF McKIM, MEAD & WHITE AND THE
DEVELOPMENT OF THE SOUTH SHORE OF LONG ISLAND

Mosette Glaser Broderick

THE EARLY COMMISSIONS OF McKIM, Mead & White on Long Island are closely related to the development as a fashionable resort of that fish-shaped body of land moored at an angle nearly parallel to the Connecticut coast (Fig. 1). Surprising as it may seem, Long Island did not really come into vogue until the turn of the century. Books on summer resorts in the Northeast of the 1870s give scant notice to Long Island.[1] Indeed, in the late 1870s, members of the "Tile Club,"[2] that short-lived artistic group given to sketching and the making of ceramic tiles, proposed a tour to the eastern end of Long Island, "because nobody goes there."[3] The artists made the journey by train, then by boat, to Easthampton and other old-fashioned, out-of-the-way areas on the South Fork.

Around 1875 the chic places for New Yorkers to summer included the bluffs at Long Branch, New Jersey; the Hudson River Valley; and to a lesser extent the Maine coast and Newport, Rhode Island. Three factors were influential in the rise of Long Island as a fashionable resort: the establishment of the Southside Sportsmen's Club near Islip on the South Shore; the eastward expansion of the Long Island Railroad under Austin Corbin; and the sport of golf in the Shinnecock Hills near Southampton.

The Southside Sportsmen's Club on the Connetquot River at Oakdale (Fig. 1), incorporated in 1866, was originally formed to "protect, increase and capture . . . game birds and fish for the promotion of social intercourse among its members,"[4] who numbered among them the men who had built or would build large country seats in nearby Islip: W. K. Vanderbilt (elected 1878), George Lorillard, Henry B. Hyde, James D. W. Cutting, and August Belmont, as well as Charles L. Tiffany, father of the artist, and William Sidney Mount, the painter. The region around the club developed as a spring and fall horse-farm and fishing area. In the summer, yachts could anchor in Great South Bay. William Kissam Vanderbilt's country house at Oakdale was one of the earliest estates on the South Shore of Long Island. Known as "Idlehour," it sat back from the bay at the top of an inlet.[5] It was here in 1876 that Richard Morris Hunt began his career as architect to the Vanderbilt clan.[6]

In addition to the Southside Sportsmen's Club,

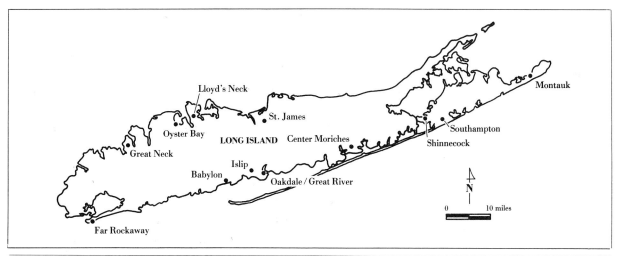

the Long Island Railroad played a decisive role in changing the character of Long Island from farm to resort, from sparsely settled to populous. The Long Island Railroad was begun as a link between Jamaica and Brooklyn in 1832. By 1850 the line was in receivership, a condition that would recur again and again throughout the nineteenth century as various companies organized rail service to parts of Long Island too unpopulated to provide revenue for the line.[7] But in 1881 the Long Island Railroad elected Austin Corbin as its president,[8] and to Corbin goes much of the credit for developing Long Island as a resort area with hotels and summer colonies—all to be serviced by the railroad.

In 1874 Corbin vacationed at the Oceanic Hotel in the established resort of Far Rockaway;[9] he hoped that the vigorous ocean breezes could aid the recovery of his son, who had been ill since winter. Immediately seeing the great potential of this beach area so close to New York City, he purchased five hundred acres of land at Manhattan Beach. He intended to upgrade the prevailing type of summer visitor by improving the accommodations on the train and building a grand seaside hotel, the Manhattan Beach (demolished),[10] which opened in the summer of 1877. He filled the hotel with Eastlake-style furniture and made it convenient to members of the Union and Union League clubs as a summer branch. In 1880 he built another grand wooden hotel nearby, the Oriental, also now demolished.

With two hotels completed and the Long Island Railroad under his control, Corbin next decided to bring the fashionable crowds closer to another section of Long Island where he owned great amounts of property—Babylon on the South Shore.[11] Here, after forming the Long Island Improvement Company (whose directors included men with business interests in Great Britain), he had bought "Blythebourne," the 1850s country villa of E. D. Litchfield. The firm of William Field & Son of Brooklyn was commissioned to build on the site of "Blythebourne" a 198-room hotel 270 feet in length. The new hotel, named the Argyle,[12] was set in a seventy-acre park landscaped with waterfalls and a lake with a rustic boat house.

In 1883 Corbin commissioned Price & Freeman[13] (a year-long partnership between Bruce Price and G. A. Freeman) to build ten cottages on the hotel grounds. Thirteen cottages actually were built and attempts were made to fill them on a seasonal basis. But the hotel and cottages failed to attract the kind of clientele Corbin and his associates desired and proved to be expensive failures for the company. A resuscitation attempt was proposed in 1888 when the Long Island Improvement Company hired McKim, Mead & White, with Taylor and Elmslie as contractors, to build a casino on the property west of the hotel (discussed below, page 187).

In the same year that the Argyle Hotel was opened, Corbin came up with a bold idea for increasing traffic on the Long Island Railroad. He would turn Montauk Point into an embarcation point for Atlantic crossings by extending the rail line from Bridgehampton to Montauk; travelers would board crack trains for the trip to Montauk, whence steamships would whisk them to Milford Haven in Wales.[14] The idea came to nought, and it was some years before service was brought to Montauk. In 1895 Corbin and C. M. Pratt bought 5,500 acres in Montauk area from the heirs of Arthur W. Benson for $200,000.

Earlier—in 1881—Corbin and the Long Island Improvement Company had bought Arthur Benson's estate at Shinnecock in an attempt to upgrade the Shinnecock Hills[15] near Southampton (Fig. 1). The stimulus that changed Southampton from a simple country place to a stylish resort was the discovery that the nearby hills of Shinnecock were perfectly suited to the game of golf.

With the exception of a small course in Yonkers, New York, there was as yet no proper golf course in the United States, and until the 1890s few people knew of the game's existence. While wintering in the south of France, Edward Spencer Mead of Southampton had noticed the game being played in Pau. Once back on Long Island he discussed the game (which he insisted should be pronounced "goff,"[16]) with Samuel Longstreth Parrish and suggested that a Scotsman be imported to help establish it in some suitable place near Southampton. In 1891 William Dunn was brought from Scotland to Long Island where he and Samuel Parrish inspected the land at the eastern edge of the Shinnecock Hills. Dunn declared the terrain too fierce for cultivation as a golf links and explained to Parrish, who knew little about the game, how the land should be. The latter, who was fond of riding his horse through the Shinnecock Hills, instantly hit on the correct location—about three miles west to the section of the hills just north of the present location of Southampton College.[17] Brought there, Dunn pronounced the area perfect for the game. On August 4, 1891 Dr. Gaillard Thomas, Hampden Robb, George R. Schieffelin, Charles T. Barney, Samuel Parrish, and Charles L. Atterbury met at Edward Mead's cottage to organize a club. These men purchased eighty acres of land from the Long Island Improvement Company in September 1891. Forty-four people registered as members of the club and they selected McKim, Mead & White to build their clubhouse. Stanford White was interviewed for the commission and seemed to be very enthusiastic about building a clubhouse for a new game he had never heard of before. The firm sent a presentation watercolor to the members which still hangs in the clubhouse. The building was begun in March 1892 and officially opened with a tea dance on July 2, 1892. Thus, the Shinnecock Hills Golf Club became the first officially organized association owning a tract of land for the purpose of the sport, with a course laid out by a golf professional (Willie Dunn) and a proper clubhouse. As early as June 1892 members dressed in red woolen coats with white collars and brass buttons played the game on the rolling hills overlooking Peconic Bay.[18]

Corbin's dream of increasing the value of Long Island property and bringing revenue to the railroad came to an end in 1896 when he was killed in an accident on his estate in Newport, New Hampshire. Four years later, the Pennsylvania Railroad bought the line and provided terminal facilities for it in Pennsylvania Station, built to the designs of C. F. McKim and William Symmes Richardson in 1902 to 1911.

BABYLON

In 1888, before Corbin's death, the Long Island Improvement Company commissioned McKim, Mead & White to design a casino on the grounds of the Argyle Hotel. The *casino*, a type of social hall popular in the late nineteenth century, derived its name from an Italian word describing a pleasure house set in a garden where concerts, theatrical performances, and balls were given. The casino of the late nineteenth century might also contain a café or restaurant and a gaming hall. The building type was popular with McKim, Mead & White, who had built the Newport Casino for James Gordon Bennett, Jr. (1879–1881); the Short Hills Music Hall (1879/80); the Narragansett Pier Casino (1884–1886); the Kansas City Casino (1887/88); the Stockbridge Casino in Stockbridge, Massachusetts (1887); they would go on to rebuild the Garden City Casino and Louis Sherry's Casino at the Narragansett Pier (1904/5).

A single extant photograph of the Argyle Hotel casino, which burned in 1954 after having been converted into a residence, shows it to have been a rectangular wooden building with a steeply pitched roof and four rounded corner pavilions with Norman roofs, a popular type for McKim, Mead & White and others in the 1880s. In its rectangularity, it resembles the Stockbridge Casino of a year earlier, but with Shingle Style, not Colonial, detail. Further, to suit its location at the shore, an open, one-story porch surrounded the building, which had a pedimented entrance and Chinese rama screens at one end. Eyebrow windows poked from the overpowering mass of its roof.

McKim, Mead & White also had two small commissions in Babylon. In 1882, early in the firm's career, James G. DeForest, a member of the DeForest family of New York and Cold Spring Harbor, a banker active in South American trade, and a member of the Union League Club, commissioned a house. Set at the head of Sumpawam's Creek, it appears on Long Island maps as a rather small building surrounded by a great extent of grounds. The firm's account books show tiny sums of $100 and $400 spent on the project; one cannot be sure what the money was used for. A picture of what may well be the DeForest house when it became the Brooklawn Hotel does not clarify the situation.[19] The house appears to be earlier than 1882 and the $500 may have been spent on decorative work on the interior or on alterations to the exterior.[20]

Equally mysterious and unlocated is the set of house plans for which George S. Moulton paid the firm $75 in June 1883, probably a prototype design for cottages to be built near the Argyle Hotel (perhaps the three additional cottages built on the hotel grounds beyond the ten done by Price & Freeman). McKim, Mead & White occasionally did sell prototype designs to developers who built them on their own, a practice that left its mark on Garden City and other Long Island places.

ROCKAWAY

Austin Corbin had summered at Manhattan Beach in the Rockaways as far back as 1874, even though the hotels there did not attract an exclusive clientele, perhaps because of their proximity to the city. However, several prominent families owned land in a section of the Rockaways near the Jamaica Turnpike. Edward Nicoll Dickerson,[21] H. F. Clark, and John H. Cheever lived in this area, which they named Wave Crest for its situation atop the inlet near where the Marine Pavilion Hotel had been. Cheever's house was built shortly after the fire of 1864 on the site of the hotel. Cheever, who was president of the New York Belt and Packing Company, had a daughter, Gertrude, who was known for her horsemanship. In 1885 Gertrude Cheever married John Elliot Cowdin of Elliot C. Cowdin & Co., silk importers. A particularly handsome gentleman (Fig. 2) and a polo champion, Cowdin must have been a most eligible bachelor in New York Society. He is pictured here in his costume for the celebrated ball given by Mr. and Mrs. William K. Vanderbilt at their New York house in March 1883.

As a wedding present, Cheever gave the newly married couple a parcel of his land at Wave Crest, and in 1885 he commissioned McKim, Mead & White to provide a suitable house.[22] The

Cheever/Cowdin house (demolished) (Fig. 3) sat atop a bluff on the Rockaway inlet. Curved to follow the line of its circular drive, the house was entered through a centrally placed Federal-style doorway, somewhat like the one McKim had used at the house of the Misses Appleton in Lenox, Massachusetts, of 1883 to 1885 (cf. below, p. 247), a residence that similarly wrapped around its driveway. In keeping with the summer character of the Cheever/Cowdin house, an open double-deck porch completed the western wing. The oval windows were another Federal motif found here, but they were not enclosed in rectangular wooden frames as at the firm's Cyrus McCormick house in Richfield Springs, New York. Instead, the windows were cut into the gray shingles of the second floor. Small eyebrow windows set in the broad roof ventilated the attic space, constituting one of the earliest applications of such windows in the firm's work. The two-story house was brick to the second floor and shingle above. The beach side had a large glazed conservatory with Federally detailed arched windows wrapped around the facets of the curve of the house.[23] The modified eighteenth-century detailing, coexisting with the exuberant Shingle Style features, perhaps was suggested by the Boston ancestry of Mr. Cowdin.

SOUTHAMPTON

The town of Southampton[24] (founded 1640) on the eastern end of Long Island (Fig. 1) was a whaling port until the mid-nineteenth century, when farming became the principal economic force in the region. The first urban refugee to move to Southampton in the years following the Civil War was Leon Depeyre DeBost who remembered Southampton from childhood visits made to his mother's family. DeBost's maternal grandfather

was the Rev. David Schuyler Bogard, a Presbyterian divine who often donated his services to the Southampton community.

When DeBost and others came to Southampton to shoot game—Southampton was known for its wild ducks—they boarded in farm cottages or in boardinghouses in the village. In 1875 DeBost purchased a farmhouse on the east side of Main Street and built a summer house on property just to the south of the village.[25] In 1877 he lured his family doctor, the prominent New York physician, T. Gaillard Thomas, to Southampton. South of DeBost's verandahed, three-story residence, Thomas built an even larger house—right at the ocean dune of Gin Lane. It was a four-story house with a double-deck porch on all four sides.[26]

Just west of the village, running at an angle almost to the ocean, is the town pond, where residents occasionally sailed their small cat-boats. On the west bank of the pond, Mr. and Mrs. William S. Hoyt purchased a plot of land from a local family, the Halseys, in 1872. Mrs. Hoyt, daughter of Chief Justice Salmon P. Chase, was an amateur artist who would later join the handicraft circle of Candace Thurber Wheeler of the Associated Artists. Mrs. Hoyt saw the potential for painting bucolic open-air scenes on the peaceful pond, so she decided to summer at Southampton and arranged to have a house built to resemble a Colonial residence with a gambrel roof.[27] The Hoyt house, called "Windibourne," was the first built on the west bank of the pond. Later sold to Charles T. Barney,[28] it burned in 1901, destroying Mrs. Hoyt's paintings of the pond, which had covered the first-floor walls.[29]

George R. Schieffelin, and his cousin, William H. Schieffelin, who enjoyed duck shooting at Southampton with their friend, Colonel Louis

P. Siebert, purchased a lot of fifteen acres[30] and built summer homes on the west bank of the pond. Frederick Holbrook Betts and his brother, C. Wyllys Betts, also built houses on the pond's west side. The latter bought the old windmill at the Good Ground (near Shinnecock inlet) and had it moved to Dune Road. There he remodeled it and attached a cottage, thus creating a very unusual summer house. A Village Improvement Society was formed and the town pond became Lake Agawam—"the place of shells." With the start of sailboat racing, on the 4th of July each year, lakeside residents would festoon their docks with Japanese paper lanterns in different color combinations to identify the family home for the "Yorkers" when they made for shore after an evening sail on the lake. At night the air was filled with refrains from popular ballads.[31]

In 1879, a small Episcopal church was founded for the summer community. C. Wyllys Betts donated a plot of land at the south of Lake Agawam on the protected side of an ocean dune. Dr. Thomas, who had a lifesaving station on his property, donated the wood-frame building, which was moved to the Betts's dune and transformed into the nave of a church.[32] After Sunday services, this summer chapel's minister would lead the gowned ladies and flannel-dressed gentlemen to the beach for an afternoon on the dunes.

Year by year, more cottagers came to Southampton.[33] By the early 1880s, the circle consisted of artists, authors, lawyers, clerics, and doctors. Lists of summer cottagers included Dr. Richard H. Derby, a close friend of Charles McKim and son-in-law of Anna C. Alden, and the architects C. C. Haight and R. H. Robertson. These professional men could not leave their practices in the hands of a clerk when they vacationed; they had to find a summer resort within commuting distance to New York so they could take the train out on Friday evenings and return to the city Tuesday mornings. The families of these men remained in Southampton during the week. It is this necessary attachment to New York City via the umbilical cord of the railroad that distinguishes Long Island resorts from watering spots such as Newport and Maine. Summer vacationers at the latter two spots rarely needed to manage their own business interests; they entrusted the day-to-day problems to others. Thus in the last quarter of the nineteenth century, a split arose between the resort property owners of Long Island and those of Newport/Maine, between those who had to work during the summer and those who did not.

In 1885 McKim, Mead & White built their first Southampton house on the now prestigious west bank of Lake Agawam. The client, James Hampden Robb, was born in Philadelphia a year before McKim (who was born in nearby Isabella Furnace, Pennsylvania). He left the Lawrence Scientific School at Harvard in May 1866, the same month that young C. F. McKim commenced his studies there for the qualifying examination. Robb, a member of the New York State Assembly and future state senator, served on the City Parks Commission from 1887 to 1890.[34] His shingle-covered house, called "The Dolphins" (Fig. 4), is not unlike the Watts Sherman house of a decade earlier by Henry Hobson Richardson. Described as "English-looking" in the newspapers of the day (New York *Tribune*, July 22, 1890), it has a much more restrained facade than many other McKim, Mead & White houses of the early 1880s. A one-story porch circles the house on three sides. On the west side is a set of stairs especially designed to help riders

4. *"The Dolphins" (James Hampden Robb House), South-ampton. McKim, Mead & White, 1885. (Photo: Herbert R. Broderick.)*

climb on and off their horses. The southeast corner of the house, which faces the ocean dunes, was originally rounded, with windows and built-in window seats to accommodate the view. The principal drawing room has a central fireplace[35] flanked on either side by windows offering a view of the lake and providing a contrast of flame and water on a cool evening. The fireplace has a flattened "aesthetic" sunflower motif at either side. As is typical of the Shingle Style, the fenestration is planned to reflect the internal needs of the house, not to enforce exterior symmetry. The principal staircase is paneled and rises inside against a tall rectangular window. The porch breaks the height of that window on the outside of the house. The library walls were originally covered above the wainscot level with orange and blue stencil designs in a Japanese pattern, giving the interior an aesthetic flavor characteristic of

the 1880s. The house must have pleased Mr. Robb and his family, since four years later he commissioned the firm to build a city house at 23 Park Avenue (now the Advertising Club of New York). The Southampton house remained in the family until 1952 when it was sold by the family of Goodhue Livingston, Jr. (Mr. Robb's daughter had married the architect Livingston of the prominent twentieth-century firm of Trowbridge & Livingston.)[36]

Houses at Southampton, like those of this period at Newport, were designed to fit in with the Colonial character of the towns. Southampton, which proclaims itself "the oldest English settlement in New York State," had several saltbox houses as well as vernacular farm dwellings. Mrs. Hoyt, it will be remembered, designed her house in the Colonial manner in the early 1870s. As a venerable Southamptonite wrote in his old

5. *Edward Spencer Mead House, Southampton. McKim, Mead & White. (Photo: The New York Public Library.)*

age, "The particularly severe style of colonial architecture chosen for the buildings was quite predominant, on the South shore, in the early days among the better classes of homes, and I might add, was expressive of solidity and long life, but the 'tout ensemble' reflected a bare setting at that time, no trees, no shrubs, no hedge, no vegetation of any kind."[37] The Colonial detail, however, gave the illusion that, despite the sense of newness, the houses blended in with the atmosphere of the place.

When it came to designing a Southampton house for Edward Spencer Mead in 1886 (Fig. 5), McKim, Mead & White followed the example it had itself set at Newport with the H. A. C. Taylor House, begun in 1882. The Taylor House completed in 1886 and now demolished, was a New England Colonial building with peaked roof, widow's walk, dormer windows, and Federal de-

tailing. The firm designed Mead's house for a flat fee of $100.[38] Only one entry in the account books seems to refer to a design for a whole house, and it may have been in fact a renovation of an earlier house; certainly the architects had no control over the execution of the design.

E. S. Mead, a partner in the publishing house of Dodd, Mead, followed Mrs. Hoyt in looking to the Dutch gambrel-roof farmhouse for inspiration. His residence stands on Hill Street at the corner of Halsey Neck Lane. A Federal doorway (not unlike the door at Wave Crest in the Cheever/Cowdin house) bisects the rectangular box of the facade. A large peaked pediment protrudes from the roof at midsection. Approached, as is usual in Southampton, by a semicircular driveway, the originally barren grounds are now lushly planted.

In the fall of 1886, Charles R. Henderson hired McKim, Mead & White to design a house for his

family at Southampton. Called "White Caps," it was built by Mead & Taft, a respected construction firm, and completed by spring of 1887. The house must have been supervised by the architects, since they billed the client for travel to the site.

McKim, Mead & White's houses at Newport were mostly in the Colonial Revival style thought appropriate to their surroundings, whereas in nearby Narrangansett, Rhode Island, the firm's work of the 1880s, such as the Cresson House, tended to be idiosyncratic. At Southampton, three of the four known houses by McKim, Mead & White are Federal, Dutch Colonial, or restrained Shavian in detail. Only the C. R. Henderson house (Fig. 6, lower left) was openly in the simple Shingle Style. The Henderson house, on a dune above the lifesaving station/church, seemed singular in contrast to the houses of the newly fashionable left bank of the lake, just as Henderson himself, president of the Matteawan Manufacturing Company, differed from the usual club-and-family-related clients of McKim, Mead & White at this time. The house, however, with its daring design, did suit its bold setting atop a dune. (Fifty-two years after its erection, during the hurricane of 1938, the house was washed into the Meadow Club.)

The Henderson house, two and a half stories high, curved slightly around the driveway. It had a corner porch tower, characteristic of the period, and an internal open verandah reached by walking up east or west stairs. This twin-stair entrance, much like the entry at St. Andrew's Dune Church (Fig. 6, upper right) nearby, may have contained a storage room, since a window penetrated the mass. Three dormer windows extended through the roof and a porthole window pierced the house on the eastern side.

Charles McKim, with three commissions in Southampton in two years, probably decided in 1887 to summer at Captain Rogers Boarding House in the hope that Southampton might develop more rapidly.[39] McKim's holiday did not bear fruit for two years, but early in 1889 he designed and built a large summer house (Fig. 7) for Samuel Longstreth Parrish. Parrish, who had begun to summer at Southampton, boarded at cottages for three years until he decided to build on First Neck Lane across from J. Hampden Robb.

The Parrish house resembles the Charles T. Cook house of 1884/85 at Elberon, New Jersey, though it lacks the latter's round corner towers capped with pointed roofs, and is more Colonial. Thus, a Federal oval window is set to the right of the entrance door and three dormer windows break the roof line. The arrangement is reminiscent of the H. A. C. Taylor house, where two regular dormers frame a central one surmounted by a similar scrolled pediment with a central finial. This dormer arrangement of broken pediment and regular pyramid coverings can also be seen in Newport at the William Edgar House. The Taylor House also had a Federal oval window in the side flank of the house, but set in a rectangular frame. A photograph of the Parrish House in the New-York Historical Society's McKim, Mead & White Collection shows this house with its new, nonweathered shingles and barren-looking grounds. Penciled in the picture are lines indicating changes in the dormer arrangement. Pencil drawings on photographs of completed buildings seem to have been a working habit at the McKim, Mead & White office and can be seen in other examples.

In March 1892, John F. Pupke, a coffee merchant from New York and member of the Lieder-

6. Sketches of Southampton. "White Caps" (Charles R. Henderson House), labeled "A characteristic Dune House," is at lower left. (Illustration: Harper's Weekly, August 27, 1892, p. 832.)

kranz Club, who had boarded at cottages in Southampton since 1889, decided to build a house. Pupke purchased several plots of land, including two acres for $10, from Pyrrhus Concer, "widower." Concer was part Shinnecock Indian and the man who plied the old boat which crossed the lake from the summer colony of "Yorkers" and the beach to the southern end of town.[40]

One entry follows in the McKim, Mead & White account book[41] for a large house and stable to cost $16,000, representing the most expensive house built by the firm in Southampton. The house, unsupervised, rose between Cooper's Neck Road and Cooper's Neck Pond, west of the Meadow Club. The house was two and a half stories high and was located just south of "Meadowmere," the home of Henry G. Trevor. A two-year search for pictures of the house has been fruitless. The Pupkes died early in the 1900s and around 1911 the house passed to Emily M. Davies; it is said to have burned sometime thereafter.

Southampton was indeed undergoing a transition from its humble roots. Charles White, a former whaling captain, had returned from sea to his family cottage in Southampton and gradually had transformed his home into a boarding house

where he hosted city folk. One evening, after seeing to the needs of his guests, he strolled to the pond to get some fresh air. The old captain's tranquility, however, was broken by an eerie sight. As a cloud passed across the moon, he suddenly spied a sea monster, something low, long, and dark swishing by. The serpent had a tall, erect head and a tail. Horrified, Captain White raced home, where Judge Kilbreth, his prize boarder, laughingly assured him that all was well—the monster was only Mrs. Frederick Betts's new gondola (Fig. 8), which she had had shipped to Southampton from Venice to ply the pond.[42]

Although increasingly larger houses were built at Southampton—such as McKim, Mead & White's Jimmy Breese house, "The Orchard," begun in 1898—development was not nearly as rapid or grand in the 1890s and 1900s as at Newport. Starting as a modest country retreat, Southampton had changed by the end of the nineteenth century into a discretely fashionable resort.

SHINNECOCK

As discussed earlier, one of the principal factors in the transformation of Southampton was the discovery that the nearby hills of Shinnecock were ideally suited to the game of golf.

McKim, Mead & White's clubhouse at Shinnecock of 1892 was originally a two-story, shingle-covered structure consisting of a long, nave-like section bisected twice by gabled "transepts." A large, steeply pitched roof covered the building, and an enclosed porch was formed by columns supporting the gables in teams of fours. The gables were pierced by Palladian windows. Rather modest originally, the clubhouse was enlarged by the firm in 1895 (Fig. 9) and again in the twentieth century as the Hamptons and the game of golf soared in popularity. McKim, Mead & White's solution to the design of the clubhouse derived from the small casino buildings it had done from 1879 through the 1880s, but here omitting all the corner towers and asymmetrical turrets in favor of Colonial Revival fenestration and a dignified, sober composition.

McKim, Mead & White's first work in the Shinnecock Hills was a modest one. Frances Key Pendleton, attorney and partner of Charles L. Atterbury, asked the firm in 1887 to give him a house design in return for a flat fee of $25. Pendleton's house was across the road from Mrs. Hoyt's and directly south of the future home of the golf club. (Unfortunately, no picture could be located of this house.)

The following year, Atterbury, who had long-standing connections with the Hamptons, commissioned the firm to build him a house south of Pendleton's on the bluff overlooking the ocean. Following completion of the Long Island Railroad route to Bridgehampton, he bought acreage in the area from the local farmers at good prices. Hampden Robb, it will be remembered, had purchased his land at Lake Agawam from Atterbury. Atterbury's law firm[43] handled legal problems for the

railroads, and thus he was well aware of the influence of the railroads in improving the value of property.

Atterbury was closely tied to McKim, Mead & White. With the architects, the sculptor Olin Warner, the painter Albert Pinkham Ryder, and the art dealer Daniel Cottier, he had founded the short-lived Jereboam Club.[44] For him, McKim, Mead & White designed a house in the manner of H. H. Richardson's Ames Gate Lodge of 1881/82.[45] It was low and heavy, and curved slightly in a gentle U-shape around the driveway. The walls were built of stones left in their natural state. A low, heavy roof with a flattened pitch sat atop the stones. An off-center archway pierced the house allowing a view of the water to those who drove around the driveway in front. All that remains of the house today are the brickwork supports for the arches.

The next commission at Shinnecock involved Mrs. Hoyt, the art lady, yet again. In 1890, Mrs. Hoyt decided to attempt to lure William Merritt Chase to Shinnecock to give open-air painting classes in the summer. Mrs. Hoyt and Mrs. Henry Porter of Pittsburgh, another summer resident, gave Chase some land for a house on a bluff overlooking the bay, not far from the future site of the golf club. The land, less desirable because it was near the railroad, suited Chase, who asked McKim, Mead & White to build him a summer house and studio there. The commission, done gratis for a fellow artist, was unrecorded in the firm's account books.[46] The house was finished by 1892 (Fig. 10) and occupied that same summer, making it a close parallel in time to the golf club nearby. The house for the financially plagued Chase, a fellow member of the Tile Club with Stanford White, was indeed modest. A Dutch gambrel roof like that at the Mead house dominates the composition, covering the porch area that lies behind seven stout columns rather like those at the golf club. Dormer windows pop out of the roof, showing the living area as distinct from the northward-facing studio on the ground floor.[47]

MONTAUK

East of the Hamptons, on the farthest point of Long Island, is Montauk (Fig. 1).[48] City folk came to the tip of the island following the purchase for $151,000 of a large tract of land in 1879 by Arthur W. Benson, the developer of Bensonhurst in Brooklyn.

Two years later the Montauk Point Association was formed with Henry G. DeForest as treasurer. DeForest, of Cold Spring Harbor on the North Shore, in conjunction with Alfred M. Hoyt, Arthur W. Benson, William L. Andrews, Henry Sanger, Alexander E. Orr, and Dr. Cornelius R. Agnew, built houses in the development. For the benefit of association members, a clubhouse (Fig. 11), stable, and laundry were built in 1881/82. The lower floor of the clubhouse, which burned in 1933, had a large hall and dining room. The upper floors contained rooms for guests of association members. Cottages and lawn tennis sets were put around the club and all meals were taken at the clubhouse.[49] The clubhouse itself, executed by the contractors Mead & Taft, was a simple, two-story building. Unpretentious and suited to the rolling lands of Montauk (kept trim by grazing herds of cattle), the design owes its

interest to the taut surfaces. Belying the rustic simplicity of the clubhouse, butlers were on hand to attend to guests.

McKim, Mead & White built seven houses between 1882 and 1883 on a ridge overlooking the Atlantic Ocean. These ranged in size from the simple cottages of Benson, Andrews, and Orr to the bigger houses of Sanger, DeForest,[50] and Agnew. The largest and grandest of them all was the Alfred M. Hoyt house.[51]

Montauk was isolated. Located twenty-four miles beyond the end of the railroad line, the cottagers were really away from the crowds of New York. In splendid and self-contained isolation, the association members fished to their hearts' content. Yet daily contact with New York was needed for these city-related men. Every day Isaac Conklin of Easthampton ran an express service between the association clubhouse and East-

hampton where connections were then made to Sag Harbor. Conklin left at 4:00 A.M. and returned with the mail picked up in Easthampton from New York City at 10:00 P.M. The trip was arduous, requiring two teams of horses going in each direction, but the mail came through.

QUOGUE

Traveling west beyond Southampton, just before reaching Westhampton, one passes through the village of Quogue. In the 1880s Samuel Davies Craig, the most prominent member of the community and a New York City attorney, decided to encourage the establishment of a small Episcopal chapel at Quogue for the summer community, to be named the Church of the Atonement. Craig donated land for the building across the street from his residence, "PenCraig." The Craigs had lived at Quogue for a long time. The present "PenCraig" is a replacement of the family's earlier house, which was destroyed by fire around 1873.

The church commission was given to Sidney V. Stratton in conjunction with McKim, Mead & White in 1884. Sidney Stratton, a close friend of McKim's from their student days in Paris, where they both trained in the *atelier* of Honoré Daumet, was loosely connected with his friend's firm in the early 1880s.[52] During this period of association, some of Stratton's commissions came into the McKim, Mead & White account books with the notation on the page that a "check to Stratton" was to be paid. Here at Quogue, Stratton made the connection to Craig perhaps through another Stratton/McKim, Mead & White client, James K. Gracie, who commissioned a house at Oyster Bay. Commemorative plaques to Gracie and Stuyves-

ant Fish, yet another Stratton/McKim, Mead & White client in New York City, stand in the Quogue church.

The Quogue church was built by Mead & Taft to the Stratton/McKim, Mead & White design. The half-round, fishscale shingles which cover the exterior and the walls and ceilings of the interior are said to have been requested by Mr. Craig. The church, which exudes a slightly Scandinavian feeling, may be Stratton's tribute to his old master, Hunt, whose Church of St. Mark was just being completed in Islip, but could equally be a reflection of the client's wishes.

Samuel Davies Craig's sister, Henrietta Craig, was the wife of Robert Colgate, Jr.[53] Colgate and Craig must have decided to continue with McKim, Mead & White, for Colgate commissioned the firm to build a house for himself and his wife on

Craig land just north of the church. The house of 1885 was called "Sandacres" and was a modest house with, I suspect, a Dutch gambrel roof. "Sandacres" passed on to Helen Colgate, and her husband Samuel Vernon Mann, who loved the house and whose ashes were sprinkled on the water near the house where the family had canoed. The house was sold c. 1919 to Herbert F. Eggert and remains in the Eggert family; in 1920 it was extensively remodeled (Fig. 12).[54]

———————

This essay began with Long Island's South Shore as a fledgling community and, by ending in the mid-1890s with the smaller houses, it has followed the region's pattern of growth. From the late 1890s, when McKim, Mead & White produced a house like "The Orchard" for James L. Breese at Southampton, which looks as if the original modest farmhouse had swallowed Alice in Wonderland's magic elixir, onward to the Second World War, Long Island had become the "Gold Coast." Large estates numbering in the hundreds were built across the island as it became increasingly fashionable. In one hundred years Long Island was transformed from a place where no one wanted to go into a place where, judging from the traffic on today's Long Island Expressway, far too many people now go.

While there are, as we have seen, no major discernible stylistic differences between the early domestic commissions of McKim, Mead & White on the South Shore of Long Island and their work elsewhere, what was distinct was their clientele. More often than not, their clients were the kind of men who could not leave their businesses wholly unattended during the summer months, nor were they likely to be able to choose one location for the early and late parts of the summer and yet another spot for the weeks in between, as did

some of the extremely wealthy in the later nineteenth century.[55] Unlike the vacationers at Newport or the Maine coast, the wealthy people who came to the South Shore of Long Island early in its development came either for specific, usually sporting, activities or they did not come at all. And they were not the people of vast fortune and exalted social position who competed in places like Newport.

This study of McKim, Mead & White's early commissions on Long Island has attempted to show how closely connected the firm's work there was to the development of the South Shore as a fashionable resort, as well as how small and interconnected the social and professional circles were there in the 1880s.

Notes

For Mr. Hitchcock–who enjoys a good trip to Long Island. I would like to thank Professor Sarah Bradford Landau of New York University for her constant assistance and guidance over the years.

1. For example, Long Island is included in Appleton's *Handbook of Summer Resorts* (New York, 1876) in a small paragraph at the end of the book with only Rockaway Beach noted as a resort.

2. Members of the club included at various times Augustus Saint Gaudens, Edwin Austin Abbey, Elihu Vedder, J. Alden Weir, Frank Millet, John Twachtman, Stanford White, and William Merrit Chase. See Mildred H. Smith, "The Tile Club," *Long Island Courant* 3 (1967): 7–17.

3. William Oliver Stevens, *Discovering Long Island* (New York, 1939), p. 145.

4. Southside Sportsmen's Club, *Annual Report*, February 1, 1878, Constitution.

5. Across the inlet from "Idlehour" at Great River on Nicoll's Point was a large house, now demolished, created for George Campbell Taylor (1835–1907), the son of Moses Taylor, out of a preexistent simple, rectangular Georgian house. This is a mysterious commission that may be related to the firm of McKim, Mead & White. Unlike his brother, Henry Augustus Coit Taylor, a five-time client of McKim, Mead & White and a respected businessman, George C. Taylor never engaged in business. The George C. Taylor House is Anglo-Palladian transformed into a seaside mode by amazing double-deck porches. The open porches remind one of the Moses Taylor House at Elberon, New Jersey (1876/77), one of the earliest houses known to be by C. F. McKim at this

growing seaside resort. The porch-covered house was only one of the many buildings on the estate, which is now part of Heckscher State Park, including a stable and barn complex that survives today from the 1880s. It is difficult to determine if this complex is the commission referred to in the McKim, Mead & White bill books at the New-York Historical Society for June of 1884 for George C. Taylor. The bill books list the house as being at Moriches. Problematically, Taylor bought 225 acres on the Great South Bay at Mastic on the Moriches inlet near Robert's Point to the west of Pattersquash Creek in July 1883, just across the point from St. George's Manor. The tract of land included buildings and improvements. Perhaps Taylor did not like Moriches. There is no record of his life there and no trace of a grand $30,000 house built there by McKim, Mead & White. In December of 1884 he bought the tract of land in Islip which he increased by buying a neighboring tract in 1886. In 1887, as revealed by a deed search in the County Offices at Riverhead for this and other real estate transactions discussed in this paper, he sold his entire property at Moriches to Benjamin W. Morrill of East Orange, New Jersey for $5—a net loss of $29,995 on the transaction. The deed for both transactions lists dwellings on the property in 1883 and those on it when he sold it in 1887.

Although it is impossible to tell for certain if the $30,000 commission listed in the McKim, Mead & White records is the enlargement of the Great River house, interior views of the house seen in an album kept at Heckscher State Park look like they could be by the architects. The staircase, for example, has a paneled hall reminiscent of other McKim, Mead & White interiors of the 1880s.

My thanks go to Mr. O'Neil of Heckscher State Park for sharing photographs and information on this house.

6. It is unknown how the grandson of the Commodore and his southern-born wife came to select Hunt as their architect, but the country house Hunt built for them between 1876 and 1878 must have pleased them, for upon the death of the Commodore and the settlement of his estate, they had Hunt design and build their François I chateau on Fifth Avenue at 52nd Street. Oakdale, the site of "Idlehour," was an inexpensive and not yet fashionable place for a summer cottage. The house itself was a rambling ensemble in the Stick Style, perhaps the largest one ever built in that mode, and marks the culmination of the skeletal and half-timber framing technique begun by Hunt at the J.N.A. Griswold House of 1861–1863 at Newport. Hunt provided open one-story porches as well as many erratic dormer projections and an ogive-capped tower on the entrance facade of the house. The projections and rambling roof line at "Idlehour" are reminiscent of the F. W. Andrews House at Newport of 1872, now demolished, by H. H. Richardson. For the Andrew's house, see the pictures reproduced in Richard Guy Wilson's "The Early Work of Charles Follen

McKim," *Winterthur Portfolio*, 14 (Autumn, 1979), fig. 4. The first "Idlehour" burned in 1899 and was replaced by a large stone mansion designed by Hunt & Hunt, now part of Dowling College. For the original "Idlehour," see Paul R. Baker, *Richard Morris Hunt* (Cambridge, Mass. and London, 1980), fig. 61. "Idlehour" has one touch which is mysterious and unusual for the period. There are curved decorative projections, possibly Japanese in origin, on the ends of the roof ridge poles. This is most atypical and is echoed later in the Scandinavian ringerike-style finials on the ridge poles of the Episcopal Church of St. Mark by Hunt which the Vanderbilts donated in East Islip. Hunt was in Scandinavia in 1867, but no stave church detail exists in his other buildings. For the church, see *American Architect and Building News*, February 14, 1880, p. 58.

7. The story of the Long Island Railroad can be found in Mildred H. Smith's *Early History of the Long Island Railroad, 1834–1900* (Uniondale, L. I., 1958).

8. Born in Newport, New Hampshire, Corbin graduated from Harvard College and Harvard Law School before moving west to Indiana to start his career. He returned to New York a successful banker. In 1873 he organized the Corbin Banking Co. He became the receiver of the Long Island Railroad in 1880, its president the following year.

9. In 1833 Far Rockaway was considered such a beautiful and healthful rural spot—only a coach ride from the city—that a hotel, the Marine Pavilion, was built there to the designs of Alonzo Reed, Town, Davis & Dakin. A print of the hotel, showing a central cupola and grand colonnade, can be found at the New-York Historical Society. The Marine Pavilion, one of the earliest resort hotels in the country, flourished until a fire of 1864 destroyed it. On the site there developed a fine residential community, following the establishment of a railroad link in 1869. Dubbed "Wave Crest" in 1881, residences for New York businessmen were built there; see *Long Island Illustrated* (New York, 1884).

10. See *The Story of Manhattan Beach* (New York, 1879).

11. In 1877 Corbin bought a large farm in Babylon two miles distant from August Belmont's country place. Belmont had bought property as a nursery and stud farm at Babylon in 1864 where he had Detlef Lienau build him a plain but commodious twenty-four-room mansion in 1867/68 (demolished). Corbin remained content with a local farm dwelling surrounded by great acreage.

12. Named, supposedly, but incorrectly, for the family whose seat, Inverary Castle, is in Argyllshire, Scotland. There is no evidence that the family of the duke of Argyll had anything to do with the Argyle (spelled wrong) Hotel (letter from the duke of Argyll, 3 December 1979). The identification of the architect of the Argyle Hotel was kindly brought to my attention by the ever resourceful Dennis S. Francis, who showed me the announcement for the hotel's construction in the Building Intelligence section of the *American Architect and Building News*, February 18, 1882. Sadly,

as this paper was being typed, Dennis fell ill and died. His generous sharing of the fruits of his labor will be remembered by all who knew him.

13. The names of the architects of this project were once again kindly supplied by Dennis Francis.

14. David Landman, "Montauk: Phantom Rival to New York Port," *New York History* 33 (1952): 115–137.

15. Local newspapers of 1887 (*Mail & Express*, August 26, 1887) report Corbin was building a cottage at Shinnecock. Evidently, this cottage never was built.

16. Through the kindness of Mrs. Henry G. Trevor, "Memoirs of a Southampton Child," unpublished manuscript, hereafter cited as Mrs. Trevor's manuscript.

17. Southampton College of Long Island University is on the site of the second house of Mrs. William S. Hoyt (see the section of this paper on Southampton), built when she sold her Southampton house to C. T. Barney. Arthur B. Claflin had Grosvenor Atterbury build him a large house on the site of Mrs. Hoyt's home which is today the main building of the college.

18. Samuel L. Parrish, *Some Facts, Reflections and Personal Reminiscences Connected with the Introduction of the Game of Golf into the United States—More Especially as Associated with the Formation of the Shinnecock Hills Golf Club* (New York, 1923).

19. My thanks to Albert Maction, the son of the hotel's owner, who sent me pictures of the building, and to Ann D. White librarian at the Babylon Public Library, who located Mr. Maction for me. Thanks also to Theresa Bouquet of the Village of Babylon Historical & Preservation Society for her assistance.

20. The picture bears a resemblance to an odd photograph in The New-York Historical Society, McKim, Mead & White photo album, Record Work 674, which shows a small boy standing in front of a similar house.

21. Dickerson hired McKim, Mead & Bigelow to build him a town house at 64 East 34th Street between 1877 and 1879; see Leland M. Roth, *The Architecture of McKim, Mead & White, 1870–1920, A Building List* (New York, 1978), #34. The commissions of McKim, Mead & White on Long Island cited in the present article—and in its sequel concerning those on the North Shore of Long Island, to be published separately—come from a study made of the firm's account books in the McKim, Mead & White Collection at the New-York Historical Society. This study was made before the publication of Professor Roth's invaluable opus and concerns itself with the small-fee commissions omitted in that work.

22. McKim, Mead & White had worked in Far Rockaway earlier. For $200 they sold a set of designs for a cottage group to the attorney, Charles C. Beaman (the firm of Prescott Hall Butler), who had close connections with McKim, Mead & White. I could not trace these cottages, but there might have been several built at Wave Crest when the community was formed c. 1881.

23. G. W. Sheldon, *Artistic Country Seats* (New York, 1886/87), entry 121.

24. This section owes a great debt to Mr. and Mrs. Charles P. Stevenson and Mrs. Cary Potter who were extremely kind and generous with their time and papers. Also of great assistance was Richard B. Foster, the Southampton Village Historian.

25. Edward Henry Moeran, "Southampton's First Vacationists," *Long Island Forum*, April, 1943, pp. 87–88.

26. After the house was badly damaged in the devastating hurricane of 1938, it was moved behind the dunes to prevent further destruction. Dr. Thomas later commissioned McKim, Mead & White to build some houses on St. Ann's Avenue in the Bronx in 1886.

27. William S. Pelletreau, "The New Southampton," *Long Island Magazine* (October 1893): 89.

28. Barney commissioned McKim, Mead & White to build two New York town houses in 1880 and 1895.

29. The winter residence of Mr. and Mrs. Hoyt at Twin Islands, Pelham, is illustrated in *Artistic Houses* (New York, 1883–4), in the fourth section, pp. 143–144. Like the Southampton house, the Pelham house was done without benefit of architect.

30. The purchase was conveniently divided into three parcels with lots chosen by George Schieffelin's young daughter. The three men had local builders do their homes for them. Life for these first "cottagers," according to Mrs. Henry G. Trevor's "Memoirs of a Southampton Child," was very simple and unpretentious. After a day out of doors, the evening meal would be the day's catch, while conversation centered on the neighbor's attempts to improve the "fields" and make the barren grounds of the cottages look more as they did before being cleared for construction.

31. Mrs. Trevor's manuscript.

32. North and south transepts were added in 1883; choir and aisles done by Edward H. Kendall in 1887/88; reredos, altar, and decorations by Robert Henderson Robertson in 1893.

33. In 1880, for example, Salem Wales (1825–1902), a prominent New York City publisher and politician, bought land and built a house at the northwest corner of Lake Agawam, naming his place "Ox Pasture." Wales, an unsuccessful Republican candidate for mayor of New York, was president of the Board of Park Commissioners from 1880–1885. To the south of Wales's property, his daughter and son-in-law, Elihu Root, commissioned a summer house from the architects Carrère & Hastings.

34. Robb served as president of the commission. It was probably through Salem Wales that Robb came to Southampton. Robb purchased the land from Charles L. Atterbury.

35. Interestingly, it resembles the one in the dining room of the James A. Burden house in Troy, New York, of 1880, by Potter & Robertson. See Sarah Bradford Landau, *Edward*

T. and William A. Potter: American Victorian Architects (New York/London, 1979), p. 475 and fig. 293.

36. Livingston designed the house next door, "Old Trees," which stands on half the original Robb property. Assistance on the original entrance front of the house and its interior decoration was graciously given by its current owners, Mr. and Mrs. John Sullivan. My thanks also go to Goodhue Livingston, Jr., for his memories of the family and the house.

37. Edward Henry Moeran, "The Genesis of Southampton's Summer Colony," *Long Island Forum*, 1943, p. 73.

38. Account book 2, page 301, reads "To commission as agreed on house at Southampton."

39. The major growth of Southampton occurred during World War I when pleasure travel to Europe ceased and America's wealthy had to develop indigenous watering holes.

40. Land transactions at the Deed Office, Suffolk County, Riverhead, Long Island, liber 365, p. 180, March 19, 1892. The anecdote about Concer from Mrs. Trevor's Memoirs.

41. Book 4, p. 233, McKim, Mead & White Collection, New-York Historical Society.

42. "A Venice of the Sand Dunes," New York *Herald*, July 21, 1889.

43. One of his partners was Betts of the Southampton Betts family.

44. L. Effingham DeForest and Anne Lawrence DeForest, *The Descendants of Job Atterbury* (New York, 1933), pp. 64–66. Atterbury's son, Grosvenor Atterbury, who excelled at tennis, played with the young W. B. Dinsmoor, classicist and founder of the Department of Art History at Columbia University. Atterbury became a prominent twentieth-century architect.

45. A badly faded picture of the Atterbury house exists in the McKim, Mead & White Collection, New-York Historical Society, but its quality is too poor for reproduction.

46. Katherine Metcalf Root, *The Life and Times of William Merritt Chase* (New York, 1917), p. 162.

47. The art colony and school Chase agreed to participate in were located three miles east of the artist's house. The land used for the art village was really not very valuable (Mrs. Hoyt had owned some of it) and was located just across the road from the Shinnecock Indian reservation. The Shinnecock Indians, native to the region, had all but expired by the time the New York colony moved in. Although the reservation survives to this day, frequent intermarriage had ended the purity of the tribe, as was noted in the nineteenth century (see John Gilmer Speed, "An Artist's Summer Vacation," *Harper's*, June 1893, pp. 7–8).

The students lived and worked in the colony until 1902 when the school was closed, but the buildings of the art colony survive. Although the art school ended, Chase continued to use his house through the teens of this century. My thanks go to Ronald G. Pisano, Curator of the Parrish Museum in Southampton, for telling me where to find the Chase house, which, though sadly deteriorated, is still standing. Chase, fond of this house among the bayberry and sand dunes, painted the region frequently. The basic account of Chase's summers in Shinnecock can be found in Katherine Metcalf Root, *The Life and Times of William Merritt Chase* (New York, 1917).

48. Pronounced by locals, Mun*tauk*.

49. "A New England Colony in New York," *Harper's Magazine*, 1892, p. 35.

50. The Henry G. DeForest house had sandalwood carvings which were probably imported by his cousin Lockwood.

51. Hoyt later asked McKim, Mead & White to design a town house at 934 Fifth Avenue, built 1883 to 1885, now demolished. Alfred Miller Hoyt was a member of Jesse Hoyt & Co., which owned great tracts of land in the Northwest. Information from Carleton Kelsey of the Amagansett Free Library and Mrs. Momeyer, a current owner of the house.

52. Stratton, like McKim, returned from Paris to an architectural office in New York: Stratton to R. M. Hunt's office, McKim to Richardson's. They both took rooms at 57 Broadway in the 1870s. Also in Daumet's *atelier* was Robert Swain Peabody of Peabody & Stearns.

53. Information on the Craigs and Colgates thanks to Craig Colgate, Jr., and Mrs. John K. Colgate.

54. My thanks to Mrs. Walter B. Potts of Quogue, daughter of Mr. Eggert, for her assistance.

55. Jacob Schiff, for example, had summer homes in Sea Bright, New Jersey, and Bar Harbor, Maine; see Stephen Birmingham, *Our Crowd* (New York, 1967), p. 216.

TWENTIETH-CENTURY ARCHITECTURE

THE NEW TRADITION AND
THE NEW PIONEERS

ANTONIO GAUDI'S INTERIOR SPACES

George R. Collins

THE SORT OF INTERNAL ENVIRON-ment that Antonio Gaudí appeared to be evolving early—and perhaps uniquely—in his residential buildings anticipated in certain ways twentieth-century concepts about internal spaces, particularly as regards continuity of effect and ambiguity in compartmentalization.

It may be that Gaudí was originally stimulated to search out what he did in this respect because of the nature of the patronage that he enjoyed; that is to say, he was seeking to satisfy the aspirations regarding life-style of the families who commissioned him to work for them.

In the late nineteenth century, Catalonia as a region was industrializing, urbanizing, and prospering. Its wealthy upper middle class and titled families were seized by the memory of the one-time power, in the later Middle Ages, of the Aragonese empire. As Catalans were rather frustrated politically in modern times, these urges were expressed more culturally and socially than politically—in the encouragement of Catalan language, music, and especially architecture. There arose a movement then known as the *Renaixensa* ("renascence," i.e., rebirth) that asserted itself in many ways, including a literary and artistic periodical of that name.

The *Renaixensa* movement was both urbane and vernacular. In the first sense it was reflected in a great upsurge of planning and building activity. For instance, about 1860 the engineer Ildefonso Cerdá designed a remarkable plan for the future expansion (*ensanche*) of Barcelona with radically open blocks and public spaces, and, in fact, actually coined the term "urbanization" that is so typical of the dynamics of late-nineteenth-century in-city migration. At first, the buildings in this *ensanche* of the city tended to follow styles popular elsewhere in Europe, but suddenly in the 1870s the patrons and their architects burst out with an unparalleled originality and lushness of effect that persisted for several decades.

In their eclecticism of the day, government buildings and museums tended to be designed in Greek, Roman, or Renaissance classicism and in the Baroque. Churches and castle-villas, in a Gothic that politically conformed to the period of ascendency of their region, Aragon. Educational institutions, often in the Romanesque. As regards residences, however, whatever palatial style may have been adopted for the exteriors, it would seem that the most advanced ideas about domestic high life in the 1870s and early 1880s were based on the Muslim manner that Spain's own earlier monarchs had adapted from Granada (the Alhambra especially) and elsewhere in Andalusia.

Take, for instance, these two interiors by Gaudí (Figs. 1,2). There is no architectural style term that one can apply accurately to their design, but the life-style of the inhabitants of the earlier one can be described by the term "Mudéjar."

"Mudéjar" refers to those Muslims who in one way or another came under Christian authority and even largely adapted the ways of their conquerors in the later Middle Ages. The Mudéjares were renowned for their farming, craftsmanship, and building—the last done largely in what Spaniards considered to be the "inferior" materials of brick and tile. The term "Mudéjar" only began to be applied systematically to architecture, however, beginning in 1859 with the entrance speech into the Academia de San Fernando de Madrid of José Amador de los Rios, a prominent authority on things Hispano-Mauresque; it has commonly been used since for almost any Muslim mix.

In the Romanticism and the spate of travel books of the early nineteenth century, Spain was known as the romantic land *par excellence* because it seemed to northern Europeans to be still quite medieval—and in some regions distinctly Muslim. Théophile Gautier, Victor Hugo, Richard Ford, Owen Jones, David Roberts, J. F. Lewis, the Dumas, Gustave Doré, Washington Irving, and even Eugène Delacroix were among those who contributed to this image of the Spain they visited. Spanish authors and artists also caught on to this and perpetuated the picturesqueness in several extended series of increasingly scien-

tific, but popular, books of "travel." In any case, Spaniards themselves began to think the Muslim—or at least the Spanish-Muslim mixture—was part of their own heritage and not just of their enemy or servant, as had been the case when Muslims still lived in the peninsula. In the 1870s, the prominent Catalan architect Lluís Domènech i Montaner, teacher and rival of Gaudí, published a learned article on the essence of Spanish national architecture, stressing the Muslim and Romanesque ingredients. A latter-day Mudéjar style emerged in Spain in those years as one of the most unique and creative European eclecticisms

3. *Bath, the Alhambra. Plan and section. (Illustration: Jules Goury and Owen Jones,* Plans, elevations, sections, and details of the Alhambra . . . , *1834–1845, Vol. I.)*

4. *Mariano Fortuny,* Le Kief, *watercolor, 1868. (Illustration:* Fortuny 1838–74, *pl. 16.)*

of the century.

The Contreras family, conservators of the imperishable Alhambra, supplied plaster casts of Granadine ornamental wall reliefs for exposition pavilions, interiors, and especially smoking rooms, including that in the Royal Palace at Aranjuez. Owen Jones and Jules Goury's detailed sections of the Alhambra (Fig. 3) were used then, as they are still today, in publications on the subject, and the Jones-Goury monograph was to be found—among other places—in the library of the school of architecture in Barcelona. "The Alhambra Palace that the Genies have gilded like a dream and filled with harmonies," its title page reads.

Catalans were leaders in this Mudéjar revival, although they had not historically been as much occupied by the Muslims as had other parts of Aragon that had reveled in (and profited from) *mudéjarismo* until the final ejection of the Moors in the early seventeenth century. Actually, a certain mythology about Muslims and Berbers obtained in Catalonia. This was in part because of the reputation of a couple of famous Catalans who had "gone native" in North Africa. Also, Catalans were much involved in the military campaign in Morocco led by General Prim, himself an important political figure from Gaudí's home town of Reus; and that campaign had been painted, largely from the point of view of its native Muslim ingredients, by another Reusian, Mariano Fortuny (Fig. 4).

In any case, the Catalan upper classes felt that they deserved a very special form of residential living, and their architects struggled to produce it for them. For instance, Gaudí's younger competitor, Josep Puig i Cadafalch, designed a house with Muslim décor for the Baron Quadras of Barcelona that was illustrated (Fig. 5) and described in a Barcelona periodical in 1907 as follows:

5. *Casa Quadras, Barcelona. Josep Puig i Cadalfach, 1904. Interior. (Illustration:* Ilustració Catalana, *1907.)*

6. *Gustave Moreau,* King David, *painting, c. 1878. (Courtesy The Armand Hammer Foundation, Los Angeles.)*

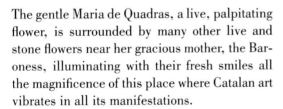

The gentle Maria de Quadras, a live, palpitating flower, is surrounded by many other live and stone flowers near her gracious mother, the Baroness, illuminating with their fresh smiles all the magnificence of this place where Catalan art vibrates in all its manifestations.

And the French painter Gustave Moreau in some of his paintings of interiors came as close as anyone to the eclectic Moorish effects that are to be seen in the homes of Gaudí's patrons (Fig. 6).

Gaudí obtained especially palatial qualities in all of his residences, whether for an extended family, for a religious group, or as an urban apartment building. In the first case, we have the Palacio Güell, built in the late 1880s for Eusebio Güell, his major patron, on a narrow street in the old city center of Barcelona, looking somewhat like the protruding galleries that one finds in the Muslim world (Figs. 7, 8).

As has often been pointed out, the central core of the Palacio Güell, from its *piano nobile* to roof (Fig. 9), was set up similarly to a section of the Alhambra (Fig. 3), and the front gallery outside the core (Fig. 10) looks much like another bit of Granada (Fig. 11). The domestic quarters upstairs open onto and illuminate the central core through traditional Muslim jalousies (*mashrabiyas*), and the perforated upper cupola (Fig. 12) resembles starlit Arab baths (Fig. 3, right). A contemporary monograph on the Palacio Güell described the effect of the interior: "as if by magic art and by virtue of the wand of some Schehera-

7. *Palacio Güell. View of façade on the Calle Conde de Asalto. (Photo: Foto MAS B113.)*

8. *Street, Tulun quarter, Cairo. (Photo: Collins' Catalan Archive, N.Y.C.)*

zade all the dreams of oriental tales had taken body, leaving them suddenly materialized and converting them into tangible fact." The dynamic views which can be seen at all levels as one ascends the stairs, through various apertures that also allow exterior light to pass, are impossible really to illustrate here (Fig. 13); they must be experienced to be believed. Gaudí was apparently fascinated with the possibility of producing a spacious central core with galleries around it at several levels, accessible by open-lit stairways—the whole exhibiting a free interpenetration of space through what might be called transparen-

cies—flowing interior space with light penetrating from the outside. At this stage his technique seems to be quite Muslim, that is, Mudéjar, as we also saw in the painting by Moreau (Fig. 6).

The Episcopal Palace in Astorga (1887–1894) also was designed with a central core which, if it had been completed according to Gaudí's drawings, would actually have cascaded more light into its center because of the clerestories on the upper and wider floor (Fig. 14).

But the Teresian convent and school in Barcelona (1888–1890) is even more remarkable. We see it here in plan (Fig. 15), transverse sec-

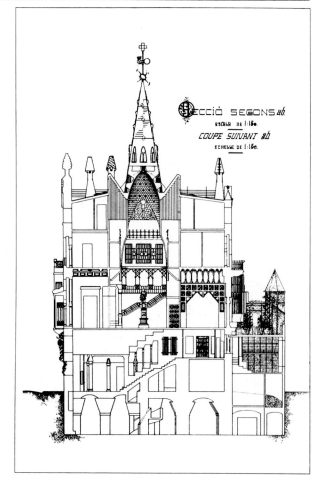

9. Palacio Güell. Section drawn for 1910 Paris exhibition of Gaudí's works. (Photo: Amigos de Gaudí, Barcelona, Planos 1.)

tion (Fig. 16), and an interior detail (Fig. 17). In this structure Gaudí lit the long interior passageways by dropping a pair of internal longitudinal light courts, each about one-third of the way in and each about a tenth of the length of the "corridor." Tall windows also admitted light at both the corridor ends. On the *piano nobile* the passageway is one-third wider and is composed of tall, slim, narrow arcades that flank the inner courts as they pass them, making up a naturally lit cloister for the nuns. Thus the convent school achieved from its top and end lighting an illumination—even radiance—in what would ordinarily be tunneling, dark corridors. One is reminded of the methods of Giovanni Lorenzo Bernini for illuminating the *Ecstasy of Santa Teresa* in the Cornaro Chapel in Rome, and one wonders if Gaudí by any chance had that miracle in mind for her *colegio* here.

But, functionally, what has happened is that sunlit patios and a cloister have been introduced into the central core of a massive multistoried building, similarly to the intentions of passive solar designing by such of our contemporaries as Gunnar Birkerts.

In his apartment buildings Gaudí applied these general procedures to the elevator stairwells and courts. The use of two light courts in front of and behind the wide stairway with its open-ironwork elevator carriage in the Casa Calvet in Barcelona (1898–1904) allowed considerable internal illumination, as we can see (Figs. 18, 19).

Actually such lightwells associated with elaborate elevator cages are a commonplace in southern Europe and also were developed in Belgium by Victor Horta and others, but the way in which Gaudí funneled outside natural illumination into the apartments in the Casa Batlló in Barcelona (1904–1906) is certainly unique. This building

was actually a rehabilitated apartment house in which major changes made were in the façade, internal stairwell, top floor, and *piano nobile.* About half the façade windows were left essentially as before, and half were considerably enlarged in expanse: those of the ground floor, *piano nobile*, and the two flanking windows of the second floor (Fig. 20). The skeletal piers of the ground floor allow light to flood into the interior entrances (Fig. 21). But more remarkable is what is done to the building's stairway core (Fig. 22). It is almost half again as long a court at the top floor as at the lower floors, and those windows of

the apartments that give onto the stairwell vary in expanse, being twice as large at the lower floor as they are at the top. The whole is, for protection, covered with a metal and glass skylight (Fig. 23), and the sheathing of the stairwell walls, composed of alternating white and bluish undulant tiles, is bluer at the top and whiter at the bottom (Fig. 24) in order to even out the illuminative qualities and tone (Fig. 25).

The Casa Milá, designed from scratch by Gaudí to fit the champfered (*chaflan*) intersections of Cerdá's plan is, in its organic way, a machine or mechanism for such amenities (Figs. 26, 27). One can see from the different ornamental de-

11. *Generalife, Granada. View of vestibule. (Illustration: Rafael Contreras*, Del arte arabe en España, *1875, p. 280.)*

12. *Palacio Güell. Interior. Central core, view looking upward toward domestic quarters and cupola. (Illustration: Salvador Tarragó*, Gaudí, *1974, p. 37.)*

13. *Palacio Güell. Interior. Entrance stairs at ground floor level. View illustrating connecting windows and arcades. (Photo: Foto MAS G1 36342.)*

vices on the roof that a variety of stairways, chimneys, and miscellaneous vents service the interiors below, and it is observable in the plan of any floor level that the occupied spaces undulate in such a manner that nearly all of them open through the perforations in their walls on to one or other of the two interior courts of the building. And Gaudí's ornamental effects reinforce this continuity between internal environment and external nature. The façade is a wave-pounded rocky escarpment (Fig. 28), the bedroom floors are paved with concrete tiles (*baldosas*) of geometricized marine design (Fig. 29), and the ceilings are fan-

14. *Episcopal Palace, Astorga. Gaudí, 1887–1894. Transverse section through central core. (Original blueprint. Photo: Collins' Catalan Archive, N.Y.C.)*

15. *Colegio de Santa Teresa de Jesús, Barcelona. Gaudí, 1888–1890. Plan of* piano nobile, *as drawn for the architect Lluis Bonet Gari. (Illustration: Roberto Pane,* Gaudí, 1964, *Fig. 161.)*

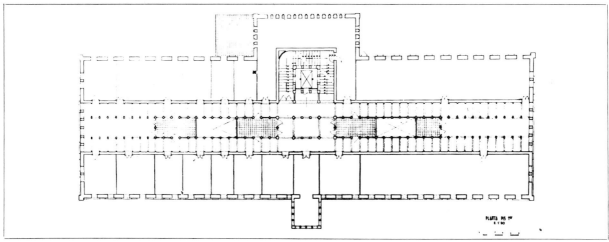

16. *Colegio de Santa Teresa de Jesús. Transverse section, as drawn for Bonet Gari. (Illustration: Pane, Gaudí, Fig. 163.)*

17. *Colegio de Santa Teresa de Jesús. Interior. Cloister corridor, with lightcourt at the right. (Illustration: Laura Vinca Masini, Antoni Gaudí, 1969, pl. 15.)*

18. *Casa Calvet, Barcelona. Gaudí, 1898–1904. Interior. Elevator stairwell with view of flanking lightcourts. (Illustration: César Martinell, Gaudí, 1967, Fig. 320.)*

19. *Casa Calvet. Interior. View from stairwell into lightcourt. (Illustration: Vinca Masini, Antoni Gaudí, pl. 19.)*

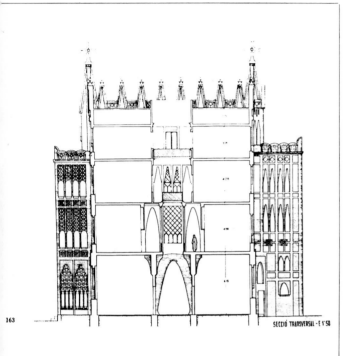

20. *Casa Batlló, Barcelona. Gaudí, 1904–1906. Exterior. View of façade. (Photo: Foto MAS C-4977.)*

21. *Casa Batlló. Interior. View of entry vestibule. (Photo: Amigos de Gaudí, Barcelona, Bat. 1.)*

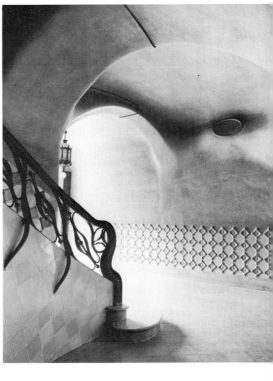

22. *Casa Batlló. Transverse and longitudinal sections, showing lightcourt and stairwell. (Photo: Amigos de Gaudí, Barcelona, Plano 5.)*

23. *Casa Batlló. Interior. View from attic corridor into covering skylight. (Photo: Collins' Catalan Archive, N.Y.C.)*

24. *Casa Batlló. Interior. View of lightcourt walls and windows. (Illustration: Oriol Bohigas,* Arquitectura Modernista, *pls. 217–220.)*

25. *Casa Batlló. Interior. View of lobby at top of grand stairway access to piano nobile. (Photo: Foto MAS C-48893.)*

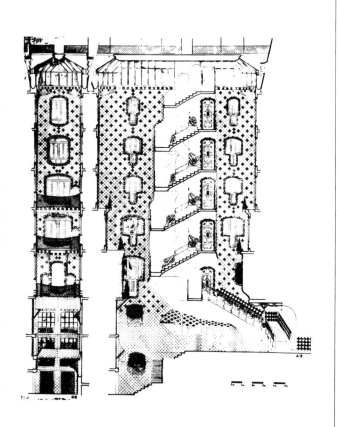

tastically plastered in the form of ocean-wave actions (Figs. 2, 30) with, in some cases, ceilings penetrated to transmit light between adjacent rooms in a suite (Fig. 30). The whole, then, is flooded with natural light with the impression of its origins in nature.

Thus, in Gaudí's later designing there is not only the functional desire to introduce exterior

26. *Casa Milá. Exterior. View of façade. (Photo: Foto ALEU, Barcelona, Mil = 1.)*

27. *Casa Milá. Plan of ground floor. Drawn by the architect César Martinell. (Photo: Juan Polo.)*

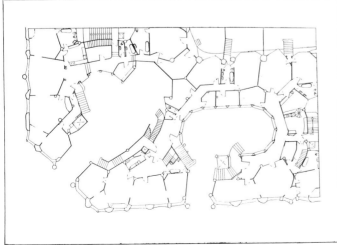

28. Casa Milá. Exterior. Detail of façade. (Photo: Foto ALEU, Mil=2)

29. Gaudí, sketch for concrete tiles used in Casa Milá. (Illustration: Ráfols and Folguera, Gaudí, 1929, p. 184.)

light into the very core of his structures, but also to reduce distinctions between the exterior and interior environment. He achieves this in various ways. Thematically or ornamentally the Casa Milá is, as we have seen, Nature all through—from the piers that step out onto the street (Fig. 31), to the metallic kelp strewn over the sine-curving balconies that undulate as if they were breaking waves (Fig. 28), to the interior floor tiling whose dynamic naturalism is strictly controlled by a geometry of hexagons and spirals (Fig. 29). Structurally and experientially it is hard to say when one ceases being inside or outside. For instance,

in looking obliquely at the Casa Batlló's treelike supporting piers (Fig. 32), which of the planes that one can imagine passing through the façade-work are external and which are internal? Likewise, looking into its skylight structure (Fig. 23), how many definite sensations of closure does one see? Suspended in front of the façade like a *bird* (Fig. 33), there is a proto-cubist (already 1904) indeterminacy and transparency of depth effects, while seated inside like a *person* (Fig. 34), where does the "room" terminate? In the posts? In the indulating glazing? Or at the external mullions of the window enclosure? Unlike a painting, how-

ever, there is no ambiguity or indeterminacy as regards the materials employed or the structural statements: both are unusually emphatic—and, indeed, a bit Alhambra-like.

So what can we conclude?

That Gaudí, at least early in his career, responded to certain demands of a Catalan elite class which, in trying to reevoke the late medieval grandeur of Aragon, turned in its residences to the only sumptuous and comfortable residential lifestyle of the Middle Ages—the Muslim—as its model. The resultant modern hybrid build-

30. *Casa Milá. Interior. View of apartment on* piano nobile. *(Photo: Foto HER, Barcelona.)*

31. *Casa Milá. Exterior. View of lower portion of façade on the* chaflan *of the Paseo de Gracia and Calle Provensa. (Photo: Foto ALEU, Mil=3)*

ing style can be called Mudéjar—that is, post-Muslim Muslim.

In the nineteenth-century buildings that we have seen, Gaudí tried in his characteristic way to design an architectural totality of solids, spaces, ornament, and texture that in its screen transparencies, spatial continuities, and general ingenuity appears to be more of our century, despite the period décor that is so dated as to seem almost surreal in context.

During his last decades Gaudí continued on this trajectory, leaving behind most of his former patrons and his fellow architects. He was in-spired by nature but did not really copy nature: in nature's "built" forms, for example, trees, there is usually no strong line between "outside" and "inside." In Gaudí's buildings he has also sought an identity of architectural form and architectural structure, not in the minimal sense of an engineer's bridge, but by analogy to the rich identity in nature of form and structure, an identity which he believed to have been achieved via the geometry that he considered to underlie both nature and art. His earlier angular bracketed décor (Fig. 1) became in the early twentieth century organic with its building mass (Figs. 31, 32), the whole

remarkably warped in ways that appear willful and arbitrary but are actually ordered in terms of related families of geometrical and mathematical equations that, in part because they are quadric, not Platonic, give a sense of continuity and ambiguity to his resultant spaces.

33. *Same, detail of façade at* piano nobile *level. (Illustration: Tarragó, Gaudí, p. 82.)*

34. *Casa Batlló. Interior. View looking out from* piano nobile. *(Illustration: Tarragó, Gaudí, p. 83.)*

BERLAGE OR CUYPERS?
THE FATHER OF THEM ALL

Helen Searing

CHARACTERISTICALLY, HENRY-RUSsell Hitchcock was the first to point out the true significance of the Dutch architect, Eduard Cuypers. Already, in the first edition (1958) of his monumental *Architecture: Nineteenth and Twentieth Centuries*, Hitchcock had noted that Cuypers "has perhaps as much right as [H. P.] Berlage to be considered a father of the Amsterdam School."[1] We have learned a great deal more about Dutch architecture of this period since Hitchcock penned these words, but his insight remains correct. Although Berlage's towering stature[2] has made it customary to credit him as the source of almost every twentieth-century trend spawned in the Netherlands, we now know that view to be oversimplified.[3] In the case of that group of Dutch Expressionists whose housing work of the teens and twenties Hitchcock considered "internationally . . . the greatest Dutch contribution to modern architecture,"[4] it would seem to be Cuypers who is the immediately crucial figure.

Working in Cuypers's office during their formative years were the three founders of the Amsterdam School—Michel de Klerk, Pieter Lodewijk Kramer, and Johan van der Meij—as well as lesser-known architects who would become allied with the group, among them B. T. Boeyinga, Jan Boterenbrood, Dick Greiner, G. F. LaCroix, Nicolaas Lansdorp, and J. M. Luthmann.[5] This surely is no coincidence. Yet Cuypers remains a shadowy presence even in his native land.[6] By describing the nature of Cuypers's theory and practice and the intellectual and artistic atmosphere of his *atelier*, it is my purpose, within the confines of this brief essay, to account for his seminal role in the evolution of the Amsterdam School, with particular reference to its most brilliant member, de Klerk, who was discovered by

Cuypers at the age of fourteen and who remained in his employ from 1899 to 1910.[7]

Cuypers received his own architectural training in the office of his uncle, Petrus Josephus Hubertus Cuypers, deservedly the most renowned Gothic Revivalist in the Netherlands.[8] Dubbed with good reason the "Dutch Viollet-le-Duc,"[9] the elder Cuypers's own rationalism was nevertheless deeply tinged with fantasy. Furthermore, he blended the structural rationalism so dominant in nineteenth-century French architecture with the English concern for craftsmanship and evocative detail.[10] In such major buildings as the Rijks Museum (1876–1885) and the Central Station (1882–1898), both in Amsterdam, he fused Neo-Gothic and Neo-Renaissance elements into a powerful but picturesque new idiom and brought to the Dutch townscape an exuberant vitality that had not been seen since the early seventeenth century. The nephew, with his penchant for plastic manipulation of the building masses and his devotion to the ideal of the *Gesamtkunstwerk*, would prove himself a worthy heir.

In 1878 Eduard Cuypers set up an independent practice in Amsterdam. For the next twenty years he worked in the historical modes—chiefly Dutch Renaissance—that were then the rule in the Netherlands. Around 1897, however, he was caught up in the new spirit sweeping Europe that would result in the diverse national manifestations known collectively as the Art Nouveau,[11] a movement which rejected revivalism and sought an integration, free of historical borrowings, of the building and decorative arts. The Netherlands had its own rather sober, rectilinear version—*Nieuwe Kunst*—which flourished in Amsterdam, and a Franco-Belgian variety, centered in The Hague around the painter Jan Toorop and

1. House, Jan Luykenstraat 2–4, Amsterdam. Eduard Cuypers, 1899. Plan. (Illustration: Het Huis, January 15, 1903, pl. 1.)

the architect H. P. Mutters, whose works are informed by curvilinear rhythms derived from plant life.[12] Cuypers offered a third, more international and synthetic approach. An art historian of the period described him as "one of the first to accept modern [Art Nouveau] conceptions. His earliest works in this style are related to Belgian and English art . . . and he has developed his own personal notions in a large number of buildings."[13] Cuypers's responsiveness to Austrian and German design of the turn of the century also should be noted, as well as a typically Dutch fascination with Indonesian art, which in the Netherlands was an important ingredient of the Art Nouveau.[14]

Indeed, it is Cuypers's very inclusiveness that constitutes the most "personal" element of his style. With this in mind, one must qualify the judgment of the anonymous necrologist who summarized his career in these terms: "Cuypers was a talented epigone rather than a pioneer, following the manifold art currents rather than creating one of his own."[15] At a time when the dominant approach to architecture in his country was a narrow, rather moralistic one, as evidenced, for example, in the austere *Sachlichkeit* of Berlage and his school,[16] Cuypers deliberately chose a broad-ranging eclecticism that must have been very liberating for the young men in his office. One of the major characteristics of the Amsterdam School would be the eagerness of its members to employ motifs from a wide variety of visual sources, and ultimately they would be even more successful than their master in assimilating and transforming their borrowings.

Three houses which are striking departures from the norm of Dutch domestic architecture of the time will serve to illustrate Cuypers's methods and artistic origins. The combination residence-

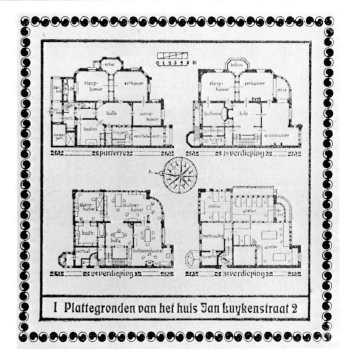

atelier that he built for himself in 1899 on Jan Luykenstraat 2–4, in Amsterdam (Figs. 1–3), may most succinctly be termed—following Hitchcock's well-known practice of turning proper names into adjectives—"Berlagian Queen Anne," or "Berlago-Shavian." The plan (Fig. 1), with irregularly shaped rooms grouped around a large living hall containing stairs, attests to a familiarity with the work of Richard Norman Shaw. Cuypers justified his use of such a plan by explaining that it avoided the boring enfilade of rooms and "lent itself to the making of spaces with surprising 'cosy-corners' [sic] in them."[17] Also Shavian are the asymmetrical composition and the fenestration; each elevation (Fig. 2) is unique and the windows reveal the variety of interior functions and spaces. The generous expanse of glass at the upper stories where the *ateliers* (Fig. 3) are located was unusual in the Netherlands at this time, as were

the multiple small panes; in England, however, the Queen Anne studio-house fitted out with large window-walls was a popular building type.[18] On the other hand, the tautness of the surfaces is very Dutch, and specifically shows the impact of Berlage, as does Cuypers's treatment of the masonry: red brick with white *stone* (rather than plaster or terra-cotta) trim kept flush with the wall plane. Also Berlagian are the segmental brick arches framed by stone blocks over the ground-floor windows, and the stepped corbel of the northeast corner, which transforms an oblique angle into a 90-degree angle. Like Berlage, Cuypers preferred to design in the round whenever

3. House, Jan Luykenstraat 2–4. Interior, Atelier for architecture. Woodcut. (Illustration: Het Huis, *January 15, 1903, pl. 8.)*

4. House, van Eeghenstraat 22. Cuypers, 1902/3. Exterior. Perspective rendering. (Illustration: Het Huis, *March 15, 1903.)*

possible. He professed his satisfaction that the house had only one party wall (on the west); this gave him the opportunity to make three main elevations in place of the one facade that architects were commonly restricted to in tightly built-up Amsterdam.[19]

The interiors, fitted with inglenooks and tiled fireplaces, evoke chiefly English precedents. According to Cuypers, they were "designed for maximum comfort with inexpensive means; there is a lot of warmly colored wood and the walls are plastered and painted. Everything has been done to make the house hospitable, warm, and friendly."[20] In this sentiment he departed markedly from Berlage, who used exposed brick within as well as without, and who sought monumentality and severity in place of warmth. Nor does the living hall have as much prominence in Berlage's houses as it does here, where Cuypers has clearly based the organization of the plan on the Anglo-American type called by Hitchcock "agglutinative."[21]

The residence of 1902/3 at van Eeghenstraat 92 in Amsterdam (Fig. 4) reveals another source of inspiration. It clearly has connections with the work of the Viennese Joseph Maria Olbrich, who settled in the Kunstlerkolonie at Darmstadt in 1899.[22] While a number of Berlagian features survive—smooth red-brick walls dressed with stone, and a corner entrance marked by medievalizing piers—these typically are confined to the lower stories. Above, Austro-German influence is visible, especially in the broad expanse of plaster surfaces painted yellow with red geometric trim, and the gambrel roof. Such features call to mind Olbrich's own house and the Keller residence, both built at the Darmstadt artists' colony in 1900. The interiors of van Eeghenstraat 92, as well as others designed by Cuypers in the same years, also reflect the impact of the

5. Villa in Dordrecht. Cuypers, 1903. Plan of ground floor. (Illustration: Het Huis, *January 15, 1904, pl. 1.)*

6. Villa in Dordrecht. Plan of upper floor. (Illustration: Het Huis, *February 15, 1904, pl. 7.)*

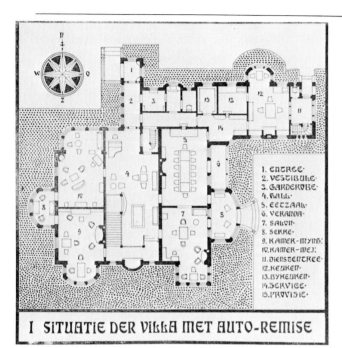

I SITUATIE DER VILLA MET AUTO-REMISE

1. ENTREE·
2. VESTIBULE·
3. GARDEROBE·
4. HALL·
5. EETZAAL·
6. VERANDA·
7. SALON·
8. SERRE·
9. KAMER-MYHR·
10. KAMER-MEJ·
11. DIENSTENTREE·
12. KEUKEN·
13. BYKEUKEN·
14. SERVICE·
15. PROVISIE·

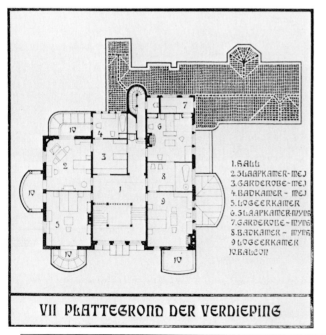

VII PLATTEGROND DER VERDIEPING

1. HALL
2. SLAAPKAMER-MEJ
3. GARDEROBE-MEJ
4. BADKAMER-MEJ
5. LOGEERKAMER
6. SLAAPKAMER-MYHR
7. GARDEROBE-MYHR
8. BADKAMER-MYHR
9. LOGEERKAMER
10. BALCON

Glasgow-Vienna-Darmstadt axis. The interior decorative motifs based on Olbrich's work as well as the lively massing and the polychromatic surface patterns of the exterior made a lasting impression on Cuypers's young employees, as can be discerned when one views the independent work of members of the Amsterdam School.

A well-documented luxury villa in Dordrecht of 1903 (Figs. 5–11)[23] provides a perfect illustration of Cuypers's exhaustive approach to residential design. The house earns the designation of *Gesamtkunstwerk*, not only in the usual sense of an harmonious completeness of detail in relation to the whole (Cuypers designed all the interior fittings and most of the furniture), but most of all in the way that space and light have been masterfully coordinated to complement the aesthetic idea. In this freestanding building Cuypers not only was unhampered with respect to the four elevations but had no external restraints with regard to the plan (Figs. 5, 6), and he used his freedom to enhance to the maximum the total architectural effect.

The spacious living hall (marked *4* in Fig. 5, *1* in Fig. 6; cf. pp. 321–337) is the starting point of the composition, but it lacks the picturesque looseness of its English Queen Anne forebears. It unites the central area of the house vertically, and extends uninterruptedly through the house in the horizontal dimension from the entrance to the garden facade, a planning principle manifest in American resort houses of the 1880s.[24] Also reminiscent of American houses of this decade, especially those by McKim, Mead & White—for example, the Commodore William Edgar and the H.A.C. Taylor houses in Newport, Rhode Island—is the subtle symmetry of the organization, with the hall itself forming the principal axis and the surrounding rooms attached to it in a very

7. *Villa in Dordrecht. Interior, living room. View looking north, toward dining room and conservatory.* (Photo: Het Huis, *April 15, 1904, pl. 22.)*

8. *Villa in Dordrecht. Interior, living hall. View looking south.* (Photo: Het Huis, *May 15, 1904, pl. 28.)*

disciplined manner. However, Cuypers's manipulation of interior space tends to be three-dimensionally more complex. The rooms to either side of the hall—on the west, the separate sitting rooms for the master and mistress of the house (marked respectively *9* and *10* on Fig. 5); on the east, the dining room and the salon (*5* and *7*)—are partially interwoven via the projecting conservatories (*8* in Fig. 5), which help to dilate and illuminate the space of the more formally arranged rooms to which they are appended (Fig. 7). In the living hall itself (Figs. 8, 9), light enters directly from the north and south, and indirectly through interior leaded glass windows which transmit diffused light from the rooms on either side.

The various interior volumes are clearly articulated in the massing, and the central position of the hall is made very legible, especially on the quasi-symmetrical garden front (Fig. 11). The loftiness of the hall is communicated here by the trio of long windows connected by low pedimental forms; this constitutes a rather special motif that will be elaborated later in some of de Klerk's independent projects (cf. Hillehuis, Amsterdam, 1911/12, Fig. 12)[25] and perhaps one can discern the hand of that youthful draftsman in this part of the design. The garden front (Fig. 11) is the most successfully composed facade, being less restless than the others. Again the lower portions of the house and the chimneys are Berlagian, while the half-timbered upper walls and picturesquely grouped roofs derive from the English Queen Anne, itself an amalgam of themes from various traditions.

These three houses, and several others from Cuypers's flourishing practice, were published in a periodical that he launched in 1903. This was a "house organ" in every sense of the word. Only

22 WOONKAMER

28 HALL

9. *Villa in Dordrecht. Interior, living hall. View looking north. (Photo:* Het Huis, *May 15, 1904, pl. 29.)*

10. *Villa in Dordrecht. Exterior. View from northwest. (Photo:* Het Huis, *January 15, 1904, pl. 4.)*

29 HALL

4. GEVEL ⅋ STATIONSWEG
MET BRUG EN HOOFDINGANG

commissions from Cuypers's office were included, and the magazine, initially called simply *Het Huis* (The House), was to be devoted primarily to domestic architecture. This was the architect's favorite building type because it gave him the maximum control over every detail, and the program allowed for great variety in massing and materials. Under the rubric of "house" was included applied art, which Cuypers believed indispensable to proper residential design (in 1900 he had supplemented his architectural practice by founding an *atelier* for interior furnishings, also called "Het Huis"; Fig. 13).[26]

Cuypers explained his venture as follows:

In recent years the interest in the arts has grown not only more widespread but deeper and more comprehensive. . . . English, German, and French periodicals publish numerous descriptions and illustrations of the useful arts, yet while many Netherlanders also find themselves involved in this area, we lack a journal of our own.[27]

This overstates the case somewhat. From time to time articles on the applied arts appeared both in architectural journals and in reviews of a more general nature.[28] In 1898, three of Cuypers's near contemporaries—William Bauer, J.L.M. Lauweriks, and K.P.C. de Bazel[29]—initiated a serious and sumptuous magazine called *Bouw- en Sierkunst* (Architectural and Decorative Art) that anticipated *Het Huis*; when it ceased publication after two years, Cuypers moved to fill the gap. Doubtless Lauweriks and de Bazel had come by their enthusiasm for craftsmanship and the applied arts via the same route as Cuypers, for they too had trained in his uncle's office. Interestingly, one year after the first issue of *Het Huis*

there appeared Berlage's first book on architecture and furniture design,[30] and the character of its black-and-white illustrations is strikingly similar to those in Cuypers's magazine. But the two men approached the issue from opposite directions. While Berlage thought of each piece of furniture as a building in miniature, Cuypers tended to think of each building as a huge piece of furniture. The difference is significant; Berlage emphasized sturdy and rational construction when he designed furniture; Cuypers stressed refinement and individuality of detailing in architecture no less than in furnishings, presaging a similar attitude on the part of members of the Amsterdam School.

If not the very first periodical to deal with the decorative arts in the Netherlands, *Het Huis* was the most enduring.[31] Although self-serving in the beginning in that it advertised Cuypers's own products and point of view, the magazine became more inclusive in 1905, when he shifted to a larger format and expanded the name to *Het Huis Oud en Nieuw* (The House, Old and New). Articles by learned scholars on old buildings and on the history of the decorative arts were featured, and reviews of relevant Dutch and foreign

12. *Hillehuis, Johannes Vermeerplein, Amsterdam. Michel de Klerk, 1911/12. Exterior. (Photo: Helen Searing.)*

13. *Cuypers, designs for lamps and fireplace accessories, 1903. (Woodcut:* Het Huis, *May 15, 1903, pl. 30.)*

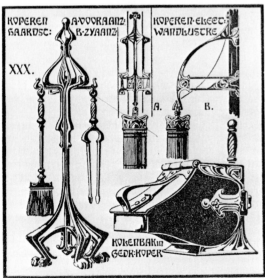

books and periodicals became a part of the text. As far as contemporary design was concerned, however, only work from Cuypers's architectural and decorative *ateliers* was represented.

During the early years of publication, *Het Huis* carried a number of essays by Cuypers which cast light on his ideas about architecture, ideas that would be reflected in the words and works of his employees. For example, in a period of growing functionalism, Cuypers continued to insist that architecture was first and foremost an art, and that the architect had an almost sacred mission to create a beauty that would transcend the pragmatic realities of program and resources:

> In the main a good building should fulfill the requirements of beauty, hygiene and convenience, but each of these three categories must be analyzed in terms of a great number of small details. This makes architecture into an art which

is already bound by its very nature to so many laws that the architect, in regard to the large conception and the forms in which he wishes to express his ideas, cannot be tied to narrow paths. Every significant work of art, then, can only be the free, unfettered expression of the artist who, influenced alone by the best that preceded him, mirrors in his own creation the cultural attitudes of his time.[32]

The notion of "free, unfettered expression" was developed further in the essay "Is there a modern style?"[33] In contrast to those who concluded from the architectural pluralism prevalent at the turn of the century that there was no contemporary style, Cuypers found precisely in such diversity the key constituent of the modern aesthetic. Twentieth-century culture, he argued, was dominated by the ethos of individualism and therefore the only common stylistic denominator was the requirement that the artist express his own personality. This idea was anathema to Berlage and his followers, who saw it as an "unbearable manifestation of bourgeois individualism,"[34] but it would become a fundamental credo of the Amsterdam School.

A corollary concept was Cuypers's belief in visually differentiating buildings according to program and context. He insisted that the specific function of each commission be symbolically expressed as well as formally accommodated, and that the design take into account the existing setting, be it natural or man-made. Such a position was diametrically opposite that of Berlage, who sought to forge a universal style applicable to every location and building type. While his viewpoint would triumph among the New Pioneers (see introductory essays), Cuypers's attitude would be reasserted by the Amsterdam School, especially de Klerk, who in his one published utterance criticized Berlage on the grounds that

> his work totally lacks representational character, in the choice of materials as well as in the indication of use. His urban houses for the wealthy are not differentiated in essence or type from his country houses or workers' dwellings; his office buildings are scarcely distinguishable from his union headquarters or stores. They all lack that special visual embodiment of purpose.[35]

When de Klerk further complained that Berlage did not infuse into his work the "sparkingly new, the thrillingly sensational . . . that which characterizes the properly *modern* [his italics],"[36] he was also echoing sentiments that Cuypers had proclaimed in the article on the modern style.

Yet around 1905 Cuypers himself seemed to retreat from such a provocative vision of modern architecture. The change coincided with the conversion of *Het Huis* from a precious "little magazine" to a more historically oriented journal. At the same time, it probably reflected Cuypers's response to the widespread academic reaction against the Art Nouveau. Tradition was reasserted in his architecture no less than in the work of numerous colleagues, as can be seen in the two variant projects of 1906 for a villa near Haarlem (Figs. 14–16). Still, it would be erroneous to read the change as a complete regression to the strict revivalism of Cuypers's early years, when he practiced in the Dutch Renaissance mode. Although the dominant motif is the scrolled gable, the work is not based on those Netherlandish facades of the sixteenth and early seventeenth centuries most recently analyzed by Hitchcock.[37] Rather, the domestic architecture of Stuart Eng-

14. Cuypers, project for a villa near Haarlem, 1906. Ground floor plan. (Illustration: Het Huis Oud en Nieuw, 1906, p. 149.)

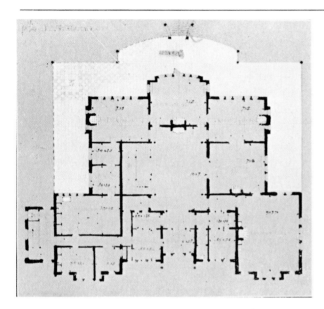

14. Cuypers, project for a villa near Haarlem, 1906. Ground floor plan. (Illustration: Het Huis Oud en Nieuw, 1906, p. 149.)

land, with its lively combination of Dutch and Italianate elements, is recalled in the layout, decoration, stone quoining, and Palladian and bull's-eye windows of the villa.[38] Cuypers's actual sources may have been more contemporary however, for architects of the Late-Victorian/Edwardian period like Shaw and William Lethaby had already added seventeenth-century English themes to their design vocabulary. Illustrations of their residential work were readily accessible to Cuypers, not only in periodicals but in the monumental *Das Englische Haus*, which had been reviewed in *Het Huis Oud en Nieuw* in 1905.[39]

The plan (Fig. 14) of the Haarlem villa, however, is more formal than anything published by Hermann Muthesius,[40] and represents a further stage in the development that commenced with the Dordrecht house (Fig. 5), when Cuypers set about disciplining the "agglutinative" plan. In the project of 1906, the living hall remains the center of the circulation but the symmetry is more pronounced and the massing more compact, giving stateliness to a composition that nevertheless retains a picturesque vitality.

On the exterior, a curious form crowns the second-story windows of each variant. It may be described as a brick "arch," almost flat along the intrados, the extrados shaped into a broad pediment. The "arch" is framed by stone impost blocks which, in the Berlagian manner, do not project from the wall. This motif appears at a larger scale over the doors of the garage belonging to the villa (Figs. 17, 18); here, bull's-eye windows are merged with the impost blocks. As befits its humbler function, the garage is simpler in silhouette and detail than the house. The curving gables of the front and rear facades are devoid of applied ornament, decorative interest being supplied through the skillful manipulation of the materials. The wall is smoothly taut and the composition unified by the rhythmic repetition of a very few motifs. An equilibrium is struck between originality and historical allusion that suggests, in embryo at least, those qualities that will characterize the New Tradition (see introductory essays) and the mature work of de Klerk and the Amsterdam School.

When rendering the perspectives and elevations of the villa, de Klerk presumably followed the directives of his employer, though he slyly inserted his signature into the fenestration of the second story. In the case of the garage, however, surely the drawings are in conception as well as execution entirely de Klerk's and comprise the first extant design completely from his hand. In the same year, 1906, appeared the second, a competition entry for a "railway station for a small municipality" (Fig. 19),[41] which attracts attention purely through the bizarre detailing. The design is arbitrary and unresolved, and the "arch" form, now covering circular windows, creates an unsettlingly anthropomorphic effect. The jewelrylike centerpiece, which destroys the scale and

15. *Project for a villa near Haarlem. Perspective. (Illustration:* Het Huis Oud en Nieuw, *1906, p. 145.)*

16. *Variant of Figure 15. Elevation. (Illustration:* Het Huis Oud en Nieuw, *1906, p. 151.)*

integrity of the Edwardian gable, is an Art Nouveau survival; so are the downward-tapering openings, which exist uncomfortably with the other motifs.[42]

A comparison of the two projects suggests that in 1906 de Klerk still needed the guidance of Cuypers and the reaction of his peers. Thus the opportunity to receive criticism from the master and to exchange ideas with like-minded contemporaries was a crucial aspect of employment at Jan Luykenstraat 2. Also attractive was the extensive library which Cuypers reputedly encouraged his draftsmen to utilize.[43] Especially for de

17. De Klerk, project for a garage for a villa near Haarlem. Front facade. Elevation. (Illustration: Het Huis Oud en
Nieuw, 1906, p. 157.)

18. De Klerk, project for a garage. Rear facade. Elevation. (Illustration: Het Huis Oud en Nieuw, 1906, p. 157.)

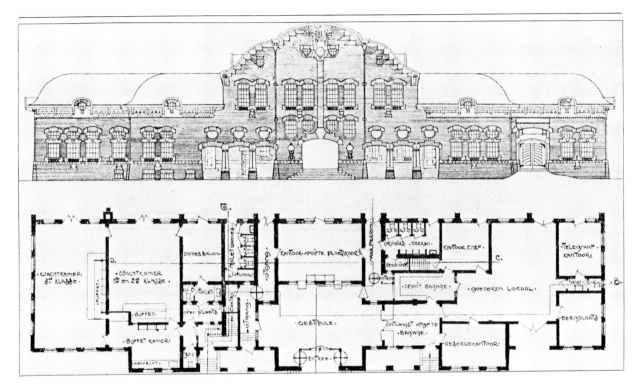

Klerk and Kramer, who were virtually autodidacts, Cuypers's office was, in Kramer's words, "the best school you could have wished for as a young architect."[44]

But ambitious young architects yearn for independence and one by one those most responsible for fashioning the style of the Amsterdam School left Cuypers's employ. Van der Meij, who had arrived in 1897, remained until 1906; de Klerk left in 1910, while Kramer was in and out of the Jan Luykenstraat *atelier* from 1903 to 1913.[45] In 1912 these three collaborated on designing an artistically satisfying inner and outer mantle for the reinforced-concrete skeleton of the Scheepvaarthuis (Figs. 20, 21), an office building for a group of shipping companies. Their joint achievement conveys the exotic excitement associated with ocean travel, and the extraordinarily varied and imaginative detailing in brick,

molded terra-cotta, stone, and wrought metal creates an overwhelmingly dramatic effect. Many of the motifs suggest the art of the Dutch East Indies with which Cuypers's draftsmen, because of his own keen interests, were so familiar.[46] All in all, the experience *chez* Cuypers must have been essential preparation for the attainment of such high levels of craftsmanship and invention. The completion in 1916 of this architectural tour de force heralded the emergence of the Amsterdam School as a recognized phenomenon.[47]

Commercial commissions, however, were an anomaly in the *oeuvre* of the Amsterdam School. Its members would more usually make their mark handling the large-scale housing projects constructed en masse in the teens and twenties with government funds provided via the Dutch Housing Act (*Woningwet*).[48] Thus Cuypers's former apprentices continued to be involved with do-

mestic programs, though now—since opportunities to design single-family dwellings were rare—in terms of *housing* rather than "the house." But they transformed this conventionally utilitarian building type into a means of expression of personal fantasy for collective enjoyment, justifying Cuypers's sustained conviction that the modern style could accommodate personal diversity and that architecture was indeed an art.

The title of this contribution, no less than the method of its author, has been inspired by Hitchcock.[49] While in any consideration of twentieth-century Dutch architecture the influence of the powerful Berlage cannot be ignored, it has become clear that he was not the only protagonist of importance active when the first generation of modern architects was being trained. The extraordinary variety of Dutch architecture during the 1910s and 1920s becomes far more comprehensible when one recognizes that in the early years of the century conflicting architectural philosophies were available, philosophies that allowed for the concurrent development of divergent trends like Expressionism and Functionalism. For the Amsterdam School one must indicate as significant, besides Berlage, Willem Kromhout, de Bazel, Lauweriks, and indubitably Eduard Cuypers. Although largely forgotten now, Cuypers at many points seems to have been a rival worthy of Berlage and, in the case of the Amsterdam School at any rate, "the father of them all."

Notes

the major architects of the early twentieth century." Hitchcock, *Modern Architecture: Romanticism and Reintegration* (New York: Payson and Clarke, 1929), p. 119; (rep. ed., New York: Hacker Art Books, 1970).

3. Three recent exhibition catalogues have greatly expanded and to a certain extent revised our view of Dutch architecture in the early twentieth century. These are P. Singelenberg and M. Bock, *H. P. Berlage, bouwmeester: 1856–1934* (The Hague: Gemeentemuseum, 1975); M. Bock, *Architectura: 1893–1918*, text in German and Dutch (Amsterdam: Architectuur Museum, 1975); and A. Venema, E. Bergvelt, F. van Burkom, and W. de Wit, *Amsterdamse School: 1910–1930* (Amsterdam: Stedelijk Museum, 1975). See my review in the *Journal of the Society of Architectural Historians* 38 (December 1978): 305–306.

4. Hitchcock, *Architecture: Nineteenth and Twentieth Centuries*, p. 357. In *Modern Architecture*, Hitchcock placed the Amsterdam School with the New Tradition.

5. There is as yet no single comprehensive publication in English on the Amsterdam School, but see chapters in Wolfgang Pehnt, *Expressionist Architecture* (New York: Praeger, 1973), and Reyner Banham, *Theory and Design in the First Machine Age* (London: Architectural Press, 1960). The indispensable work on twentieth-century Dutch architecture is Giovanni Fanelli, *Architettura moderna in Olanda 1900–1940* (Florence: Marchi e Bertolli, 1968; rev. ed. translated into Dutch by Wim de Wit, *Moderne architectuur in Nederland* [The Hague: Staatsuitgeverij, 1978]). For de Klerk and the Amsterdam School see also two unpublished doctoral dissertations: Suzanne Shulof Frank, *Michel de Klerk: An Architect of the Amsterdam School*, Columbia University, 1970; and Helen Searing, *Housing in Holland and the Amsterdam School*, Yale University, 1972.

6. There is a brief consideration of Eduard Cuypers in the catalogue *Amsterdamse School* cited in note 3.

1. Henry-Russell Hitchcock, *Architecture: Nineteenth and Twentieth Centuries* (Baltimore: Penguin, 1958), p. 357.
2. Hitchcock first wrote of Berlage that "in Holland, the New Tradition is almost entirely dependent upon him and has brilliantly developed the many tendencies inherent in his personal manner into a general national style that has been admired and emulated by the rest of the world. He is unquestionably to be considered with Wright . . . as one of

7. Except for a brief trip to England in 1906.
8. The elder Cuypers himself played the godfather role to several important architects of Eduard's generation, among them K.P.C. de Bazel and J.L.M. Lauweriks, as well as to a number of decorative artists who would help to realize the ideal of the *Gesamtkunstwerk*. There is no definitive monograph on P.J.H. Cuypers in English, but see Hitchcock, *Modern Architecture*, pp. 118–121; idem., *Architecture: Nineteenth and Twentieth Centuries*, pp. 199–201 (he uses for both uncle and nephew the alternative spelling, Cuijpers); and most recently the essay by Richard Padovan, "Building Towards an Ideal: Progressive Architecture in Holland," in Frank Russell, ed., *Art Nouveau Architecture* (New York: Rizzoli International, 1979), pp. 138–141.
9. After Eugène-Emmanuel Viollet-le-Duc (1814–1879).
10. Cuypers was instrumental in founding in Amsterdam several schools of applied art for the craftsmen and artists he needed to decorate his public commissions. In 1879 the Quellinusschool was established, and in 1881 two training *ateliers* were set up in the unfinished Rijksmuseum, one to teach drafting and the other applied art. These provided essential training for Dutch decorative artists, whose collaboration was eagerly sought by many architects until the mid-1920s.
11. Again we must turn to Hitchcock for one of the first reappraisals of Art Nouveau architecture. See his essay in P. Selz and M. Constantine, ed., *Art Nouveau* (New York: Museum of Modern Art, 1960).
12. See L. Gans, *Nieuwe Kunst: De Nederlandse Bijdrage tot de Art Nouveau* (Utrecht: A. Oosthoek, 1960); Ernest Braches, *Het boek als Nieuwe Kunst* (Utrecht: A. Oosthoek, 1973); and the essay by Padovan cited in note 8.
13. E. Gugel, *Geschiedenis van de Bouwstijlen in de Hoofdtijdperken der Architektuur*, Part II, 4th ed., expanded by J.H.W. Leliman, Rotterdam: D. Bolle, n.d. [1920]), p. 413. "Cuypers behoorde tot de eersten die de moderne opvattingen aanvaardden. Zijne vroegste werken in dien trant . . . zijn verwant aan belgische en engelsche kunst. Bij een zeer groot aantal bouwwerken . . . is een eigen opvatting ontwikkelde."
14. Fanelli, op. cit., p. 339, believes that "Commercial ties with the Orient and the subsequent development of an exotic taste had notable influence on Dutch culture from the sixteenth century on. . . . One of the reasons for the singularity of Dutch "fin-de-siecle" and early twentieth-century art is the exotic Javanese component."
15. *De Groene Amsterdammer*, June 11, 1927: "Hij was talentvol epigoon, geen pionier. Bij hem was het meer een talentvol volgen der onderscheiden kunststromingen dan een zelfscheppen."
16. For Berlage and the concept of *Sachlichkeit*, see Pieter Singelenberg, *H.P. Berlage, Idea and Style* (Utrecht: Haentjens, Dekker, and Gumbert, 1972); and Helen Sear-ing, "Berlage and Housing, 'the most significant modern building type,'" in *Nederlands Kunsthistorisch Jaarboek* 25 (1974), especially note 42.
17. *Het Huis* I, no. 1 (15 January 1903):18: "zich bijzonder leenen tot het inrichten van verrassende hoekjes–den cosy corner."
18. For the Queen Anne see Mark Girouard, *Sweetness and Light: The 'Queen Anne' Movement 1860–1900* (Oxford: Clarendon Press, 1977).
19. *Het Huis* I, no. 1 (15 January 1903):16.
20. Ibid., p. 18: "is er naar gestreefd met weinig kostbare middelen zekere behagelijkheid te bereiken. De betimmeringen zijn van warm getint vuren-hout, de wanden . . . in de kalk geschuurd en beschilderd. [Alles werd] met zorg behandeld, opdat zij er recht huiselijk uit zouden zien: een gedachte aan vriendelijkheid en gastvrijheid, dient de eerste indruk te zijn."
21. Hitchcock, *Architecture: Nineteenth and Twentieth Centuries*, p. 262.
22. See, for example, Ian Latham, *Joseph Maria Olbrich* (New York: Rizzoli International, 1980).
23. The entire second volume (1904) of *Het Huis* is given over to illustrations—seventy-two in all—of this villa.
24. The classic discussion of these houses is in Vincent Scully, *The Shingle Style* (New Haven: Yale University Press, 1955; rev. ed., 1971).
25. Hillehuis, a middle-class apartment block that still stands on the Johannes Vermeerplein, was de Klerk's first executed independent commission. A number of its features seem to have originated from designs for interior details made in Cuypers's office during the period de Klerk was there. For example, the curious tentlike forms that project over the end bays of the main facade resemble certain fireplace projects illustrated in *Het Huis*, but these in turn have formal similarities with earlier decorative designs by Olbrich. The wrought-iron railings of Hillehuis—and wrought-iron architectural details were among the products supplied by Cuypers's ornamental *atelier*—resemble in many respects those on the Glasgow School of Art by Charles Rennie Mackintosh (1868–1928), which de Klerk probably knew from drawings or photographs published in international periodicals like *The Studio* or *Moderne Bauformen* with which Cuypers's library was abundantly supplied. Hillehuis is discussed and generously illustrated in my dissertation.
26. At first the "Atelier for Interior Design" was located upstairs next to the architecture studio on Jan Luykenstraat; in 1904 business was so successful that it became necessary to move "Het Huis" to its own quarters at Kerkstraat 310–314. Again, it is not so much the fact that Cuypers believed the decorative arts to be essential to architecture that is singular, but the synthetic, international character of his designs. "Het Huis" had been preceded by Jan Toorop's "Arts and Crafts" shop, established in The Hague in

1898; it was contemporary with "'t Binnenhuis," which Berlage with several decorative artists set up in 1900. But these two establishments sold items made by a variety of artist-craftsmen, while Cuypers created his designs to order and controlled every aspect of production.

27. *Het Huis* I, no. 1 (15 January 1903):2–10: "Het is een verblijdend feit, dat de belangstelling voor kunst in de laatste jaren niet alleen algemeener, maar tevens breeder en dieper werd. . . . Terwijl Engelsche, Duitsche, en Fransche kunsttijdschriften uitvoerige besprekingen en afbeeldingen van zulke 'gebruikskunst' brengen, ook in ons land talrijke lezers vinden en niet zelden zich met onze kunst bezig houden, blijft ons toch nog een eigen, een Nederlandsche orgaan ontbreken."

28. Among the important professional magazines were *Architectura*, which commenced publication in 1893, and *Bouwkundig Weekblad*, which first appeared in 1881. Both of them were organs of architectural organizations which held competitions for decorative arts projects as well as for more large-scale designs. Among the general periodicals, *De Kroniek*, a cultural-political review, carried numerous articles about the decorative arts during the 1890s. It was edited by the social democrat, P. L. Tak; discussions of the useful arts and of socialism in the same forum had a healthy precedent in England, where the Arts and Crafts Movement was inseparable from social reform. The works of John Ruskin (1819–1900), William Morris (1834–1896), and Walter Crane (1845–1915) were well known in late-nineteenth-century Holland.

29. Discussion in English of the work of these men is sparse, but see my dissertation and the article by Padovan cited in note 8. The most recent consideration in Dutch (with a German translation provided) is the exhibition catalogue *Architectura: 1893–1918*, cited in note 3.

30. H. P. Berlage, *Over stijl in bouw- en meubelkunst* [On Style in Architectural and Furniture Design] (Amsterdam: A. P. Soep [1904]; subsequent editions, Rotterdam: Brusse, 1908, 1917, and 1921).

31. With interruptions in 1917, 1918, 1920, and 1929, it ran from 1903 to 1931.

32. *Het Huis* IV (1906):155: "In hoofdzaak moet een goed bouwwerk beantwoorden aan alle aesthetische, hygiënische en gemakseischen, doch elk dezer drie hoofdbegrippen is nog in een groot aantal kleinere factoren te ontleden. Dit maakt de architectuur tot eene kunst, die uit den aard reeds aan zoovele wetten gebonden is, dat de bouwmeester, wat betreft de groote conceptie en de vormen, waarin hij zijne gedachten wenscht uit te drukken, niet aan te nauwe banden gelegd mag worden. Elk belangrijk kunstwerk kan dan ook slechts de vrije, ongebonden uiting wezen van den kunstenaar, die alleen beïnvloed door het geen vòòr hem als het beste tot stand gebracht is, in zijn werk de afspiegeling geeft van het beschavingsstandpunt van zijnen tijd."

33. "Bestaat er een moderne stijl?," *Het Huis* II, no. 11 (November 1904).

34. The phrase, "ondragelijke verschijningen van burgerlijk individualisme" is from Berlage, *Normalisatie in Woningbouw* (Rotterdam: Brusse, 1918). Berlage's feelings on this point are discussed in Searing, "Berlage and Housing."

35. *Bouwkundig Weekblad* XXXVI (1916):331–332: "Mist ook zijn werk ten eenemale, karakteristiek en uitbeelding, zoowel in zijne materiaal verwerking als in zijne gebruiksaanduiding. Zijne stadsheerenhuizen verschillen in wezen en typeering niet van zijn land- of volkswoonhuizen, zijn kantoorgebouwen onderscheiden zich weinig van vereenigings of winkelgebouwen, zij missen allen dat speciaal bijzondere, het typeerend uitbeelden hunner bestemming." However it should be acknowledged that precisely at the time these words were written, Berlage was in fact working toward a more expressive imagery. In a brilliant and insightful paper ("Berlage and the Amsterdam School, 1914–20: Rationalist as Expressionist," not yet published), H. Paul Rovinelli of the Columbia School of Architecture has shown that Berlage was not consistently the *sachlich* architect he is so often made out to be. Around 1915 he designed a number of buildings that were "physical expressions [of ideas] articulated directly through the manipulation of architectural form" (p. 14). Rovinelli sees Berlage not only influencing the Amsterdam School but also responding to it, absorbing in his turn some of the formal strategies of its members.

36. *Bouwkundig Weekblad*, loc. cit: "Het tintelend-nieuwe, het sensationeel-schokkende . . . wat het eigenlijke *moderne* kenmarkt . . ."

37. H.-R. Hitchcock, *Netherlandish Scrolled Gables of the Sixteenth and Early Seventeenth Centuries* (New York: New York University Press, published for the College Art Association, 1978).

38. See, for example, Swakeleys, Middlesex, of 1638, and Raynham Hall, Norfolk, c. 1635. These are discussed and illustrated in John Summerson, *Architecture in Britain: 1530–1830* (Baltimore: Penguin, 1953; 4th rev. ed., 1963).

39. Hermann Muthesius, *Das Englische Haus* (Berlin: Wasmuth, 1904). Volune II was reviewed by W. Vogelsang, *Het Huis Oud en Nieuwe* III (1905):128.

40. The English architect whose house plans were most formal in these years was Sir Edwin Lutyens (1869–1944). Interestingly, Pevsner observes, "If I look for continental parallels to what is most valuable in Lutyens's work, I find some similarity with Berlage and his Dutch successors, especially de Klerk. . . . Here is the same origin in picturesque traditions, the freedom of handling . . . the occasional jazziness of detail and also . . . the keen interest in a variety of materials and in craftsmanship." ("Building with Wit: The Architecture of Sir Edwin Lutyens," in Alistair Service, ed., *Edwardian Architecture and its Origins* [London: The Architectural Press, 1975], p. 467.)

41. The villa near Haarlem was published in *Het Huis Oud*

en Nieuw in July 1906 (III, pp. 145–160). The results of the competition for the railway station were reported in *Bouwkundig Weekblad* in late 1906 (XXV, p. 301), so presumably the garage design antedates de Klerk's competition submission. Between 1906 and 1911 when his first building—Hillehuis—was executed, de Klerk entered eight competitions.

42. See, for example, the Rotterdam Insurance Society building in Amsterdam, c. 1901, by Johannes Verheul Dzn. (1860–1948).

43. Unhappily, the library was destroyed by fire.

44. E. G. Emeis, interview with Pieter Kramer, *Week in Beeld*, November 11, 1951: "de beste leerschool die je als jong architect zou kunnen wensen."

45. Giovanni Fanelli, *op. cit.*, biographical catalogue.

46. Cuypers had a number of commissions in the Netherlands Indies (he did a great deal of work for the Java Bank) and so was unusually familiar with the art and architecture of these colonial possessions. There were also articles in *Het Huis* about artifacts from the Malay Archipelago, a place which cast a spell on many Dutch architects during this period.

47. Wim de Wit, *Amsterdamse School*, p. 51, believes that the term was first used in 1916.

48. For the *Woningwet* see Catherine Bauer, *Modern Housing* (Boston: Houghton Mifflin, 1934); H. Searing, "With Red Flags Flying: Housing in Amsterdam 1915–1923," in ed. Henry A. Millon and Linda Nochlin, *Art and Architecture in the Service of Politics* (Cambridge, Mass.: MIT Press, 1978); and idem., "Amsterdam South: Social Democracy's Elusive Housing Ideal," in *VIA, IV: Culture and the Social Vision*, Architectural Journal of the Graduate School of Fine Arts, University of Pennsylvania (Cambridge, Mass.: MIT Press, 1980).

49. With a little help from his friends (viz., Virgil Thomson et al.; see note 3 of my Introductory Essay, above, p. 7). The title of the concluding chapter of Hitchcock's groundbreaking *Early Victorian Architecture in Britain* (New Haven: Yale University Press, 1954) is "Ruskin or Butterfield? Victorian Gothic at the Mid-Century."

FRANK LLOYD WRIGHT'S
DIAGONAL PLANNING

Neil Levine

ALMOST HALF A CENTURY HAS passed since Henry-Russell Hitchcock published *In the Nature of Materials*,[1] yet the full sweep of the work of Frank Lloyd Wright is still imprecisely charted and its contemporary meaning still obscured by the tendency to think of him, as Philip Johnson once put it, as "the greatest architect of the nineteenth century."[2] One reason simply may be that historians and architects alike have been so transfixed by the stunning originality and power of the buildings of Wright's Oak Park years that they just have not paid the same kind of attention to his later work. Another reason, and the one to be addressed here, is that the later work often appears so inconsistent and so idiosyncratic that, lacking any discernible principle of design, it offers no real sense of logical development and one is hard pressed to see the historical continuity of Wright's career as a whole.

The Wasmuth portfolio of 1910 presented an image of extraordinary coherence from the point of view of planning, but the same can hardly be said for the two issues of *Architectural Forum*—January 1938 and January 1948—that are devoted to Wright. While the German publication gave such an impression of discipline and unity that it could immediately be accepted as a textbook of modern architecture, the later collections offer an almost bewildering variety of geometric forms. Gone is the rigorous orthogonal plaiting that characterized both public and private buildings of Wright's earlier years and gave his planning an almost mesmerizing sense of logical necessity. Instead, there is Fallingwater, with its open series of staggered, rectilinear elements; or the Hanna House, with its hexagonal grid fanning out in a pattern of reflex movement; or Taliesin West, with its spiky projections from an elongated spine; or the Guggenheim Museum, with its spiraling, closed, circular forms; or, finally, Florida Southern College, with its rotated, multilayered square grid, edged by angular paths pivoting on circles and projecting out into space. The radically different geometries emphasize the particularity of each project and appear to deny any form of consistency. But their very use depends on an underlying principle of order, common to all Wright's later work, which is the diagonal axis.[3] Whether or not the diagonality is made explicit in the geometry of the plan, as in the Hanna House, it is always implicit in determining the spatial experience of the building and its relation to the site.

"When Dad builds," wrote Wright's son John in 1946, "he sees things out of the corner of his eye. He never looks straight at them."[4] In his Prairie Style buildings, Wright's desire for free-flowing space led him to open up the corner and deny its role of containing and bounding interior space. But only after 1920 did the diagonal axis become the positive organizing principle of his planning, bringing a new depth and meaning to his work.[5] The supple principle of diagonality allowed for that new sense of freedom, breadth, and openness Wright sought after leaving the suburban world of Oak Park behind and moving to Taliesin in the hills of southern Wisconsin. When seen against the background of his early work, the emergence of diagonality helps chart the course of his career more accurately and clarifies the changing values of his architecture.

While it is true that the diagonal axis has played an important role in planning throughout history —and here one immediately thinks of the Acropolis in Athens, Hadrian's Villa, and the radiating avenues of Baroque cities and gardens[6]—

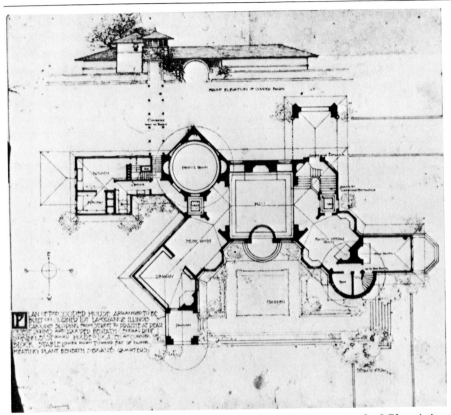

it is also fair to say that its systematic use in the design of buildings themselves is a relatively modern development. One might resort to the diagonal when faced with the structural problem of a dome, or a particularly difficult site, or, especially as the eighteenth century went on, in order to produce an intricate and animated solution; but, to the classically trained architect, the diagonal implied irregularity and irrationality. Its consistent use in the rib vaults, canted piers, and flying buttresses of medieval cathedrals was a major reason for the traditional criticism of Gothic architecture.[7] However, by the later nineteenth century in America, the desire for more picturesqueness and casualness, particularly in domestic architecture, made the use of diagonal shifts in axis almost common practice until the

renewal of Classicism in the 1890s redirected the Shingle Style toward greater discipline and order.[8] It is in this context, as Vincent Scully pointed out long ago, that we can understand Wright's early work and its extraordinary resolution of the opposed pressures toward freedom and order.

Wright employed diagonal shifts in axis from the very beginning of his career as a way of opening up the plan and giving direction to the interior space. The house he apparently designed in 1887 (Fig. 1) and showed to Louis Sullivan when applying for a job—he proposed to build it three years later for the Cooper family in La Grange, Illinois—has three wings projecting at 45-degree angles from the corners of a square central hall. The "butterfly plan," as it was called in late-Vic-

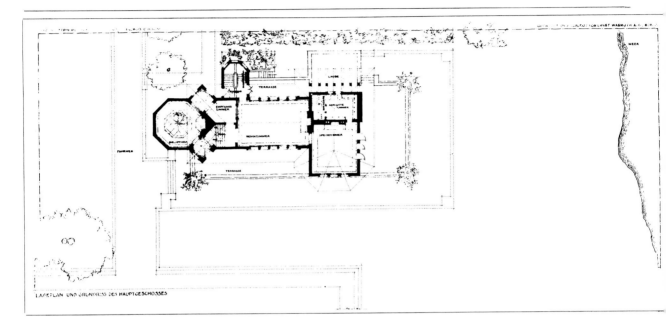

torian England, had an obvious source in the
project for a townhouse by E. E. Viollet-le-Duc
published in his seventeenth *entretien* in 1872
and in Bucknall's English translation in 1881.[9]
It was used almost immediately by McKim, Mead
& White, first in the Colonial-detailed Misses
Appleton House at Lenox, Massachusetts, built
in 1883/84, and then in the shingled house for
John Cowdin at Far Rockaway, Long Island (see
also pp. 188–189, above), both published in
Sheldon's *Artistic Country Seats* in 1886/87.[10]
In Wright's design the loose and picturesque handling of the parts is tightened up and the changes
in direction are articulated with greater clarity
and assertiveness. The hall, with its fireplace on
axis, is preceded by a partially enclosed garden,
gently skewed toward the corner entrance; and
each separate wing is assured privacy as well as
light on three sides.

Wright's drive to give ever greater focus and
order to his architecture soon led him away from
the dispersive tendencies of the "butterfly plan"

and toward much more compact solutions. In the
Blossom House in Chicago, of 1892, and especially the Winslow House in River Forest, Illinois, of the following year, the rooms are grouped
around a central fireplace. Oblique views from
room to room break up the apparent symmetry
and give a dynamic, pinwheeling effect to the
space, as in the house and studio he built for
himself in Oak Park in 1889.

Following the almost Classical statement of
principles in the Winslow House, Wright then
designed two other houses in the Sullivanian
mode in which he returned to the explicit use of
45-degree angles. Both the McAfee House of
1894 (Fig. 2) and the Devin House of 1896 were
designed for narrow lots on the shore of Lake
Michigan, and angled projections were obviously
provided to take advantage of the view. In the
McAfee House, the shifts in axis are integrally
related to the spatial movement of the plan, giving it a dynamic pistollike shape. The two square
vestibules, rotated within the reentrant angles of

3. *Frederick C. Robie House, Chicago, Illinois. Wright, 1908/9. Living room. (Photo: Neil Levine.)*

the octagonal library and entrance area, provide a fork in the main axis and echo at a distance the symmetrical projections of the dining room and arbor.

By the turn of the century, as his work reached full maturity, Wright began to eliminate any such graphic representation of axial inflection but continued to use the rotated square as the terminating projection of the orthogonal axes themselves. The earliest fully developed instance of this is the Ward Willits House in Highland Park, Illinois, of 1901/02.[11] The main axis of the dining room ends in a triangular bay; a cross-axis projects out through the low front wall of the porch to form a conservatory just under the edge of the overhanging eaves. Since the apex of the dining-room bay window lines up with the far wall of the porch, half the view from that room is directed outward onto the garden while the other half is contained within the open porch. In this way, the pointed axial terminations extend the interior out into a half-indoors, half-outdoors space. Their diagonal shape gives physical form to Wright's idea of manipulating space as the plastic medium of architecture. Indeed, it is as if the interior space had literally been pulled out from the center and stretched taut between one's thumb and forefinger.

The Robie House in Chicago, of 1908/09, culminated Wright's use of the diagonally set bay to define and extend the spatial axes. Here, the living room (Fig. 3) and the dining room are pulled out from the central fireplace into prowlike extensions under the soaring eaves. Inside, the effect is rather like that of Classical one-point perspective. The angled planes of the projecting bay establish a vanishing point and the three pairs of piers, set parallel to the direction of the space,

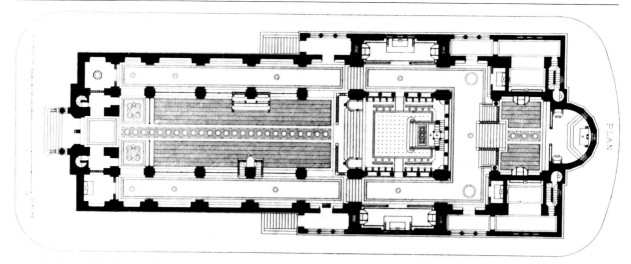

recede into depth, enforcing the telescopic effect. While the corner is in fact denied its role of containment, the eye is not allowed to look out on the diagonal. The slots of space created by the inset piers *in antis* give the illusion of space seeping out at the corners while actually channeling the view and focusing it on the middle. This method of giving a feeling of openness and extension to the interior space through the use of inset piers and corner slots of space was characteristic of Wright's Prairie Style and could occur with or without the diagonally set projections. The effect is fundamentally unidirectional and relates to classical methods of Beaux-Arts axial composition and framing, as can be seen in comparing the plan of the Martin House in Buffalo, of 1904, or the project for the Ullman House of the same year, to the plans of Sullivan's teacher, Emile Vaudremer, for the Parisian churches of St. Pierre de Montrouge or Notre-Dame d'Auteuil (Fig. 4).[12]

There were, however, a few instances during these early years when Wright made more radical use of the diagonal axis. It is perhaps no coincidence that the Glasner House in Glencoe, Illi-

nois, of 1905, which is often cited as a prototype for the later Usonian houses with their combined living-dining space, has a plan that develops along two main diagonal axes, realizing, as it were, the full implications of the earlier McAfee project. The eccentrically placed fireplace in the living room is located on a 45-degree line of sight from the corner entry, and the same angle defines the diagonal disposition of the bedrooms and octagonal sewing room which step out over the sloping site. A longitudinal axis defined by the two larger octagons of the library and projected tea house, however, stabilizes the plan in a rectilinear fashion.

Much more radical in their use of the diagonal axis and rotated square, as well as more prophetic of later developments in Wright's work, are the Hillside Home School, built for his two aunts Jane and Ellen in Spring Green, Wisconsin, in 1902, and a Studio House planned for himself in the following year. In the former, Wright rotated the square balcony 45 degrees within the main square space of the assembly hall (Figs. 5, 6). The aggressively diagonal spatial cut causes the ceiling to appear unsupported at the corners and

the space to flow out in all directions. In the extraordinary Studio House project of 1903, Wright set the dining room, living room, and studio all on a 45-degree diagonal perpendicular to the diagonal axis from the entry hall to the porch, and then expressed the diagonal deflection of the space by an eccentrically placed fireplace, open at three of its four corners (Fig. 7). The experimental quality of this very personal design was obviously subdued for the Glasner House, just as the aggressiveness of the Hillside Home School was modulated in Unity Temple.

It is quite apparent that at this point in his career Wright considered the use of diagonality very unconventional and confined its most radical expression to buildings for himself and his family. This is even more apparent in the decade following his return from Europe. Between 1910 and 1920, Wright's planning became more and more Classical, emphasizing rectilinearity, closure, and formality. While the symmetrical courtyard plans of Midway Gardens in Chicago, of 1913/14, and the Imperial Hotel built in Tokyo in 1916 to 1922 are the most notable examples, this development can also be seen in his domestic work, beginning with the Coonley Playhouse in Riverside, Illinois, of 1911/12, and culminating in Hollyhock House, built for Aline Barnsdall in Los Angeles in 1919 to 1921. The summer house for Joseph Bagley at Grand Beach, Michigan, of 1916, gives perhaps the best indication of the extent to which Wright tried to impose an abstract geometrical order (Fig. 8). Each function is zoned in a separate pavilion, and these

6. Hillside Home School. Assembly Hall plan, balcony level.
(Ausgeführte Bauten . . . , pl. 10.)

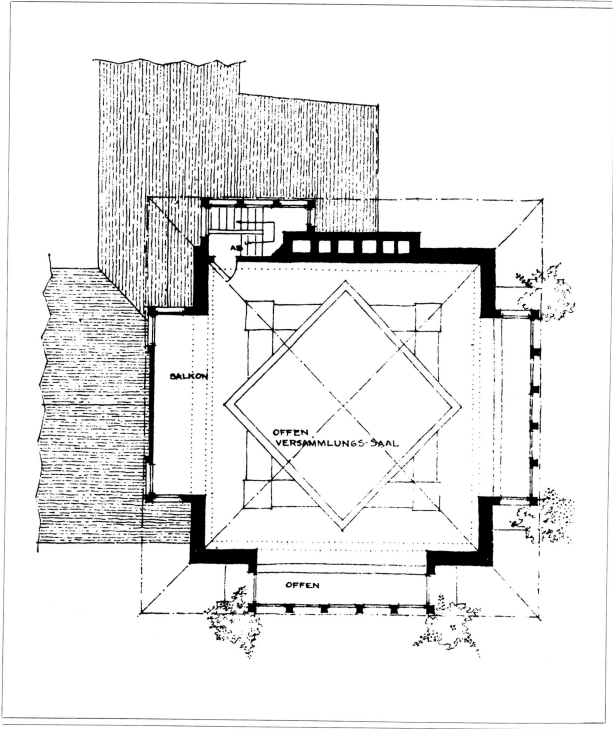

BALKON

OFFEN
VERSAMMLUNGS-SAAL

OFFEN

7. Wright, project, *Studio House*, *Oak Park, Illinois, 1903.*
Plan. (H.-R. Hitchcock, In the Nature of Materials . . . , *fig.*
80.)

8. *Joseph J. Bagley House, Grand Beach, Michigan.* Wright,
1916. Plan. (Hitchcock, In the Nature of Materials . . . , fig.
210.)

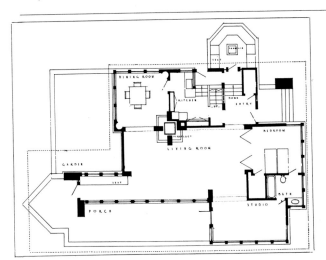

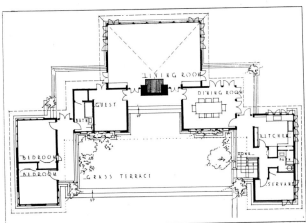

are all connected at their corners. The five sym-
metrically disposed pavilions describe a right-
angle triangle which thus contrasts in its complete
regularity with the seemingly casual arrangement
of the Glasner House or the Studio House project
of 1903.

A few houses of this period, such as the projects for Arthur Cutten and Sherman Booth of
1911 or the second Little House at Wayzata, Minnesota, of 1913, display a more freewheeling relation to the site. But the casualness is once again
a pale reflection of the assertive diagonality of a
building Wright designed for his own use. Taliesin, built in 1911 on the next hill over from the
Hillside Home School, stands out from all his
other work of this period in the way it blends in
with the landscape and almost literally becomes
part of it. It is organized around a court in a
loosely connected series of wings following the
contours of the hill, just below its crown, and
forming, as Wright explained, a brow for the hill
itself.[13] The rough stone laid up in strata imitates
the outcrops of the surrounding hills, but the fundamental sense of oneness with the land is most
fully expressed in the commanding view from the
living room out over the valley below.

The rectangular living room, perched out over
the hillside, is entered through a loggia off the
corner of the court diagonally opposite the main
view. The great fireplace and the bookshelf seat,
forming a nook in the path of entry, immediately
define the implied axis, while the notched corner
and diagonally placed piano at the far end of the
fireplace wall reinforce the angled line of sight.
When Taliesin was rebuilt after the tragic fire in
1914, Wright increased the importance of the implied diagonal by pushing the window-wall opposite the fireplace out two bays. At the same
time, he enlarged the farm buildings and set
them at a 45-degree angle, echoing the visual
axis of the living room. And after the fire of 1925
(Fig. 9), Wright even further increased the effect
of the diagonal by setting a stone pier just inside
the far corner and opening the corner out onto a
balcony.

The view upon entering the room now cuts
across the space and over the hills in one great,
effortless, arching movement which seems to follow the curve of the earth itself, as the stone
fireplace to the rear mirrors the pier in the far
corner and anchors the vista back in the hill behind. The catercornered placement of the stone

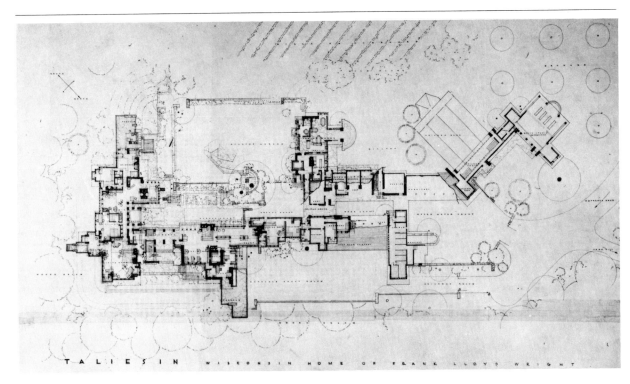

uprights helps give the impression of shearing along the diagonal; and, with the planes of the hipped ceiling spreading above and the floor sliding out toward the light, one has the boundless sense of being in the center of things, in a space turned inside out. Recalling the times when as a boy he would pick flowers on the hillside now occupied by the house, Wright later described how, "when you are on the low hill-crown, you have the feeling of being out in mid-air as though swinging in a plane, the Valley . . . dropping away from you leaving the treetops standing below all about you."[14] In this house built for himself on his family's land, it is almost as if Wright had consciously set himself the task of creating an architectural equivalent of nature.

For whatever reasons, Wright was not to offer a client anything quite like Taliesin until Fallingwater in the mid-thirties. But in the mountains and desert of California, for which he developed the textile-block method of construction just after returning from Japan, Wright began to experiment more and more with diagonal planning until it became the norm rather than the exception in his work. The first indications are the grandiose projects for the Edward H. Doheny Ranch Development in the Sierra Madre Mountains, of 1921 (Figs. 10, 11); the A. M. Johnson Desert Compound and Shrine in Death Valley, designed in the following year; and the Tahoe Summer Colony at Lake Tahoe in the Sierra Nevada Mountains, also designed in 1922 (Figs. 12, 13).[15] The multiple concrete-block houses that form the terraced hillsides of the Doheny project take their cue from Taliesin in leaving, as Wright noted, the "contours of the hills undisturbed."[16] Some become arched bridges over ravines, others stretch out in long horizontal platforms, while still others

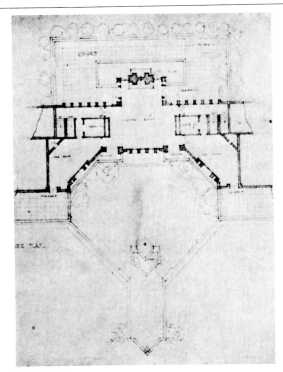

emerge like natural promontories from an existing chasm. Wright obviously felt that a nonorthogonal geometry was more accommodating to such a terrain. One of the most spectacular houses develops around an open court defined by the splayed, angled walls of a natural cleft (Figs. 10, 11). The chamfered square court is rotated 45 degrees and is then set like a cut diamond in the hillside. The diagonals define the major axes. The transverse one forms terraces to the left and right, following the contours of the hill, and the longitudinal one reaches out from the fireplace, set in a pool deep in the cavelike living room, to a projecting hexagonal terrace.[17] Its wedge shape reflects the conical hill behind, while, below, its angled planes split to allow a mountain stream running under the court to cascade down the ravine.

In the project for the Tahoe Summer Colony,

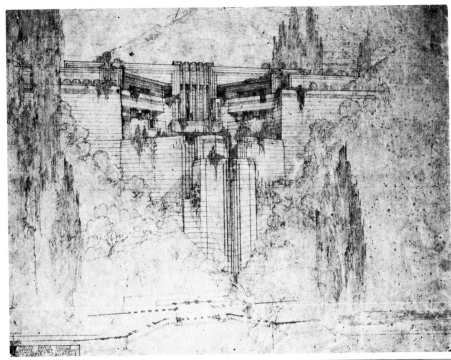

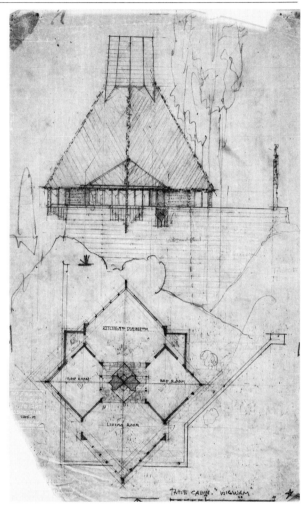

Wright pursued the obtuse geometry and open-angled plan in a number of the shore cabins. In others (Figs. 12, 13), he went even further in developing some of the implications of the 45-degree angle that had appeared in his work between 1900 and 1909. The Big Tree, or Wigwam, Type Cabin, for instance, is composed of one square rotated 45 degrees within another, like the assembly hall at the Hillside Home School, but now the rotated square projects through the outer casing to emphasize the extent of the diagonal. The Family Barge, with its double prow, restates the central shape of the Robie House plan, while the smaller Barge for Two is composed of three interlocking hexagons, with the central axis extending from point to point. Now also, for the first time, the diagonal geometry is not limited to the plans but is reflected in the sections and elevations as well, thus echoing the shape of the surrounding conifers and referring to traditional forms of nomadic shelter.

Wright's experimentation with diagonal planning in California culminated in the following year (1923) in two buildings that together form a watershed in the development outlined so far. The first, the Kindergarten and Playhouse (Figs. 14, 15) designed for Aline Barnsdall's estate on Olive Hill, and called the Little Dipper because of its shape, was only partially built and then partly demolished; the second, the Samuel Freeman House (Figs. 16, 17), also in Los Angeles, was completed in 1924. Both were designed for precipitously sloping sites and both were constructed of 16-inch-square concrete blocks set into a square grid of steel reinforcing rods. The Little Dipper was sited halfway down the slope from Hollyhock House to Studio Residence B at a 45-degree diagonal to the main east-west axis. The schoolroom angles out from the hill and is

entered on the diagonal down a narrow ledge connecting it to the driveway above. The plan, while obviously deriving from the Hillside Home School and the Tahoe Big Tree Cabin, represents the most integrated expression of diagonality Wright had achieved so far. Movement down the slope is gently deflected by a series of three 45-degree bends. Two offset, elongated hexagons define the overall length of the building and determine the first two 45-degree shifts. Then, at the crossing of the two major hexagons, within the deformed square of the school room, the axis is once again

14. *Little Dipper Kindergarten and Playhouse. (Aline Barnsdall House), Los Angeles, California. Wright, 1923. Perspective. (Collection, The Frank Lloyd Wright Foundation.)*
15. *Little Dipper Kindergarten and Playhouse. Plan. (De
Fries, Frank Lloyd Wright, p. 56.)*

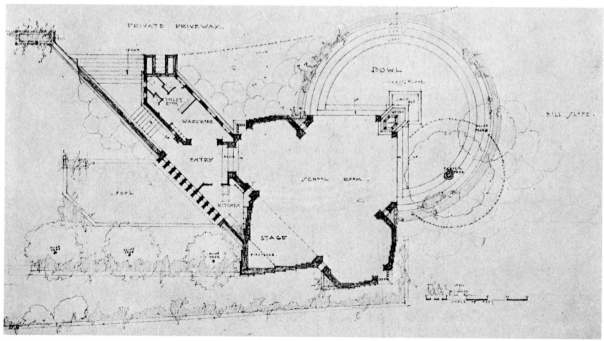

16. *Samuel Freeman House, Los Angeles, California. Wright,*
1924. Perspective. (Collection, The Frank Lloyd Wright
Foundation.)
17. *Samuel Freeman House. Living room. (Hitchcock,* In
the Nature of Materials . . . , *fig. 259.)*

shifted 45 degrees to angle out through the corner opened up by two diagonally placed piers. The main axis of the schoolroom, under the clerestoried central section, opens out at either end in vertical slots of perforated concrete block as in the preliminary project for the much later First Unitarian Church in Madison, Wisconsin, of 1947. The cross-axis reaches back into the deep-set fireplace to carry the eye out through the corner hexagonal pool and surrounding sandbox in an arc of 270 degrees over the bowl of seats defining the southern horizon.[18] The connection of fire and water to earth and sky along the diagonal axis resembles the Doheny house project described above, and one must assume that Wright felt that the thrust of the diagonal into space provided the means to effect that natural union at the scale of the landscape itself.

While the diagonal axis could be a carrier of elemental symbolic power, the sense of depth it projects could also be translated onto the domestic plane to produce a more dynamic spatial experience of openness and breadth. Here, the contemporary Freeman House is a perfect case in point. It terraces down the hillside, like the Little Dipper, but in the form of a square ladle (Fig. 16). Its narrow entry passage also aligns with the rear wall of the main space to become the back of a fireplace. But, whereas the entry into the Little Dipper was deflected 45 degrees along the side of one hexagon and the fireplace was set on the diagonal in the corner of another, the entry into the living room of the Freeman House is through a corner and the fireplace is located in the middle of one side of an absolutely square room. Piers on either side of the fireplace support two deep beams that extend across the space to the great expanse of windows overlooking Los Angeles. The piers opposite the fireplace are matched by others along the side walls inset equidistantly from the corners. The corners are left completely open; the horizontal sheets of plate glass are butted directly with no vertical mullion in one of Wright's first true corner windows (Fig. 17).[19] The view from the entry out the far corner is thus unimpeded and has an immediate and powerful impact. The diagonals of the square define the axes of the space, like an early Gothic rib vault, extending the space outward beyond the perimeters of the square; and the room takes on the virtual shape of the Little Dipper schoolroom, something one can imagine by making the rotated square balcony of the Hillside Home School equal in size to the room itself, as Wright had just done the year before in the Big Tree Cabin.

The spatial experience of virtual or implied diagonality in the Freeman House immediately recalls the contemporary Diamond paintings by Piet Mondrian, just as the explicit diagonality of the Little Dipper reminds one of the diagonal "counter-compositions" by Theo Van Doesburg of 1924/25 (Fig. 18). Mondrian adopted the diamond format as early as 1918/19 for a series of grid paintings continuing through 1921.[20] Then, in 1925/26, perhaps in reaction to Van Doesburg, he produced another group of four works (Fig. 19) in which the square central space projects a sense of dynamic continuity without, however, forsaking the orthogonal structure of vertical and horizontal lines. Van Doesburg, on the other hand, just after completing a series of architectural designs with Cornelius Van Eesteren in 1922/23, translated the 45-degree geometry of their axonometric projections onto the flat, rectangular picture plane and declared the resulting diagonality the basis of a new Elementarism.[21] The issue of explicit diagonality became so divisive that Mondrian left the De Stijl group in 1925.

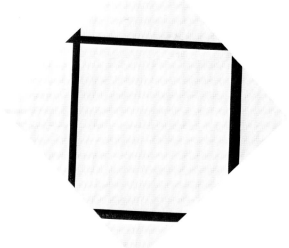

It is fascinating to recall that the second major European publication of Wright's work occurred at just this time, in the Dutch magazine *Wendingen* in 1925. Although the relation between Wright's bird's-eye perspective of the orthogonal Freeman House and the explicitly diagonal plan of the Little Dipper makes us think of Van Doesburg's strikingly similar translation of axonometric projection, it should be apparent immediately that for Wright explicit and implicit diagonality were not mutually exclusive and, indeed, would continue to coexist throughout his work as they do in the Little Dipper and Freeman House. Diagonality was never a polemical issue for Wright as it was for the Dutch. Van Doesburg ascribed to its dynamic form a spiritual, "space-time" dimension and believed that its incorporation in works of art would help break down the traditional barriers between art and life.[22] While such ideas were hardly inimical to Wright's project for a pyramidal Steel Cathedral for a Million People of 1926, or the Gordon Strong Automobile Objective and Planetarium of 1924/25, where the circular geometry is given a dynamic spiraling form by the application of the diagonal in section, Wright did not adopt the principle of diagonality for theoretical or ideological reasons. Rather, it was the specific topographical conditions he faced in California in 1921 to 1924 and the means of construction he developed in response to those conditions that led him to formalize a spatial idea in a method of planning that had previously appeared only incidentally in his work. Once having adopted a modular system, with the square grid directly expressed in the lines of the adjoining blocks of the floor, it was almost a natural reflex to draw the diagonal from corner to corner to define the greatest internal dimension.

The next important development also came about as a result of working in a radically different environment. In 1927, while in Arizona to help his former student Albert Chase McArthur on the design of the Arizona-Biltmore Hotel, Wright met Alexander Chandler, who commissioned a project for a winter resort to be called

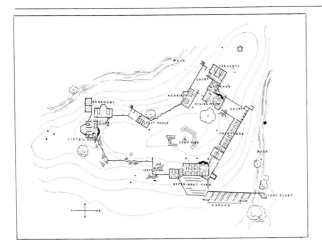

San Marcos-in-the-Desert. In response to the local topography, Wright began using the 30/60-
degree triangle. In the temporary camp he built
for himself and called Ocatillo, a series of small
wood and canvas structures were connected by a
continuous low wall that angles in and out, following the contours of the "low, spreading, rocky
mound" and rising in the center to a triangular
campfire (Fig. 20).[23] "The one-two triangle used
in planning the camp is made by the mountain
ranges themselves around about the site," he wrote,
"and the magical one-two triangle is the cross-
section of the talus at their bases. This triangle
is reflected in the general forms of all the cabins
as well as the general plan."[24] For the San Marcos
resort, Wright used the 30/60-degree triangle to
make "a far-flung, long-drawn-out building" rather
than an enclosure. It was to be, in Wright's words,
a form of "great nature-masonry rising from the
great mesa floor," like "an abstraction of this
mountain region itself."[25] The extended range of
rooms, stepped back in three terraces against a
slope, bridges a ravine before skirting a spur in
a 30/60-degree triangle.

In conjunction with the main hotel, Wright also
designed a group of private houses set into the
surrounding mesas. In the project for Owen D.
Young (Fig. 21), the rectangular geometry of the
enclosed spaces is set off against the diagonal
projection of an elongated hexagonal terrace, while
the diamond pattern of the concrete blocks echoes
the distant mountain peaks. In the house for Wel-
lington and Ralph Cudney (Fig. 22), called the

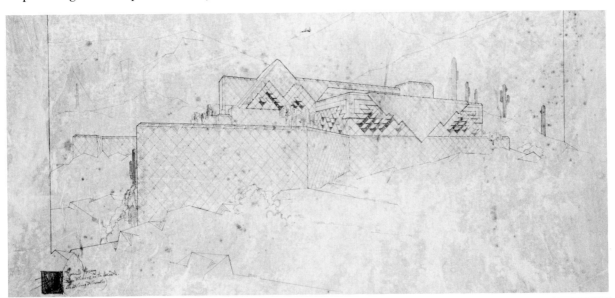

"Sahuaro," the plan is based on a diagonal grid, making the house appear as an extension of the jagged cliff-face behind it. As in all these designs of 1927/28, the diagonal serves to echo in the building the natural shapes of the environment and to direct the eye outward to those shapes across the vast expanse of the desert.

Wright eventually was to prefer the 30/60-degree triangle over the right-angle triangle for the more dynamic, more varied, and more supple relations it allowed. Its characteristic effect on his work can be seen in the next and last major project he undertook before the Depression, the St. Mark's Tower for New York City, of 1929. Here, within the constrictions of an urban situation, Wright gave new life to the Tahoe Big Tree Cabin paradigm of a square rotated within a square by reducing the degree of rotation from 45 to 30

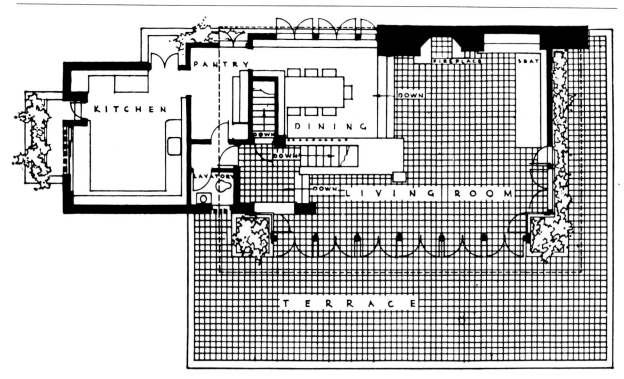

degrees. The gaps are used for exterior balconies and projecting fire stairs. The apparent shift and dislocation of each duplex apartment, with its mezzanine balcony set at a 30/60-degree angle, gives an effect of great variety and enormous sweep to the interior space, as can be appreciated in the similar apartments in the Price Tower, built in Bartlesville, Oklahoma, in 1952 to 1956.

The Depression cut short Wright's activity in the Southwest as well as such projects as the St. Mark's Tower. The final phase of his career, often referred to as his renaissance, began in 1932 with the commission for the Malcolm Willey House in Minneapolis, coinciding with the International Style exhibition held at the Museum of Modern Art in the fall of that year. While Wright's work of the thirties, forties, and fifties grew directly out of his introduction of diagonality in the previous decade, there now appeared a much greater

degree of complexity in the intersection of implied axes and a much looser relation between them and the actual definition of spatial boundaries. This increased openness undoubtedly owed something to the example of European modernism, and in particular Mies, but it also must be understood in terms of the unparalleled facility and virtuosity Wright had achieved in the shaping of architectural space.[26]

The site of the Willey House is a small lot at the southern end of a north-south street on a bluff overlooking the Mississippi River, which flows on a diagonal from the northwest to the southeast. The first project of 1932 (Fig. 23), which proved too costly, called for a two-story building with the living and dining rooms raised on a base of bedrooms and opening out onto a cantilevered terrace with splayed sides. The house, sited east-west, has floor-to-ceiling glass doors running the

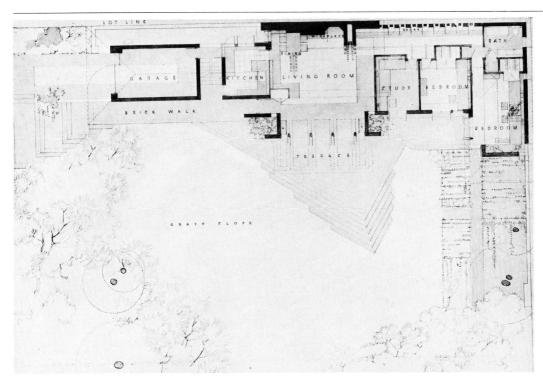

entire length of the south-facing living room and wrapping around both ends, with indented corner windows containing planters in the reentrant angles. From the entry into the living room at the top of the stairs, the view continues straight across the space, through a pair of glass doors, over a walled garden on the east. The fireplace is positioned at a 45-degree angle to the southwest corner of the room and at a 60-degree angle to the southeast corner window. The northeast corner of the living room is entirely closed by the fireplace and wraparound seat. The view out from this corner, toward the Mississippi River to the southwest, follows an arc whose chord is the major diagonal axis of the space, which runs from the far northwest corner of the dining room at a 30-degree angle out through the southeast corner window, paralleling the river below and thus tying the small house to the ends of the horizon.

To meet the demands of the budget, Wright completely redesigned the house two years later (Fig. 24). The only feature the two designs have in common is the diagonal axis that relates the house to its site and the river below, but even that was given an entirely different definition. The house was reduced to one story, with the walled garden turned into a bedroom wing forming an ell, and the living and dining rooms combined into one open space at the center. From the street, a series of steps, decreasing in width at an angle of 30 degrees, rises up to a level brick walk to form a monumental processional entrance. Just before the door, to the right of a planter, the brick mat angles out 30 degrees into a triangular terrace carrying the eye out to the end of a brick wall at the eastern edge of the property. Upon entering the living room, a diagonal axis is immediately defined by the corner fireplace (Fig.

25). The view through the passage to the bedrooms is at an angle of 30 degrees, literally mirroring the view along the edge of the outside terrace. The opposing diagonal cutting across the fireplace parallels the 30/60-degree angle of the terrace, thus skewing the whole space of the room toward the southwest. As you turn around in that direction, the terrace appears to swing out from under your feet as if hinged to the edge of the brick walk, and the diagonal vista it opens up extends the view out far beyond the confines of both house and garden. The edge of the terrace parallels the course of the river below and thus locks the house into the site, causing the one to

pass through the other and, as it were, making the space of the house an aspect of a much larger whole. It was the first realization of Wright's ultimate goal to make the house, as he said, "itself parallel to the ground, companion to the horizon."[27]

The Malcolm Willey House introduced two new developments in Wright's use of diagonality. The first is the multiplication of visual axes and their overlapping in space, resulting in a constant shifting of focus. One can now begin to distinguish not only between explicit and implicit axes but also between the objective, or compositional, axis and the subjective, or experiential, axis. The

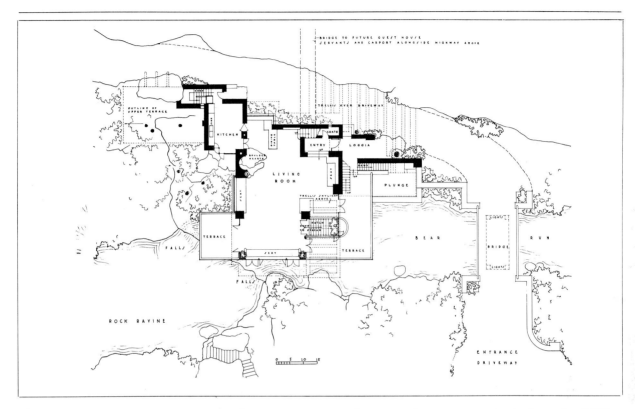

subjective experience of space is no longer coextensive with the axial definition of that space, or, as Wright's student Curtis Besinger remarked, "the vistas are generally oblique to and—in effect—independent of the geometry of the house. This independence suggests to the occupant a freedom of movement in any direction" for now "the occupant is always the center of the space and not an onlooker."[28]

The second novel aspect of the Willey House, clearly relating to the first, is the change from rotating a plane around a central axis to pivoting a plane from a point along its outer edge. With the point of deflection now located on the perimeter, the centrifugal power of the core—be it solid or space, fireplace or hollow—finally disappears from Wright's work and is replaced by a progres-

sively expanding space. And thus the Willey House is the first instance in which the edge of the pivoted terrace is perceived as a portion of the radius of a circle, containing the house in a sector and having for its circumference the horizon.

The idea of pivoting immediately became the basis of the project for the Stanley Marcus House in Dallas, Texas, of 1935; the Herbert Johnson House, called "Wingspread," just north of Racine, Wisconsin, of 1937; and Wright's own desert compound of Taliesin West in Scottsdale, Arizona, begun in 1938. In all these cases the terraces swing out at 30 degrees or 45 degrees to expand the interior space out into the landscape. In the plan of Florida Southern College, of 1938, the buildings themselves act either as the hinges or

27. *John C. Pew House, Shorewood Hills, Wisconsin. Wright,*
1940. Plans, ground floor and upper floor. (F. L. Wright,
The Natural House, *p. 131.)*
28. *John C. Pew House. Living Room, view to terrace.*
(Photo: Ezra Stoller, © ESTO.)

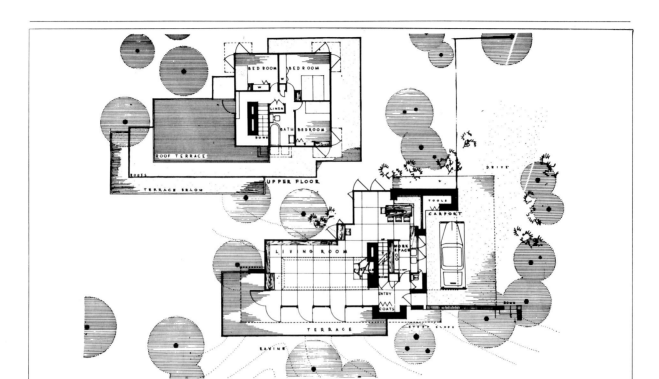

as the leading edges of space. But in Fallingwater (Fig. 26), designed in 1935/36 and the masterpiece of this period, Wright reversed the roles of building and terrace to effect the most astounding integration of architecture and landscape conceivable. Instead of pivoting a terrace out from the house, Wright pivoted the house itself out from the rocky cliff, angling it 30 degrees to the southeast out over the water to create, as he said, "an extension of the cliff beside a mountain stream."[29] The house becomes a stack of indoor-outdoor terraces projecting from a stone wall which parallels the rocky ledge behind and seems to be part of the earth itself. All the floors are flagstone, inside and out, and the sense of a plane angling back into the earth is literally expressed at the fireplace, where a boulder projects through the floor to become the hearth.

The diagonality of the plan of Fallingwater is extremely subtle. The staggered, rectilinear elements create a rhythmic pattern which seems at first closer to the International Style of Mies, as in the Barcelona Pavilion or the Tugendhat House, than to anything we have seen before in Wright's own work. But Wright himself was obviously aware of the internal logic that led to the plan of Fallingwater, and his organization of the January 1938 issue of *Architectural Forum* provides a number of important clues. The section devoted to Fallingwater follows after the Willey House, but between them Wright inserted two projects that could have no other purpose than to make his development of diagonal planning the link. The first is a perspective and plan of the Little Dipper Kindergarten, drawings not previously published in the United States; following that is a project of 1937 for a Memorial to the Soil, a chapel designed for southern Wisconsin, whose diagonally sliced space and asymmetricality Wright con-trasted with the rectilinearity of the much earlier Unity Temple.[30] The first two images of Fallingwater are a raking-angle view of the open corner window to the left of the chimney mass and a distant view on the diagonal taken from below the first waterfall. The Little Dipper and the Memorial to the Soil mark the poles of explicit and implicit diagonality in Wright's planning; the corner window immediately recalls the Freeman House which, along with Taliesin, is the clearest precedent for Fallingwater.

Like the Freeman House, the weekend house for Edgar Kaufmann is a two-sided building, presenting a nearly solid face to the hill behind and a series of terraces overlapping down the slope. Both are entered from the rear and then open out into a sweeping diagonal vista across the main living space. In Fallingwater, a series of crevices in the stone wall lead to the entry where you turn left, go up three steps, and then look out across the space of the living room along a 45-degree diagonal which is extended as far as the eye can see by the terrace projecting out over the ravine. The raised stone floor and recessed ceiling give a lift to that diagonal, recalling the great arching vista at Taliesin. But the basic shape of the living room, as in the Freeman House, is a square, here expressed in the form of an atrium by the four stone piers (the fourth being the fireplace) supporting the indirectly lit, coved ceiling. Unlike the Freeman House, the square is off-center, shifted back toward the powerful corner fireplace; set diagonally opposite the hatch leading down through the floor to the water below, its semicircular cavity and spherical kettle are reflected in the curved parapet enclosing the stairway on the east terrace, thus defining the 30/60-degree cross-axis.

The two major diagonals, from entry to west

terrace and from fireplace to hatch, do not intersect in the center of the square at 90 degrees, as in the Freeman House. The plan of Fallingwater is more complex than those of the twenties in maintaining the continuity of interior and exterior space. The main diagonal axis from the entry follows the stream of water below; while the 30/60-degree cross-axial diagonal, running due east-west, following the rocky ledge and drive, parallels the datum line from which the house was originally pivoted into position. This suggests the metaphorical content Wright had already ascribed to the diagonal axis in the Little Dipper and perhaps explains why he chose to introduce the world to Fallingwater through that image. A single straight line joins all elements in the earlier building, but in Fallingwater the diagonal from the entry to the far west terrace connects the rocky earth ledge, from which the house springs, to the sky above, while the cross-axis joins the elements of fire and water on a line that internalizes the conjunction of architecture and nature. Both more dynamic and more subjective than the relationships established in the Little Dipper, the meaning of Fallingwater nonetheless grows out of that background just as the idea of placing the house over a waterfall goes back to the Doheny project.

Fallingwater derives its unique immediacy of impact and oneness with the landscape from the transcendent order of the diagonal axis. While the special circumstances of such a commission produced a highly charged symbolism, its formal principles could be reused by Wright whenever he was presented with such a tight, steeply sloping site that the only way to relate building to environment was to dramatize the situation and ensure continuity through the purely visual effects of implied diagonal axes. Among the group of Usonian houses known by their owners as "Little Fallingwaters," the George Sturges House in Brentwood Heights, California, of 1939, may be the most dramatic, but the John Pew House in Shorewood Hills, Wisconsin, built in 1940 (Figs. 27, 28), is the most moving.[31] Perched precariously at the edge of Lake Mendota, it is set diagonally on its site to take fullest advantage of a mere 75-foot frontage. The house is planned, based on Fallingwater, as a series of rectangles overlapping a square. The roof terrace, living room, and lower terrace slide out from under the top bedroom story and are offset on a 30-degree diagonal pointing in the direction of the lake. The house is tiny but the scale is gigantic. The living room is only 26 feet long by 16 feet wide. The sense of space and its extension into the landscape is due to the powerful action of the main diagonal axis linking the house at its very foundations in the hillside to the far horizon. An uninterrupted visual axis runs from the rear corner of the stone dining nook, out across the fireplace, on a continuous 30-degree diagonal course out through the corner window of the living room to the far shore of the lake (Fig. 28). The eye traverses this space in a flash and perceives in an instant the sense of oneness with nature. The diagonal, as at Fallingwater, cuts across boundaries and makes connections immediate.

For more typical sites, Wright would ask, "Where does the garden leave off and the house begin?" and then answer, "Where the garden begins and the house leaves off."[32] The total integration of interior and exterior that Wright achieved in the diagonal planning of his later Usonian houses could be expressed through whatever geometric module seemed most appropriate. The first two Usonian houses, the Herbert Jacobs House in

30. Paul R. Hanna House, Stanford, California. Wright, 1936/37. Plan. (Architectural Forum, January 1938, pp. 70–71.)

29. Herbert Jacobs House (I), Madison, Wisconsin. Wright, 1936/37. Plan. (Architectural Forum, January 1938, p. 81.)

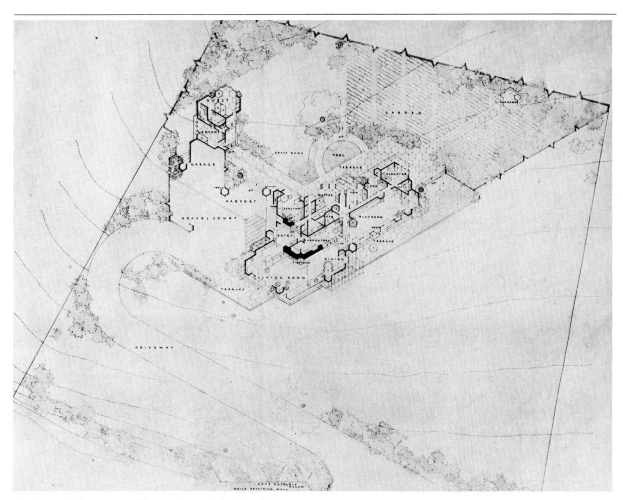

Madison, Wisconsin (Fig. 29), and the Paul Hanna House in Stanford, California (Fig. 30), were both designed in 1936 and completed in the following year. The one is based on a double-square-rectangle module, etched in the concrete floor mat, and the other on a hexagonal one. Like the Little Dipper and the Freeman House, the one is the obverse of the other.

The first house Wright built for Herbert Jacobs is sited on a suburban corner lot. It turns its back to the street and opens out in an ell to the south, enclosing a garden between the living-room and bedroom wings. The basically rectangular shape

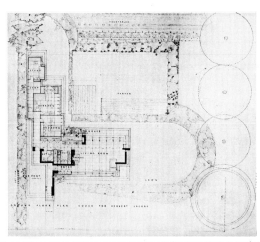

of the living room is sheared into thirds along a 30/60-degree diagonal, with the upper part pushing out toward the garden terrace through wraparound floor-to-ceiling glass doors, and the lower part, closed to the street, sliding back in toward the entry. This shearing creates a virtual rhomboid out of the rectangle, with its two 30/60-degree diagonal axes—the one from the entry to the upper corner of the living room, and the other from the dining nook to the lower corner—crossing just in front of the fireplace. While the diagonal from the entry gives a sense of openness and direction to the relatively small communal space of the house, the cross-axial diagonal leads the eye back across the fireplace to the bedrooms, thus tying the two wings of the house together at their hinge in the utility core. That same axis is extended to define the jog of the bedroom corridor out to the lot line, while parallel axes drawn due east from the offsets of the living room—the first from the glass slot between the L-shaped pier and the flat one, and the second from the outside corner of the brick mat of the terrace—locate the two main setbacks of the bedrooms and define an imaginary 30/60-degree triangle between the two garden fronts. The hypotenuse of that triangle stretches across the garden from east to west, embracing the southern horizon and making the house, "itself parallel to the ground, companion to the horizon." It is as if the house had spread out like a fan hinged at its utility core.

The method Wright used in planning the Jacobs House remained characteristic of all his later work. Sometimes the rectangular shape of the house might be set diagonally on its site in order to take advantage of a particular view, as in the Pew House or the house built for Alma Goetsch and Katherine Winkler in Okemos, Michigan, in 1939; at other times it might be aligned on the diagonal in order to create a sense of vista and expanse where there was none, as in the Albert Adelman House at Fox Point, Wisconsin, of 1948, or the Isadore Zimmerman House in Manchester, New Hampshire, built in 1950. The Jacobs House, however, physically conforms to its orthogonal suburban lot. The larger-scaled, superimposed diamond grid of 60/120 degrees, defined by the intersecting diagonal axes, is only virtual. Its actual effect, however, can be visualized in Wright's bird's-eye perspectives, which seem almost to illustrate the ways in which an explicitly diagonal grid, such as he was to use in many of his later houses, would allow the wings to fan out 120 degrees or fold in 60 degrees in response to more irregular sites.

The hexagonal plan of the Hanna House (Fig. 30), as it fans open from its utility core to embrace the hillside, merely makes explicit the shearing of space in the Jacobs House. "Here," wrote Wright, "the thesis changes, not in content but in expression."[33] The obtuse angles of the plan have a "reflex" action, as noted by Wright, causing the plan to appear to flip in and out of perspective. The impression is that of looking at a flattened-out axonometric projection of a rectilinear pattern, much as Van Doesburg had done in his paintings of the twenties, and almost naturally arising from Wright's own typical bird's-eye perspectives. Clearly, Wright's most important reason for adopting an explicitly diagonal module was to be able to fit the house more snugly into its environment. The site of the Hanna House presented the broad sloping arc of a hillside, and the 120-degree angle of the court allows the house to follow its contours in a gently accommodating fashion. The existing trees were left untouched and the house cuts in and around them like an Oriental screen, producing, as

Wright noted, an effect of great "repose."[34] For the Sidney Bazett House in Hillsborough, California, of 1939, located at the point of a steep hill, Wright set the two wings 60 degrees to one another to enclose a garden at the head of the rising triangular piece of land; at the Carlton Wall House in Plymouth, Michigan, of 1941, the hexagonal living room and terrace form a headland above a lake while the open 120-degree angle of the court cups the broad plateau behind.

The reemergence of explicit diagonality in the Hanna House indicates Wright's increasing insistence on the organic integration of building and landscape, most strikingly realized in Fallingwater, along with the corollary idea of the building itself growing and expanding like nature, first given tentative expression in the diagonal pivoting of the Willey House. Wright compared the hexagonal grid of the Hanna House to "a cross-section of honeycomb" and maintained that its "flow and movement" give a reflexiveness to the space allowing it to open and close, expand and contract, and, indeed, almost to return back on itself in a continuous curve.[35] The angled space between the two hinged wings of the Usonian house, be it 60, 90, or 120 degrees, is under-

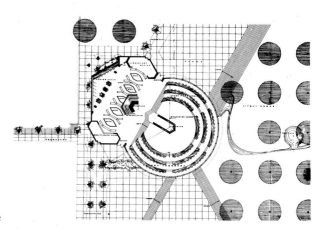

stood as the sector of a circle, and it is therefore not surprising that, the year after the completion of the Hanna House, Wright returned to the circular plan for the first time since the Gordon Strong project of 1924/25, as a logical extension of the principle of diagonality.[36]

Implied diagonal axes almost always determine the internal organization of Wright's circular buildings as well as their relation to the site. The sketch of the Ralph Jester House for Palos Verdes, California (Fig. 31), a project of 1938 and the first of these designs, shows how the positions of the different cylindrical volumes were established by two contiguous 30/60-degree triangles. The first has its long side forming the diameter of the pool and its hypotenuse running from the servant's room to the living room through the center of the dining room; the second has its hypotenuse along the gate and its long side defining the axis from the bedroom to the dining room. In the final project, the patio was widened and the living room set back 15 degrees on a diagonal perpendicular to the main 45-degree axis extending from the bedroom at the rear of the house across the swimming pool and down the length of the valley opening out into the Pacific Ocean.

In that same year, 1938, Wright produced the master plan for Florida Southern College, using circular and semicircular forms to articulate the joints of the diagonal covered walks. The Library (Fig. 32), completed in 1941 and the first of Wright's circular designs to be built, is located at the entrance to the campus in the 60-degree angle formed by the main axis leading to the Chapel and central triangular plaza. For this pivotal spot, Wright reused the Little Dipper plan (Fig. 15), aligning the axial walkway with the hexagonal schoolroom, placing the periodical shelves where the fireplace was, and enclosing

the bowl of seats to form a circular reading room around the projecting hexagonal reference desk which replaces the pool and sandbox.

The Florida Southern Library graphically illustrates the direct link between Wright's diagonal planning and his later circular designs. Few of these were ever to be as explicit in their diagonality. More characteristic is the Guggenheim Museum, built in 1956 to 1959 though originally designed in 1943/44, where only traces of the diagonal remain in the implied axes, which orient the visitor and relate the building to the site. The integral expression of the circular form is overriding, yet one of the first studies of 1943 (Fig. 33) shows the building as a hexagon rotated 30 degrees around an interior hexagonal court aligned with Fifth Avenue. A circular ramp, the same size as the court, overlaps the northern wall of the main hexagon; its projecting half is treated as a dodecagon, matching the dodecagonal administration wing at the northwest corner of the site. Whereas the Florida Southern Library conjoins circular and hexagonal spaces as in the earlier Little Dipper project, the first studies for the Guggenheim illustrate the progressive transfor-

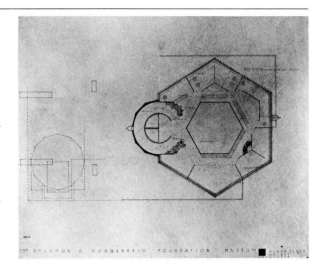

33. *Solomon R. Guggenheim Museum, New York City, New York. Wright (1943/44), 1956–1959. Plan, scheme "C." (Collection, The Frank Lloyd Wright Foundation.)*

mation of the hexagon into a circle through a process of continuous rotation that finally results in a completely circular design. These cylindrical volumes, varying in size from those containing the restrooms and ducts, through the small administration building, to the main gallery itself, are related to one another along the lines of overlapping 30/60-degree triangles, and the final plan is a mirror image of the Ralph Jester House.

From the entrance to the Guggenheim Museum, under a loggia, the axis is defined at a 30/60-degree angle to the Fifth Avenue sidewalk by the two-tiered opening into the Grand Gallery. This is crossed in the center of the space by another 30/60-degree axis, extending from the end of the ramp and elevator to the southwest corner of the building where a large window provides the only view out and a point of orientation. Otherwise, the spiraling form of the museum is a closed circuit, constantly rotating around a vertical axis. The sense of infinite extension in space is linked to the feeling of suspension in time. According to Wright, "it is this extraordinary quality of the complete repose known only in movement that characterizes this building," a "complete repose similar to that made by a still wave, never breaking, never offering finality to vision."[37]

Timelessness, the vision of endlessness, the oneness of experience—this is what the embracing immediacy of the diagonal had meant to Wright. It is therefore impossible not to see the Guggenheim Museum as an urban translation into the vertical dimension of Wright's compelling vision of the desert, a space "beyond reach of the finite mind," in the winter home he built for himself just east of Phoenix and called Taliesin West (Figs. 34, 35).[38] Appearing to Wright as if it belonged "to the Arizona desert as though it

had stood there during creation,"[39] it was completed just about the time the Guggenheim was designed. The site of Taliesin West is a high mesa just below McDowell Peak to the north. The tent-like structures branch off both sides of an elongated circulation spine paralleling the range of mountains (Fig. 34). The main working and living quarters face south off the hypotenuse of a great triangular terrace that swings out over the desert to the west, its hinge marked by a boulder set on a prow-shaped ledge to the right of the steps at the entrance. The upper part of the apprentices' court twists in response to this movement, while the pivoting of the main diagonal axis is checked at 45 degrees by the counterbalancing entrance office and shop building, rotated 45 degrees at the base of the entrance court. The continually changing angles of approach, the 30/60-degree slope of the exposed redwood trusses of the canvas roofs, and the canted "desert stone" walls, all echo the shapes of the surrounding mountains, while the right-angle triangle of the terrace seems to cast the shadow of McDowell Peak onto the vast plane of the desert below.

"Just imagine," Wright thought, "what it would

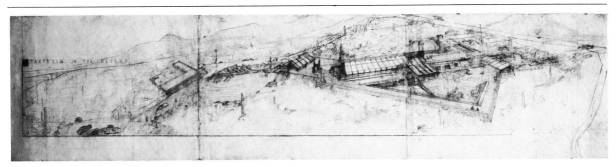

be like on top of the world looking over the universe at sunrise or at sunset with clear sky in daylight between" (Fig. 35).[40] The 45-degree diagonal from the boulder at the entrance carries the eye down the gravel terrace, past the drafting room on the left and the pool and the sunken garden, and then, all of a sudden, the "great prow running out onto the Mesa" with the "wide desert below" becomes, as Wright said, "a look over the rim of the world."[41] The diagonal links everything together in a glance—buildings, mountains, desert—and in its arc produces, in Wright's words, "an esthetic, even ascetic, idealization of space, of breadth and height and of strange firm forms and a sweep that was a spiritual cathartic for Time if indeed Time continued to exist in such circumstances."[42]

The diagonal fans out across the distant horizon and makes the slice of space palpable and its measure of distance instantaneous. The space is sensed in depth, not through an intellectually reconstructed series of layers or planes perpendicular to the line of sight, but immediately, instantaneously.[43] It is this absolute experience of space as depth that finally brought Wright's quest for continuity to its ultimate realization in the endless expanse of the desert. Beginning with his first exposure to the desert in the twenties, in California and then at San Marcos, Wright saw a spiritual factor in the space opened up by the diagonal axis and, indeed, like his contemporary Van Doesburg, attributed a temporal dimension to it. But in Wright's work, the concept of "space-time" never became an intellectualized simultaneity, ultimately deriving from Cubist painting. Rather, as he translated the axonometric vision of simultaneous points of view into the reality of diagonally defined space, Wright eventually achieved in his architecture of the thirties and forties an expression of instantaneity as powerful as nature itself.

The diagonal axis was never just a compositional device for Wright. It implied a rootedness to the earth along with a sense of liberation in space. And thus at Taliesin West, the diagonal that carries the eye out across the vast desert space has its "reflex" in the 45-degree cross-axial diagonal which turns back on itself to the mountains behind, passing along the far side of the triangular pool and then through a dark passage marked on the left by a boulder set on axis with McDowell Peak and on the right by the chimney of the drafting-room fireplace.[44] As in Fallingwater, and even earlier in the Little Dipper, the relation between earth, sky, fire, and water described by the diagonal axis gives both a physical and spiritual depth to Wright's work that it never had before.

But it is perhaps only in Taliesin West that one can see so clearly retraced the various stages in Wright's development and the overall pattern of his life's work. The 45-degree shifts in axis, though now progressive and linear, go right back to the plan for the house shown to Sullivan in 1887. The rotated squares and prowlike projections, though now disconnected and dispersed, find their source in the Ward Willits House and the Hillside Home School of 1901/2. The canted roofs and explicit diagonality recall Lake Tahoe, San Marcos, Ocatillo, indeed, all those many projects and few buildings of the twenties in which Wright laid the groundwork for his renaissance.[45] And, finally, there is the pivoted terrace, open plan, sheared space, and reflex diagonal of the Willey House, Fallingwater, the Jacobs and Hanna houses, all directly preceding Taliesin West.

Clearly, there is a consistency and a continuity to Wright's work after 1909. While it is not to be presumed that the principle of diagonality explains all, its reappearance in the work of Louis Kahn, Robert Venturi, Charles Moore, and now Peter Eisenman, with his axonometrically projected House El Even Odd, makes the relevance of just this one aspect of Wright's work all the more apparent. And if Wright's use of diagonality can be seen as one measure of the coherence of his later work, then it does go some way toward explaining the shift in emphasis that took place in his architecture after his flight from Oak Park to Europe in 1909 and the interregnum of the following decade. If the Oak Park years may be characterized as a search for types—images of the home, work, or worship[46]—the later work reveals a quest for a more profound synthesis of architecture and nature. The shift represents a turning outward from a concentration on the inner workings of things to their integration in the larger order of nature. Like the radiating avenues in Baroque gardens and town planning, the diagonal extends the view out to the horizon, but, in pivoting around to follow its curve, Wright's diagonal makes the building itself "companion to the horizon" in an expression of continuity unparalleled in the history of modern architecture.

Notes

1. The basic study of Wright still remains Henry-Russell Hitchcock's *In the Nature of Materials: The Buildings of Frank Lloyd Wright, 1887–1941* (New York: Duell, Sloane and Pearce, 1942; reprint ed., with a new foreword and bibliog., New York: Da Capo Press, 1973). Since then, of course, much important work has been done by Reyner Banham, H. Allen Brooks, Arthur Drexler, Edgar Kaufmann, jr., John Sergeant, Norris Kelly Smith, and William Storrer. My greatest debt, however, goes to Vincent Scully, whose writings and lectures helped form my understanding of Wright. This essay grew out of a trip I made across the United States in the summer of 1976 to study Wright's architecture. It was supported in part by a grant from the Harvard Graduate Society Fund, Harvard University. Of the many people who went out of their way to help my work, I would like to thank, first of all, Bruce Brooks Pfeiffer, Director of Archives, The Frank Lloyd Wright Memorial Foundation; and Virginia Kazor, Curator, Hollyhock House. Of the many, many owners of Wright houses who allowed me to visit their homes, I would like to thank the following: Mr. and Mrs. Albert Adelman, Mr. and Mrs. Altay, Mr. James Bridges, Mr. Gus Brown, Dr. and Mrs. Fineberg, Mr. Louis Frank, Mr. and Mrs. Samuel Freeman, Mr. Harvey Glanzer, Miss Elizabeth Halsted, Mr. and Mrs. Bruce Haynes, Miss Ellen Johnson, Mr. Jack Larsen, Mr. and Mrs. William Miller, Dr. and Mrs. Franklin S. Nelson, Mr. and Mrs. John C. Pew, Mr. and Mrs. Harold C. Price, Jr., Mr. and Mrs. Joe D. Price, Mrs. Alice Shaddle, Mrs. Donna Taylor, Mr. and Mrs. William Walker, Mr. and Mrs. Carlton Wall, Mr. Thomas Walsh, Jr., Mr. and Mrs. David Wright, and Dr. and Mrs. Isadore Zimmerman.

2. Philip Johnson, "The Seven Crutches of Modern Architecture," *Perspecta* 3 (1955): 44.

3. Cf. Bernard Pyron, "Wright's Diamond Module Houses: His Development of Non-Rectilinear Interior Space," *Art Journal* 21 (Winter 1961/62): 92–96; B. Pyron, "Wright's Small Rectangular Houses: His Structures of the Forties and Fifties," *Art Journal* 23 (Fall 1963): 20–24; Edgar Kaufmann, jr., "Centrality and Symmetry in Wright's Architecture," *Architect's Yearbook* 9 (1960): 120–31; John Sergeant, *Frank Lloyd Wright's Usonian Houses: The Case for Organic Architecture* (New York: Whitney Library of Design, Watson-Guptill Publications, 1976), esp. pp. 183–187; and H. Allen Brooks, "Frank Lloyd Wright and the Destruction of the Box," *Journal of the Society of Architectural Historians* 38 (March 1979): 7–14.

4. John Lloyd Wright, *My Father Who Is on Earth* (New York: G. P. Putnam's Sons, 1946), p. 127.

5. On the importance of the decade of the twenties in Wright's work, see Reyner Banham, "The Wilderness Years of Frank Lloyd Wright," *Journal of the Royal Institute of British Architects* 76 (December 1969): 512–519.

6. For a discussion of Michelangelo's fortifications in relation to Wright's use of the diagonal, see Vincent Scully, "Michelangelo's Fortification Drawings: A Study in the Reflex Diagonal," *Perspecta* 1 (1952): 38–45.

7. In one of the first important reappraisals of Gothic architecture, Jacques-Germain Soufflot, in his "Mémoire sur l'architecture gothique," read to the Lyons Academy in 1741, stressed the significance of the diagonal in the creation of characteristic Gothic spatial effects (reprinted in Michael Petzet, *Soufflots Sainte-Geneviève und der Französische Kirchenbau des 18. Jahrhunderts*, [Berlin: Walter de Gruyter and Co., 1961], pp. 135–142).

8. See Vincent Scully, *The Shingle Style and the Stick Style: Architectural Theory from Downing to the Origins of Wright*, rev. ed. (New Haven: Yale University Press, 1971), esp. pp. 71–164.

9. Eugène-Emmanuel Viollet-le-Duc, *Entretiens sur l'architecture*, 2 vols. (Paris: Vve A. Morel, 1863, 1872), 2: 283–290; English translation by Benjamin Bucknall, *Lectures on Architecture*, (Boston: James R. Osgood, 1881). For the "butterfly plan," see Jill Franklin, "Edwardian Butterfly Houses," *Architectural Review* 157 (April 1975): 220–225.

10. Vincent Scully remarked on the similarity between the Appleton House and Wright's Hanna House in *The Shingle Style*, p. 145.

11. On Wright's planning of this period, see Richard MacCormac, "The Anatomy of Wright's Aesthetic," *Architectural Review* 143 (February 1968): 143–146; H[einrich] de Fries, ed., *Frank Lloyd Wright: Aus dem Lebenswerke eines Architekten* (Berlin: Ernst Pollak, 1926), pp. 70–75 (de Fries, "Die Grundriss-Gestaltung des Architekten Wright").

12. On Wright's debt to the Beaux-Arts tradition, see H.-R. Hitchcock, "Frank Lloyd Wright and the 'Academic Tradition' of the Early Eighteen-Nineties," *Journal of the Warburg and Courtauld Institutes* 7 (January–June 1944): 46–63.

13. Frank Lloyd Wright, *An Autobiography* (1932; rev. ed., New York: Horizon Press, 1977), pp. 192–195.

14. Ibid., p. 191.

15. See esp. de Fries, *Wright*, pp. 45 ff.

16. This is noted, in Wright's hand, on the overall perspective of the project. See Arthur Drexler, *The Drawings of Frank Lloyd Wright* (New York: Bramhall House, 1962), p. 296.

17. On the source of this in the fireplace of Wright's Hollyhock House, completed just prior to the Doheny project, see my forthcoming article, "Hollyhock House: Frank Lloyd Wright's California Romanza." Wright had previously set an indoor pool diagonally opposite the fireplace in the entrance hall of the Susan Dana House in Springfield, Illinois, of 1902/3, and the F. C. Bogk House in Milwaukee, Wisconsin, of 1916, but had never placed the hearth within

the pool itself until the house built for Aline Barnsdall in 1919 to 1921.

18. On the plan reproduced in *Architectural Forum* 68 (January 1938): 33, the square sandbox is mislabeled as the pool.

19. The corner windows of the south-facing side of the Ennis House dining room are contemporary; the only earlier example seems to be the canted, leaded windows of the playroom projecting from the nursery of Hollyhock House, apparently done by 1921. All Wright's earlier corners have a vertical mullion.

20. See E. A. Carmean, Jr., *Mondrian: The Diamond Compositions* (Washington, D.C.: National Gallery of Art, 1979).

21. See Hans L. C. Jaffé, "The Diagonal Principle in the Works of Van Doesburg and Mondrian," *The Structurist* 9 (1969): 14–21; Donald McNamee, "Van Doesburg's Elementarism: New Translations of His Essays and Manifesto Originally Published in De Stijl," ibid., pp. 22–29; and Theo Van Doesburg, "Painting: From Composition to Counter-Composition," "Painting and Sculpture: About Counter-Composition and Counter-Sculpture. Elementarism (Fragment of a Manifesto)," trans. in H. L. C. Jaffé, *De Stijl* (New York: Harry N. Abrams, 1967), pp. 201–217.

22. Van Doesburg, "Painting and Sculpture: Elementarism (Fragment of a Manifesto)," pp. 213–217. This was written between December 1925 and January 1927. For Wright's connection with European art at this time, see Heidemarie Kief, *Der Einfluss Frank Lloyd Wrights auf die Mitteleuropäische Einzelhausarchitektur: Ein Beitrag zum Verhältnis von Architektur und Natur im 20. Jahrhundert* (Stuttgart: Karl Krämer, 1978), esp. pp. 100 ff.

23. Wright, *Autobiography*, p. 332.

24. Ibid., p. 335.

25. Ibid., pp. 338, 333, 339.

26. On Wright's debt to the International Style, see Vincent Scully, "Wright vs. the International Style," *Art News* 53 (March 1954): 32–35, 64–66; and E. Kaufmann, jr., "Frank Lloyd Wright's Years of Modernism, 1925–1935," *Journal of the Society of Architectural Historians* 25 (March 1965): 31–33.

27. Frank Lloyd Wright, in *Architectural Forum* 68 (January 1938): 83.

28. Curtis Besinger, "To Appreciate the Pleasures of this House," *House Beautiful* 105 (January 1963): 101, 103. This special issue of *House Beautiful* was devoted to the Hanna House.

29. Wright, in *Architectural Forum* 68 (January 1938): 36. Donald Hoffmann pointed out Wright's use of the 30/60-degree triangle in siting the house in his fascinating recent book, *Frank Lloyd Wright's Fallingwater: The House and Its History* (New York: Dover Publications, 1978), p. 18.

30. *Architectural Forum* 68 (January 1938): 32–35.

31. On all these houses and, in particular, the Pew House, see Sergeant, *Wright's Usonian Houses*, esp. pp. 66–71.

32. Wright, in *Architectural Forum* 68 (January 1938): 83.

33. Ibid., p. 68.

34. F. L. Wright, quoted in "Frank Lloyd Wright Designs a Honeycomb House," *Architectural Record* 84 (July 1938): 60.

35. Wright, in *Architectural Forum* 68 (January 1938): 68.

36. The semicircular Jacobs House, designed in 1943/44 and built in Middleton, Wisconsin, in 1946 to 1948, is a direct development of the idea of hinging and pivoting. The module of the house is a 6-degree sector of a circle whose center is the middle of the circular sunken garden. As Vincent Scully noted, "its arc partly encloses a deep earth hollow, and it sends its overhangs out to pick up the continuities of the prairie horizon" (*Frank Lloyd Wright*, Masters of World Architecture Series [New York: George Braziller, 1960], p. 30). My interpretation of Wright's late work is to a large extent based on Scully's.

37. F. L. Wright, in *Architectural Forum* 88 (January 1948): 137.

38. Wright, *Autobiography*, p. 478.

39. Ibid., p. 480.

40. Ibid., p. 478.

41. Ibid., pp. 479, 477.

42. Ibid., p. 478.

43. Cf. Colin Rowe and Robert Slutzky, "Transparency: Literal and Phenomenal," *Perspecta* 8 (1963): 45–54.

44. This was first pointed out by Scully in *Wright*, pp. 28–29.

45. Again, see R. Banham, "The Wilderness Years."

46. See Norris Kelly Smith, *Frank Lloyd Wright: A Study in Architectural Content* (Englewood Cliffs, N. J.: Prentice-Hall, 1966), esp. pp. 55–100.

JEANNERET AND SITTE:
LE CORBUSIER'S EARLIEST IDEAS ON URBAN DESIGN

H. Allen Brooks

CHARLES-EDOUARD JEANNERET (Figs. 1, 2) later known as Le Corbusier, began to research his first book in April 1910. Yet it was never published and in later years even he believed that the manuscript had been lost. Only the title seemed to survive, *La Construction des Villes*—The Building of Cities—a topic of immense import in view of his later publications and influence in this field.

While doing research for a book on Jeanneret's formative years, I discovered the long-lost manuscript. It is unfinished and therefore presents a complicated puzzle that can be pieced together only with difficulty. The pieces include two or perhaps three outlines of the book, nearly 135 manuscript pages divided into several chapters, many pages of notes and drafts, and more than 150 drawings intended as illustrations. To add to the problems, some of the chapters are written in

a hand other than Jeanneret's, others were rewritten at uncertain dates, and many of the drawings have nothing whatever to do with the text.

Some of these complexities must be set in order before discussing the text, and therefore we will begin by trying to establish a chronology within the work in the hope of putting its various parts into a more meaningful relation. Since no internal evidence for dating exists, we must turn to Jeanneret's correspondence for clues, and in this regard I have been fortunate in finding scores of letters whose existence was hitherto unknown.[1]

Jeanneret was born at La Chaux-de-Fonds, Switzerland, where he studied at the Ecole d'Art (the local applied-arts school) and there came under the influence of the painter and teacher Charles L'Eplattenier. After designing and building his first house (the Villa Fallet) he set off on a four-year period of travel and apprenticeship. These travels began in September 1907, when he was just short of his twentieth birthday, with a trip to Italy, the winter spent in Vienna, and some twenty months in Paris where he worked part-time for the brothers Perret. The early months of 1910 saw him again at La Chaux-de-Fonds where he decided to live, alone, in an old farmhouse outside of town. It was at this time that L'Eplattenier proposed he write a booklet on the construction of cities, a subject with which he himself was particularly concerned. Thus in this casual manner began Jeanneret's lifelong preoccupation with urban design, with all of its implications for those of us in the twentieth century.

Once the winter months were over Jeanneret left for Munich, and on April 16, 1910 he sent L'Eplattenier a four-page outline entitled "Thèse : La Ville : La Chaux-de-Fonds" with each page containing a column for L'Eplattenier's comments and corrections. Its brevity makes dif-

ficult a detailed comparison with the subsequent manuscript, but the basic form and general program is there, that is, an historical, analytical section to be followed by a case study of the town of La Chaux-de-Fonds. Some remarks in the outline do not reappear later, phrases like "common people and aristocrats; crisis–then 19th century industrialism to excesses; social crisis; disequilibrium," yet these thoughts are significant premonitions of Le Corbusier's outspoken socialist and syndicalist views of the 1920s and 1930s. Finally, at the end of the outline, a note says that

he intends to "cite plans and views in the manner of Camille Sitte."

From Jeanneret's letters in May and early June we learn that he is unable to buy Sitte's book; it is out of print. He asks if L'Eplattenier can spare his copy; he cannot. Jeanneret is referring to the French edition (*L'art de batir les villes*, Paris, 1902) as translated by his countryman Camille Martin in which there is an added chapter, "Streets," a subject that plays an important role in Jeanneret's manuscript.[2]

On May 19 Jeanneret wrote L'Eplattenier that he had begun to write "notre brochure." On June 2 he said it was nearly complete, while on June 7 he said that the illustrations were collected but he had not decided whether to prepare them as rapid sketches or as tracings; the rest of his work was complete. The latter was apparently an overstatement, because on June 29 he broke the news to his parents (he and L'Eplattenier had kept the project secret for fear the local authorities would find out) and said he hoped to finish the research in fifteen days and would then come home and visit his parents at their summer place in Les Eplatures while continuing to work on the manuscript. From the same letter we learn that "This study will be published as a brochure, the importance of which surpasses my expectations. . . . It will be signed by L'Eplattenier and by me, and will have a greater than local interest. . . . Today it is almost ready. But it is written in such abominable French that I greatly count upon the quiet of the countryside to give me the chance to improve it."

"J'ai une peine épouvantable à l'écrire en français," he had written to L'Eplattenier on June 2, and this was absolutely true. He simply could not write well, or even correctly, in his native language, as anyone who has read his *Voyage d'ori-*

ent (posthumously published but largely written in 1911) well knows. His parents and friends repeatedly pointed this out to him, and for him it became a source of acute embarrassment. For years he battled with the problem and finally, in the early twenties, surmounted it by adopting an abbreviated style of writing that did not depend upon complete sentences.

In mid-June Jeanneret visited Berlin where he attended the Allgemeine Städtebau-Ausstellung and the Deutscher Werkbund meetings. He was apparently well received and even went to a reception given by Hermann Muthesius at his home. As a result of this trip, his first to Berlin, he decided he wished to apprentice under Peter Behrens, Bruno Paul, and Sitte's follower, Hermann Jansen.

Earlier, while in Munich, Jeanneret learned that L'Eplattenier had arranged for the Ecole d'Art to provide him with a traveling scholarship in order to prepare a study on the decorative arts in Germany. The report was published in 1912 as *Etude sur le mouvement d'art décoratif en Allemagne* and served to reinforce L'Eplattenier's views on how the curriculum at their school should be restructured. Incidentally, of course, the scholarship served to finance Jeanneret's work on *La Construction des Villes*, a book which, because of its intended attacks on hometown authorities, would never have won financial support from the commune.

By midsummer Jeanneret returned to La Chaux-de-Fonds and there helped plan the extensive celebrations which marked the early September dedication of L'Eplattenier's allegorical statue, *La République*. He designed costumes for some of the representations, while his brother Albert wrote the music. As previously noted, some of his manuscript chapters are written in a different

hand, which may lead one to assume that, since L'Eplattenier was planning to cosign the work, these chapters were his contribution. However, a check of the handwriting discloses that it is in Jeanneret's mother's hand; she, during the summer, had helped her son by transcribing part of the text.

In the accompanying chart I have endeavored to reconstruct the table of contents as it may have existed in the summer of 1910. It is based upon an incomplete table prepared by Jeanneret, as well as the various chapter headings, outlines, and notes that he left. Some of the headings were later changed or crossed out, which compounds the confusion; it also implies that Jeanneret was not clear in his own mind as to the final organization. In the margin I have added three items of information: (1) the numbering, if any, which Jeanneret assigned to the section; (2) the number of manuscript pages in the section; and (3) by the letter M or J whether the manuscript is in the mother's or Jeanneret's handwriting. The fact that Jeanneret's numbering system indicates omissions that are not apparent from his Table of Contents or outlines raises the issue of whether (as I expect is the case) parts of the manuscript have yet to be recovered.

The book included a statement of his thesis (*Thèse*), but later he discarded this section on the grounds that it was unnecessary. It contained a general discussion about mankind's need to group together in a social order, and how the changes wrought during the nineteenth and twentieth centuries must necessarily affect the design of cities. It concluded with a lament about the failure of government to recognize the worth of art and artists, and an assertion that we must allow art to enter into our daily lives.

Part One, which follows the *Thèse*, consists of

PROPOSED RECONSTRUCTION OF TABLE OF CONTENTS				
La Construction des Villes		Labeled by Jeanneret as No.	Number of pages of manuscript	Whose handwriting?
Thèse		Thèse	8	M
I Partie				
Chap. I Considèrations Générales		1	4	M
1) Destination de cette étude				
2) Principes généraux				
Chap. II Des Eléments Constructifs de la Ville				
1) Introduction (relabeled "Avant-Propos") Avant		5	7	J
2) Des Chéseaux		5	8	J
3) Des Rues		6	29	M
4) Des Places		7	33	J
5) Des Murs de Clôture		9	4	M
Chap. III Des Moyens Possibles (including a chapter labeled "Chap. Second" but relabeled "Chap. Troisième."		12 13 14 15 }	24	M M J J
II Partie : Application critique: La Chaux-de-Fonds.			16	J
(various drafts and notes)			±15	J
(Avertissement)			13	J

three chapters and several subsections. Chapter I (*Considérations Générales*), subsection 1 (*Destination de cette étude*), begins with the sentence: "This study, written for no other reason than to state the procedures for embellishing our existence in cities, is addressed, especially, to the authorities." He continued by regretting that the great era of city-building, dominated by rulers from Ramses to Louis XV, is past and has been supplanted by unimaginative administrators whose designs are based on mechanical patterns of straight lines rather than the dictates of the landscape or upon human considerations. This jab at civil servants was hardly likely to win for Jeanneret the support of his intended readers.

Chapter II, *Des· Eléments Constructifs de la Ville*, includes five sections comprising the major portion of the intended book: (1) *Introduction* (this text was later relabeled *Avant-Propos*); (2) *Des Chéseaux* (Parceling of Land or Lots); (3) *Des Rues* (Streets or Roads); (4) *Des Places* (Plazas or Squares); (5) *Des Murs de Clôture* (Enclosing Walls).

The short *Introduction* is carefully composed and written, and is the one place in the manuscript where we obtain a general picture of Jeanneret's vision of an ideal city rather than merely comments concerning its individual parts. He

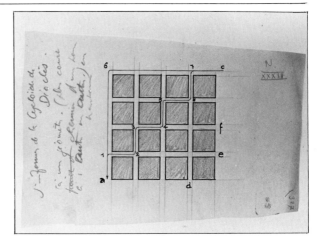

3. Jeanneret, grid pattern of streets. Sheet size approx. 14 × 22 cm. (Fondation Le Corbusier, Paris.)

sees the city as being divided into major zones for industry, commerce, and residence with the actual positioning of these zones determined by landscape, prevailing winds, and considerations of hygiene. And even at this early date he reveals his concern for isolating various types of traffic: "The lack of concordance between the actual means of locomotion and the layout of our cities *à l'américaine* has created in many places an untenable situation." He then concludes, "The problem is to find the shortest route, for vehicles on the one hand, for pedestrians on the other: *two interlacing networks* [*réseaux*] *without the one interfering with the other*" [italics underlined in the original].

The second section discusses *Des Chéseaux*, or the layout and parceling up of residential lots, and concludes that the elongated rectangle or parallelogram is the most advantageous shape because of the practicality of its long parallel sides (Jeanneret favors a deep lot because of the lengthy views it affords) combined with the possibility of gaining frontage when the lot faces on a curved street. He cites Hampstead (see Fig 6. below), Bournville, and Hellerau for their excellent residential layout, and praises Siegfried Sitte for his ingenious scheme (published in the journal *Der Städtebau*, Heft 10, 1906, p. 131) for locating schools in the center of large blocks where the classrooms may enjoy quiet, trees, and open spaces with only the entry and administrative offices facing on the street.

The third section concerns streets—*Des Rues*. This is the most thoughtfully written portion of the entire book and it clearly expresses Jeanneret's enthusiasm and devotion for his subject. His opening sentence confirms that "This chapter is the most important of all because it is from the design [*aspect*] of streets that the impression of

either charm or ugliness of a city is gained." Fortunately for us, this is the one chapter for which Jeanneret added nearly complete figure numbers to the texts, and for which many of the illustrations can (although coming from a totally different collection) be identified.[3] Reference is made to figure numbers (Roman numerals) as high as 60, thus implying that at least this many existed, or were contemplated, at one time; about half that many can be accounted for at present. These numerals are written by both Jeanneret and his mother, which probably implies that the sketches they refer to were already prepared in 1910.

The theme of this section on streets is easily summarized: streets should be curved, their width and slope should vary, views along them should be closed, and symmetrical or geometric layouts must be avoided. Jeanneret specifically states that "The lesson of the donkey is to be retained" (La leçon de l'âne est à retenir) and urges planners to learn from the donkey how to design roads which respect and enhance the landscape and are never tiring to ascend because of the variations in their slope. (Years later, after making an about-face, it is precisely this analogy of donkey paths with which Jeanneret chose to

4. *Jeanneret, Weissenburg. Sheet size approx. 16 × 19.5 cm. (Fondation Le Corbusier, Paris.)*
5. *Jeanneret, Munich, detail. Sheet size approx. 7.5 × 20 cm. (Fondation Le Corbusier, Paris.)*
6. *Jeanneret, Hampstead. Sheet size approx. 28 × 17 cm. (Fondation Le Corbusier, Paris.)*

mock Sitte's views on planning.)

This chapter, however, warrants discussion in greater depth. Jeanneret's first sentence calls it the most important in the book, and further on in the same paragraph Sitte is quoted in support of Jeanneret's views. He then draws his *première conclusion*: "the width and slope of streets can and must vary; systems of streets of equal width are to be condemned." He continues by denouncing the grid or checkerboard plan *à l'américaine* (his phrase) for its monotony and absence of visual appeal, its impracticality in terms of either vehicular or pedestrian circulation, and its lack of respect for the landscape (Fig. 3 which indicates how ridiculous it is to get from *c* to *a* by either going *c-b-a* or by the route 7–6–5–4–3–2–1-a). Although he praises the right angle ("L'angle droit est le plus beau, le plus monumental") and elsewhere says that "Two impressions are associated with the right angle: the impression of the grandiose; the impression of beauty," yet he hastens to observe that "the straight line, the most noble line in Nature, is justifiably the rarest of all!" And so it must be in the planning of cities. He cites the Avenue des Champs-Elysées in Paris as a prime example, saying that a city like Paris, the mid-nineteenth-century planning of which he greatly admires, "can support one such noble street but small towns should not try to emulate it. An occasional straight street, which is short and closed at both ends, is permissible, but long straight streets without a nearby visual terminus are deplorable." Figure 4 illustrates this, using as an example the town of Weissenburg; Jeanneret comments that while the tower dominates the center of the street, "the town hall [at the left] was not placed on the axis of the street, because two important buildings standing at two extremities of a straight street create a trite

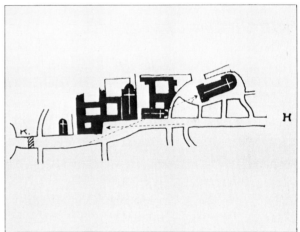

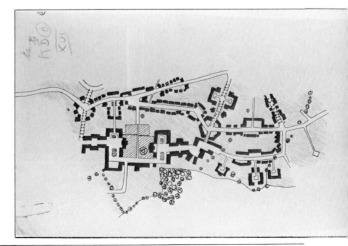

7. *Jeanneret, diagram showing alternate types of curved streets. Sheet size approx. 11 × 20 cm. (Fondation Le Corbusier, Paris.)*

8. *Jeanneret, diagram showing possible placement of major building on a curved street, and how it may be screened. Sheet size approx. 18 × 26 cm. (Fondation Le Corbusier, Paris.)*

impression that other epochs have carefully avoided." Here, as elsewhere, Jeanneret draws a lesson from the past.

It is the curved and the irregular street for which he finds almost unconditional praise. Again citing former times, he praises Soleure in Switzerland for the visual richness and variety of its streets, and singles out Neuhauserstrasse in Munich as an example of how to close a view by projecting a building into the line of sight along a straight stretch, and also to demonstrate what a splendid view of church towers (Frauenkirche) is gained while passing in the opposite direction (Fig. 5). From modern times he cites Hampstead

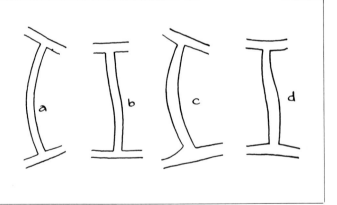

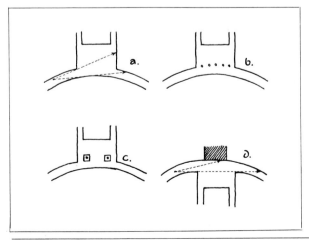

Garden Suburb as a superb example of the application of these same laws (Fig. 6).

Much of Jeanneret's discussion is devoted to demonstrating the pros and cons of various types of curved and irregular streets, or showing how to modify existing straight streets in order to make them visually more attractive. Citing Karl Henrici, he agrees that the longer a street seems to the person moving along it, the less pleasant and successful it is as a design: it pleases most by seeming short. By being curved, streets appear to be closed at both ends while offering a continuously unfolding view of the approaching facades along the concave perimeter. Figure 7 indicates how they might be designed; *c* and *d* are superior to *a* and *b* because of their varying width and often asymmetrical junctions. Figure 8 indicates other means of enlargement, especially where there is a building of particular importance. The scheme in diagram *a* is not recommended because one's view of the building is spoiled while approaching it; this bad situation can be improved by planting trees (*b*) or erecting monuments (*c*). It is preferable, however, that the enlargement be on the convex side of the street (*d*), where one can step back and properly admire the building. By contrast, if the road is straight, it is preferable to have the building set back as in figure 9*a* rather than 9*b*, in order not to interrupt the line of houses. Double enlargement is also possible, that in *d* being preferable to *c*. Another demonstration is presented in Figure 10 where in *a* (which recalls Munich, see Fig. 5) and *b*, "The beauty of this solution surpasses the need for commentary." Solution *c* is "froid" (cold) because of its symmetry but is considerably improved in *d*.

The themes and viewpoints expressed by Jeanneret are heavily dependent upon Sitte's book,

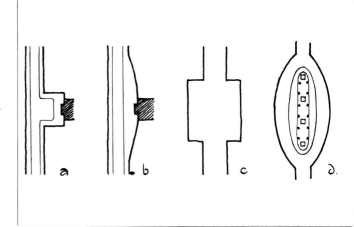

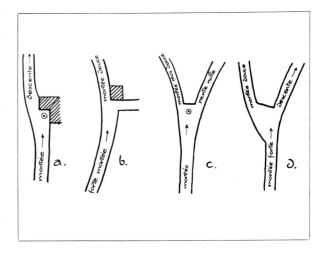

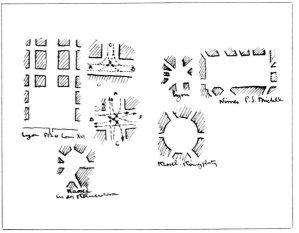

whether the sections by Camillo Sitte himself or the added chapter on streets by Camille Martin. What Jeanneret has contributed on his own are the more creative aspects, that is to say, the visual demonstrations, often abstract in nature, showing how and how not to design streets and how to enrich them by the artistic placement of buildings, monuments, and trees. The precedent for this is partly due to the journal *Der Städtebau*, which Jeanneret singles out for special praise and highly recommends to his readers.

Indeed, much more than just Jeanneret's section on streets owes a debt to Sitte's book. The titles of the two books are somewhat similar, and the division of their contents into two parts is identical—the first part being an historical, analytical analysis, and the second a case study (Vienna in Sitte's book, La Chaux-de-Fonds in Jeanneret's). Also, major chapters in both books are devoted to plazas and streets. Jeanneret copied many of Sitte's illustrations, in some cases tracing them directly, in others making sketches. Whether these were intended for reuse in his own book is unclear, yet the extreme care taken in their execution implies as much. The careful tracings were most often of squares and plazas. The less careful tracings or sketches include Sitte's plan of the Acropolis at Athens, the Piazza San Marco at Venice, and the series of sketches in Figure 11.

Sitte's followers are also accorded praiseworthy mention in the text. These include Werner Hegemann, Karl Henrici, Théodor Goecke, Paul Schultze-Naumburg, and Sitte's son Siegfried.

Jeanneret's section on Plazas—*Des Places*—is more spontaneous and less tightly argued than that on streets; the thirty-three manuscript pages are in his hand, rather than his mother's, and there are various marginal sketches, notes, and charts, factors which may suggest a slightly later date for the writing, when he had less time for editing or for transcription by his mother. Many figures are mentioned in the text but a blank space, rather than a number, follows the word "Fig.," thus making identification, except where place names are mentioned, nearly impossible.

"More so even than in the case of streets, the layout of plazas during the nineteenth century was unaesthetic . . . " So opens section 4. Jeanneret then lists three reasons why plazas are needed: to create a peaceful public area within the city's network of busy streets; to "mettre en valeur" an important or particularly handsome building; to serve as the junction for several streets as in a round point or major intersection ("la place créée pour elle-même; la place pour l'édifice; le carrefour"). After discussing these types he insists that "we must . . . hear the lessons of the past," and for Jeanneret this often meant the Middle Ages rather than the Renaissance. He cites the Piazza San Marco, Venice (the plan of which he had copied from Sitte), the market squares at Dresden and Stuttgart, and Piazza della Signoria, Florence (Fig. 12). He is particularly concerned that plazas should be closed—so that one cannot see out either at the corners or along the sides. This requires that streets enter at an angle or be curved. He condemns the nineteenth century's preference for "monotonous" geometrical plazas—often with a building at the center—and restates Sitte's argument that the major building in a plaza should be imbedded into the surrounding fabric and should have low structures around its base in order to give an optical impression of greater size.

At variance with his medieval predilections, however, was Jeanneret's preference for unity

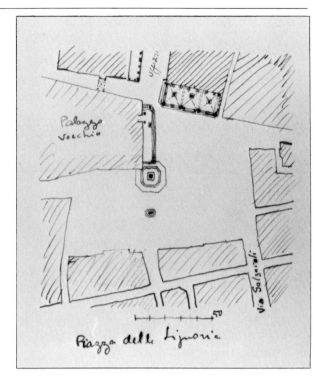

Piazza della Signoria

based upon the repetition of architectural motifs. Probably this derived from his protracted stay in Paris, where he specifically cites the Cour du Louvre and Place des Vosges for the restful qualities which their repetitive facades educe.

The fifth and final section of Chapter II is entitled *Des Murs de Clôture* (Enclosing Walls). "A wall is beautiful, not only because of its plastic form, but because of the impressions it may evoke. It speaks of comfort, it speaks of refinement; it speaks of power and of brutality; it is forbidding or it is hospitable;—it is mysterious. A wall calls forth emotions." Jeanneret pleads for high walls—at least 3 or 4 meters high—and denounces low ones or metal grills (the latter being only for the parvenu). He extols the wall at the Hôtel de Cluny: "The court behind the wall, under its great chestnut tree, is an oasis of tranquil refreshment which visitors to the museum

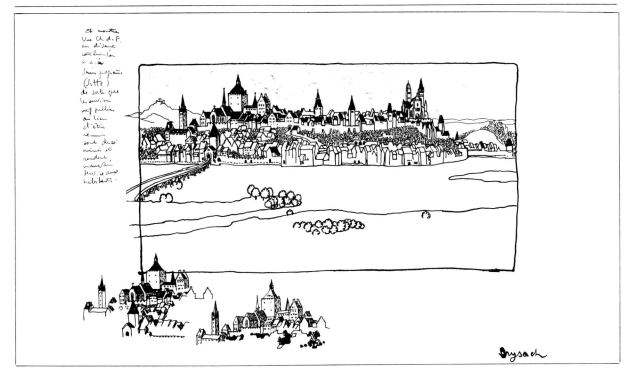

may well appreciate." The more important the space, the higher should be the wall, and to prove this he cites the cathedral square at Pisa.

This fifth section is very short, only four manuscript pages long. Later, on L'Eplattenier's advice, he agreed to add sections on other subjects, but these will be considered in due course.

Chapter III is entitled *Des Moyens Possibles*, and if my reconstruction is correct it consists of two manuscripts. The first is written in Mme. Jeanneret-Perret's hand and has as its only caption "Chap. Troisième" (this was subsequently crossed out and the word "Second" [sic] substituted in Jeanneret's handwriting, an alteration probably made in 1915; see below). The other manuscript is written in Jeanneret's hand, and although it lacks a caption, it does have a covering sheet which says: "I. Partie / Chap. TROISIEME / Des moyens possibles." Three factors

suggest that this is a continuation of the other text: (1) it deals with the same themes; (2) the subject (city administration), with which the first part ends begins the second part; and (3) the system of numerical designation seems continuous (12, 13 and 14, 15) between the two parts. It should also be noted that the second manuscript ends with the words "fin de la I partie," which corresponds with my reconstruction of the Table of Contents.

Jeanneret ends the section (second part) by saying, "One word will summarize all: the process of developing our cities must be returned to those who are alive and responsive. It must be taken from the bog [*cloaque*] of administration where all is dead, anonymous, sterile." This theme, already expressed in Chapter I (*Considérations Générales*), is restated in various forms in this rather repetitive section which is more of a crusade than anything else. "L'administration n'a pas plus le respect de l'art qu'elle n'a celui du terrain." Jeanneret argues that art *is* compatible with economy, with hygiene, with utility. He denounces administrators who tear down old buildings on the grounds that what is new is better. He rages against competitions and the juries that judge them. He says that we do have the means of improvement: we must appoint architects to design our city extensions; we should make models rather than designing cities on paper; and we must make use of new materials in our buildings. He again praises the planners of Hampstead (Fig. 6) and also extols the grouping of buildings at Breisach as it appeared in a seventeenth-century print he had found and copied (Fig. 13).

It is in this chapter, while discussing art and utility, that we find Jeanneret's earliest praise of the machine aesthetic. He distinguishes between two kinds of beauty. To the first kind belong those things that are "susceptible to beauty" (a favorite phrase of his); to the other kind belong those things of which it can be said, "beauty is the perfect conformity of their construction to their intended purpose." Thus a factory, aqueduct, or dam can be beautiful, but if ornament is applied they will become ugly. (He contrasts the brute force of a factory chimney with one which has been decorated with pilasters.) He also observes that "We admire the 'temporary beauty' of a locomotive or airplane, of a dynamo or a racing car because no superfetation distracts the viewer from their anatomy." This sentence, however, he later deleted.

Thus concludes Part I of the book. Part II is an *"Application critique"* devoted uniquely to "La Chaux-de-Fonds" with the subtitle, "Son développement actuel et son plan d'extension;

Comparaison des moyens employés avec ceux exposés dans la I partie." The heavily edited sixteen pages of text are written in Jeanneret's hand. From notes and letters we know that he intended to use forty-three or more plans and photographs (which he had taken in March) as illustrations, but these do not seem to have survived.

La Chaux-de-Fonds was, and still is, a clean-industry town (watchmaking) of fewer than 40,000 inhabitants. After a fire in 1794 destroyed most of the original village, the town's future extension was laid out as a grid with its long, thin blocks set parallel to what later became the double-laned (with trees in the central mall) rue Léopold-Robert, which runs down the center of the valley. Nothing infringed upon the grid of streets except the stairs built on the very steep sides of the valley (Fig. 14).

The chapter on his birthplace begins with yet another blast at "les géomètres," which is Jeanneret's euphemism for administrators who create town plans. "Nowhere in the plan of La Chaux-de-Fonds does one find a single layout which creates a pleasant view," and, "There is not a single public or private building in the town that is favorably situated in the manner proposed in Part I." There is much truth in his statements, yet they can do nothing but antagonize the reader whose sympathies he is trying to win. It is not until the latter part of the chapter that his criticism becomes constructive, and there he makes some very worthwhile observations about the remarkably inartistic grid layout one finds at La Chaux-de-Fonds and proposes some reasonable ways to ameliorate it.

Among the manuscript pages there are a few sheets of rough, often overlapping study sketches which can be identified with La Chaux-de-Fonds

14. La Chaux-de-Fonds, map dated 1908. (Fondation Le Corbusier, Paris.)

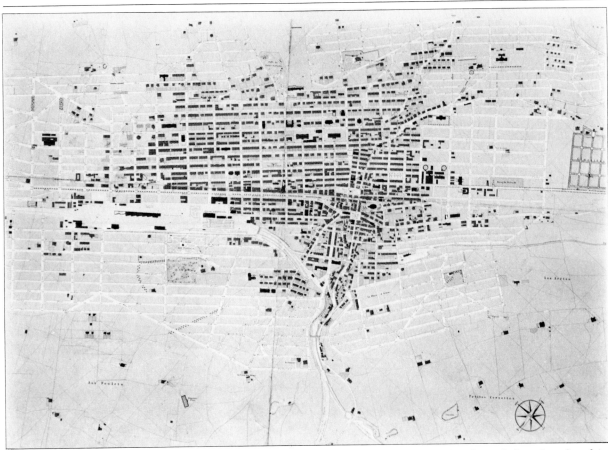

and these give some idea of Jeanneret's thoughts. In general he wished to create closed, intimate views and to develop focal points within them. Three sketch-plans appear to represent the eastern end of rue Léopold-Robert where Jeanneret proposed to create a more enclosed space around the fountain by throwing a visual barrier, penetrated by two traffic lanes, across the boulevard at a point near where Léon Perrin's sculpture (dedicated to Léopold Robert) now stands (Fig. 15). A similar type of solution was envisioned for the Place de la Gare, where, Jeanneret justifiably observed, neither the railroad station nor the newly completed post office was displayed to advan-

tage. His most fully developed drawing for this was enclosed in a letter, dated October 1, 1910, to L'Eplattenier (Fig. 16). The open, rather nebulous space in front of the station is here tightly structured with carefully controlled, intimate views which celebrate the major public buildings.

With this chapter on La Chaux-de-Fonds Jeanneret concluded his book on *La Construction des Villes*, a book that, while heavily dependent upon Sitte's earlier work, nevertheless contributed a great deal more by way of translating analysis (of old towns) into specific "rules," with accompanying diagrams, that could actually be applied to the designing of cities. His text, how-

15. *Jeanneret, sketches of how to modify the terminus of Avenue Léopold-Robert, La Chaux-de-Fonds. Sheet size approx. 30 × 21 cm. (Private collection.)*

16. *Jeanneret, project for the modification of Place de Gare, La Chaux-de-Fonds, with letter dated October 1, 1910. Sheet size approx. 10.3 × 12 cm. (Fondation Le Corbusier, Paris.)*

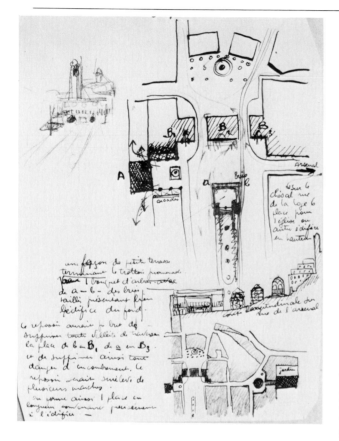

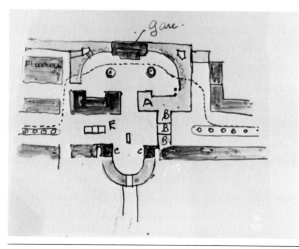

ever, was marred by his unremitting damnation of the municipal authorities who were responsible for city extensions, and this certainly detracted from the value of the whole. For a young man of twenty-two, he possessed more than his share of self-righteous indignation when it came to condemning others.

Before returning to Munich after the dedication of *La République*, Jeanneret discussed his manuscript with L'Eplattenier, who recommended adding five more sections to Chapter II: (6) bridges, (7) trees, (8) gardens and parks, (9) cemeteries, and (10) garden cities (reported in a letter to Jeanneret's friend, August Klipstein). These titles were dutifully noted in the manuscript but the texts probably were never written. From Munich, on October 1, Jeanneret wrote that he was finding documentation on gardens and cemeteries, but not on bridges. Subsequent letters make no mention of either research or writing, these activities apparently being superseded by his impending employment in Peter Behrens's office.

En route to Berlin, Jeanneret stopped to visit his brother at Hellerau (October 21–24). Judging from his letters he was tremendously impressed with the plan, layout, and architecture of the town; yet the fourteen pages of his sketchbook devoted to Hellerau are primarily concerned with economics and the factory system. After entering Behrens's employ on November 1, Jeanneret lived in Neu-Babelsberg, which he described enthusiastically as a garden city, and his sketchbook contains several sketches of houses (rather English in appearance) in the Nicholasee suburb of Berlin.

Obviously, Jeanneret's interest in urban design was not dead, but some five years passed during which his manuscript, *La Construction des Vil-*

17. *Jeanneret, project for Arnold Beck for a subdivision near Les Crétets in La Chaux-de-Fonds. Signed and dated "mai 1914 / Ch E Jeanneret." (Drawing: Fondation Le Corbusier, Paris.)*

les, lay idle. What happened during those years?

In the spring of 1911 he left Behrens in order to visit, with Klipstein, the Balkans, Turkey, mainland Greece and the islands, and southern and central Italy—his *Voyage d'orient*—before returning to La Chaux-de-Fonds to accept a teaching appointment, arranged by L'Eplattenier, at the Ecole d'Art. Shortly thereafter (1912) he published his *Etude sur le mouvement d'art décoratif en Allemagne*, in which he praised the garden-city movement and singled out the Städtebau exhibition in Berlin (1910) for its decisive role in demonstrating that streets should be curved and respectful of the terrain.

In 1912 he also designed two houses, one for his parents and the other for Georges Favre-Jacot in Le Locle. These were no longer characterized by the Jura regionalism that had influenced his earlier work, but rather by his own growing interest in a simplified Classicism such as had existed about 1800 and was being revived in the early twentieth century. This, however, is a point to which we shall return.

Jeanneret's first commission for an actual urban extension—a 120-house subdivision in La Chaux-de-Fonds (Fig. 17)—came from Arnold Beck in June 1914. The unexecuted plan gives us concrete proof that Jeanneret's ideas remained basically unchanged since the writing of his book in 1910. The design, including that of the houses, is almost pure Hellerau—with a bit of Barry Parker and Sir Raymond Unwin thrown in. Curved roads, like donkey paths, follow the contour of the landscape and break completely with the contiguous grid of the town.

By the following summer (1915) the war was raging in Europe, and although Switzerland was not militarily involved, building activity there

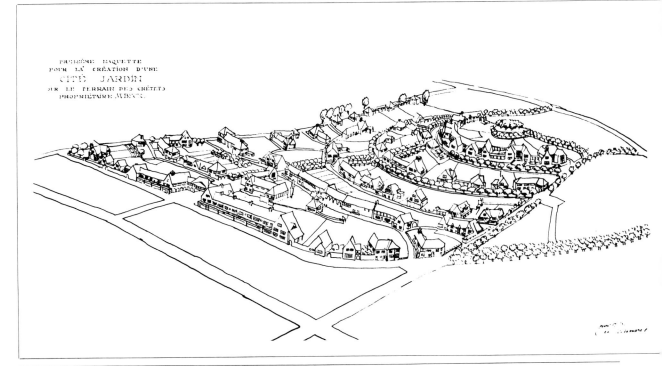

declined. Jeanneret, who had resigned his teaching post the previous year over a curriculum dispute, had designed no houses since 1912 yet managed to keep reasonably busy as an interior decorator and furniture designer; he also devoted an inordinate amount of time to working out the Dom-Ino project in collaboration with the engineer Max Du Bois. But by the summer of 1915 time hung heavy on his hands.

At this moment phase two of our story begins. On June 15, 1915 he wrote Du Bois, saying that because the war had destroyed so many cities, the time seemed ripe to find a publisher for *La Construction des Villes*—which "is all written." It was probably immediately after that that he took the manuscript out of storage and, on rereading it for the first time in five years, apparently felt that much of what was said was repetitious. Across the section entitled *Thèse* he wrote "Probalement inutile, 23 juin 1915," and it must have been during this month that some of the minor editing of the text took place. Apparently it was also at this time that the sixteen-page *Avertissement* was written. The latter seems to be an outline summary of what was *already* written, with the correct pagination carefully noted. It could, of course, be an outline for writing the book in the first place, but this seems improbable for various reasons including the quick, tight, almost illegible style of handwriting.

On June 30 Jeanneret wrote Auguste Perret that he would soon be in Paris in order to seek a publisher. He remarked that although the book was well advanced, it was written in a tight and tortuous manner and would have to be completely revised. After this date there is a gap in Jeanneret's letter copy book until July 20, then another gap until September 21, and a third until September 30 after which his ever-active correspondence resumes with one letter mentioning that virtually his entire summer was spent in Paris. Thus it seems clear that, except for two brief visits home, he spent the three months of July, August, and September 1915, in Paris. A July letter to Klipstein informs us that he has again taken up his study on the construction of cities, that he is working at the Bibliothèque Nationale, and that he is torn between discouragement over the vastness of the subject and the encouraging thought that the book will be useful and timely.

A file box at the Fondation Le Corbusier in Paris, subsequently marked "Bibliothèque Nationale," contains the fruits of his summer's work plus other materials such as the drawings already discussed, which clearly are earlier in date and have more to do with the State Library in Munich than with Paris. An in-depth analysis of the contents of this box would easily fill a book, but our chief concern is with Jeanneret's written ideas rather than the notes and drawings he made, except insofar as they inform us about how his mind was working.

The box contains several sheets of bibliography, many Bibliothèque Nationale and Département des Estampes call slips (listing "15, Av. de Trocadéro"—Max Du Bois's apartment—as his Paris address), scores of small blue cards that comprise an index of the drawings, larger yellow ones on which are both notes and drawings, and—most important of all—some 150 sheets of sketches and tracings including those we have already discussed. His method of filing these was ingenious. Each sheet was placed in his 1914 copy of the *Schweizerisches Bau-Adressbuch* with the notation of the page number on the drawing sheet—thus the fragile drawings could be indexed, filed, and refiled with relative ease.

18. *Jeanneret, parterre, Nancy, after Callot. Sheet size approx. 21.3 × 25.6 cm. (Fondation Le Corbusier, Paris.)*
19. *Jeanneret, Tuileries, Paris, after Patte. Sheet size approx. 16.5 × 25 cm. (Fondation Le Corbusier, Paris.)*

Wholly unexpected, in light of our earlier discussion, are the numerous drawings of eighteenth-century sites, with Place Stanislas/Cour Carrée at Nancy heading the list (Fig. 18). Jeanneret's research at the Bibliothèque Nationale had effectively opened his eyes to eighteenth-century urban design. And why not? We already noted a similar trend in his architectural works of 1912, and this was even more obvious in his furniture designs and interior decorations in the years that followed. By 1915 order, geometry, axial control, and monumentality had become his new gods in urban planning (and for an architectural example, see his Villa Schwob, La Chaux-de-Fonds, of 1916). Sitte, with his medieval town squares, was superseded by Pierre Patte and his *Monuments érigés en France à la gloire de Louis XV* of 1765 and other eighteenth-century works (Fig. 19).

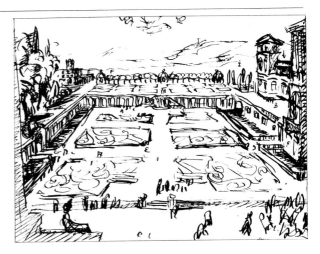

Jeanneret's bibliographies bear this out. One was copied from the *Discours sur la nécessité de l'étude d'architecture* of 1754 by Jacques François Blondel. Another, apparently Jeanneret's own, includes Philibert de l'Orme, Abbé Marc-Antoine Laugier (his *Observations sur l'archi-*

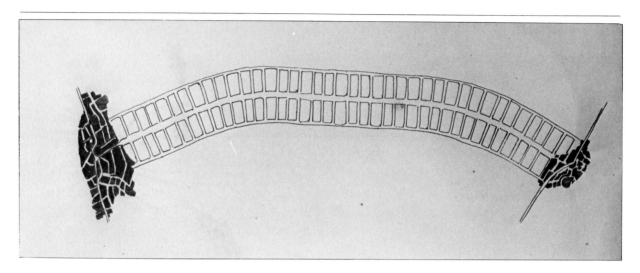

tecture, The Hague, 1765), plus a roster of more contemporary names such as Eugène Hénard, Georges Benoît-Lévy, Raymond Unwin, and Otto Wagner (his *Moderne Architecktur* of 1896).[4]

Drawings copied from the early books tend to be larger (frequently on 25.6 × 21.3-cm. sketchbook sheets), more quickly executed, and sometimes covered with Jeanneret's own notations, all in sharp contrast to the painstakingly careful renderings he had prepared five years earlier. It is probable that most of these were intended for study and reference rather than with immediate publication in mind (Figs. 18, 19).

Included among the drawings is one that deserves special note. It is a tracing, appropriately made on a long narrow sheet, of a series of illustrations (plans, sections, block layouts, etc.) of Arturo Soria y Mata's linear city (Fig. 20), thus confirming Jeanneret's knowledge of the Spaniard's work.

One of the last pieces in our complicated puzzle is a twenty-three-page section, entitled *Appropriation*, in Jeanneret's so-called "A-2" sketchbook of 1915.[5] Most of these pages contain only brief headings that he intended to develop later, but clearly this is an outline for rewriting his book. Although it begins with urban matters ("L'Acropole . . . Venise Piazza . . . Piranèse place St. Pierre . . . le plan de Paris de Patte . . .") it soon becomes a more theoretical work with emphasis upon architectural expression. It is notable that classical sites are more frequently mentioned than medieval ones.

Two pages of this outline are more thoroughly annotated than the others and here Jeanneret lists (under "question de race ou de tradition") various civilizations or cultures (Rome, Assyria, France, Japan, Asia, Islam) and equates certain characteristics with each of them. For example, of Rome he says "imperial instinct / unity of decision"; of Japan, "poetry / the gods / grace which is noble rather than picturesque"; and of France (the country with which he identified himself), "La raison plus intellectuelle et *raisonneuse*." He also makes a strong point about the need to express "the spirit of the epoch," as Louis XIV did at Versailles. In such statements we see the basis for his architecture of the 1920s, wherein he united the machine aesthetic (which he saw as the spirit of the age) with the (in his mind) specifically French characteristics of intellectualism and rationalism, which find their highest expression in the order of geometry. We should also note that he is continuing to use Sitte's method of historical analysis. And finally, we observe that his thought process (but not his conclusions) relates to that of ten years earlier when he advocated a Jura architecture that would be based upon regional (natural) forms and the cultural expression of the Suisse Romande (the French-speaking part of Switzerland which is located in, and just south of, the Jura mountains).

It is evident, therefore, that Jeanneret's summer of research at the Bibliothèque Nationale in 1915 was of tremendous significance to him. It completed his reorientation toward the classical (whether antique or of the sixteenth to eighteenth centuries) values of order and geometric control, and reinforced his earlier views that artistic expression had a national/cultural/epochal basis in the past and therefore should have such a basis in the future. His summer's work, however, did not result in the publication of his book prior to the end of the war (thus possibly gaining for him a role in the reconstruction), even though as late as June 17, 1918 he wrote to his brother that he had found a publisher for *La Construction des Villes*. Yet upon returning to La Chaux-de-Fonds at the end of September, 1915, it seems that he again put actual work on the book aside, this time for some six or seven years.

The third time that Jeanneret took up the project he did succeed in getting it published, at first rather piecemeal in *L'Esprit Nouveau* and then, in 1925, as the book *Urbanisme*. The latter is well known and therefore beyond the scope of this study, but it is important to note certain distinctions and similarities with his earlier work.

The major difference between the 1910 and 1925 texts is the complete reversal of Jeanneret's position. Indeed, one could interpret *Urbanisme* as Jeanneret's personal cathartic rather than a book intended to instruct its readers. He mercilessly lashes out against his (unnamed) self as well as against his earlier idols—and accordingly entitles his first chapter "The Pack-Donkey's Way and Man's Way" (Le chemin des ânes, le chemin des hommes). The inordinate amount of space devoted to this subject can only be appreciated in terms of his earlier dictum: "The lesson of the donkey is to be retained." And while "les géomètres" represented the devil in 1910, by 1915 and 1925 geometry was the god of order, harmony, and beauty in the universe. "Order," which was one of the generative words in the 1915 outline, reappears as the title of Chapter II in *Urbanisme*, and "sensibility," which originates from the same source, is the title of Chapter III. Meanwhile Chapter X, *Nos Moyens*, has its affinity with Chapter III of *La Construction des Villes* which was entitled *Des Moyens Possibles*. The interrelation between all three "books" is therefore apparent and one can appreciate why Jeanneret—by then his other self: Le Corbuiser— must have been happy that his first text was never published.

There are also important structural similarities that link the earlier and later works. If we compare Jeanneret's early Table of Contents (rather than my reconstruction, which is partly based on the manuscripts) with that of *Urbanisme*, it is evident that the latter is a direct outgrowth of the former.

Part One in both works is the same. Parts Two and Three are interchanged in sequence but in each instance are an analysis of a specific city— of La Chaux-de-Fonds on the one hand and of

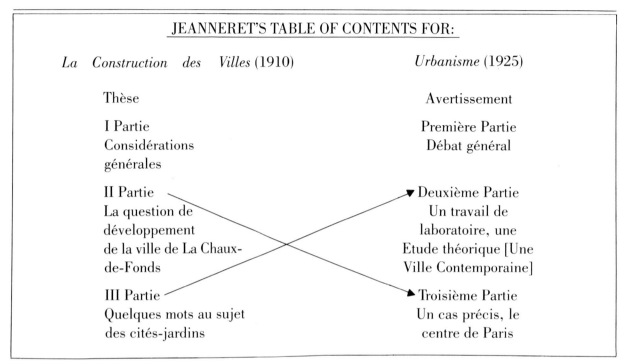

JEANNERET'S TABLE OF CONTENTS FOR:

La Construction des Villes (1910)	*Urbanisme* (1925)
Thèse	Avertissement
I Partie Considérations générales	Première Partie Débat général
II Partie La question de développement de la ville de La Chaux- de-Fonds	Deuxième Partie Un travail de laboratoire, une Etude théorique [Une Ville Contemporaine]
III Partie Quelques mots au sujet des cités-jardins	Troisième Partie Un cas précis, le centre de Paris

Paris on the other (we recall that Sitte wrote about Vienna). A third heading is devoted to a case study of a modern city type; in the early manuscript it is garden cities and in *Urbanisme* it is Jeanneret's own Contemporary City for Three Million Inhabitants. Such parallels are too close to be overlooked.

And finally, the illustrations. These also found their way into *Urbanisme* (and various subsequent publications). Included are a plan of Ulm (see page 7 of *Urbanisme* [1925]); plans of La Cité, Les Invalides, and L'Ecole Militaire, Paris (p. 8); a bird's-eye view of Altdorf (p. 25), which was intended as Figure IX in Jeanneret's earlier manuscript and is in the same style of drawing as our Figures 4 and 13; a plan of the Place Vendôme (p. 147); and a sketch after Patte (see Fig. 19) of the view from the Tuileries looking toward the future Place de la Concorde (p. 251). Although Jeanneret published over the years many

of these *Construction des Villes* drawings, he more often than not used them to demonstrate, or prove, a point which was exactly contrary to that which he had in mind when he created them. They, like he himself, had the freedom to represent a totally different cause, a freedom which the 1910 manuscript could never possess.

Postscriptum. Times have turned full circle now that Rob Krier, a hero of the younger generation, has written *Urban Spaces* (1979, with Foreword by Colin Rowe; first published 1975 as *Stadtraum*) "In memory of Camillo Sitte." Therein the author repeatedly castigates the plans of Le Corbusier for having "generated an unforgivable epidemic of 'urban blight'" (p. 75). Krier, who like Sitte and Jeanneret devoted the last section of his book to an historical case study (Stuttgart), would surely have been enthusiastic about *La Construction des Villes*. The two books are strikingly similar in several respects—including illustrations which in some cases are the same—except that Jeanneret's text is more thematic, analytical, and persuasive. How different our mid-twentieth-century cities might be if Jeanneret had published his book in 1910, an act that in all probability would have committed him to a stance on urban design at variance to the one he finally assumed.

Notes

1. This research, supported by both Guggenheim and Canada Council fellowships—to which organizations I am deeply indebted—is part of a larger study on the early, formative years of Charles-Edouard Jeanneret, that is, the little-known period prior to 1920 when he reached thirty-three years of age. Thus it includes his youth and early career at La Chaux-de-Fonds and his first years in Paris (1917–1919) when he and Amédée Ozenfant founded the Purist movement. The working title for my book is *Le Corbuiser's Formative Years.*

2. The standard English translation is by George R. Collins and Christiane Craseman Collins, *City Planning According to Artistic Principles*, along with their accompanying volume *Camillo Sitte and the Birth of Modern City Planning* (both N.Y.: Random House, 1965). The German edition, *Der Städtebau* (Vienna, 1889 and subsequent editions), was also known to Jeanneret.

3. The drawings (see more detailed discussion below) are at the Fondation Le Corbuiser in Paris. The manuscript belongs to a private European collector who prefers to remain anonymous.

4. I wish to acknowledge the valued assistance of Catherine MacKenzie, who as a graduate student studied this dossier in depth.

5. See *Le Corbusier Sketchbooks*, vol. 1, New York and Cambridge, Mass., 1981, figs. 55–77.

EXCAVATION, RESTORATION, AND ITALIAN ARCHITECTURE OF THE 1930s

William L. MacDonald

THE USE OF CLASSICAL FORMS throughout the long history of architecture in Italy is notorious, and the selection of elements of design from ancient buildings by architects of the Fascist period hardly surprising. However, it was not on the whole the grand tradition of design with the classical orders that these architects exploited. More often they turned to a style characterized by primary geometric shapes, largely unadorned, that had flourished during the Roman Empire, a style the regime's vast programs of excavation and restoration revealed in quantity. The forms of the often undistinguished official buildings of the 1930s are worth examining, partly in order to call attention to certain essential formal qualities of a somewhat neglected phase of Roman art, but chiefly because they provide evidence for the extraordinary persistence, throughout so much of Western history, of cardinal themes from Roman architecture.

Although it is misleading to divide Roman architecture arbitrarily into two parts—one with, and one without, the orders—the polarities implied by such a division are correct. Roman design ranges from the fundamentally Hellenistic, with rich displays of classical detailing, to an almost undecorated functionalist mode represented by such building types as apartment houses (*insulae*), warehouses, and local baths. In between there is a broad array of combinations of trabeated and vaulted work, of hidebound tradition and startling creativity, of buildings either strongly externalized or strongly internalized. What is significant here is the nontrabeated end of the spectrum, where buildings with little if any classical detailing are grouped and where the temple-front motif, if it is used at all, appears only in relief around a doorway or a niche. Much

of this architecture is of brick-faced concrete, and much, though by no means all, is vaulted. It is an architecture that has emerged from the buried ruins of antiquity only in this century, almost entirely through the work of Italian archaeologists. Examples had been known previously but their significance was obscured by their non-Vitruvian aspect; they lacked decorum and therefore when they were considered at all were not thought very important. But twentieth-century excavation at Ostia, Porto, Rome, and other sites revealed how pervasive this unadorned architecture had been, and the widespread new evidence could not be ignored.[1] At such sites the column with its capital often took a back seat; at others, such as major bath buildings and Hadrian's Villa near Tivoli, the orders were seen to dance to a Roman, not a Greek, tune.

So those who wanted modern architecture to harmonize with Italian tradition, rather than follow the prescriptions of domestic or transalpine modernists, were given ammunition by the results of the archaeologists' work.[2] The mandarins of official architecture were expounding the relevance of the past to the creation of forms that would echo the state's claim to be a latter-day Roman empire just at the time when a little-known and, for antiquity, nontraditional architecture was being exposed in quantity on Italian soil. Two state-sponsored activities—archaeological and architectural—turned toward each other in a kind of historical tropism. It may even be that the influence worked both ways, in that touches of the thirties style can be seen in certain archaeological restoration; more about that later on. In any event, restoration went swiftly forward, partly out of sheer necessity, so great was the quantity of half-wrecked structures from which the protective debris of centuries was removed. It was spurred also by the twin needs of modernizing the capital and of making the most out of the great sites and monuments, now isolated from their postantique surroundings and charged with a fresh if ephemeral symbolic weight.[3] Postantique buildings also were restored at this time, many of which—for example, S. Sabina—have strong formal affinities with the Roman plain style.

Thus the effect of the tangible presence of antiquity, always high in Italy, was increased during the Fascist era. Propagandists touted it, the government embraced it insinuatingly, and architects hoping for official commissions ignored it at their peril. The stage was set for the absorption of non-Greek elements from ancient buildings into contemporary architecture. The process itself was probably speeded by the fact that students of architecture and engineering worked at archaeological sites and on restoration projects alongside the professionals.[4] Many paper restorations were published, especially drawings of ancient streets and buildings made by the indefatigable Italo Gismondi. These were more accurate than the restorations of long-familiar monuments that had been made by Luigi Canina and others during the previous century, when gross guesswork was often necessary. And useful plaster models of ancient buildings and city districts proliferated; even the whole of ancient Rome as it appeared at the end of the imperial age was re-created in a huge model at a scale of 1:250—surely the most photographed and widely publicized architectural model ever. A major impetus behind this painstaking work was the preparation of models and graphic reproductions for various expositions, beginning with the Mostra Archeologica of Rodolfo Lanciani in 1911, held in the Terme, and continuing with the establishment in 1927 of the Museo

dell'Impero Romano. These collections were included in the influential exposition that opened in September, 1937 to celebrate the two-thousandth anniversary of the birth of Augustus Caesar (the Mostra Augustea della Romanità).[5] That effort formed in turn the basis of the instructive Museo della Civiltà Romana housed at the Esposizione Universale di Roma (EUR), whose sixty galleries contain scores of models of plain, unadorned buildings for study.[6]

Before examining the motifs and elements that ancient buildings and official architecture of the

2. Tomb of Marcus Virgileus Eurysaces, Rome. (Photo: Fototeca Unione, Rome.)

1930s have in common, two more factors in their relationship should be mentioned. The first is the effect of the predilection of several architects of the period for designs of major public buildings based quite directly on the work of Filippo Brunelleschi, Andrea Palladio, Giacomo Vignola, and so on.[7] These buildings, from which most moldings and ornament have been eliminated, exhibit a kind of undressed historicism. There are many examples of this substyle, which lies part-way between unabashed revivalism and the other thirties buildings under discussion. They are curious structures, neither fish nor fowl stylistically, but in their day they contributed through their quality of simplification to the movement that advocated bringing monuments and motifs from the past up to date. Another point, not an inconsiderable one, is that some ancient buildings originally encased in elaborate marble colonnades and embellished with temple fronts large and small had, by the time they were exhumed, lost much or all of their marblework. As a result only their towering structural bones were revealed, powerful concrete structures of uncluttered shape of the kind seen, for example, at the Palace of the Caesars on the Palatine (Fig. 1), the Temple of Venus and Rome (Fig. 14), and the newly laundered hulks of the huge imperial baths. Although they bear little resemblance to the complete original buildings, their lucid, planar forms may have helped to lead architects of the Fascist period toward those echoes of imperial antiquity they hoped to capture.

The kinds of forms under discussion can be seen clearly in the tomb of the baker Eurysaces that stands just outside the Porta Maggiore (Fig. 2).[8] Built of travertine toward the end of the first century B.C., it was encased in late antique fortifi-

cations until 1838. Its three horizontal zones are divided by courses made of travertine slabs that project slightly from the body of the whole to form continuous bands or oversized fillets. The surfaces of these bands are unfeatured in the traditional sense, although the upper one carries dedicatory inscriptions. This laconic geometry of forms appears on three sides of the building; in the zones between the bands, cylindrical shapes that represent grain measures are set both vertically and horizontally (there were forty-two originally). A nod was made to polite design at the top of the tomb, in the form of simplified pilaster

3. *Monument, Gianicolo, Rome. I. Jacobucci, 1941. (Photo: William L. MacDonald.)*
4. *Casa dei Cavalieri di Rodi, Rome. Quadriporticus. View before restoration. (Photo: Fototeca Unione, Rome.)*

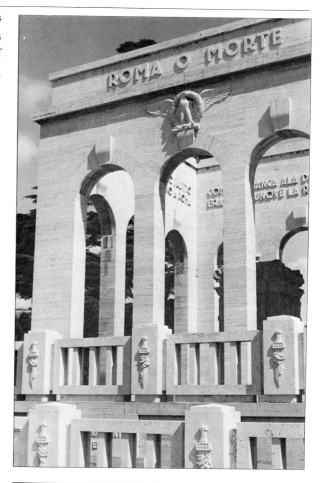

capitals, a sculptured frieze, and a more or less traditional cornice, but the broad, plain shapes below almost overwhelm this small amount of classical detail. The overall geometric bulkiness of the structure is outlined and broken up by the slightly projecting bands and by the prismatic corner elements, and its effect is lightened by a sense of perforated structure ingeniously evoked by having the vertical measures suggest columns and the horizontal ones interior hollows.

These direct, nontraditional attitudes toward form, typical of the novel, unadorned structures of antiquity, are recapitulated in twentieth-century buildings. Consider for example the monument of 1941 on the Gianicolo by I. Jacobucci that honors those who fell in the struggle for Rome from 1849 onward (Fig. 3). A freestanding, arched *cortile* of travertine, it is composed of plain, largely undetailed surfaces, semicircular arches, and banding, all of the simplest kind, sparsely accented with legionary short swords and with eagles based on the one from Trajan's Forum now in the porch of the SS. Apostoli. A counterpart in the plain style is the arched and banded quadriporticus of the time of Domitian (A.D. 81–96) incorporated in the later House of the Knights of Rhodes hard by the Forum of Augustus; Figure 4 shows it before the careful restoration begun in 1940.[9] Related, influential sets of forms can be seen in the courtyards of *insulae* and warehouses at Ostia, which are fundamental examples of Mediterranean construction (Fig. 5).[10]

The repetition of plain, unmolded arches to form lengthy arcades was common in both periods. In Rome, I. Guidi's Anagrafe on the Via del Teatro di Marcello (formerly the Via del Mare, a Fascist creation) is a case in point, as is the blocks-long prewar section of the Stazione di Termini by A. M. Del Grande (Fig. 6). The latter, with its

aqueductlike progression of unmolded arches large and small, is built up from three design elements only: the flat, unfeatured wall, the arch, and the plain running band. This combination of forms appears throughout Italy and in its former colo-

nies overseas; the examples are nearly endless and here it need only be stressed that they are all, in respect of architectural form, closely related to ancient structures.

Of greater interest are more fully articulated arcades that carry on dialogues with ancient monuments nearby. An instructive example is the arcaded, brick-faced retaining wall built against the northeastern part of the Velia ridge when it was partly cut away to make a level course for the new Via dei Fori Imperiali (ex-Via dell'Impero, connecting the Colosseum with the Piazza Venezia, inaugurated in 1932).[11] Looking southeast from the end of the colonnade of the Vittoriano one sees the Velia wall (at the center of Fig. 7) facing on the opposite side of the street the awesome remains of the Basilica of Maxentius and Constantine, one of the many ancient structures

7. *Via dei Fori Imperiali, Rome. View looking southeast. (Photo: William L. MacDonald.)*

8. *Velia buttress, Via dei Fori Imperiali, Rome. A. Muñoz (?), 1931. View looking east. (Photo: William L. MacDonald.)*

which with their dependencies were cleared and renovated during the hectic archaeological work accompanying the construction of the new street.[12] The Velia design has eleven niches, marked by brick banding and slight reveals, with a fountain in the central concavity (Fig. 8). The top of the stone-faced plinth and the levels of the platforms above are marked by travertine bands of the usual kind, and the motif is repeated in staccato segments of coping for the merlonlike railing piers. Huge, niched, buttressing walls have many counterparts in antiquity. The Velia arcade is closely related to the one standing a street's width from the northeast flank of the basilica (Fig. 9). This splendid example of late antique design may also have included fountains originally, for some of its niches were decorated with mosaic, a combination of form and décor that very often indicates the presence of a water display. Of equal relevance are the basilica's triads

of enormous windows, their jambs and sills restored after postantique additions were removed (Fig. 10). These openings, each some 5.4 by 8.2 meters, embody the essence of the plain style: sharp-edged, monumentally scaled, simple geometric form.

9. *Arcade behind Basilica of Maxentius and Constantine, Rome. View looking southeast. (Photo: Fototeca Unione, Rome.)*

10. *Basilica of Maxentius and Constantine, Rome. Westernmost bay of aisle, view looking north. (Photo: William L. MacDonald.)*

Another way of making useful connections between the two periods is to look at the omnipresent Fascist towers. The ones with square plans, of obvious historical background, need not detain us. But the ones that project, singly or in pairs, at right angles from their buildings and then modulate to semicylindrical form, very common in both Italy and the former colonies, surely derive chiefly from Roman plain-style military gateways.[13] Prime examples of the latter are the pairs of rounded towers, such as those guarding the Porta Asinaria (Fig. 11), added early in the fifth century to the massive Wall of Aurelian (A.D. 270 ff.) that still circles much of the historical center of Rome; there are many other examples in Italy and beyond. Figure 12 shows the facade of the R.A.I. Auditorium building (c. 1935; E. Del Debbio?) at the Foro Italico (ex-Foro Mussolini), which is typical of this kind of composition. The new towns of the Agro Pontino are sprinkled with

11. *Porta Asinaria, Rome. View looking northeast. (Photo: William L. MacDonald.)*

12. *R.A.I. Auditorium Building, Foro Italico, Rome. E. Del Debbio (?), c.1935. Facade, view looking southwest. (Photo: William L. MacDonald.)*

this motif, which as part of the baggage of Fascist design turns up in such widely separated places as Naples (the Stazione Marittima of 1936), Sabratha in Tripolitania (the museum), and Rhodes (the central cinema; Fig. 13). All these have emphatic banding; the Stazione also boasts flattened-out, bloodless metal horses that may be descendants of those of San Marco in Venice.

Other major plain-style features were almost equally influential, for example, the large semidomed exterior niche, of the kind seen in tombs and fountains at Pompeii, in the porch of the Pantheon, and in the monumental back-to-back apses of Hadrian's Temple of Venus and Rome (Fig. 14). The remains of the temple were cleared during the early 1930s, when the removal of part of the Velia gave them a considerably greater elevation than before.[14] The apses were of course not originally intended to be seen the way they are today, isolated and uncovered, but the transformations brought about by such a long lapse of time have done nothing to lessen their expressive power (cf. Fig. 1). This motif can be seen on a monumental scale at S. Michele in Aprilia, where the facade frames a lofty apse like those of the Temple of Venus and Rome, though divided into zones by travertine bands and lacking Hadrian's swirled coffering (Fig. 15). Again other examples are found in distant places, as at the Hôtel des Roses (ex-Albergo delle Rose) at Rhodes, of 1927 (Fig. 16).

Whatever influence these ancient structures had on Italian architects before the establishment of the regime, it was soon increased by the discoveries and publications of the archaeologists working at Ostia, the port city of ancient Rome.[15] Few could have been prepared for what was revealed there: scores of buildings that bore almost no resemblance to the better-known discoveries

13. *Cinema, Rhodes. Flores Fano Di Fausto (?) (Photo: William L. MacDonald.)*

14. *Temple of Venus and Rome, Rome. Originally designed (A.D. 120s) by Hadrian, partly reconstructed in the early fourth century A.D. Eastern apse, view looking west. (Photo: Fototeca Unione, Rome.)*

at Pompeii. Structures of the classical, Vitruvian tradition turned out to be few and far between at Ostia, which was exposed as a city largely executed in the plain style, its buildings faithfully mirroring those of the nearby capital now almost entirely lost (Fig. 17). Though founded in the fourth century B.C. and for long a small town of traditional buildings, Ostia had been almost completely rebuilt under the empire, with much reconstruction taking place under Hadrian. The moving force behind these discoveries, and behind their publication until almost the time of his death in 1946, was Guido Calza, who began publishing his studies in 1915.[16] Systematic excavation at Ostia had begun in 1909 and continued methodically over the next three decades. In 1938 the tempo of work was greatly increased, in anticipation of an international exhibition planned for 1942; during that four-year period Calza and his workmen uncovered about half of the thirty-odd hectares of buildings that can be seen today.

In the imperial age Ostia was a city where most buildings were characterized by plain, even brickwork, unmolded window and door openings, and uncomplicated architectural shapes. The orders were there, in official buildings such as temples, the theater, and the larger baths, and they were lined up along some of the main streets. But in *insulae*, markets, warehouses, and most other kinds of buildings there was little if any use of traditional classical motifs except for some decoration in terra-cotta. Gismondi, working closely with Calza, made reconstruction drawings of these Ostian buildings that began to be published at least as early as the mid-twenties.[17] One drawing, frequently reproduced, of the Casa di Diana, c. A.D. 160, was a major source for the model of the building in the EUR museum (Fig. 18); it was first published at least as early as

15. San Michele, Aprilia. Facade. (Photo: William L. MacDonald.)

16. Hôtel des Roses, Rhodes. M. Platania, 1926. (Photo: William L. MacDonald.)

1925. Figure 19, where the draftsman has extended the information found in a photograph of the remains of one of the flanks of the Casa di Diana, is a 1960s interpretation. The vertical development, planar wall surfaces, nature of the door and window openings, string courses, and ubiquitous relieving arches (as they are usually but erroneously called) are all typical of imperial *insulae*. The balcony here is exceptional; unfeatured walls of the kind seen to the left in Figure 17 are almost always found in the hundred-odd examples visible at Ostia.

From these buildings it is instructive to turn to modern housing at Latina (ex-Littoria) in the Agro Pontino (Fig. 20). Though there are differences from the Ostian structures there are also telling similarities, for example, the general proportions, the blocklike forms, the segmental arches, and certain ground-floor dispositions. This is an Italianate form of great antiquity, though it may

have come to the twentieth century partly by way of a living tradition never entirely lost in Italian cities and towns. In any event, it is difficult to look at these buildings without feeling that their forms are too closely related to those of Roman times to have been the result of wholly independent evolutions.[18]

The shapes in question had been studied before Euclid, but it was he who set out their properties canonically, in Books 11–13 of his *Elements* (c. 300–290 B.C.). He cared nothing for practical applications of his work, but Archimedes, writing a generation or two later, took a less lofty attitude and, generally speaking, writings on geometry and mensuration tended to include more practical information as time passed. The widely read work of Heron of Alexandria (first century A.D.) contains much useful data about solving practical problems, including calculations that the architect and builder needed to master.[19] Mixtures of practical and theoretical material can be found in the works of Pappus of Alexandria (early fourth century) and of Anthemius and Isidorus, the creators of the Hagia Sophia.[20] The chronology of the texts, which clearly

changes ancient architecture underwent meanwhile. By the time the Palestrina complex was built, about 100 B.C., post-Euclidian treatises contained didactic examples of a familiar kind, and now and then an actual building was mentioned; the material is not unlike that given in the first section of the Kidder-Parker *Handbook*[21] for some twenty editions now. The properties of planes, rectangular prisms, cylinders, spheres, and so on would have been second nature to architects and builders, and structures composed of such shapes appeared ever more frequently as time passed.

Other factors were at work, such as the rapid increase in the use of brick and concrete (so amenable to the construction of forthright geometric forms) and the requirements of extensive building programs needed to accommodate expanding population and trade, but the intervention of the manuals may have been crucial. Architecture was, after all, taught in the classroom.[22] What is certain is that the plain style was a success. It was used in almost all public and private building types, sometimes in combination with the orders (which are undergoing major changes). By the second and third centuries A.D. only the venerable temple form, by then close to the end of its tenure—for the time being—had resisted translation. The other quintessentially Roman building types succumbed: the curia, the basilica, the local bath building, even the magnate's villa.[23] And although the austere shapes of the Wall of Aurelian were largely determined by its function, the fact remains that it was then, and remains, exceptionally potent both formally and symbolically, a paradigm of the plain style (Fig. 11).

In turning again to connections with Italian architecture of the thirties, it should be stressed

were aimed at specialists, shows that such information was not readily available until well after classical Greek architecture had reached maturity, that is, only in Hellenistic times. Practical manuals of solid geometry became commonplace at the same time as the Romans were establishing themselves around the Mediterranean, a fact which helps to make sense out of the wide variety of architectural form found in the Greco-Roman world. The publication of the *Elements* falls about half-way between the date of the Parthenon and that of the Sanctuary of Fortune at Palestrina, monuments which underline emphatically the

18. *Casa di Diana, Ostia, c. A.D. 160. Model in the Museo della Civiltà romana, EUR, Rome. (Photo: William L. MacDonald.)*
19. *Casa di Diana, Ostia. Flank along Via dei Balconi, looking southeast. (Photo/drawing montage: Duane Thorbeck, architect.)*

that this plain architecture, largely free of complex building techniques, did not disappear with the collapse of Roman authority. Examples can of course be found in several periods of Western architecture. It may be that Carlo Lodoli (see pp. 31–37), the Abbé Laugier, Claude-Nicolas Ledoux, Etienne-Louis Boullée, whose work shows archaeological influences, and other writers and architects interested in elemental or functional architectural shapes had an effect on Italian designers, but the subject lies outside the limits of this discussion. Another influence might have been that of the work of Giorgio de Chirico, whose first one-man show in Italy was held in Rome in 1919; until then he had been little known in his homeland, having lived in Paris from 1911 to 1915.[24] Discussions of the nature and origins of his architectural forms by critics and historians are brief and the subject needs further investigation. His early works abound with examples of plain, bold, geometrically formed architecture, usually painted in whitish grays, their stark shapes set off by deep, dark shadows. These forms are sometimes said to have been inspired by the piazzas and streets of Rome, Florence, and Turin as they existed early in the century. But the evocative, scrupulous clarity of the shapes of his arcades and other buildings, in paintings and drawings from 1910 to 1915, stems from brightly lit, broad, and undifferentiated planes and a lack of moldings and details, not from the more complex buildings he knew as a youth (which he seems to have transcribed only rarely). It is true that plain-style forms, mostly medieval, can be seen in the gates, towers, and piazzas of such cities as Viterbo, Susa, and San Gimignano, and in vernacular buildings throughout Italy, but the architecture de Chirico painted was even simpler.[25] Whether or not any link can be made between

his work and the official architecture that would soon appear seems moot. But it is clear that there are close formal similarities between the two.

There are of course other kinds of relevant historical continuities than formal ones. For example, building with brick and mortar, as well as with concrete—which did not cease in post-Roman times though the quality dropped off badly—never stopped in Italy from the time of Augustus onward (Figs. 8, 10, 11). Brick walls and piers have always flourished there. Travertine, the building stone *par excellence* of Rome, has already been mentioned; half the monuments of the city are built of or faced with it. Because of its rich texture, brilliant color, and light-reflecting qualities it goes extremely well with matte brickwork and stucco, combinations never abandoned. Building in this tradition, with most individual parts cut or molded to rectilinear shapes, contributed to the continuities in question.

The restoration of plain-style buildings was easier and less expensive than the restoration of elaborate marble monuments. The Italians were so good at this that one can be misled by restoration in brickwork done before it became generally accepted that such work should be made clearly distinguishable from ancient construction by one means or another; it has been said that "sometimes the restoration [at Ostia] is rather too Roman than not Roman enough."[26] Sometimes, through the refacing and extension of walls and vaults that could not otherwise resist the elements, the sense of plain-style forms is much augmented, as on the Palatine (Fig. 1), where a fair part of the brick skin is modern. And where restoration, in fact or on paper, influenced other buildings, the subject becomes directly relevant. We have seen that reconstructions of the *insulae* of Ostia could have influenced the design of housing in the Agro Pontino. There are cases of

more direct inspiration. An example is that of the 1934/35 restoration of the Castello in Tripoli, Libya, by Armando Brasini, who later designed the Forestale building at EUR. This, in large part finished but then destroyed after the war, repeated the Castello's grand scale and high, open arches riding above a lofty, battered, and impenetrable ground story.[27] Restorations on paper by experts such as Gismondi, and by less well-informed, entrepreneurial draftsmen such as Giuseppe Gatteschi, circulated widely from the early 1920s onward; they also contributed to the evolution of a style harmonizing with antiquity.

The influence of Gatteschi's book of 1924, *Restauri della Roma imperiale, con gli stati attuali*, with explanatory texts in four languages, was considerable.[28] His reconstructions, crude and sometimes absurd, nevertheless created a widespread impression of what ancient Rome looked like (photographic teaching collections drew upon them heavily). Gatteschi was not much affected by the discoveries made at Ostia after 1909, and his versions of grand civic monuments now lost relied on those of Canina—a weak reed by Gatteschi's time—and on his own imagination.[29] Even so, historical illustrators, designers of theater and cinema sets, and at least one or two architects turned to the book for guidance.[30] The designer of the Serbatoio Idrico on the Via Eleniana, of 1934, for example, seems to have reassembled the motifs Gatteschi composed for his hypothetical Entrance to the Gardens of Adonis on the east slope of the Palatine, spreading them across walls of highly rusticated stonework (themselves reminiscent of the surfaces of the nearby Porta Maggiore).[31] Gatteschi's book was more effective than Gismondi's responsible but less comprehensive work in forming popular notions of the appearance of a major Roman city.

The intersection of Fascist propaganda and requirements with excavation and restoration produced results which, though easily as curious as those resulting from the circulation of Gatteschi's stale and inaccurate reconstructions, are worth noting because they help show how closely the two periods became intertwined architecturally. Two examples may suffice. The back of the restored stage wall of the Roman theater at Sabratha in Tripolitania has a strong look of the thirties to it—blocky, monumental, stark, complete with strips of banding. The effect is not unlike that of the looming buildings lining de Chirico's haunted streets, with their anonymous surfaces that seem to await the decorator's additions.[32] More extraordinary is the way the new bricks (made to ancient dimensions) used in the restoration of the Domus Augustana on the Palatine were stamped AEF XII M (the twelfth year [1934] of the Fascist era, M[ussolini?]), in direct imitation of the consular brickstamps of the empire.

Much evidence, then, points to a close connection between the two periods, evidence of varying kind and quality but justifying the claim of a community of form. Other sources of the style of the thirties can be identified, such as the hope of creating an impression of modernity by eliminating historical detail. But in Italy history could not be denied, and, ironically enough, the rediscovery and display of uncolumned ancient buildings, together with the allure of Italic vernacular forms, shaped the regime's presumptively up-to-date architecture.

That architecture is the essence of simplicity compared to most historical styles. But simplicity, perhaps its key quality, created complications. Because the broad surfaces of the buildings are rarely broken up by any decorative, small-sized elements defining easily read subdi-

visions or patterns, true scale can be hard to apprehend. Interruption of the surface continuity of the major formal elements is largely limited to fenestration and arcading, usually composed of regularly repeated primary forms. Since there is little or no plastic mediation between these shapes and the starkly plain walls or piers that surround and define them—no detailed moldings and few small-scale shadow lines—the eye has chiefly to deal with an unrelieved giant's geometry, a world without many visual moorings, an effect strengthened by the broad, straight-edged shadows these buildings cast. Because there are so few indications of scale, in contrast with the comparatively elaborate systems that establish scale in most styles, the buildings can look like models or stage sets—which by their nature are composed of simplified forms. This effect is particularly noticeable when several structures are grouped together, as in the civic centers of the Italian new towns of Cyrenaica.[33] Simplicity at almost any cost can be self-defeating.

The same factors often create a sense of a lack of depth in walls and facades. Windows and arcades tend more to suggest blank voids than to imply usable interior spaces because the eye is given so little guidance as to the relationships between unarticulated openings and the bulk and surface of the building. Joining two plain, flat surfaces at a precise right angle revealed to the eye only by shadow and the sharply defined line of juncture does not do much to develop the artistic character of a building or to emphasize the tangible qualities of its forms. And if that is not done, the building is less architecture than a rather uncohesive assembly of shapes. Moldings around an arch strengthen the sense of the axis of the opening by suggesting planes parallel or leading to that axis; a clear case of this effect is found in the high Gothic portal. Without moldings, the planes of piers and the soffits of arches are so incorporated into the surrounding fabric they cannot properly suggest an axis to the interior or the potentiality of passage; the needed sense of how one part is related to another is missing. In a negative sense, this is one of the governing principles of the buildings in question. Composed of expansive surfaces reaching uninterruptedly from edge to edge, of broad forms lacking in subtlety of description or definition, they are deprived of all but a simplistic, somewhat dehumanized kind of architectonic character.

Layering horizontal zones and framing large rectangular surface areas by broad, running bands produces neither patterns nor articulation; the expanses between bands are too large for that (Figs. 6, 15). In any event, these bands—of plain, rectangular section—are not true moldings but discrete architectural elements (Figs. 2, 4, 8). Unlike proper fillets, they are independent tectonic members, often of a different material and texture than the adjoining fabric. A proper fillet is much smaller, a slightly projecting part of a structural block, and is normally one of a group of elements that function together visually across a wall or around an entire building. The distinction is important because the running bands or projecting ribbonlike elements used as cornices in the fashion just described are often called moldings, which they are not. They are basic design elements, like arches, or towers with semicircular ends, quickly singled out by the eye because of their relative size and because there are no other features at their scale to vie for attention. Their major function is to emphasize the shape and extent of the big, simple forms of the building, rather as the external reinforcing boards that are nailed along the edges of a wooden ship-

ping crate emphasize the uncompromising boxiness of the underlying volume. Both rectilinear and circular windows are often banded, but the flatness of the bands and the shallowness of their reveals do little to differentiate the plane of the window opening from that of its surrounding wall surface; the band tends to emphasize the flatness of the surrounding wall-plane rather than its penetration by the window. Copings, made of flat slabs of travertine projecting noticeably beyond the outlines of their foursquare supports, are common; they are a kind of banding (Fig. 8). Even the preferred style of lettering was formed of rectilinear bars (Fig. 3), and the band form was common also in the architectural background of contemporary painting.[34]

An elemental geometry of forms, then, organized to a degree by running bands but free of almost all other surface articulation, characterizes this kind of architecture, one of whose sources was austere Roman design. Clearly it is different both from works that imitate in varying degrees specific historical models, such as the churches of the Addolorata (1930; G. Astorri) and S. Eugenio (begun in 1942; E. Galeazzi and M. Redini), as well as from those that are defined by stripped classicism seen, for example, in modern buildings at the ends of the Via della Conciliazione. But is it really an architectural style? It fits uncomfortably under the designation "modern," partly because of its historical associations.[35] Yet it does in a sense fall in with the modernists' fulminations against ornament, which shows once again how difficult it is to determine what "modern" architecture was or is. What happened in Italy was that modern-looking buildings were wanted, and simple geometry seemed to go a long way to fill that need while at the same time having the capacity to evoke Old Italy and the putatively ancestral empire as well. But the result was submodern rather than modern, an ambiguous quasi-style, not a proper one. It was not as creative as it probably seemed to be at the time, partly because of its historical genealogy and partly because of its artistic limitations. It really had no system or philosophy, just a fairly limited repertory of acceptable forms not infrequently out of harmony with each other in relative scale. Such disharmony affects proportions, and in that respect a number of these buildings seem decidedly idiosyncratic because their forms are awkwardly related: naked geometric forms are hard to handle satisfactorily. Many monumental buildings of the high and late empire, such as the Pantheon, the Baths of Caracalla, and the Basilica of Maxentius and Constantine (Fig. 10), are essentially built up from such forms, but in their original state these buildings were made more apprehensible by the effects both of well-thought-out proportions and of readable, properly-scaled decoration and detail. Lacking these, the 1930s buildings are less successful. They come closest to success when they reflect unpretentious traditional forms (Figs. 21, 22).

Columns and their trappings usually were avoided because they appeared on just about every major building in the land from the early fifteenth century onward, and those were not the buildings that state architecture was meant to recall. Some colonnades were built in the 1930s, with the ancient forms of the capitals faintly recorded by innocuous quarter-round ring moldings; the orders, however, do not strip attractively (Piazza Augusto Imperatore and the EUR Museo in Rome; Via Roma in Turin). But columns hardly ever appear in official buildings of the kind being considered, and pilasters are rare. The result is a kind of late-antique modern,

21. *Central square, Pomezia. (Photo: William L. Mac-Donald.)*

vaguely tangential to sophisticated modern architecture but substantially anchored in the Roman austere manner. It was sufficiently deprived of historical fancywork to satisfy the undiscriminating in need of an architecture for their time, while it was carefully protected from any infection from the International Style. The situation was hardly novel, given the propensity of architects to come up with dusted-off historical forms trying to look up to date.

The buildings do manage to speak of Italy, of the long and splendid history of Italian art, but not in a particularly accomplished way, and they cannot be contemplated without thoughts of the ghastly sides of the Fascist regime. Many have aged rapidly, both in the sense of the nearly complete loss of that modishness they were once thought to possess, and in the physical sense as well. Although they tend to sit firmly on the ground, as stable building-blocks do, they utterly lack electricity, the capacity to generate positive responses. On the other hand, the columnless, plain-style buildings of the Romans can engage our attention because they were strikingly original, succeeding in the teeth of an omnipresent and entrenched classicism, and because they ap-

22. Arcade, Pomezia. (Photo: William L. MacDonald.)

peared in response to new social and practical needs.[36] They hold our interest also because they sponsored so many subsequent architectural events, while the political and social realities of the Roman world that produced them are too far distant to influence opinion very much. The buildings of both periods use many of the same design elements, but on the whole these were not judiciously or interestingly composed by the architects of the 1930s. In the last analysis, many of their run-of-the-mill official buildings are just awkward—ill-proportioned and out of step both historically and artistically—though there are honorable exceptions, both in Italy and overseas.

The amount of building carried out in the twenties and thirties was surprisingly large in view of Italy's poverty and limited industrialization. Costs were reduced somewhat by the fact that much work was done in traditional building materials put up in traditional ways. By these means the Fascist presence was signaled in due time in every town by the forms of official buildings. This activity was by no means limited to Italy and the home islands, for many buildings were built overseas, especially in Libya.[37] The Italians had been there since 1912 but comparatively little was accomplished until the energetic administration of Italo Balbo, beginning in the early 1930s. Waves of emigrants were sent from Italy, and large projects were put in hand. New towns were built, as they were in the Agro Pontino and Sardinia, and Tripoli and Benghazi were enlarged with new quarters and buildings. Hundreds of farmhouses were erected for settlers, and fancy hotels put up for visitors. Money was made available for archaeology, and Italian expertise in excavation and restoration was involved on a large scale; work at Lepcis Magna, Sabratha, Cyrene, and Apollonia produced re-

sults of major significance.[38]

The Italians had been in the Dodecanese also since 1912 and in the city of Rhodes had built some charming work in a semi-Liberty style. In time all the major islands got Italian buildings, some of historiated design, some in the new manner. Rhodes was enlarged and a score of new official buildings erected. Kos and Patmos got smaller, pleasant streets and buildings chiefly in a generalized Mediterranean style. So when Mussolini proclaimed the re-creation of the Roman empire there was an element of truth in his boast: as the Romans had taken their architecture to the provinces, so had twentieth-century Italians.[39] The Romans however had adopted or selected trends from regional artistic forces, absorbing many ancient elements and principles. This give-and-take of stylistic energies helped to create the very architecture that Italian architects took overseas so much later, to form a brief chapter in the story of the apparently unending persistence of ancient architectural forms.

This official architecture in the colonies followed in general the lead of the homeland, although there seem to be proportionately more arcaded streets in Libya. Government housing for settlers looks much the same there as that for farmers in the Mezzogiorno: blocky, efficient, plain structures with arched enclosures and rigidly foursquare silhouettes.[40] The new additions to the cities overseas were on a quite grand scale, with broad arcaded avenues lined with palms, and extensive, landscaped seaside prospects. Savings banks sprang up beside venerable mosques. In Tripoli, Balbo was housed in a domed neo-Byzantine mansion that would have been quite at home in the grounds of the Great Palace of Constantinople. In general these colonial buildings are less totalitarian in appearance and effect than those in Italy. It is difficult to say why, for the forms are much the same except that banding is less evident. In Libya perhaps it is because the buildings are in the off-white, buff, and sand-colored tints of the African soil and landscape and are therefore less aggressively obtrusive than the richer, brighter colors often used in Italy.

Walking along the Via dei Fori Imperiali from the Colosseum to the Vittoriano, examining the buildings discussed here and other instructive sights nearby, one can find most of the facets of that complex body of architecture we gather into the word "classical," as well as the various results of later Italian interpretations of it. There are seven churches, ranging in date from early medieval to high Baroque, four of them installed in republican or imperial remains. There are works of the thirties other than those mentioned above, such as the stair system at the northwest end of the Velia buttress, and its counterpart across the street that leads up to the elevated terrace of the Temple of Venus and Rome. Toward the end of the journey the Campidoglio can be gained by the stairs of the 1930s that run up alongside the northeast flank of the Temple of Concord and past the end of the great gallery of the Tabularium. Once atop the hill one can examine, in a niche centered at the base of the facade of the Palazzo Senatorio, an ancient polychrome statue of a helmeted goddess, a restored orb of the earth in her outstretched left hand. *Urbis Romae simulacrum*, the inscription says, but the fact is that she is not Roma at all but Minerva, gotten up as a stand-in for Roma long ago. It was this would-be Roma that was copied, much enlarged, and set atop the Italian Pavilion at the New York World's Fair of 1939, an act that comprehends the whole range of the relationship of the art of the times to ancient forms: restoration, appropriation, imitation, and, sometimes, misapplication.[41] Antiquity, as so often happens, supplied the form, but its effective use proved elusive.

Notes

1. For these buildings, see A. Boëthius, *The Golden House of Nero* (Ann Arbor, 1960), chapter 4; H. P. L'Orange, *Art Forms and Civic Life in the Late Roman Empire* (Princeton, 1965), pp. 9–18; and W. L. MacDonald, *The Architecture of the Roman Empire*, vol. 1, *An Introductory Study* (New Haven, 1965), chapter 4. In order to focus on the center of archaeological and architectural activity, most of the buildings cited here are in Rome; locations usually are given only for buildings elsewhere. For additional illustrations and information, see E. Nash, *Pictorial Dictionary of Ancient Rome*, 2d ed., 2 vols. (London, 1968); and A. Boëthius and J. B. Ward-Perkins, *Etruscan and Roman Architecture* (Harmondsworth, 1970), Parts Two and Three. For illustrations of twentieth-century buildings, see for example A. Muñoz, *Roma di Mussolini* (Milan, 1935); F. Sapori, *Architettura in Roma, 1901–1950.* (Rome, 1953); *Edilizia Moderna* LXXXI (1963); as well as various other works cited in the notes that follow. I would like to thank Professors Spiro Kostof, Henry Millon, John Pinto, and Helen Searing for advice and criticism.

2. For the archaeologists, see H. A. Millon, "The Role of History of Architecture in Fascist Italy," *Journal of the Society of Architectural Historians* 24 (January 1965): 53; and S. Kostof, *The Third Rome, 1870–1950: Traffic and Glory* (Berkeley, 1973), pp. 29–33. For architecture and the regime, see also C. De Seta, ed., *Giuseppe Pagano, Architettura e città durante il fascismo* (Rome, 1976); G. Veronesi, *Difficoltà politiche dell'architettura in Italia, 1920–1940* (Milan, 1953); C. De Seta, *La cultura architettonica in Italia tra le due guerre* (Rome, 1978); S. Kostof, "The Emperor and the Duce: The Planning of Piazzale Augusto Imperatore in Rome," in *Art and Architecture in the Service of Politics*, eds. H. A. Millon and L. Nochlin (Cambridge, Mass., 1978), pp. 270–325; and D. Y. Ghirardo, "Italian Architects and Fascist Politics: An Evaluation of the Rationalist's Role in Regime Building," *Journal of the Society of Architectural Historians*, 34 (May 1980): 109–127; and cf. S. Danesi and L. Patetta, eds., *Il razionalismo in Italia durante il fascismo* (Venice, 1976).

3. See Kostof's thorough "Emperor and Duce," an analysis of one of the major projects of the Fascist attempt at *renovatio*; for the immense changes Rome underwent, see his *Third Rome*, where on pp. 85–86 the earlier, rather thin basic literature is cited.

4. This had begun at least by the turn of the century; see for example V. Reina and U. Barbieri, "Rilievo planimetrico ed altimetrico di Villa Adriana . . . ," *Notizie degli scavi* VIII (1906): 314–317.

5. Over 3,000 models and casts had been made (Fig. 18); for these see *Palladio* I (6, 1937):201–240; and cf. J. Packer, "Pierino Di Carlo, Master Model Builder," *Curator* 22 (3, 1979): 185–198. For the 1937 exhibition there is the 2-volume *Mostra augustea della romanità, Catologo* (Rome, 1938), of which the first is a room-by-room guide to nearly a thousand pages, the second an *Appendice bibliografica*. For the propagandistic implications of the Mostra, see Kostof, "Emperor and Duce," pp. 302–304.

6. The story of these successive exhibitions and museums is outlined in A. M. Colini's Preface (pp. vii–xiv) to the handbook entitled *Museo della civiltà romana, Catologo* (Rome, 1964). The model of Rome, covering some 200 m.^{2}, was created by Gismondi and his assistants; it is in Gallery 37 (pp. 406–409 in the *Catologo*) and has been partly brought up to date in the light of recent scholarship.

7. For example, A. Foschini's Convent of S. Giacomo on the Corso del Rinascimento (1931, based on Brunelleschi and others), and his SS. Pietro e Paolo at EUR (1938, Albertian principles); the Cathedral at Benghazi, by O. Cabiati and G. Ferrazza (c. 1934, Palladio and Vignola); and, at the end of the period, S. Eugenio on the Viale delle Belle Arti, by E. Galeazzi and M. Redini (1942 ff., Vignola, Guidetti), where beyond the historiated facade the flanks are in the Fascist plain style. There are some playful examples, such as the would-be "Temple of Minerva Medica" erected beside the harbor at Rhodes, and some utilitarian ones, such as the facade of the regional market on the Via Baccina.

8. See P. C. Rossetto, *Il sepolcro del Marco Virgilio Eurisace* (Rome, 1973), *I monumenti romani* V, for a detailed description. The grain measures are sometimes erroneously called ovens. A model of the tomb is illustrated in *Palladio* I (6, 1937): 208; a direct copy of the zone of the vertical measures can be seen in a thirties building at Settecamini, just east of Rome and hard by the Via Tiburtina.

9. See G. Fiorini, *La casa dei Cavalieri di Rodi al Foro di Augusto* (Rome, 1951), pp. 91–96 and figs. 61–66; cf. the similar, arcaded pavilion in Paul Herrmann's painting, "November 9 Celebration at the Hall of Generals," illustrated in B. Hinz, *Art in the Third Reich* (New York, 1979), p. 212. Starkly plain arcades were popular in Italy in the thirties, and appear for example beside Foschini's SS. Pietro e Paolo at EUR, and in the nave of the church of the Pontificio Collegio Ungarico by B. M. Apollonj Ghetti (illustrated in Sapori, *Architettura*, p. 207).

10. For this form see G. Calza, "Contributi alla storia della edilizia imperiale romana. Le case ostiense a cortile porticato,'" *Palladio* 5 (1, 1941): 1–33; cf. R. Meiggs, *Roman Ostia*, 2d ed. (Oxford, 1973), ch. 12.

11. For the Velia cut, see A. Muñoz, *Via dei Monti e Via del Mare* (Rome, 1932), esp. pls. 23 and 31; Muñoz may have designed the retaining wall, for he shows an elevation drawing of it (p. 7) over his name. Another example of this kind of dialogue is that between the Porta Maggiore and the Serbatoio Idrico of 1934 on the nearby Via Eleniana, which share a number of features; cf. note 30, below.

12. For the Via dell'Impero, see G. Calza, "The Via dell'Impero and the Imperial Fora," *Journal of the Royal Institute of British Architects* 41 (1934): 489–508; and Kostof, *Third Rome*, pp. 27, 60–63. For the Basilica, A. Minoprio, "A Restoration of the Basilica of Constantine, Rome," *Papers of the British School at Rome* 12 (1932): 1–25. Muñoz, *Via dei Monti*, describes and illustrates extensively the excavation and restoration of the building and of its flanking street (plan, pl. 21), the northeast wall of which (on the left in Fig. 9 here) was also built as a retaining wall against the Velia.

13. These go back at least to the fourth century B. C., as at Norba (Boëthius and Ward-Perkins, *Etruscan and Roman*, pl. 59) and were common under the empire (M. Todd, *The Walls of Rome* [London, 1978], pp. 72–83). The U-shaped building wing or projection with a semicylindrical end had been popular with the expressionists (W. Pehnt, *Expressionist Architecture* [London, 1973], p. 120 [Mendelsohn], p. 175 [Sant'Elia], and p. 177 [Chiatonne]), and it appears in Italian architecture of the thirties as well (Veronesi, *Difficoltà*, figs. 49 and 52; and Danesi and Patetta, *Razionalismo*, figs. 102, 110, 230, 271, etc.).

14. A. Muñoz, *La sistemazione del Tempio di Venere e Roma* (Rome, 1935). Other examples of major ancient niches: that of the nymphaeum in the Piazza Vittorio Emmanuele II (G. T. Grisanti, *I "Trofei di Mario . . ."* [Rome, 1977], *I monumenti romani* VII); and the apse in the Basilian church in the House of the Knights of Rhodes (Fiorini, *Casa dei Cavalieri*, p. 40); cf. the entrance to S. M. degli Angeli.

15. Meiggs, *Ostia*, chs. 1, 2, and 6. The typical reaction of historians was that of D. S. Robertson, *A Handbook of Greek and Roman Architecture*, 2d ed. (Cambridge, 1943), p. 308: "The general impression of the whole town . . . is astonishingly modern: it is clear that Rome in the late imperial age differed far less in outward appearance from a twentieth-century city than has usually been supposed." For the architectural elements of which Ostia is largely composed, see C. Buttafava, *Elementi architettonici ostiensi* (Milan, 1963). For proof that Ostia properly reflects the appearance of much of imperial Rome, see G. Gatti, "Caratteristiche edilizie di un quartiere di Roma del II secolo d. Cr.," *Quaderni dello Istituto di Storia dell'Architettura* XXXI–XLVIII (1961) (*Saggi . . . in onore del Professore Vincenzo Fasolo*): 49–66; cf. J. Packer, "La casa di Via Giulio Romano," *Bulletino della commissione archeologica communale di Roma* LXXXI (1968–1969): 127–148.

16. *Dizionario biografico degli Italiani* XVII (1974): 45–47. With his "La preminenza dell'insula nell'edilizia romana," *Monumenti antichi* XXIII (1915): 541–608, he opened the subject of the plain-style apartment house, which he returned to in subsequent publications, such as "Gli scavi recenti nell'abitato di Ostia," *Monumenti antichi*

dei Lincei XXVI (1920): 321–430. He wrote about his principles of restoration in "Assetto e restauro delle rovine di Ostia Antica," *Atti del III convegno nazionale di storia dell'architettura*, 1940, pp. 343–348, and in *Scavi di Ostia, Vol. I: Topografia generale* (Rome, 1953), pp. 43–52, a volume he edited (with others). Most of his *insulae* were lined at ground-level with simple *tabernae*, shops with nearly square entranceways, of the kind that has never died out in southern Europe (Boëthius, *Golden House*, ch. 4); numerous ancient examples still can be seen in Rome (at the Forum of Caesar and the Markets of Trajan, and on the Via dei Cerchi). At the EUR the two government buildings that face each other across the Piazzale delle Nazioni Unite, their incurving facades reminiscent of the *exedrae* of Trajan's Forum, are faced at ground level with repeated simulacra of *tabernae*.

17. For example in Calza's *Ostia. Guida storico monumentale* (Milan and Rome, n.d. [1924 or 1925]), fig. 20; this or a predecessor began the series of Calza's Ostian guidebooks and pamphlets of which a recent government guidebook (*Ostia*, 5th ed.) is the direct descendant (Gismondi's drawing is still in place). Most handbooks have reproduced his work, for example Robertson, *Handbook*, figs. 129 and 130; Boëthius and Ward-Perkins, *Etruscan and Roman*, fig. 111; L. Crema, *L'archittura romana* (Turin, 1959), *Enciclopedia classica*, sec. 3, vol. 12, Bk. 1, figs. 582, 583, 585, 589, 590, etc.

18. For these relationships, in addition to Boëthius, *Golden House*, cited above, note 16, see G. Calza, "Le origini latine dell'abitazione moderna," *Architettura ed arti decorativa* III (1–2, 1923): pp. 3–18 and 49–59; G. Giovannoni, *Vecchie città ed edilizia moderna* (Turin, 1931); *L'architettura*, August 1940, pp. 387–392; and De Seta, ed., *Giuseppe Pagano*, pp. 197–227; and cf. A. Mioni, "Le città e l'urbanistica durante il fascismo," *La rivista* II–III (1978): 29–64; and R. Mariani, *Fascismo e "città nuove"* (Milan, 1976), chs. 4 and 5 (I owe these last two references to the courtesy of Professor Millon).

19. The *Oxford Classical Dictionary*, 2d ed. (1970), pp. 509–510, lists his writings and evaluates his learning. There is additional information in A. G. Drachmann, *The Mechanical Technology of Greek and Roman Antiquity* (Copenhagen, 1963), pp. 12, 19–21 (Drachmann gives a translation of Heron's *Mechanics*). Cf. T. H. Martin, *Recherches sur la vie et les ouvrages d'Héron d'Alexandrie . . .* (Paris, 1854), *Mémoirs . . . à l'Académie des inscriptions et belles lettres*, 1st series, IV.

20. G. Downey, "Byzantine Architects, Their Training and Methods," *Byzantion* XVIII (1946–1948): 99–118; idem, "Pappus of Alexandria on Architectural Studies," *Isis* XXXVIII (1948):197–200; and G. L. Huxley, *Anthemius of Tralles. A Study in Later Greek Geometry* (Cambridge, Mass., 1959), *Greek, Roman, and Byzantine Monographs*, I, esp. pp. 1–5. Cf. Agathias, *The Histo-*

ries, trans. J. F. Frendo (Berlin and New York, 1975), Book 5.

21. The late F. E. Kidder and Harry Parker, *The Architects' and Builders Handbook*, 18th ed. rev. (New York, 1931); originally published in 1884 as *The Architects' and Builders' Pocket-book*.

22. See, in addition to the citations in notes 19 and 20, above, the life of Severus Alexander by "Lampridius" in the *Scriptores Historiae Augustae*, ch. XLIV, 4: "To . . . engineers and architects he paid regular salaries and assigned lecture rooms" and subsidized impoverished free-born students (Vol. II, trans. D. Magie, [London and New York, 1924], p. 267); cf. F. E. Brown, "Vitruvius and the Liberal Arts of Architecture," *Bucknell Review* XI (1963): 99–107. Fortifications could have been another source for the plain style: F. E. Winters, *Greek Fortifications* (London, 1971), and discussions of Roman city walls and gates in the handbooks and in I. A. Richmond, *The City Wall of Imperial Rome* (Oxford, 1930).

23. See the references in note 1, above.

24. J. T. Soby, *Giorgio de Chirico* (New York, 1955), where architectural forms and possible sources for them are discussed on pp. 34–41. Once in a while de Chirico transcribed an actual building—the castle at Ferrara, for example, in *The Disquieting Muses* of 1917—and he frequently included simplified temple fronts and other traditional forms in his work (Soby, pp. 104, 140, 141, etc.).

25. His arcades, for example, because they are the wrong color, of the wrong proportions, and utterly unarticulated, cannot easily be seen as derived from the arcades of Turin and other cities. Italian traditional forms such as the ubiquitous *barchesse* approximate de Chirico's; see M. O. and K. Hooker, *Farmhouses and Small Provincial Buildings in Southern Italy* (New York, 1925). The Porta Savoia in Susa is typical in displaying a number of plain-style elements from various periods.

26. Meiggs, *Ostia*, p. 6; see also note 16, above.

27. G. Guidi, *Il restauro del Castello di Tripoli negli anni XII e XIII* (Tripoli, 1935). The incomplete Forestale, still visible in March, 1955, was an overscaled, Palatine-esque near ruin, just northeast of the Ospedale S. Eugenio. For Brasini's career, see the *Dizionario biografico degli Italiani* XIV, (1972): 64–66; and L. Brasini, ed., *L'opera architettonica e urbanistica di Armando Brasini . . .* (Rome, 1979); cf. *The Listener* 59 (1950): 650.

28. Published in Rome, it is the most ambitious of the many "Rome as it was and as it is" genre, wherein photographs of ruins face, or are overlaid with, restoration drawings.

29. L. Canina, *Gli edifizi di Roma antica*, 6 vols. (Rome, 1844–1856); cf. T. Ashby in W. J. Anderson, R. P. Spiers, and T. Ashby, *The Architecture of Ancient Rome* (London, 1927): "Is it too much to hope that Roman architecture may at length be entirely emancipated from Canina, who has to be quoted, *faute de mieux*, in so many cases?" (p.

viii).

30. For example, Gatteschi's vision of the Roman Forum (p. 12) was built in 1963 in Spain at full scale, column for column, for the film *The Fall of the Roman Empire* (released in 1964), with the addition of the so-called Arch of Trajan at Timgad for good measure; this sort of thing is common (it can be done right, though, as it was for the sets of *Caesar and Cleopatra* of 1946). Such matters are important because of the immense influence they have had on popular opinion about historical architecture. Ironically, the eastern, colonnaded flank of the Museo della civiltà romana at EUR was used in the 1950s as a ready-made backdrop for inexpensive historical films; praetorians in full fig could be seen parking their Fiats nearby (cf. A. Powell's splendid scene in *At Lady Molly's* [Harmondsworth, 1963], pp. 147–148).

31. Gatteschi's garden entrance appears on p. 35; cf. P. Grimal, *Les Jardins romains*, 2d ed. (Paris, 1969), pp. 184–188. The Serbatoio displays other Porta Maggiore elements such as the floating pediment, pronounced attic, and oversized keystones.

32. G. Caputo, *Il teatro di Sabratha* (Rome, 1959), *Monografie di archeologia libica*, VI, fig. 42.

33. For the new Libyan towns, see the periodical *Africa italiana*; J. Wright, *Libya* (London, 1969), chs. 14 and 15, and figs. 13 and 22; C. G. Segrè, *Fourth Shore: The Italian Colonization of Libya* (Chicago, 1974), chs. 4–9.

34. See for example fig. 12 in Veronesi's *Difficoltà*. Lettering: A. Bartram, *Lettering on Architecture* (New York, 1976), pp. 147–157.

35. See the material cited in note 2, above; cf. Pevsner's remarks in his *Outline of European Architecture*, 7th ed., (Harmondsworth, 1968), p. 411.

36. See the references in note 1, above. Despite the efforts of Calza and others, the plain style was not much known outside Italy until after the Second World War.

37. In addition to the citations in note 32, above, see D. Mack Smith, *Mussolini's Roman Empire* (New York, 1976), pp. 36–43, who points out (p. 41) that, in Cyrenaica at least, the "subject population . . . became largely a sub-proletariat for the road works and building operations of the fascist empire."

38. For overviews of these results, see D. E. L. Haynes, *The Antiquities of Tripolitania* (Tripoli, 1965); and R. G. Goodchild, *Cyrene and Apollonia. An Historical Guide* (Tripoli, 1959). For the story of archaeology in Libya, Goodchild's "A Hole in the Heavens" (in *Libyan Studies. Selected Papers of the Late R. G. Goodchild*, ed. J. Reynolds [London, 1976], pp. 269–341) could hardly be bettered; the focus is on Cyrenaica. A museum was installed in the Castello in Tripoli (Guidi, *Castello*, pp. 31–82). Brasini n. 26, above, enclosed a near duplicate of the Lepcis Magna basilica in the Italian Pavilion at the 1930

Paris Fair (*Emporium* LXXIV [1931]: 238–239).

39. The Italian Empire was proclaimed in May 1936. Imperial trophies appeared in the provinces: the huge arch (31 m. high) by the south shore of the Gulf of Sirte (F. de Fausto, 1937—the "Marble Arch" of the Second World War); the propylon just north of the Gate of Amboise at Rhodes; heads of Mussolini (one, in the Imperial War Museum in London, is in a *moderne* style, built up of circular rings of moldinglike forms so that the dictator's profile appears irrespective of one's viewpoint); the twin columns of Brasini's Shar'a Adrian Pelt (ex-Lungomare Conte Volpi) in Tripoli, counterparts of Trajan's Columns at the end of the Via Appia in Brindisi (cf. Hinz, *Third Reich*, p. 184); and so on. The process had begun before 1936; see Veronesi, *Difficoltà*, fig. 67 (A. Limongelli's triumphal-arch facade for a pavilion at the 1928 Fiera di Tripoli; cf. the entrance to the Mostra Augustea of 1937 [*Catologo*, 1938, pl. 1; and Da-

nesi and Patetta, *Razionalismo*, fig. 99]). For the parallels drawn in the 1930s between Mussolini and Roman rulers, see Kostof, "Emperor and Duce," pp. 302–303; for a play by Mussolini about Napoleon, see D. Holloway, *Playing the Empire. The Acts of the Holloway Touring Company* (London, 1980).

40. Wright, *Libya*, fig. 14.

41. The World's Fair building, by M. Busiri Vici, is illustrated in R. Wurts et al., *The New York World's Fair 1939/1940* (New York, 1977), fig. 114. The Minerva/Roma had been used before in this way, atop the 1928 Tripoli arch; see note 38, above. Cf. Speer's diary entry for October 24, 1948: "I still find it hard to grasp the difference, beyond generalities, between classical antiquity, the Renaissance, European classicism, and my own efforts." (A. Speer, *Spandau. The Secret Diaries*, trans. R. and C. Winston [New York, 1972], p. 122.)

THREE RHODE ISLAND LIVING HALLS OF THE 1920s AND 1930s

William H. Jordy with Christopher P. Monkhouse

AT TIMES, IMPORTANT HISTORICAL discoveries so authoritatively usurp a given theme as to stifle investigation of its subsequent developments. In this connection consider the theme of the "living hall" celebrated by Vincent Scully in his book, *The Shingle Style*.[1] In the history of nineteenth-century American domestic architecture, the living hall has become associated with a special moment in vacation-house design on the East Coast which peaked in the shingle houses that spread—formally and quantitatively—along the New England seaside in the 1870s and 1880s. Not that anyone, and certainly not Scully (see above, pp. 10–13), would claim that the existence in America of this English import began and ended with these houses, but the tendency has been to consider the climax and relevance of the living hall as restricted chronologically to these two decades.

The familiar exegesis goes as follows. The openness of the living hall in, say, the Isaac Bell House of 1882/83 by McKim, Mead & White becomes rigidified in their Colonial Revival H.A.C. Taylor House of 1885/86 (both in Newport).[2] As the Colonial Revival progresses, the living hall steadily contracts until it has shrunk to a mere stairhall, losing its fireplace in the process. The expansive room has been replaced by the shrunken corridor and the theme of the living hall lost, at least to the conservative academic and eclectic tradition of domestic design in the twentieth century. Insofar as it had a future beyond its presence in Shingle Style houses, this was due, above all, to the genius of Frank Lloyd Wright who absorbed and transformed the living hall into a kind of spatial continuity that eventually wed it to the "modern movement." Such, crudely put, is the legend: convenient, dramatic, with sufficient substance perhaps to insure its perpetuation.

But is this what really happened? Not at all. Examples in refutation might be considered merely the nitpicking of the historical footnote which, given sufficient digging, invariably locates *some* obscure exception to accepted interpretation—except that, in this case, it could be argued that the living hall really attained its apogee in American domestic architecture in certain houses designed and built in the 1920s and 1930s within the academic and eclectic tradition. Such at least seems to be the case for three important Rhode Island houses designed between 1926 and 1931, in the very locale in which *The Shingle Style* is centered.

The earliest of these is the J. B. Lippincott House built in what was sketchily labeled at the time, rather contradictorily, a Norman or Provençal style (Figs. 1, 2). The Providence architect Albert Harkness designed this vacation retreat in Jamestown in 1926 for the head of the Philadelphia publishing firm.[3] The choice of style was natural to Harkness. The son and grandson of two successive professors of classics at Brown University, he had even as a child accompanied his parents in frequent European travel, and especially recalled trips with his mother that centered in Normandy. Although his design sources were eclectic, French influence dominated, especially at the beginning of his career. "The strength of what I did, if it has any, came from absorbing all I could from all the different periods in France; not so much in England, but some; and the Colonial in this country. But I did everything I could to avoid something that people could label." With this love of France and French architecture which he reinforced with regular European trips every two or three years throughout his entire professional career, it may seem surprising that he was

1. J. B. Lippincott House, Jamestown, Rhode Island. Albert Harkness, 1926. First and second floor plans, north (entrance) and south (sea) elevations. Drawing dated February 18, 1926. (Photocopied drawing: Rhode Island Historical Society, Providence.)

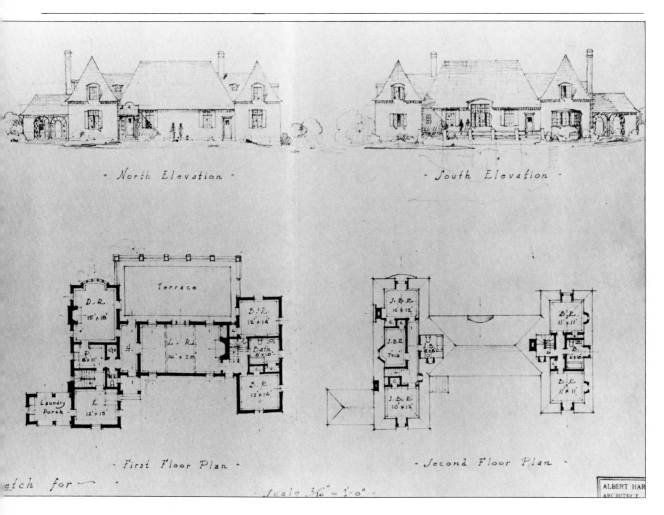

· North Elevation ·

· South Elevation ·

Terrace

· First Floor Plan ·

· Second Floor Plan ·

etch for

· Scale 3/16" = 1'-0" ·

ALBERT HAR
ARCHITECT

disinclined to give his architectural education at the Massachusetts Institute of Technology, from which he graduated in 1912, a final polish at the Ecole. This disinclination may have stemmed from his lack of enthusiasm for the teaching of Désiré Despradelle, the Ecole-trained émigré in charge of design during the time Harkness was at M.I.T., who was then in Harkness's opinion, "on his last legs." In any event, instead of finishing off his education in France he chose New York and, in rapid succession before World War I, he worked in the offices of Delano & Aldrich, Barney Mac-

gonigle, and McKim, Mead & White before returning to Providence. There he opened his own office immediately following the war, and there he practiced for the rest of his life, eventually heading one of the leading firms in Providence; immediately preceding World War II he finally edged into "modern" by making the canonical moves: from Art Deco through Scandinavian modern to the International Style. Up to World War I, however, the bulk of his work was residential and eclectically academic. Among a number of fine houses, the Lippincott House remained

one of his favorites.

It is beautifully simple: a three-part entity in an H-shaped configuration, as spectacularly sited (on a bluff overlooking a cove and out to sea from Jamestown Island) as any house in the state. A living hall fills the central unit, rising the full height of the mass right up into the steep gable roof and flanked by what are, in effect, two-story cottages at right angles to the long axis of the hall. One cottage contains service and dining rooms, plus upstairs quarters for servants; the other, two floors of bedrooms for owners and guests.

(Despite the well-heeled image the house presents on the exterior, the bedrooms are left as undisguised boards and framing in the manner of the typical "summer cottage"; only the principal rooms and the kitchen are plastered.) The entrance elevation strikes the balance sought between what appears on the exterior to be the cottagey informality of a one-story elevation with shuttered windows and high, tiled roofs with dormers and tall chimneys, and the elegant formality of a symmetrical composition disturbed only by the special treatment of the front entrance. The entrance opens into a hallway that recalls in its position and purpose the screen passage of its medieval prototypes, but without their latticed openness or the remnants of such latticing found in Shingle Style interiors. A properly prominent fireplace dominates one end of the hall itself (Fig. 3). Stairs, which figure so prominently in living halls of the 1870s and 1880s, are here moved just outside the hall itself, into the cottages to either side, thereby reinforcing their cottagey character vis-à-vis the vertical expansion of the central space right up to the apex of the ridge pole.

Did Harkness's Lippincott House inspire a very comparable house by another architect for the T. I. Hare Powel family near Newport, this time lying lower to the water in a more gardened setting and looking straight across an arm of the bay? It would seem that the influence was there, but, by a fluke of coincidence, some time after her husband's premature death, Mrs. Powel married Albert Harkness. Thus he came to know the Powel house intimately, and saw in it no direct influence. Still, interchange in this society and in this restricted professional group is constant, and who can tell? It was designed in 1927 in the office of the Providence architectural firm of Clarke & Howe, not however by Wallis Howe, a senior partner of the firm and one of the most fluent draftsmen of his generation in Rhode Island, but by Wallis's son, George Locke Howe (not to be confused with his better-known Philadelphia namesake). George had graduated in 1924 from the Harvard Graduate School of Design and after a year in New York with Helmle & Corbett had come to work in his father's office. (In the early thirties, he moved to the Washington, D.C., area where he passed the rest of his professional career.)[4] The Powel House was probably his first substantially independent commission.

Both Mrs. Powel, wife of a prominent Rhode Island banker, and her daughter were named Hope, a recurrent name in her family and one which had already called forth several houses christened "Hopelands." So "Hopelands" it was for this one as well.

Certainly whatever the indirect influence, if any, from Harkness's work, we do know from the present owners that the Powels wanted a smaller version of the very grand Norman-styled house, appropriately named "Normandie" (Figs. 4, 5), that Delano & Aldrich had completed in 1914 out on the rocks along Newport's famed Ocean Avenue for Lucy Wortham James, heiress to the Dun and Bradstreet fortune.[5] Not that the Powels needed "Normandie" for inspiration. They had developed their ideas for what they wanted in their house from extensive travel in France, but "Normandie" was close at hand as an example. In fact, a yellowed copy of the New York Herald Tribune[6] containing a spread of photographs of "Normandie," which the Powels had saved, exists today at "Hopelands" together with photocopies of the plans and some original drawings of "Hopelands" itself. As shown in the Tribune spread, the plan of "Normandie," too, is centered on what might be called a living hall, with the entrance corridor again a sort of screened passage. But because, despite its generous dimensions, it is only one story in height (although the dining room projecting out toward the sea rises through two), it seems spatially to be less in the tradition of the living hall than is the smaller hall of the Lippincott House. In another way, too, the principal living area of "Normandie" is less conspicuously identified than that for the Lippincott House, for it shares the center of the building with a row of bedrooms. Indeed, with its corri-

dorlike existence between a band of bedrooms on one side and a band of terrace overlooking the sea on the other, it becomes rather more a "zone" of activity and intercommunication than a centralizing and dominating "living hall" in the manner of that at Lippincott House.

But "Hopelands" is a different matter (Figs. 6, 7, 8). Here, even more completely than in the Lippincott house, the living hall dominates (Figs. 9, 10). It is, to begin with, a much larger room. The 16 × 28-foot "living room" indicated on the plan of the slightly earlier house becomes the 25 × 40-foot "common room" of the later house. Moreover, at "Hopelands" dining occurs, not in a separate room in the service adjunct, but in a corner of the big hall itself. Further, this living

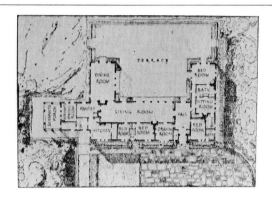

hall has a large, two-story bay projected from the slope of the roof toward the front court of the house, as the Lippincott House does not. The light-filled bay toward the entrance court balances an outsized bay opposite, which swells in a gentle curve into the clasped, arbored terrace looking on the sea. Fireplaces appear at either end of the hall, the principal fireplace being rather more grand than that at the Lippincott House. Again, stairs are pushed out of the hall into the flanking cottages (with a particularly ingenious

6. "Hopelands" (T. I. Hare Powel House), near Newport, Rhode Island. George Locke Howe, with Clark & Howe, 1927–1930. First floor plan, from a landscape scheme by Henrietta Marquis Pope. Figures on the plan refer to site elevations. (Drawing: T. I. Hare Powel estate.)

7. "Hopelands." West (front entrance) elevation, June 1927. (Pencil and watercolor drawing. T. I. Hare Powel estate.)

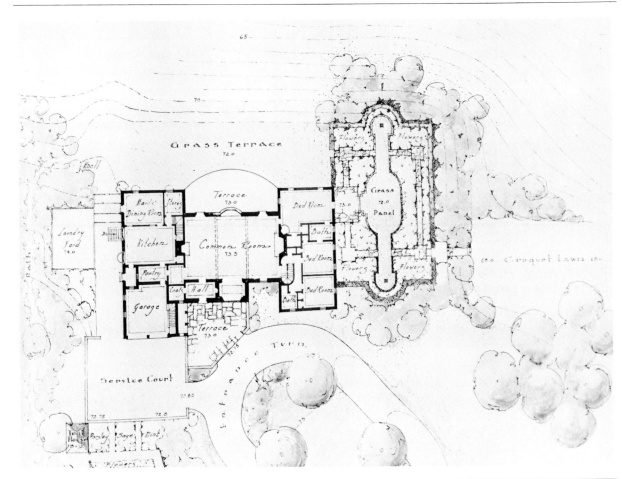

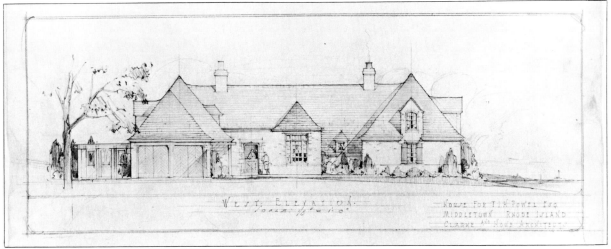

8. "Hopelands." *Exterior. View of east (sea) front. (Photo: John Waggaman.)*

9. "Hopelands." *Interior. View of living hall toward principal fireplace. (Photo: John Waggaman.)*

10. "Hopelands." *Interior. View of living hall toward the dining area. (Photo: John Waggaman.)*

curved stair in a lozenge-shaped space at "Hopelands," containing a window cutout part-way up the flight which permits a view from the living room out into a bedroom-study area in the cottage). The extreme rusticity of parts of the Lippincott interior are here treated more suavely. If the allusion to the screen passage in the Lippincott house has disappeared in "Hopelands," what with the intervention of no more than a vestibule between the entrance and the hall,[7] the very abruptness with which one steps from the vestibule into the big space makes more intense the experience of the living hall.

It is tempting not only to question what the direct connection might have been between the Lippincott and Powel houses (if any), but to push the design of both back to some earlier prototype. One thinks of Richard Morris Hunt's Joseph Busk House of 1889 to 1891 ("Indian Spring"),[8] spreading low on a rock outcropping directly across the avenue from "Normandie" (Figs. 11, 12, 13). Its focus is a living hall between two turrets which serve in the massing both as boundary markers for the central interior space and as pivots to turn the long, thin composition along the ledge. There are living spaces between flanking

11. *"Indian Spring" (Joseph Busk House), Newport, Rhode Island. Richard Morris Hunt, 1889–1891. First floor plan. (Plan: Hunt Archives, Library of the American Institute of Architects, Washington, D.C.)*

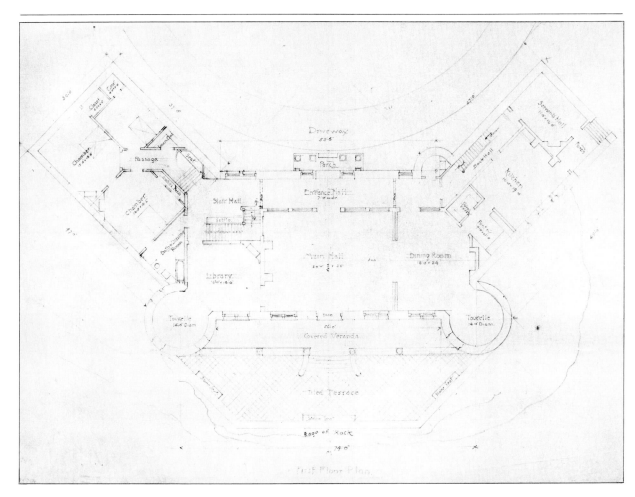

turrets at the compositional heart of other houses immediately preceding the Busk House. Consider merely a series of houses done in the early 1880s by McKim, Mead & White which disclose the sustained use of this motif for massing and plan, and which also doubtless provided the impetus for its subsequent use in the area. The motif appears in "Southside" (1882–1885) in Newport; the Charles Osborn House (1884/85) in Mamaroneck, New York; the Commodore William Edgar House (1885/86), again Newport; and, most extraordinary in this respect, their Charles Cook House (1885) in Elberon, New Jersey.[9] In this last house the squarish living hall fills the width between widely spaced octagonal towers— a vast room rather than the narrow comparatively hall-like space in the Commodore Edgar House— and the full depth of the house as well. All of which brings us back to Hunt's Busk House some two or three years later than the run of McKim, Mead & White variations on the theme. But the entire lot of them seem ultimately to derive from the most conspicuous paradigm in Rhode Island for this treatment: McKim, Mead & White's memorable frontispiece for their Narragansett Casino. Of course, the narrow bridge of space

12. "Indian Spring." Front (sea) elevation. (Drawing: Hunt Archives, Library of the American Institute of Architects, Washington, D.C.)

13. (right) "Indian Spring." Sections. (Drawing: Hunt Archives, Library of the American Institute of Architects, Washington, D.C.)

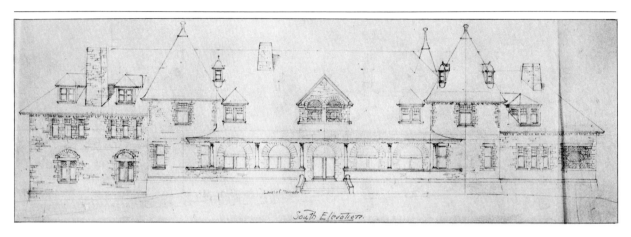

South Elevation.

straddling a road between the towers, and originally containing an open loggialike porch for a café, lacks the canonical accouterments of a "living hall" of fireplace, window bays, staircase, and (ideally as in the Busk House, but not in most of the examples by McKim, Mead & White) a room of extravagant height. Yet the kernel of the image is there, and more forcefully so since the destruction by fire of the long, thin wooden wing that once extended off one end, leaving the stone bridge between its towers as all that remained (and still remains) of the building. So vivid, indeed, was the impact of the image that it provided the logotype for a Providence whiskey firm in the early twentieth century (Fig. 14). But even the boldest of these shingle living halls are not as emphatically asserted within their compositions as those for the Lippincott and Powel houses, where Beaux-Arts hierarchical massing, discreteness in the revelation of plan, and insistent axiality all combine to make the living halls the literal cores of their houses. It is significant, after all, that the living halls in most of our early examples are subservient to the towers. In the late houses a reverse relationship holds; so assertive are they here as to become the conspicuous reason-for-being of the houses, with all else

visibly and experientially adjunctive.

Fortunately for this investigation of the post-Shingle fate of the living hall, two drawings exist of yet another—the largest of the three—which delightfully show these grand domestic spaces in use. These pencil drawings for the George Pierce Metcalf House are by Wallis Howe (Figs. 18, 19),[10] although again, as the family testifies, the designer was his son George.

Born in the state, in Bristol, Wallis Howe was the youngest of eighteen children sired by an Episcopal clergyman who eventually became Bishop of Central Pennsylvania. On completing his professional training at the Massachusetts Institute of Technology, Howe promptly returned to his native town where he made his home, with his office in Providence, for the rest of his life. He and his firm, with partners on the letterhead repeatedly changing, established themselves as another of the leading offices in the state. Of his own children (just six), only his son George followed his father into architecture. Wallis died in 1960, at age ninety-two; George, seventeen years later at age seventy-nine.

The George Pierce Metcalf House is one of several houses in the Exeter area built by children of Stephen O. Metcalf, a family once active

Section.

Section looking towards Kitchen Wing.
Section is taken on line MM.
See if first Floor Plan

in the textile industry and later in the *Providence Journal*. The house was christened "Philmoney," an allusion to the Phillips family who had once owned part of the land. In style, "Philmoney" rather suggests Philadelphia Main Line stone-and-shuttered Colonialism, a style rare to Rhode Island but possibly a recall on George Howe's part of boyhood visits to his grandfather, the bishop, in Pennsylvania. As an exquisite bird's-eye drawing in graphite and colored pencil by his father, Wallis Howe, indicates (Fig. 15), this was no compact (if luxurious) vacation retreat like the Lippincott and Powel houses, but a full-blown country estate with the substantial ramble of the fieldstone masonry main house giving out to a cluster of linked and near-linked outbuildings and cottages—a bit too full blown as it turned out, because the tail of the composition had to be reduced. The part of it that suggests the Powel house (so to speak) was separated from the main house and rotated to make a service court. Some outbuildings were omitted and others shifted about, but without fundamental change to the overall effect. At the opposite end of the house, the arched porch overlooking a formal garden became rectangularized. The porch, in turn, directly extends the living hall which butts against another gable at right angles to make the stem of the T. It is off one end of the crosspiece of the T that the composition takes off in a series of angular thrusts in order to adjust the dining room and service area to the contours of a ledge on which the entire house rests. Finally, in the process of revision, the main chimney at the juncture of the T in the bird's-eye went to one of the side walls of the living hall. But changes notwithstanding, the bird's-eye gives the sense of the house. It indicates that again the living hall is isolated as

the conspicuous climax of the house. In this instance, the space of the room as completed does not rise very far into the gable of the roof (Figs. 16, 17). It has a flat ceiling, which is strongly defined by a wide, deeply projecting cove molding. If the lowered ceiling reduces a little the sense of a medieval hall experienced in the other two houses, "Philmoney" makes up for this in part by including a "musicians' gallery" at one end of the room. Moreover, Wallis Howe's preliminary drawings for the interior of the living hall show two versions of a raftered room pushed well up into the space of the gabled roof, although short of the full height of those in the Lippincott and Powel houses (Figs. 18, 19).

The ingredients for the halls of all three houses are similar; but their varied disposition from house to house around the big box of space indicates alternative possibilities for their placement. Here the substantial fireplace and the two-story, multipaned bay face one another on the side walls. On one of the end walls French doors connect to the terrace porch. (As built, they received a Palladian treatment.) On the other end wall the medieval-inspired "musicians' gallery" appears as a new element compared to the previous examples, although its presence is not infrequent in earlier Shingle houses. It could indeed house a small musical group for a weekend dance or Christmas caroling; but its skimpy width limited its principal role to that of linking the upstairs bedrooms to life downstairs (a function which the extension of the feature as built—to almost the full width of the room—rather emphasizes, insofar as the balcony effect in the drawing took on more the aspect of a corridor as realized). All the basic ingredients of these rooms had appeared in Wallis Howe's refectory completed in 1908 for

Bird's-eye View of Estate at Exeter R.I.
for G. PIERCE METCALF ESQ
Messrs. Howe and Church, Architects Prov. R.I.

nearby St. George's School in Middletown, Rhode Island, hard by Ralph Adam Cram's chapel (Fig. 20), of which "Philmoney" is a domesticated version. Many among both clients and architects in Rhode Island had gone to St. George's, and it is interesting, among other speculations, to wonder how much boyhood memories of the big space, with its dominating fireplace, large bay at the center, and musicians' gallery at one end, might have played, ever so subtly, a conditioning role in these living halls later built in the vicinity. Yet

here at "Philmoney" one also especially feels the influence of artists' studios and barn conversions, especially in Wallis Howe's preliminary drawings, both so much a part of the country-house scene of the 1920s and 1930s. Whatever archaeological pretensions Howe might have had in the carved beaming of the ceiling roof at St. George's, he clearly vernacularized them in his preliminary drawings for the interior of the "Philmoney" living hall. As in both the Lippincott and Powel houses, here too the beams appear as simple ex-

18. "Philmoney." Sketch for living hall, viewed toward porch door, initialed and dated "W E H 32." (Drawing: Collection of the present owners.)
19. "Philmoney." Sketch for living hall, viewed toward the musicians' gallery. (Drawing: Collection of the present owners.)

Living Room for G. Peirce Metcalf Esq.

posed elements handled in a carpenter manner, although a suaver solution was in the offing.

Happily, Howe populated his interior sketches of the "Philmoney" living hall. (Stanford White did the same, but only perfunctorily, for his famous perspective of the living hall in the Watts Sherman House [Fig. 21]. White's living hall shows a spectral lady in what appears to be Elizabethan costume standing behind a chair staring moodily into the fire. Pure theater, it would seem.) How neat could we have had the real cast of characters for the living hall of the 1870s to set beside these for the early 1930s! Here they are (Figs. 18, 19): around the fireplace, a jodhpured group; in the center of the room the cocktail shaker is readied, while the miscued family terrier prepares to beg; at one end of the room a bookish guest pores over the shelves; at the other, a woman appears on the balcony with a swain below gesturing as a mock Romeo—which recalls other converted barns of the period that became "little theaters." A man in knickers, returned from hunting or hiking perhaps, puffs his Dunhill while surveying a couple in the casemented bay. There, the woman lolls in the sofa, disposed for maximum response from the man who sits on the couch facing her. Minute examination will disclose her puff of cigarette smoke caught in the light of the window.

All around are the furniture props of the period: the Colonial (or Neo-Colonial) secretaries and breakfronts with "Chippendale" or "Queen Anne" side chairs (more for show than for sitting); the Jacobethan table laden with magazines; the chandelier in wrought-iron openwork (splendid swansong to the recently defunct craft of blacksmithing); a ship model; and, scattered about, the furniture which really *was* used—those low, deep sofas at fireplaces and in bays, fronted by "coffee tables" with their freight of ashtrays, cig-

20. St. George's School, Middletown, Rhode Island, Howe, 1908. Perspective of refectory. (Illustration: Year-Book of the Rhode Island Chapter, American Institute of Architects, 1910.)

21. Watts Sherman House, Newport, Rhode Island. Henry Hobson Richardson, 1874. Perspective of the living hall, attributed to Stanford White. (Illustration: New York Architectural Sketch Book, May 1875, pl. xix.)

DINING ROOM, ST. GEORGE'S SCHOOL, NEWPORT
Clarke, Howe and Homer, Architects

arette boxes, cocktail glasses, and decorative objects. Such sofas (and equally deep, upholstered armchairs) brought the thoroughgoing comfort of the nineteenth-century men's club to the living room.

On the floors: wide boards and slightly rumpled rug, Oriental or custom-designed in some country weave and pattern. On the walls: a bit of tapestry and some "ancestral" portraits; over the fireplace, a chart done in a mock "ye olde" manner, emblazoned with exaggerated cartouches, one for the title, one for the compass with puffing winds in each quadrant, and the whole varnished to a rich golden hue. In the drawing one can just make out that it is Narragansett Bay, with the "ye olde" flavor diluted a bit by the Art Deco stepped "skyscraper" frame. Often such charts were furnished by the architect. At "Philmoney," for instance, Wallis Howe provided a bird's-eye map of the environs with all the family houses in the

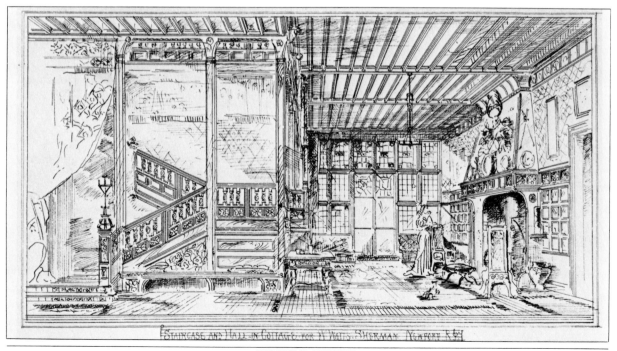

locale located on it. Smaller versions, also sometimes by architects, served as decorative maps for enclosure with invitations, so guests could find their way to all this lighthearted weekend leisure. It no longer sufficed to inform the visitor that he would be "met at the station," when he must drive through a baffling maze of local lanes directly to the door of the hideaway.

Three living halls: equivalents could of course be found elsewhere in the 1920s and 1930s. No doubt they were ubiquitous. Yet it seems particularly appropriate to use these houses as a case study. It is appropriate because they *are* in Rhode Island; because of their direct continuity with important prototypes; because of their intrinsic quality; finally, because they so compellingly indicate how much the idea of the living hall continued to influence American domestic architecture into the twentieth century. Such living halls were especially vital in houses, like these, built preemininently for recreational and entertainment purposes, but with considerable formal pretensions too. These interiors are more bland, more discreet, than the equivalents in their Shingle predecessors; they lack the palpable presence of the paneling, spindling, and latticing of those spaces, with their Victorian bulk of fireplace and staircase pitted against the exaggerated coziness of inglenooks and built-in settles. As big boxes of space, however, so decisively climaxing and centering the life of the house in a shadowed but luminous environment, they are possibly even more truly *living* halls than most of their predecessors. More truly halls for *modern* living, at least. In any event, the living hall persisted in the 1920s and 1930s, alive and well in Rhode Island, where its spaciousness eventually melded into the circumspect beginnings of local modernism.

Notes

To honor Henry-Russell Hitchcock I had originally prepared an essay on the planning of Norris by the Tennessee Valley Authority. It turned out to be too long; moreover, it may have been less appropriate for the *Festschrift* than this second effort, which relates to Hitchcock's exhibition and publication of *Rhode Island Architecture* in 1939 (see introductory essays). This essay, in fact, grows from research directly inspired by Hitchcock's pioneering work on Rhode Island architecture: an exhibition of architectural drawings, *Buildings on Paper: Rhode Island Architectural Drawings, 1825–1945*, which opened in May 1982 at three institutions in Providence: following the chronology of the material in the exhibition, these were Aldrich House, Rhode Island Historical Society; Museum of Art, Rhode Island School of Design; Bell Gallery, Brown University. The exhibition subsequently traveled to New York and Washington. In the preparation of this essay I owe much, both for data and insight, to my collaborator in this enterprise, Christopher Monkhouse, and I thank him for his helpfulness and friendship. I am also extremely grateful for the photography of another friend, John Waggaman, and for the photographic assistance of Robert Thornton of the staff of the Museum of Art, Rhode Island School of Design.

1. Vincent Scully, *The Shingle Style* (New Haven, 1955; rev. ed., 1971). For the living hall, see also Henry-Russell Hitchcock, *Architecture: Nineteenth and Twentieth Centuries* (Baltimore, 1958), chapter "The Detached House in England and America."

2. Scully, *op. cit.*, figs. 129–131, 149–150.

3. I was privileged to talk with Albert Harkness on a number of occasions in the summer and fall of 1980, shortly before his death, at age ninety-three, on January 5, 1981. Other sources of information are the Harkness Archive in the Graphics Collection, Rhode Island Historical Society and the obituary in the *Providence Journal*, January 6, 1981.

4. Information on George Locke Howe appears in Susan E. Sirillo, ed., *Bristol: Three Hundred Years* (Providence, 1980), p. 118.

5. I am grateful to Richard L. Champlin, Librarian of the Redwood Library in Newport, for this information. The house was originally named "Cherry Neck" but was early rechristened. Lucy James resumed her maiden name after her divorce from the diplomat Huntington Wilson.

6. *New York Herald Tribune*, March 8, 1929, sec. 2, p. 11. The writer for the *Tribune* commented especially on the handmade roofing tiles "splashed with patches of moss," which are also one of the beauties of "Hopelands." These leaked at "Normandie," and necessitated the extravagance of an "ordinary roof below." For fuller presentations of "Normandie," see William Lawrence Bottomley, "The Work of Delano & Aldrich," *Architectural Record* 54 (July 1923): 3–71, where "Normandie" leads the presentation; also "A House in Newport, R.I.," *House Beautiful* 55 (February 1924): 142–144.

7. A preliminary scheme in the possession of the present owners of the house shows an octagonal tower with pitched cap snuggled into the entrance corner of the elevation, with the entrance vestibule occurring within the base of the tower. This was set out from a flat wall with a row of four small windows. To pull out the wall into a deep bay, then continue the outside plane of the bay by infilling the entrance side of the projection, provided a far superior solution: more drama and more utility from the big two-story bay; more discipline in the elimination of the "cute" tower and in the assertion of the wall plane at this point; greater impact on entering, although with enough of a vestibule to provide the amenity of a transition from outdoors to in. (Preliminary scheme in the possession of the present owners of the house.)

8. It was built for William Dorsheimer and might properly be designated as such, except that he sold it to the Busk family on, or possibly even a bit before, its completion. See Paul R. Baker, *Richard Morris Hunt* (Cambridge, Mass., 1980), p. 340.

9. *Shingle Style*, figs. 126–128, 138–139, 147–148, and 140–141.

10. Information on Wallis Howe appears in Sirillo, *Bristol*, p. 119 ff.; also in his obituary *Providence Journal*, September 16, 1960. On his retirement from Howe, Prout & Ekman (the final partnership formulation in which he figured), Howe compiled a brief history of the firm which he mimeographed and distributed to its members. His son, George Locke Howe, prepared an informal memorial after his death entitled *#18* (1960) as a seven-page brochure. Information also exists in files of the Rhode Island Chapter, American Institute of Architects, deposited in the Rhode Island Historical Society.

BRUCE GOFF AND THE EVOLUTION OF AN ARCHITECTURAL IDEAL

David G. De Long

THE IDEA OF AN ARCHITECTURE shaped by personal choice rather than universal concerns has long constituted an essential component of architectural practice.[1] Yet the first major defense of this idea does not seem to have occurred until the late eighteenth and early nineteenth centuries, when it was advocated by a group of writers and architects influenced by the Picturesque point of view.[2] Since that time the term Picturesque has often been employed to signify an architecture of personal choice, and while the results are not always picturesque in the conventional visual sense of rambling, romantic images, they usually reflect an interest in pictorial values and diverse architectural modes that is consistent with the original intent of the term.

The work of the American architect Bruce Goff brings the evolution of an architecture based on personal choice to a high level of development. Seen in this context, his work assumes historic perspective and furthers understanding of an approach that has recently regained wide support.

Essential to the Picturesque point of view as it came to affect architectural practice in the late eighteenth century, and helping to form a basis for an architecture of personal choice, was an emphasis on the particular rather than the universal. Architects sought special visual effects and stressed a free approach to design that respected local conditions. The objective was personal expressiveness of the sort reflecting specific characteristics of the client and architect as well as of the site. Visual complexity was one means to such expressiveness, achieved through roughness of texture, variety in plan and elevation, and elements such as garden walls that ex-

tended into the landscape and diffused the line between building and surround.[3] As a further means of expression, a wide variety of modes were freely derived from various classical, medieval, and non-Western sources. The selection of individual modes was a matter of personal choice not bound by canon,[4] and these modes were popularized in the many pattern books of the period.[5] Included in these books were plans that recall eighteenth-century Romantic Classicism more immediately than the romantic eclecticism of the early nineteenth century, such as the "villa in the style of an abbey" (Fig. 1) by Richard Elsam or his "small house in the style of a chateau" (Fig. 2). For even at that time it was the variety of available choices that was stressed rather than adherence to any single image, and

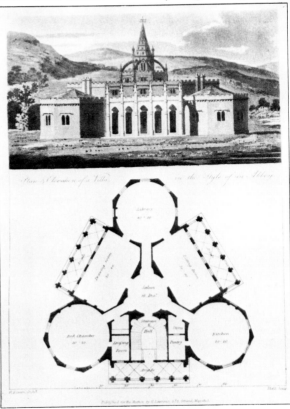

Editor's Note: Sadly, Bruce Goff died in August, 1982 as this volume was going to press.

1. *Richard Elsam, villa in the style of an abbey. Plan and elevation.(Illustration: Elsam,* An Essay on Rural Architecture, *pl. 13.)*

2. *Elsam, small house in the style of a château. Plan and elevation. (Illustration: Elsam,* An Essay on Rural Architecture, *pl. 15.)*

Plan & Elevation of a small House in the style of a Château.

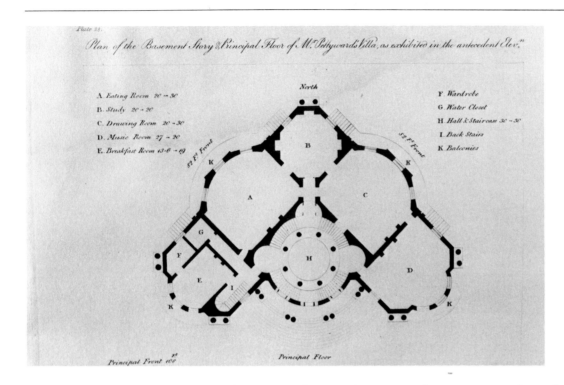

Principal Floor

Principal Front 10⁵

these choices included examples drawn from the recent as well as more distant past. Illustrating the support of relative rather than absolute values, different solutions of equal merit could be offered for the same situation; Elsam's "villa in the Italian or Roman style" has an alternate elevation "in imitation of a chateau" (Figs. 3–5).[6]

It was partly the emphasis on personal choice that led to a reaction against the Picturesque. Beginning in England in the 1830s, as evidenced by the writings of A.W.N. Pugin and John Ruskin, the free attitude toward selection of mode gave way to a more considered evaluation. It became the moral obligation of the architect to select the single mode most appropriate to a particular situation and to interpret that mode with attention to archaeological accuracy. More frivolous modes were largely abandoned.[7] The situation differed somewhat in America, where certain early-nineteenth-century attitudes took firmer root, primarily through the efforts of A. J. Downing.[8] Downing attempted to interpret these attitudes in ways that would lead to the development of a truly American architecture. Not least this meant an architecture accessible to all people and expressive of a democratic society.[9] For Downing such expression was to be achieved by encouraging personal choice, and the individual dwelling was to be its vehicle. It is fair to say that Downing did as much as any single person to establish the American ideal of a detached dwelling for each family, a personal dwelling expressive of the character of its inhabitants, its site, and its materials.[10] Downing was not untouched by Ruskin's beliefs and displayed a slight favoritism toward medieval modes as well as a prejudice against Oriental ones.[11] His American colleagues sometimes practiced a freer approach: Samuel Sloan,

for example, included a design for an Oriental villa in *The Model Architect* (Fig. 6, 7) because "our work would be incomplete without . . . one."[12]

The ideal that Downing had articulated of an architecture based on personal choice continued to inform much American architecture until the 1880s, when it was largely supplanted by an opposing attitude generated during the Academic Reaction.[13] Early examples of modern architecture depended in part on the sense of order and control stressed by the Academic Reaction,[14] and the contributing role of personal choice in the evolution of modern architecture was not much discussed during the early decades of the twentieth century. Beginning in the late 1940s, however, in a series of articles appearing in England, the free attitude toward design that had developed during the late eighteenth and early nineteenth centuries was defended as a sensible approach to design and linked to key twentieth-century examples.[15] Designs by Walter Gropius and Le Corbusier, for instance, were lauded because their architects sought a free massing that rejected conventional formulas and reflected attention to particular conditions.[16] The ability of Frank Lloyd Wright to avoid academic restraints

was praised, and underlying precepts of modern architecture were related to the Picturesque point of view.[17]

Wright's attention to the particular qualities of site and materials, and the very variety of his designs, do indeed show strong parallels with Picturesque attitudes. Moreover, his clearly stated concern with the individual dwelling as a necessary component of a healthy democracy recalls Downing's forceful interpretation of those attitudes. Yet to label Wright's work Picturesque is limiting, for it ignores his other, deeper concerns with universal principles of design and

suggests a visual quality that does not always exist in his work. What does link his work with that of architects influenced by the Picturesque point of view is a belief in personal choice as a governing determinant of design. It is choice suggested by the client and interpreted by the architect in relation to other specific conditions posed by each commission, and the objective is an expression of the particular that, in given situations, outweighs the universal.[18]

Bruce Goff goes further than Wright in seeking an architecture based on personal choice, and his work, in all its astonishing variety, suggests ultimate consequences of the ideal.[19] His fundamental belief in the ideal of choice is also apparent in his writings, where he seems to come as close to the late-eighteenth- and early-nineteenth-century defense of the ideal as has any twentieth-century architect. Like Downing, Goff believes the character of an individual house should first reflect the character of its owner, and then reflect local conditions of site and materials:

> The particular expression of my buildings usually derives from working with individual clients and using their character as part of a starting point, with the functional requirements, site, budget and climate always different in each project.[20]

> Each and every one of [the architect's] clients are individuals, or groups of individuals, in individual environments, requiring individual solutions to their needs.[21]

> One great contemporary architect has referred to the client as a mere "transient" and he considers it foolish to plan the building around the client's special needs and desires. . . . This approach seems undemocratic and denies the right of the individual by forcing him into a discipline foreign to his nature.[22]

> The client is entitled to a building which is Architecture, rather than some architect's abstract exercise.[23]

As Downing also had done, Goff supports the view that architects should feel free to design in different modes, that such modes are a matter of choice determined by the particular conditions of each problem, and that for any given problem there is the possibility of interchangeable solutions:

> Mies says that he has no use for an architect who thinks he has to invent a new style of ar-

chitecture every Monday morning; I think you have to invent one for each building, whether it is Monday morning or not. The differences in my work worried me at first because they did not seem to add up to a personal style—as did the works of Sullivan, Wright, Gaudí, Mendelsohn and Le Corbusier. . . . Now I realize that if each work of an artist has its own style, they collectively represent him.[24]

> I believe it is far more worthwhile to have each individual work the architect does become its own style . . . [and] therefore different from any other works done by him or by others.[25]

> . . . any good architect can design many solutions to any one problem.[26]

> . . . there is never just one solution. The creative artist works intuitively and instinctively with the one he feels best with: it is a matter of choice from many possibilities.[27]

As had many architects before him, Goff selects and develops various modes to create calculated visual effects. He believes that buildings complicated by extensions into the landscape and by an intricate geometry of related parts produce pleasurable sensations for the viewer. For Goff, these include an initial sense of surprise because of the unexpected appearance of the building, and a sustained sense of mystery because its secrets of composition only partly unfold over time.[28] Discussing the importance of seeking effects, he says:

> We are blamed for "striving for effect," to which we plead guilty, because effects which are not striven for are not worth having. Certainly the effects of all the *great* architecture are earned and certainly architecture must have effect.[29]

> Any artist must strive for honest effects if his work is to have effect; the important—and un-

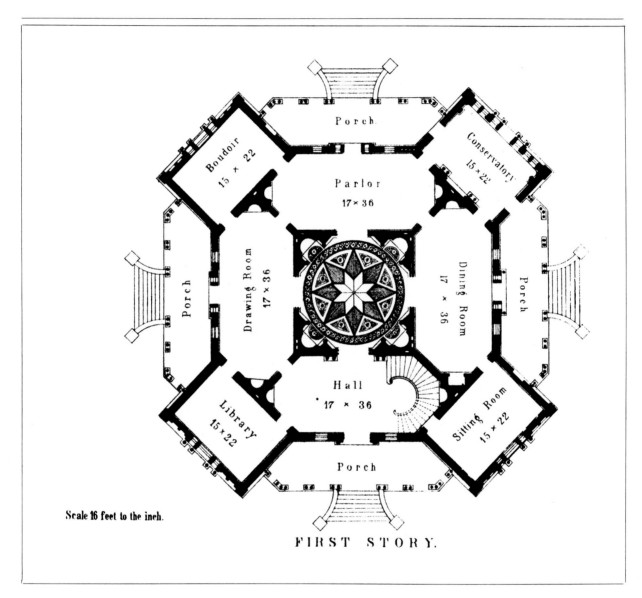

Scale 16 feet to the inch.

FIRST STORY.

usual—occurrence is when the effects come about.[30]

On complexity:

Simplicity is considered by some a virtue; but it may only disguise the absence of anything of importance. Complexity is sometimes considered confusion, when in reality this is only a matter of first appearance.[31]

On surprise and mystery:

Change brings with it the unexpected and it is this quality of surprise which engages our attention in a work of art; but since we cannot continue to be surprised by the same thing, the quality of mystery becomes necessary to sustain our interest. Mystery, however, defies analysis no matter how well we come to know a work

7. *Sloan, Oriental villa. Elevation. (Illustration: Sloan,* The Model Architect, *pl. 63.)*

7. *Sloan, Oriental villa. Elevation. (Illustration: Sloan,* The Model Architect, *pl. 63.)*

possessing it, [for] such a work, like Nature, never gives up its secrets.[32]

For Goff, such effects are not randomly achieved, but are instead the result of some underlying system of composition:

We soon tire of novelty if it lacks depth and meaning.[33]

[A building] . . . must also be complete in itself with its own character of disciplined order, no matter how "free" it may seem.[34]

Goff's systems of composition govern spatial configuration in each design, but do not lead to a rigid attitude toward the expression of structure or materials. As had many early nineteenth-century architects, he sometimes manipulates materials not so much with an eye to their inherent character as with an eye to the overall visual effect they will create. Unlike Wright, he is, for instance, willing to paint a wood building in bright colors to emphasize its shape and neutralize its structure when this suits his vision.[35] Goff's statements are slightly ambiguous regarding structure and materials, but less so regarding color:

Structure can be, and often is, beautiful and

8. *Plunkett House, Lake Village, Texas. Bruce Goff, 1970. Plan. (Where not otherwise noted, all illustrations are from author's collection.)*

9. *Plunkett House. Elevation.*

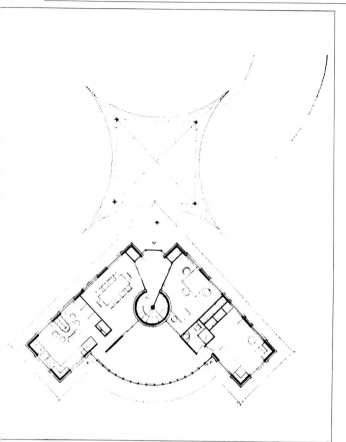

imaginative in itself, but this is not enough to make it Architecture. It does not need to be exposed to be honestly recognizable, but there should be the sense of it whether it shows or not. The human skeleton is a beautiful structure, but who wants to shake hands with it?[36]

It is not enough to use materials "honestly." . . . It is considered morally correct if our wood or our brick is used so that everyone can see that a brick is a "brick" and a board is a "board." In great Architecture the materials *are* honestly used and also help determine the forms, transcending the physical nature of materials, just as in a person we expect more than "the stuff he is made of."[37]

We can use color as limited to the natural colors of materials employed, as blending with the landscape and as quiet accompaniments of our lives, or we can use it as applied rather than integral. . . . Likewise we can use integral or applied color as a contrast with nature, complementing it as would a flower.[38]

Goff adheres to his beliefs in practice and receives enthusiastic support from his clients. Dur-

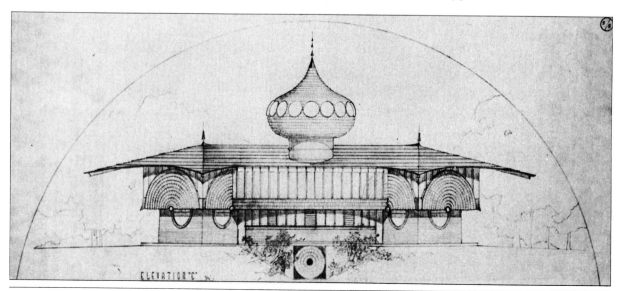

ELEVATION "C"

ing a long career that stretches back to 1916 he has designed nearly five hundred buildings; approximately three hundred are residential, almost all for rural or suburban sites.[39] Their variety reflects a disregard for convention that is essential to an architecture of personal choice and illustrates Goff's flexible manner of allowing his client's choices to affect his own. The few examples illustrated here can only suggest the range of expression they encompass.[40]

Overt references to traditional modes are rare in Goff's work, but they exist, as seen in the second Plunkett House (Figs. 8, 9), the Wakil House project (Figs. 10, 11), and the Giacomo Motor Lodge project (Fig. 12). The Plunkett House—

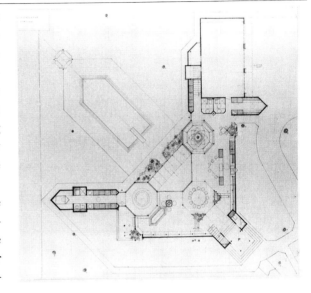

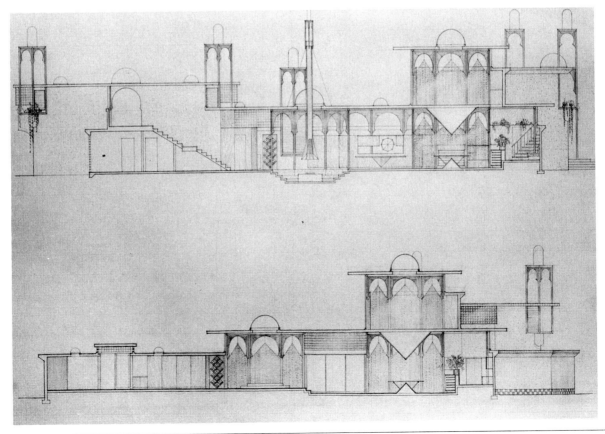

which Samuel Sloan might have termed an Oriental villa for an American land mogul—was intended for a Texas developer as a feature of his projected community of vacation houses. Goff envisioned the onion-shaped dome as a belvedere, and it would have provided appropriately framed views over the expansive Texas landscape. More importantly, it would have established a welcome mood of playful leisure, as John Nash had understood 150 years earlier.[41] The Islamic mode of the Wakil project responds to the client's request that the house recall his Middle Eastern background. The minaretlike overlooks and screened pavilions would have offered a variety of spaces related effectively to the surburban Houston site. The castellated retreat for travelers envisioned for the Giacomo Motor Lodge would have produced an extraordinary sense of place in its bleak Oklahoma setting. The client's wish for something unusual was well answered by this proposed landscape of stone towers and glass-infilled fins, all grouped around three sides of an interior garden that they protectively enclosed.

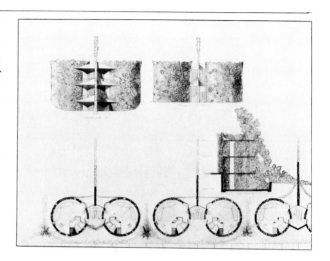

Several of Goff's designs suggest less typical modes. Among these are the Loosen Lodge project (Fig. 13) and the second project for the Nicol House (Fig. 14, 15). Proposed for Indian country, the one-room weekend lodge recalls images of American tepees.[42] The rough-textured huts of the Nicol project, raised above the ground and clustered about a central yard, have an African flavor. The client, a politically liberal banker, owned a parcel of land within the hostile territory of a highly conservative, upper-middle-class neighborhood from which he wished to retreat.[43]

Many of Goff's designs suggest not so much a particular mode as a distinctive mood recalling another time or place. His famous Bavinger House

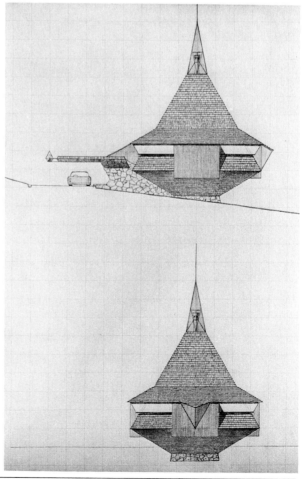

14. *Goff, second project, Nicol House, Kansas City, Missouri, 1965. Plan at second level.*

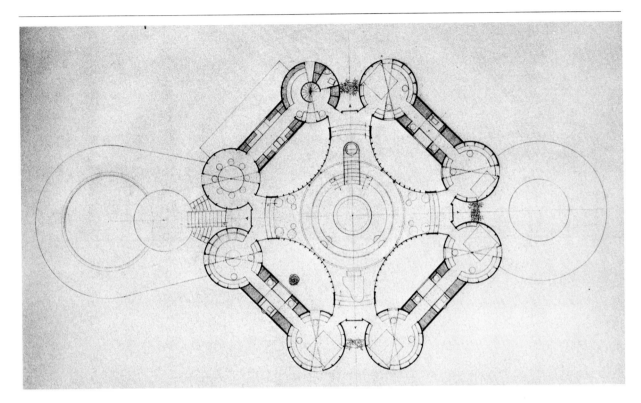

14. *Goff, second project, Nicol House, Kansas City, Missouri, 1965. Plan at second level.*

(Fig. 16), a fortified canyon villa for a university professor, evokes the romantic imagery of ruins. Inside its spiraled stone walls, the dominant presence of lush plants and extensive pools continues this theme and develops that of the grotto as well.[44] As in many of Goff's designs, the soft, picturesque image of indefinite and complicated shapes, irregular openings, finials, extended rafters, and suspended elements—all tending to diffuse the sense of edge and unite the building with its wooded setting—is at odds with the strictly controlled geometry of the plan, a logarithmic spiral with circular platforms suspended at regular intervals.[45]

Goff's exploration of various regular geometries not only generates a systematic complexity, but also contributes to the individual character of different designs and sustains various moods.

In the Darling House project (Figs. 17, 18), a turreted retreat for a flat site in a small midwestern town, the tight arrangement of circular and triangular shapes, together with the regular earth berms, reinforce the sense of snug enclosure. Like Elsam's villa that combines similar forms (Fig. 1), an exterior spire emphasizes the central focus within. In the Jones House project (Fig. 19), a belvedere for a wooded suburban site, the octagonal composition of towers and projected porches creates a variety of directed views without sacrificing a sense of protection. It answered a client's hope for views in all directions without loss of privacy. Elsam's house in the style of a chateau (Fig. 2) was similar in shape. Goff's plans are often less formal. In the McCullough House project (Fig. 20), a Hadrianic composition of loosely interlocked circles, three kinds of spaces with

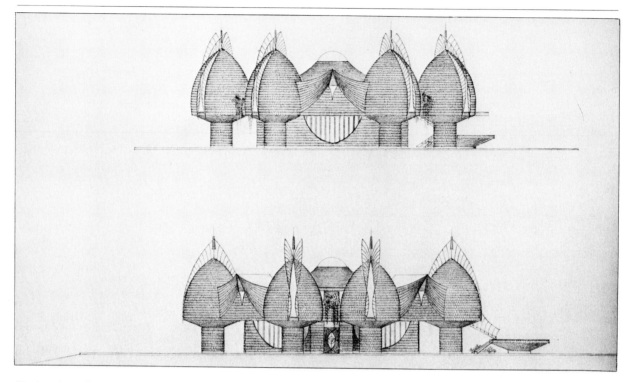

distinctive characteristics as needed by the client are developed: primary living areas in the central part of each circle, secondary living areas in the major overlaps, and services or circulation areas in the minor, or corner, overlaps. In these designs, as in many others, Goff uses geometry not as a metaphor for ideal order, but as a device to generate particular kinds of space. Goff's attitudes parallel much early-nineteenth-century practice in this sense and are distinguished from that approach to geometry in which a search is made for universal symbols.[46]

To further indicate the range of choice reflected in Goff's work, additional modes could be suggested for different designs. Several invoke images of the house of the future, as a spherical complex for an airline pilot (Abraham House project, Kansas City, 1967).[47] Others are less extreme, such as a ranch house with Colonial de-

tails for a midwestern oil executive (White House, Bartlesville, Oklahoma, 1958), a Roman porticus villa for a professor of sociology (Duncan House, near Cobden, Illinois, 1965), a Prairie Style house for the Texas developer (third Plunkett House, Lake Village, Texas, 1974), or a modern pueblo for an artist in the Southwest (second Barby House, Tucson, Arizona, 1974). Still others are coincidentally associative, such as the castle composed of grain bins for a site within a midwestern farming community (Watkins House project, Sapulpa, Oklahoma, 1956), or a house with winged roofs for a turkey breeder (Glen Harder House, near Mountain Lake, Minnesota, 1970). In all examples there are picturesque extensions into the landscape and a blurring of the edges, as in the Bavinger House. Each reflects a specific situation. Yet the actual context of each design is rarely defined in the design drawings—it is only

suggested, as in many published designs of the nineteenth-century pattern books. Partly this is a matter of graphic convention. But partly—at least with Goff—it reflects the fact that the actual sites are hardly, if ever, spectacular in themselves. The site assumes distinction through the architect's interpretation, just as his design gives tangible form to the character of the owners.

Beginning around 1960, ideas similar to Goff's began to be promoted by a group of American architects led initially by Robert Venturi and Charles W. Moore.[48] Together with a larger group of architects they have advocated the inclusion of overtly historic references in contemporary design in order to achieve various expressions relevant to particular situations.[49] Because of occasionally related attitudes, Goff might be considered a link between Downing and Wright, on one hand, and current American practice typified by Venturi and Moore on the other. Yet connections between Goff and the Venturi-Moore circle are rarely acknowledged, perhaps because critics sympathetic to that circle, as critics in general, usually consider Goff's work to be in bad taste. Probably no architecture so expressive of popular taste could be viewed as anything else by those concerned with fashion.[50] And no doubt

17. *Goff, first project, Darling House, El Dorado, Kansas, 1958. Plan.*
18. *Goff, first project, Darling House. Elevation.*

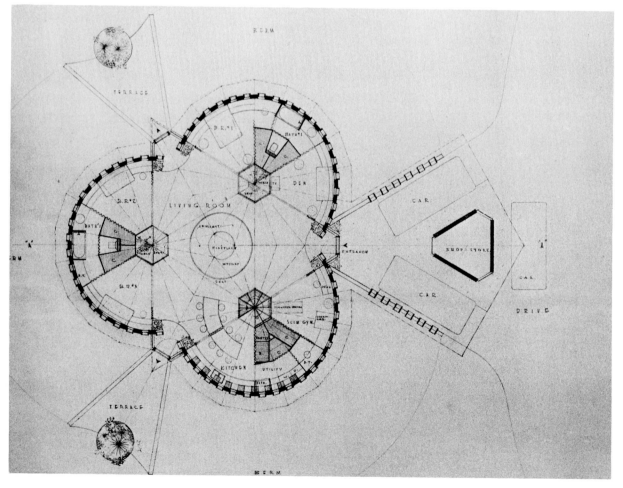

many believe Goff's work to be linked too closely with the vulgarly romantic designs produced in the 1950s by such commercial firms as those headed by Edward Durrell Stone and Minoru Yamasaki.[51] Goff's work is indeed linked with these firms, but so is the work of Venturi and Moore. In the same way, the work of Mies van der Rohe can be related to the firms of Welton Becket or Charles Luckman.[52] What is too often overlooked is Goff's creativity, and his genius for discovering new spatial patterns. These answer evolving demands of a changing society, yet they are always expressed in terms familiar to the client.

Although related beliefs establish a connection between Goff and the Venturi-Moore circle, certain differences should be mentioned which show Goff to be closer to the ideal of an architecture of personal choice and more truly responsive in seeking an architecture expressive of a democratic society.[53] First, the stated bias of Venturi and his partner and wife, Denise Scott Brown, toward an architecture based on commercial vernacular seems inherently inflexible and insensitive to essential gradations of individual taste. Moreover, they have been criticized for failing to achieve what they claim and for designing buildings that are essentially "high style" and elitist.[54] Moore seems more consistent than Venturi in supporting an architecture responsive to personal choice, but a tendency to imbue key parts of individual designs with archetypal imagery introduces the kind of regularly applied, universal principles that were consciously avoided by eighteenth- and early-nineteenth-century practitioners.[55] For them, as for Wright and Goff, such imagery was a matter of intuition rather than verbal articulation. To define it was to patronize the client's intelligence and to conventionalize design.[56] Finally, there is the question of overtly

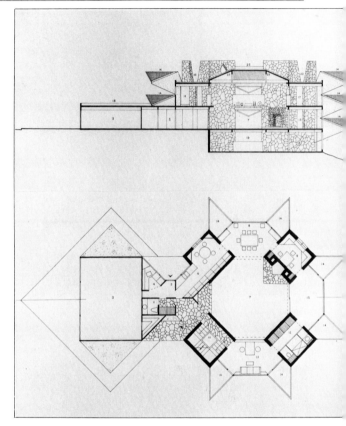

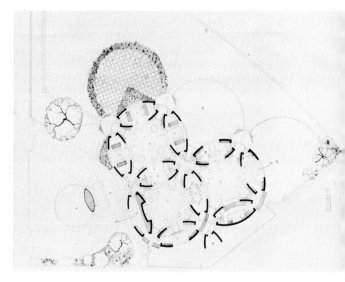

historic details. For a sizable group of architects now popularly termed "Post-Modernists," such details are applied and are meant to allude to the past.[57] For Goff, as for Wright, when historic details can be identified they are not applied, but considered integral with the whole grammar of the design. They are meant to be completely of their own time.[58]

Inherent in an architecture of personal choice is a belief that the source for a new and meaningful architecture lies with the individual client as well as with the architect. Few innovative architects have sublimated their personal preferences as effectively as Goff in achieving these ends. He is part of a significant tradition in architecture and has sustained the development of a national expression that can only occur, as Downing foresaw, if it reflects a local way of life.

Notes

1. I am grateful to Edgar Kaufmann, jr., for sharing his ideas and offering valued suggestions.

2. Although at one level merely descriptive, at a higher level—sometimes signaled by an upper case P—"Picturesque" reflects a documented point of view with clear philosophical and political roots. During the last decade of the eighteenth century the term began to be applied to buildings as well as to the landscape settings that contained them. Still fundamental to an understanding of the Picturesque is Christopher Hussey, *The Picturesque: Studies in a Point of View* (London, 1927; reprinted with a new introduction by Hussey, London, 1967). See also Nikolaus Pevsner, "The Genesis of the Picturesque," *Architectural Review* 96 (November 1944): 139–146; "Richard Payne Knight," *Art Bulletin* 31 (December 1949): 293–320; "Price on Picturesque Planning," *Architectural Review* 95 (February 1944): 47–50; and "Humphry Repton," *Architectural Review* 103 (February 1948): 58–59. All four articles are reprinted with minor revisions in Nikolaus Pevsner, *Studies in Art, Architecture and Design*, vol. 1, *From Mannerism to Romanticism* (New York, 1968), pp. 78–101, 108–125, 126–137, 138–155. For political roots, see Rudolf Wittkower, "English Neo-Palladianism, the Landscape Garden, China and the Enlightenment," *L'Arte* 6 (1969); reprinted in Rudolf Wittkower, *Palladio and Palladianism* (New York 1974), pp. 177–190. Among discussions of the

Picturesque garden outside England are Dora Wiebenson, *The Picturesque Garden in France* (Princeton, 1978); and Nikolaus Pevsner, ed., *The Picturesque Garden and Its Influence Outside the British Isles*, Proceedings of the Dumbarton Oaks Colloquium on the History of Landscape Architecture II (Washington, 1974). See also, Walter John Hipple, Jr., *The Beautiful, the Sublime, and the Picturesque in Eighteenth-Century British Aesthetic Theory* (Carbondale, Ill., 1957); and Henry-Russell Hitchcock, *Architecture: Nineteenth and Twentieth Centuries*, 4th ed. (Harmondsworth, 1977), especially chs. 6 and 15.

3. Typical of comments on such qualities are those by Uvedale Price, who, together with Richard Payne Knight and Humphry Repton, was one of the primary spokesmen for the Picturesque. Price says the effect of the Picturesque:

> . . . arises principally from its two great characteristics, intricacy and variety, as produced by roughness and sudden deviation, and as opposed to the comparative monotony of smoothness and flowing lines.

On intricacy:

> . . . intricacy in landscape might be defined [as] that disposition of objects which, by a partial and uncertain concealment, excites and nourishes curiosity.

(Uvedale Price, *Essay on the Picturesque* [London, 1794], p. 105; pp. 17–18.)

4. Choices were made with references to existing shapes within the landscape, or to ease of particular construction, or to associative values. Repton, having chosen an East Indian mode for the rebuilding of the Brighton Pavilion, supported his decision in part by demonstrating how its construction would be more rational than Greek or Gothic (Humphry Repton, *Designs for the Pavillon at Brighton* [London, 1808], pp. 21–29). Discussing his choice in a more general sense, he said:

> I was pleased at having discovered new sources of beauty and variety, which might gratify that thirst for novelty, so dangerous to good taste in any system long established [p. v].

> Yet its general character is distinct from either Grecian or Gothic, and must both please and surprise every one not bigotted to the forms of either [p. vi].

5. Between 1790 and 1835, more than sixty such pattern books were published in England according to Michael McMordie, "Picturesque Pattern Books and Pre-Victorian Designers," *Architectural History* (Journal of the Society of Architectural Historians of Great Britain) 18 (1975): 43–59. Many of these are discussed in Hussey, especially pp. 216–228. For additional discussions of these books, see Cynthia Wolk Nachmani, "The Early English Cottage Book," *Marsyas* (Studies in the History of Art) 14 (1968–69): 67–76; and Sandra Blutman, "Books of Designs for Country

Houses, 1780–1815," *Architectural History* (Journal of the Society of Architectural Historians of Great Britain) 2 (1968): 25–33. In these books, convenience of planning was stressed.

6. Richard Elsam, *An Essay on Rural Architecture* (London, 1803), pls. 13, 15, 22–25. Elsam describes the "villa in the Italian or Roman style" with its alternate elevation as ". . . interesting from its novelty of form . . . " (p. 47). He says his designs are ". . . calculated to produce agreeable and picturesque effects . . . " (p. 1), and contrasts them with formal buildings of simple shape, about which he comments: "The same dull regularity which prevails throughout wearies the sight, till at length, disgusted with the continuity of lines, it retires in search for realization to more varied and pleasing objects" [p. 3]. For a discussion of Elsam in the context of the Picturesque, see Hussey, op. cit., p. 221.

7. Pugin criticized certain modes as inappropriate to nineteenth-century England, for instance the Italian, castellated, and abbey, among others (A. Welby Pugin, *The True Principles of Pointed or Christian Architecture* [London, 1841], pp. 54–59).

   Ruskin characterized the Picturesque as "parasitical sublimity" and said:

   > The knots and rents of timbers, the irregular lying of the shingles on the roofs, the vigorous light and shadow, the fractures and weather-stains of old stones . . . are the picturesque elements of architecture: the grotesque ones are those which are not produced by the working of nature and of time, but exclusively by the fancy of man; and as also for the most part by his indolent and uncultivated fancy . . .

   (John Ruskin, *The Stones of Venice*, 3 vols. [New York, 1900], 3:135.) Volume 1 of *The Stones of Venice* was originally published in London and New York in 1851; volumes 2 and 3 were first published in London in 1853 and in New York in 1860. The various dates of publication of Ruskin's writings, their influence in America, and Wright's familiarity with *The Stones of Venice* are discussed in Henry-Russell Hitchcock, "Ruskin and American Architecture, or Regeneration Long Delayed," *Concerning Architecture; Essays on Architectural Writers and Writing presented to Nikolaus Pevsner*, John Summerson, ed. (London, 1968), pp. 166–208.

   Garbett reflected a similar attitude, and also reacted against an architecture based on personal choice. He quoted Ruskin in defining the Picturesque, and said "*novelty sought for its own sake* is the destruction of art. The end of art is truth." (Edward Lacy Garbett, *Rudimentary Treatise on the Principles of Design in Architecture* [London, 1850], p. 254.)

8. For an account of Downing's work, publications, and influence on American colleagues, see George B. Tatum, *Andrew Jackson Downing: Arbiter of American Taste,* *1815–1853* (diss., Princeton University, 1950). Tatum relates that Downing depended on English sources, especially J. C. Loudon (pp. 92–94, 109). Loudon's *An Encyclopaedia of Cottage, Farm, and Villa Architecture and Furniture* (London, 1833) is often cited as one of the culminating publications of the English Picturesque. For an account of Loudon, see John Gloag, *Mr. Loudon's England* (Newcastle-upon-Tyne, 1970); and George L. Hersey, "J.C. Loudon and Architectural Associationism," *Architectural Review* 144 (August 1968): 89–92.

   A. J. Davis anticipated some of Downing's published views in the treatise that he began in 1834 or 1835:

   > The bald and uninteresting aspect of our houses must be obvious to every traveller; and to those who are familiar with the picturesque Cottages and Villas of England, it is positively painful to witness here the wasteful and tasteless expenditure of money in building.
   >
   > Defects are felt, however, not only in the style of the house but in the want of connexion with its site,—in the absence of appropriate offices,—well disposed trees, shrubbery, and vines,—which accessories give an inviting and habitable air to the place.

   (Alexander Jackson Davis, *Rural Residences* [New York, 1838; reprinted with a new introduction by Jane B. Davies, New York, 1980], not paginated.)

   The Picturesque is related to the development of American architecture in William H. Pierson, Jr., *American Buildings and Their Architects; Technology and the Picturesque, The Corporate and the Early Gothic Styles* (Garden City, N.Y., 1978), especially chs. 1 (parts 1 and 2), 6, and 7. For a more general discussion of related American philosophies of the period, see Leo Marx, *The Machine in the Garden: Technology and the Pastoral Ideal in America* (London, 1964).

9. As discussed by Tatum, especially pp. 207–208.

10. Regarding the importance of the detached house, Downing said:

    > . . . the *individual home* has a great social value for a people. . . . those elementary forces which give rise to the highest genius and the finest character may, for the most part, be traced back to the farm-house and the rural cottage. It is the solitude and freedom of the family home in the country which constantly preserves the purity of the nation, and invigorates its intellectual powers.

    (A. J. Downing, *The Architecture of Country Houses* [New York, 1850; rep. ed., New York, 1969], p. xix.) Discussing the expression of individual character, he said:

    > . . . there are three most important truths which all Domestic Architecture should present, and without which, it must always be unsatisfactory. The first is, the *general truth* that the building is intended for a dwelling-house; the second, the *local truth* that it is intended for a town or country house; and the third, the *specific truth* that it is intended

for a certain kind of country house—as a cottage, farm-house, or villa [p. 31].

. . . the form of the building should express a local fitness, and an intimate relation with the soil it stands upon—by showing breadth, and extension upon the ground, rather than height [p. 140].

. . . the country house should, above all things, manifest individuality. It should say something of the character of the family within—as much as possible of their life and history, their tastes and associations, should mould and fashion themselves upon its walls [p. 262].

Reflecting a Picturesque-inspired attitude toward choice and visual effects:

. . . no absolute rules for guidance can be laid down here. . . . different families have somewhat various habits, and there-fore require different accommodations [p. 7].

In architecture, variety is of the greatest value, often pre-venting simple forms from degenerating into baldness, or plain broad surfaces from being monotonous, by its power in the arrangement or the decoration of details. . . . In ir-regular buildings there may also be variety in the various parts, projections, recesses, towers. . . . [p. 16].

As regularity and proportion are fundamental ideas of ab-solute beauty, the Picturesque will be found always to de-pend upon the opposite conditions of matter—irregularity, and a partial want of proportion and symmetry [p. 29].

For Downing's suggestions that verandahs and exterior sheathing of vertical boards and battens reflected American climate and construction, see pp. 47, 51, 120, 281.

11. For the slight medieval tilt, see Downing, p. 323; for the suggestion that Oriental modes did not reflect American conditions, see p. 27.

12. Samuel Sloan, *The Model Architect* (Philadelphia, 1852), p. 71. Introducing the design, Sloan says: "many persons, contemplating building, seek for a design, at once original, striking, appropriate and picturesque" (p. 71). In his *Sloan's Homestead Architecture* (Philadelphia, 1861), a slightly revised version is published, pp. 56–62. His description of it as " . . . particularly suitable for the home of the retired Southern planter" reflects his partial realization of the design for Haller Nutt: "Longwood," near Natchez, 1860, left unfinished at the outbreak of the Civil War. For addi-tional information on Sloan, see Harold N. Cooledge, Jr., "A Sloan Check List, 1849–1884," *Journal of the Soci-ety of Architectural Historians* 19 (March 1960): 34–38. Also by Cooledge, *Samuel Sloan (1815–1884), Ar-chitect* (diss., University of Pennsylvania, 1963).

13. The persistence of certain attitudes related to the Pictur-esque is discussed in Vincent J. Scully, Jr., "Romantic Rationalism and the Expression of Structure in Wood: Downing, Wheeler, Gardner, and the 'Stick Style,' 1840–1876," *Art Bulletin* 35 (June 1953): 121–142; and *The Shingle Style; Architectural Theory and Design from*

Richardson to the Origins of Wright (New Haven, 1955; reprinted as one volume, *The Shingle Style and The Stick Style*, rev. ed., New Haven, 1971). Among several works discussing the transmission of Picturesque-inspired ideals into planning are Christopher Tunnard, "The Romantic Suburb in America," *Magazine of Art* 40 (May 1947): 184–187; and Walter L. Creese, *The Search for Envi-ronment: The Garden City, Before and After* (New Ha-ven, 1966). For the Academic Reaction, see Hitchcock, *Architecture: Nineteenth and Twentieth Centuries*, es-pecially chapter 13.

14. As discussed in Scully, *The Shingle Style*, especially chs. 8 and 9; and Reyner Banham, *Theory and Design in the First Machine Age*, 2d. ed. (New York, 1967), especially chs. 1, 2, and 3.

15. Articles taking this view include Nikolaus Pevsner, "The Picturesque in Architecture," *Journal of the Royal In-stitute of British Architects*, 55 (December 1947): 55–61; and by the same writer, "C20 Picturesque," *Architec-tural Review* 115 (April 1954): 227–229. Also, I. de Wolfe (H. de Cronin Hastings), "Townscape: A Plea for an Eng-lish Visual Philosophy Founded on the True Rock of Sir Uvedale Price," *Architectural Review* 106 (December 1949): 355–362. These arguments are revived and addi-tional bibliography cited in Reyner Banham, "Revenge of the Picturesque: English Architectural Polemics, 1945–1965," *Concerning Architecture*, pp. 265–273.

16. Cited designs include the Bauhaus, Dessau, 1925/26, by Gropius and the Centrosoyus, Moscow, 1928–1936, by Le Corbusier (Pevsner, "C20 Picturesque," p. 228).

17. Ibid., pp. 227–229.

18. Among Wright's statements that suggest this ideal:

There should be as many kinds (styles) of houses as there are kinds (styles) of people and as many differentiations as there are different individuals. A man who has individuality (and what man lacks it?) has a right to its expression in his own environment.

(Frank Lloyd Wright, "In the Cause of Architecture," *Ar-chitectural Record* 23 [March 1908]:155–221, 157.)

Parallels between Wright's work and that of Downing are mentioned in Edgar Kaufmann, jr., "Texts from the Exhi-bition," *The Rise of an American Architecture*, Edgar Kaufmann, jr., ed. (New York, 1970), pp. 232–233. The coincidental resemblance between colors favored by Wright and Downing is discussed in H. Allen Brooks, "Observa-tions Concerning the Color of Wright's Plaster-Surfaced Prairie Houses," *Frank Lloyd Wright Newsletter* 2 (First Quarter, 1979): 19.

19. For a discussion of Goff's work, his critics, and his clients, see my Columbia University dissertation, *The Architec-ture of Bruce Goff: Buildings and Projects, 1916–1974*, 2 vols. (New York, 1977). For illustrations, see Takenobu Mohri, *Bruce Goff in Architecture* (Tokyo, 1970). Among

the more recent of a growing number of publications on Goff is an issue of *Architectural Design* devoted to his work, John Sergeant, guest editor, vol. 48, no. 10, 1978.

20. As quoted in Paul Heyer, *Architects on Architecture: New Directions in America* (New York, 1966), p. 69.

21. Bruce Goff, "A Young Architect's Protest for Architecture," *Perspecta* (The Yale Architectural Journal) 13/14 (1971): 330–357, 330.

22. Bruce Goff, "Notizen über das Bauen," *Bauwelt* 49 (January 27, 1958): 77–88; all quotations from Goff's original manuscript, "Notes on Architecture," June 1957, 17 pp., p. 11.

23. Ibid., p. 13.

24. Heyer, *Architects on Architecture*, pp. 68–69.

25. Bruce Goff, *Forty-Four Architectural Realizations*, unpublished manuscript, 1972, 132 pp., p. 26.

26. Heyer, *Architects on Architecture*, p. 68.

27. Goff, "Notes on Architecture," p. 1.

28. Not totally unrelated, though more intellectually contrived, are the effects Peter Eisenman seeks through what he describes as "deep structure." (Peter Eisenman, "House 1, 1967," *Five Architects: Eisenman, Graves, Gwathmey, Hejduk, Meier* [New York, 1972], pp. 15–17.)

29. Goff, "Notes on Architecture," p. 12.

30. Bruce Goff, "Goff on Goff," *Progressive Architecture* 43 (December 1962): 102–103.

31. Goff, "Notes on Architecture," p. 3.

32. Goff, "Goff on Goff," p. 102. Hussey cites the quality of mystery as a key ingredient of the Picturesque point of view (p. 186). Goff's statement that the quality of mystery does not lend itself to formula recalls the Knight-Price debate in which Knight suggested that any rules of design were contrary to the spirit of the Picturesque (Hussey, pp. 77–82).

33. Bruce Goff, "Originality and Architecture," *Kentiku* 102 (March 1969): 25–28.

34. Ibid.

35. As in Goff's Dace House, Beaver, Oklahoma, 1964.

36. Goff, "Notes on Architecture," p. 7.

37. Ibid. Regarding the use of materials in their natural state, Wright said:

> I now began to learn to see brick as brick, learned to see wood as wood, and to see concrete or glass or metal each for itself and all as themselves. Strange to say, this required great concentration of imagination. Each material demanded different handling and had possibilities of use peculiar to its own nature.

(Frank Lloyd Wright, *An Autobiography* [New York, 1932], p. 148.)

38. Goff, *Forty-Four Architectural Realizations*, p. 68.

39. The few for urban settings—such as the Viva Hotel project (Las Vegas, 1961) or the First National Bank project (Independence, Missouri, 1970)—reflect Goff's feeling that even in densely built-up areas buildings should be seen as independent units and have independent character.

40. I have selected them to reinforce my view that their variety is an essential component of Goff's vision, and not due to any evolutionary process.

41. The Royal Pavilion, Brighton, remodeled by John Nash 1815 to 1823, developed the Oriental mode first proposed for the Pavilion in 1806 by Humphry Repton (as published in 1808; n. 3 above). The Plunkett House was the second of three houses for three different sites that Goff designed for the same client. The first (Tyler, Texas, 1965) was destroyed by flood during construction; the third (Lake Village, Texas, 1974) was completed as designed; the second was built, but without its dome. The circular stair and related porch within the ell formed by the two wings (plan, Fig. 8) bear a distant resemblance to Elsam's villa design (plan, Fig. 3).

42. It also recalls Wright's designs of 1922 for a summer colony projected on Lake Tahoe; illustrated in Henry-Russell Hitchcock, *In the Nature of Materials* (New York, 1942), figs. 245–247.

43. A third and less exotic design of 1965, with clustered pavilions that recalled aspects of Indian tepees, was built.

44. The grotto theme was further developed in the Dewlen House project (Dewlen Aparture, near Amarillo, Texas, 1956).

45. The Bavinger House is fully illustrated in Yukio Futagawa, ed., *Global Architecture 33; Bruce Goff: Bavinger House and Price House* (Tokyo, 1975).

46. Among recent discussions of geometry as a metaphor for ideal order are comments in Kenneth Frampton, "Criticism," *Five Architects*, pp. 9–17. Also see a description of a design by Michael Graves: " . . . The Bennacerraf Residence Addition re-presents in architectural form aspects of the natural cosmos as the architect idealizes them. The roof terrace re-establishes the ground plane as an ideal construct." (William La Riche, "Architecture as the World Again?" *Five Architects*, pp. 39–55, p. 55.) For a discussion of geometry as an architectural device in Elizabethan England, see Mark Girouard, *Robert Smythson and the Architecture of the Elizabethan Era* (New York, 1967), pp. 39–42.

47. Among Goff's designs that have been characterized as futuristic are the Ledbetter House, Norman, Oklahoma, 1947, in "Consternation and Bewilderment in Oklahoma," *Life* 24 (June 28, 1948): 71–74; and the Ford House, Aurora, Illinois, 1948, in "Umbrella House," *Architectural Forum* 94 (April 1951).

48. As discussed in Robert A. M. Stern, *New Directions in American Architecture*, rev. ed. (New York, 1977), p. 127. See also Vincent Scully, *The Shingle Style Today, or, the Historian's Revenge* (New York, 1974), p. 17. Scully cites Robert Venturi's 1959 project for a beach house as the first clear example, and relates the underlying philosophy to American ideals. By limiting his discussion to shingled examples he identifies a major Picturesque mode

of the post-1960 period, but restricts his range of view.

49. The subtle differences between the various components of this larger group—the so-called "Whites," "Greys" (Inclusivists), and others—seem largely a matter of rhetoric rather than practice. Among articles that define these components, identify key figures, and point out the inherent similarities are Paul Goldberger, "Should anyone care about the 'New York Five'? . . . or about their critics, the 'Five on Five'?" *Architectural Record* 155 (February 1974): 113; and Rosemarie Haag Bletter, review of *Five Architects* and "Five on Five," *Journal of the Society of Architectural Historians* 38 (May 1979): 205–207. Suggestive of the developing bibliography is Manfredo Tafuri, "European Graffiti; Five × Five = Twenty Five," trans. Victor Caliandro, *Oppositions* 5 (Summer 1976): 35–74. Originally the "Whites" differentiated their work from picturesque imagery, and were thought to seek universal rather than particular forms, as made apparent in Kenneth Frampton, "Criticism," *Five Architects*, p. 10. Yet almost immediately, picturesque elements reflecting aspects of personal choice were identified in the work of the "Whites"; for example, Meier's work was likened to Downing's in Allan Greenberg, "The Lurking American Legacy," *Architectural Forum* 138 (May 1973): 54–55. Other articles in this issue, gathered together under the heading "Five on Five" as a criticism of *Five Architects* by leading "Greys" were: Robert Stern, "Stompin' at the Savoye," pp. 46–48; Jaquelin Robertson, "Machines in the Garden," pp. 49–53; Charles Moore, "In Similar States of Undress," pp. 53–54; and Romaldo Giurgola, "The Discreet Charm of the Bourgeoisie," pp. 56–57.

50. Architecture based on personal choice has rarely elicited critical acclaim; for instance, the Picturesque is linked with bad taste (though bad taste with positive aspects) in Charles Jencks, *The Language of Post-Modern Architecture*, rev. ed. (New York, 1977), p. 73. For Jencks's recent opinion of Goff, see Charles Jencks, "Bruce Goff: The Michelangelo of Kitsch," *Architectural Design* 48, no. 10 (1978): 10–14.

51. The "neohistoricism" of Yamasaki and the romanticism of Stone are discussed in Stern, *New Directions in American Architecture*, p. 7. Differentiating his own work, Venturi wrote:

> An architecture of complexity and contradiction, however, does not mean picturesqueness or subjective expressionism. A false complexity has recently countered the false simplicity of an earlier Modern architecture. It promotes an architecture of symmetrical picturesqueness—which Minoru Yamasaki calls "serene"—but it represents a new formalism as unconnected with experience as the former cult of simplicity. Its intricate forms do not reflect genuinely complex programs, and its intricate ornament, though dependent on industrial techniques for execution, is dryly reminiscent of forms originally created by handicraft techniques.

(Robert Venturi, *Complexity and Contradiction in Architecture*, The Museum of Modern Art Papers on Architecture, No. 1 [New York, 1966], pp. 25–26.) This statement is not unlike that by Ruskin, note 7 above. .

52. Such links seem to be suggested in Arthur Drexler, *Transformations in Modern Architecture* (New York, 1979).

53. Several British critics have singled out Goff as the most American of American architects. They include Ian McCallum, *Architecture USA* (London, 1959), pp. 110, 115; Ian Nairn, "The Master Builders," *A.I.A. Journal* 34 (October 1960): 47–59; Reyner Banham, *Guide to Modern Architecture* (London, 1962), pp. 64–65; and Alan Pryce-Jones, "The Serious American," *The Listener* 69 (January 10, 1963): 59–60.

54. Commenting on this, one critic wrote: "But Venturi is not advocating a landscape which combines the genuine interplay of many styles and vernaculars. Rather he is preaching the familiar line that the architectural elite consciously take from the landscape one particular set of forms in order to create a new and more 'relevant' style of building." (Michael Sorkin, "Robert Venturi and the Function of Architecture at the Present Time," *AAQ: Architectural Association Quarterly* 6, no. 2 [1974]: 31–35.) Similar criticisms are made by Goldberger and Bletter, note 49 above.

55. The objective of emulating a nineteenth-century pattern book is stated in Charles Moore, Gerald Allen, and Donlyn Lyndon, *The Place of Houses* (New York, 1974), p. viii. Among statements that suggest the idea of an architecture of personal choice:

> . . . our experience as architects leads us to believe that houses can and should be more completely suited to the lives of their inhabitants and to the specific places where they are built [p. viii].

> . . . the banishment of eclecticism [is] contrary to human nature. Every house has to be "like" something in order to mean something to its inhabitants and to give them pleasure [p. 67].

The second quotation might be compared to one by Sloan:

> . . . ancient forms and details have too long appealed to the tastes or prejudices of mankind for the architect to dream of their abandonment [*Homestead Architecture*, p. 25].

Among the archetypal images is the comparison of certain design elements to aedicula, and the discussion of their relation to "mythic recollection" and "the archetypal form of a square hut" (Moore, *The Place of Houses*, p. 60). For comments that (perhaps unknowingly) relate Moore and his colleagues to Goff, see Charles W. Moore, "Where Are We Now, Vincent Scully?" *Progressive Architecture* 56 (April 1974): 78–83; and Robert A. M. Stern, "Towards an Architecture of Symbolic Assemblage," *Progressive Architecture* 56 (April 1974): 72–77.

56. By no means does this rule out its existence, as shown, for instance, in Robert Kosta, "Bruce Goff and the New Tradition," *Prairie School Review* 7, no. 2 (1970): 5–15, 23; and Edgar Kaufmann, jr., "Precedent and Progress in the Work of Frank Lloyd Wright," *Journal of the Society of Architectural Historians* 39 (May 1980): 145–149.

57. Post-Modernism is defined in Jencks, *The Language of Post-Modern Architecture*. See also Stern, *New Directions in American Architecture*, pp. 127–129. Discussing their entry to the Yale Mathematics Building competition, 1970, Venturi and his associates explain:

> The Gothic porch (in concrete) and the quatrefoil paving in back are small stylistic appliqués on the loft like brick,

making the relation to Leet Oliver [Hall] explicit through symbolism as well as through compositional form and scale.

(Robert Venturi, Denise Scott Brown, and Steven Izenour, *Learning from Las Vegas* [Cambridge, Mass., 1972], p. 150.) This stance seems somewhat relaxed from that quoted in note 51 above.

58. Some critics have suggested that the historical allusions of applied details, in lacking depth, also lack meaning; for example, John Morris Dixon, "Revival of Historical Allusion" (editorial), *Progressive Architecture* 56 (April 1975): 59; and Joseph Rykwert, "Ornament is No Crime," *International Studio* 190 (October 1975): 91–97.

HENRY-RUSSELL HITCHCOCK: PUBLICATIONS 1967–1981

Professor Hitchcock's bibliography through 1966 can be found in two volumes of the *Papers* of the American Association of Architectural Bibliographers. The years 1927 through 1956 are covered in Volume One (Henry-Russell Hitchcock: The First Thirty Years, pp. 1–22); the years 1957 through 1966 in Volume Five (Henry-Russell Hitchcock: The Fourth Decade, pp. 1–14). The following list of Professor Hitchcock's publications from 1967 through 1981 has been compiled from the books and articles on his shelves by William Foulks.

"Frank Lloyd Wright, 1867–1967" in *The Prairie School Review* 4, no. 4 (1967): 5–9.

Review of *Victorian Architecture* by Robert Furneaux Jordan in *Architectural Design* 37 (October 1967): 444.

"Peter II Thumb and German Rococo Architecture" in *Essays in the History of Architecture presented to Rudolf Wittkower*, edited by Douglas Fraser, Howard Hibbard, and Milton J. Lewine, pp. 170–188. London: Phaidon Press, 1967.

"Frank Lloyd Wright 1867–1967" in *Zodiac*, no. 17 (1967): 6–10.

"Ruskin and American Architecture, or Regeneration Long Delayed" in *Concerning Architecture: Essays on Architectural Writers and Writing presented to Nikolaus Pevsner*, edited by John Summerson, pp. 166–208. London: Allen Lane The Penguin Press, 1968.

"Meeks's Monuments," review of *Italian Architecture 1750–1914* by Carroll L. V. Meeks in *The Yale Review* 57 (March 1968): 401–417.

"English Architecture in the Early 20th Century: 1900–1939" in *Zodiac*, no. 18 (1968): 6–10.

Rhode Island Architecture, paperback edition. Cambridge, Mass.: M.I.T. Press, 1968.

Rhode Island Architecture, reprint edition. New York: Da Capo Press, 1968.

German Rococo: the Zimmermann Brothers. London: Allen Lane The Penguin Press, 1968.

Built in U.S.A.: Postwar Architecture (editor with Arthur Drexler), reprint edition. New York: Arno Press, 1968.

Rococo Architecture in Southern Germany. London: Phaidon, 1968.

Review of *Town Planning in London; the Eighteenth and Nineteenth Centuries* by Donald J. Olsen in *Journal of the Society of Architectural Historians* 27 (May 1968): 147.

"Modern Architecture—a Memoir" in *Journal of the Society of Architectural Historians* 27 (December 1968): 227–233.

Architecture: Nineteenth and Twentieth Centuries, 3rd edition. Harmondsworth, Middlesex: Penguin Books, 1968.

"Introduction" in *Contrasts* by A.W.N. Pugin, pp. 7–18. Leicester: Leicester University Press, 1969.

Exhibition Catalogue, *Modern Architecture in England* (with C. K. Bauer), reprint edition. New York: Arno Press, 1969.

Exhibition Catalogue, *Modern Architecture International Exhibition* (with others), reprint edition. New York: Arno Press, 1969.

Review of *The Meanings of Architecture: Buildings and Writings by John Root*, edited by Donald Hoffmann in *Architectural Forum* 130 (January/February 1969): 82–83.

Exhibition Catalogue, *Paul Rudolph: an Exhibition of His Architecture*, U.S.I.S., 1969?

"American Influence Abroad" in *The Rise of an American Architecture*, edited by Edgar Kaufmann, jr., pp. 3–48. New York: Praeger Publishers, 1970.

"Cloverley Hall, Shropshire" in *The Country Seat: Studies in the History of the British Country House*, edited by Howard Colvin and John Harris, pp. 252–261. London: Allen Lane The Penguin Press, 1970.

"Architectural Publishing in Philadelphia" in *Historic Preservation* (April-June 1970): 36–40.

Architecture: Nineteenth and Twentieth Centuries, 1st paperback edition. Harmondsworth, Middlesex: Penguin Books, 1971.

Modern Architecture: Romanticism and Reintegration, reprint edition. New York: Hacker Art Books, 1970.

L'architettura dell'Ottocento e del Novecento, translation. Turin: Giulio Einaudi Editore, 1971.

"Preface" in *Schindler* by David Gebhard, pp. 7–8. London: Thames and Hudson, 1971.

"Introduction" in *A Catalogue of British Drawings for Architecture, Decoration, Sculpture and Landscape Gardening 1550–1900 in American Collections* by John Harris, pp. xi-xii. Upper Saddle River, N.J.: Gregg Press, 1971.

"The Plassenburg above Kulmbach" in *Journal of the Society of Architectural Historians* 3 (October 1972): 163–175.

Remarks, "The Chicago School of Architecture. A Symposium—Part II: the Other Panelists" in *The Prairie School Review* 9, no. 2 (1972): 16–22.

"Foreign Influences in American Painting and Architecture after 1860" in *The Shaping of Art and Architecture in Nineteenth Century America*. New York: The Metropolitan Museum of Art, 1972.

Latin American Architecture since 1945, reprint edition. New York: Arno Press, 1972.

Modern Architecture: Romanticism and Reintegration, reprint edition. New York: AMS Press, 1972.

"The Beginnings of the Renaissance in Germany, 1505–1515," in *Architectura*, 1971, no. 2, pp. 123–147; 1972, no. 1, pp. 3–16.

Early Victorian Architecture in Britain, 2 vols., reprint edition. New York: Da Capo Press, 1972.

In the Nature of Materials, 1887–1941: The Buildings of Frank Lloyd Wright, reprint edition. New York: Da Capo Press, 1973.

HHP: Buildings and Projects. Düsseldorf: Econ Verlag, 1973.

"Foreword" in *The Architecture of Frank Lloyd Wright: A Complete Catalog* by William Allin Storrer. Cambridge, Mass.: M.I.T. Press, 1974.

Die Bielefelder Kunsthalle. Bielefeld: Kunsthalle Bielefeld, 1974.

"Landscape and Cityscape" in *The Aspen Papers: Twenty Years of Design Theory from the International Design Conference in Aspen*. New York: Praeger, 1974.

"Architecture" in *Art Nouveau: Art and Design at the Turn of the Century*, new, revised edition. New York: Museum of Modern Art, 1975.

Architecture: Nineteenth and Twentieth Centuries, paperback edition reprinted. Harmondsworth, Middlesex: Penguin Books, 1975.

"Introduction" in *Kevin Roche John Dinkeloo and Associates Vol. One 1962–1975*. Tokyo: A.D.A. Edita, 1975.

"An Inventory of the Architectural Library of H. H. Richardson" in *Nineteenth Century* 1 (January 1975): 27–31; (April 1975): 18–19.

"Aalto versus Aalto: The Other Finland," reprint. New York: Garland Publishing, 1976.

"Frank Lloyd Wright and the 'Academic Tradition' of the Early Eighteen-Nineties," reprint. New York: Garland Publishing, 1976.

"Sullivan and the Skyscraper." New York: Garland Publishing, 1976.

Early Victorian Architecture in Britain (abridged), reprint. New York: Da Capo Press, 1976.

"How Nebraska Acquired a State Capitol Like No Other" (with William Seale) in *AIA Journal* 65 (October 1976): 56–61.

"An Unpublished Introduction to *Temples of Democracy*" in *Nineteenth Century* 2 (Autumn 1976): 6–15.

American Architectural Books, new expanded edition. New York: Da Capo Press, 1976.

Temples of Democracy: the State Capitols of the USA (with William Seale). New York: Harcourt Brace Jovanovich, 1976.

Architecture: Nineteenth and Twentieth Centuries, 4th edition. Harmondsworth, Middlesex: Penguin Books, 1977.

"Foreword" in *The Architecture of Frank Lloyd Wright: a Complete Catalog* by William Allin Storrer. Cambridge, Mass.: M.I.T. Press, 1978.

The International Style (with Philip Johnson), translation. Tokyo?: Kajima Institute Publishing Co., 1978.

"French Influence on 19th Century Architecture in the U.S.A." in *The Beaux-Arts* (A.D. Profiles 17). London: Architectural Design, n.d.

Netherlandish Scrolled Gables of the Sixteenth and Early Seventeenth Centuries. New York: New York University Press, 1978.

"Notes on the Architecture" (with William Seale) in *Court House: a Photographic Documentation*, pp. 165–250. New York: Horizon Press, 1978.

"H. H. Richardson's New York Senate Chamber Restored" in *Nineteenth Century* 6 (Spring 1980): 45–47.

"Foreword" in *The Villard Houses: Life Story of a Landmark* by William C. Shopsin and Mosette Glaser Broderick, pp. 8–9. New York: Viking Press, 1980.

Exhibition Catalogue, *Springfield Architecture: 1800–1900*. Springfield, Mass.: Springfield City Library, 1980.

Arquitectura de los siglos xix y xx, translation. Madrid: Catedra, S.A., 1981.

"Häuser von zwei Modernen," translation in *Bauwelt*, no. 42 (6 November 1981): 1903–1905.

German Renaissance Architecture. Princeton, N.J.: Princeton University Press, 1981.

NOTES ON THE CONTRIBUTORS

MOSETTE GLASER BRODERICK was born in 1945 on Long Island where she lived in a Shingle Style house. She received a B.A. at Finch College and an M.A. at Columbia University where she is currently enrolled in the Ph.D. program. She wrote the architectural and social history portion of *The Villard Houses* (1980). She is writing a book on Fifth Avenue houses and teaching architectural history at New York University. She is president of the New York Chapter of the Society of Architectural Historians.

H. ALLEN BROOKS is Professor of Fine Arts at the University of Toronto where he has taught since 1958. A native of Connecticut (b. 1925) he received degrees from Dartmouth, Yale, and Northwestern before moving to Canada. He is a former president of the Society of Architectural Historians, and a Guggenheim Fellow. His book *The Prairie School: Frank Lloyd Wright and His Midwest Contemporaries* (1972) received the Alice Davis Hitchcock Book Award. Other books include *Prairie School Architecture: Studies from the "Western Architect"* (1975), and *Writings on Wright: Selected Comment on Frank Lloyd Wright* (1981). He is currently General Editor of the thirty-two-volume *Le Corbusier Archive* (Garland, 1982/83), and is completing a book on Charles-Edouard Jeanneret's formative years (1887–1920), one aspect of which is represented by this essay.

RICHARD G. CARROTT, born in 1924, received the B.A. degree in 1950 from Wesleyan University where he first met Professor Hitchcock. He earned the M.A. at the Institute of Fine Arts, New York University in 1955, and the Ph.D. from Yale University (1961) where Professor Hitchcock was one of his dissertation advisors. He has taught at Sweet Briar College, the University of California, Berkeley, and since 1961 at the University of California, Riverside, where he is currently Professor of Art History. His publications include *The Egyptian Revival; its Sources, Monuments and Meaning, 1808–1858* (1978), and the exhibition catalogue, *Thomas Moran 1837–1926*. In 1966/67 Professor Carrott was National Coordinator of the Committee to Rescue Italian Art.

GEORGE R. COLLINS, Professor of Art History at Columbia University where he has been since 1946, was born in Springfield, Massachusetts, 2 September 1917, and was educated at Princeton University. On finishing his graduate education there, he served for three years overseas and a year with the UNRRA Displaced Persons operation in Germany. He has had ACLS, Guggenheim, Rockefeller, and NEH fellowships, and received the doctorate *honoris causa* from the Universidad Politécnica de Barcelona. He specializes in Spanish art since the Golden Age, and in modern architecture and town planning, especially Antonio Gaudí, linear planning, and the visionary—on which he has published thirteen books and twenty-six articles; he has edited twenty books.

JOHN COOLIDGE was born in 1913 and was educated at Harvard and at the Institute of Fine Arts, New York University, where he received the Ph.D. in 1948. He was an Instructor in the Fine Arts at Vassar College 1936–1938 and Assistant Professor at the University of Pennsylvania in 1946/47. Between 1947 and 1979 he was at Harvard, where he became William Dorr Boardman Professor in 1973; he was named Professor Emeritus in 1979. He served as Director of the Fogg Art Museum from 1948 to 1968, and as President of the Museum of Fine Arts, Boston, from 1973 to 1975.

J. MORDAUNT CROOK was born in London in 1937 and educated at Oxford University. He is the author of *The British Museum* (1972) and *William Burges and the High Victorian Dream* (1981); co-author of *The History of the King's Works, 1660–1851* (1972–1976), the standard history of Britain's later royal palaces and public buildings; and editor of Eastlake's *Gothic Revival* (revised edition 1978), another standard work. He is a Council Member of the Society of Antiquaries and the Victorian Society and has served for some years on the Historic Buildings Council for England. He was Slade Professor of Fine Art at Oxford in 1979/80 and is currently Professor of Architectural History at the University of London and President of the Society of Architectural Historians of Great Britain.

DAVID G. DE LONG teaches architectural history at Columbia University, where he is Associate Professor of Architecture and Chairman of the Division of Historic Preservation in the Graduate School of Architecture and Planning. An architect, he studied design with Louis I. Kahn at the University of Pennsylvania, receiving the Master of Architecture Degree in 1963. He practiced for several years in New York City, served as the Restoration Architect for the Harvard-Cornell Archaeological Expedition to Sardis, and taught at the Middle East Technical University in Ankara before pursuing graduate studies at Columbia, where he received the Ph.D. in Architectural History in 1976. Professor Hitchcock was a reader for his dissertation, *The Architecture of Bruce Goff*, which was published in 1977. He has also published several articles, compiled and edited fourteen volumes of *Historic American Buildings*, and is currently serving as guest curator for architecture for the 1983/84 Cranbrook Exhibition sponsored by the Detroit Institute of Arts and the Metropolitan Museum of Art.

MARK GIROUARD was born in 1931. He was educated at Ampleforth, Christ Church, Oxford, and the Courtauld Institute, University of London, where he received the Ph.D. He was the Slade Professor of Fine Art at Oxford 1975/76. His books include *The Victorian Country House* (1971 and 1979), *Victorian Pubs* (1975), *Sweetness and Light* (1977), *Life in the English Country House* (1978), and *The Return to Camelot* (1981).

JOHN HARRIS is Curator of the Drawings Collection of the Royal Institute of British Architects and an historian who has written many books and articles on architecture and gardening. Two of his recent works have been *The Artist and the Country House* (1979) and *The Palladians* (1981). He delivered the Andrew Mellon Lectures in the Fine Arts to the National Gallery of Art in Washington in 1981 and is at present preparing these lectures—on the influence of Palladio in Britain—for publication. He is currently President of the International Confederation of Architectural Museums.

WILLIAM H. JORDY attended Bard College, the Institute of Fine Arts at New York University and, eventually—after a World War II interruption—received the doctorate from Yale University in 1948. He has taught, first at Yale University and, since 1955, at Brown University where he is Henry Ledyard Goddard University Professor of Art. His publications include *Henry Adams: Scientific Historian* (1952), the two-volume *Montgomery Schuyler, American Architecture and Other Writings* (co-edited with Ralph Coe, and including an extensive introduction; 1961), and another two volumes, *American Buildings and Their Architects: Progressive and Academic Ideals at the Turn of* the *Twentieth Century* (1972) and *The Impact of European Modernism in the Mid-Twentieth Century* (1972). His most recent work, co-authored with Christopher P. Monkhouse, is *Buildings on Paper: Rhode Island Architectural Drawings 1825–1945* (1982), the catalogue for an exhibition held in Providence, New York, and Washington. He has contributed to various collections and written a number of articles and reviews.

EDGAR KAUFMANN, JR. was born in 1910. Instead of attending a university, he studied art in Europe, principally Italy. Hitchcock's *Modern Architecture* (1929) influenced his ideas. After returning to the United States he studied under Frank Lloyd Wright, who designed Fallingwater for Kaufmann's parents. Some years later he joined the staff of the Museum of Modern Art, New York. He served in Army Air Force Intelligence during World War II. In the mid-1950s he wrote and did editorial advising for the Encyclopaedia Britannica. In 1963 he began teaching architectural history at Columbia University, which recently named him Adjunct Professor Emeritus.

SARAH BRADFORD LANDAU was educated at the University of North Carolina at Greensboro (B.F.A., 1957) and the Institute of Fine Arts, New York University (M.A., 1959; Ph.D., 1978). In 1971 she seized the opportunity to study with Henry-Russell Hitchcock who had recently joined the Institute's faculty. Her doctoral dissertation, published as *Edward T. and William A. Potter, American Victorian Architects* (1979), was written under his advisement. She is also the author of *P. B. Wight: Architect, Contractor, and Critic 1838–1925* (1981) and is currently at work on a book about American Neo-Gothic architecture, for which she received an NEH fellowship (1979/80) and a Graham Foundation grant (1980/81). She is Assistant Professor of Fine Arts at New York University.

NEIL LEVINE received the B.A. in 1973 at Princeton University. He completed the Ph.D. at Yale University, where he also taught. He is presently Professor of Fine Arts at Harvard University. His publications include "The Romantic Idea of Architectural Legibility: Henri Labrouste and the Neo-Grec" in *The Architecture of the Ecole des Beaux-Arts* (edited by Arthur Drexler, 1977).

THOMAS JULIAN McCORMICK was born in Syracuse, New York, in 1925. He received the B.A. and M.A. from Syracuse University, the M.F.A. and Ph.D. from Princeton. He was Senior Fulbright Research Fellow to the Courtauld Institute of Art, University of London 1966/67 and to the Urbanisticki Zavod Dalmacije, Split, Yugoslavia 1976/77. He is the author of numerous museum catalogues, articles, and reviews, many focusing on the career of Charles-Louis Clérisseau. He has taught at Smith, Vassar, Wells, and Williams colleges and is currently A. Howard Meneely Professor of Art, Wheaton College, Norton, Massachusetts.

WILLIAM L. MACDONALD was born in 1921 and educated at Harvard and in Rome. His books include *Early Christian and Byzantine Architecture* (1962), *The Architecture of the Roman Empire* (1965), and *The Pantheon* (1976). He was the Associate Editor of, and a contributor to, the *Princeton Encyclopedia of Classical Sites*. A Fellow of the American Academy in Rome, he taught first at Yale University and then at Smith College.

HENRY A. MILLON received degrees in English, physics, and architecture at Tulane University before completing the Ph.D. in the history of art at Harvard (1964). Professor Millon taught the history of architecture at MIT from 1960 to 1974, when he went to Rome to serve as Director of the American Academy until 1977. He is presently Dean of the Center for Advanced Study in the Visual Arts at the National Gallery of Art in Washington, D.C. Among Professor Millon's most recent publications are his contribution to *Art and Architecture in the Service of Politics* (1978) and to *Studies in Italian Art and Architecture: 15th through 18th Centuries* (1978).

VINCENT J. SCULLY, JR. received the Ph.D. from Yale University in 1949. His doctoral thesis was revised and published as *The Shingle Style and the Stick Style* (1955). Some of Scully's other books are *Frank Lloyd Wright* (1960), *Modern Architecture* (1961), *The Earth, the Temple, and the Gods, Greek Sacred Architecture* (1962), *Louis I. Kahn* (1962), *American Architecture and Urbanism* (1969), and *Pueblo, Mountain, Village, Dance* (1975). He also wrote the introduction to Robert Venturi, *Complexity and Contradiction in Architecture* (1966), and the Postscript to Aldo Rossi, *A Scientific Autobiography* (1981), and at present is working on a book on French Gothic Cathedrals and seventeenth-century gardens and fortifications. Vincent Scully is the Colonel John Trumbull Professor of Art History at Yale University, where he has been teaching since 1947.

HELEN SEARING received the B.A. from Vassar College in 1954 and the Ph.D. from Yale University in 1972. In 1956/57, on a Fulbright Fellowship in Economics at the University of Copenhagen, she first became interested in modern architecture, an interest she pursued from 1959 to 1962 at the University of California at Berkeley. Traveling on a Woodrow Wilson Fellowship in 1962/63, she met Professor Hitchcock. Their friendship was renewed in 1967 when she went to Smith College where she is today Professor of Art, succeeding the irreplaceable Russell Hitchcock. She was guest curator of two recent exhibitions, "Speaking a New Classicism: American Architecture Now" (1981) and "New American Art Museums" (1982), and contributed the accompanying catalogues.

DOROTHY STROUD, M.B.E., F.S.A., Hon. F.R.I.B.A., was born in London in 1910 and was educated at Edgbaston High School. From 1930 until 1941 she was on the staff of *Country Life*, and then joined the National Buildings (now Monuments) Record on its inception in that year. Since 1946 she has been Assistant Curator of Sir John Soane's Museum. Her books include *The Architecture of Sir John Soane* and biographies of "Capability" Brown, Henry Holland, and Humphry Repton.

DAVID VAN ZANTEN was born in 1943 in New York City and educated at Princeton and Harvard, receiving the doctorate in 1970 with a dissertation entitled *The Architectural Polychromy of the 1830's*. He taught for eight years at the University of Pennsylvania and since 1980 has been chairman of the art history department at Northwestern University. He published *Walter Burley Griffin: Selected Designs* in 1970, contributed to *The Architecture of the Ecole des Beaux-Arts* (edited by Arthur Drexler, 1977), and edited the posthumous publication of Donald Drew Egbert's *Beaux-Arts Tradition in French Architecture* (1980).

INDEX OF ARCHITECTS AND ARCHITECTURAL WRITERS CITED IN TEXT

Figure numbers are in italics preceded by the page number on which the illustration appears.

nn. 5–8; 98 n. 10, n. 12, n. 22, n. 30; 99 n. 32, n. 36, n. 41, n. 42, n. 46, n. 47; 100 n. 53; 101 n. 62; 109; 123

Sturgis, Russell (1838–1909), 151; 153; 156, 162 n. 28; 163 n. 41, n. 48

Sturm, Leonhard Christoph (1669–1719), 70

Sullivan, Louis (1856–1924), 136; 137; 138; 143; 149–152; 154; 157; 158; 160 n. 1, n. 2, n. 6; 161 n. 11; 164 n. 58; 246; 247; 249; 275; 343

Tatham, Charles Heathcote (1772–1842), 7; 41; 52; 53, *1*; 54, *2*, *3*, *4*; 55, *5*, *6*; 56, *7*, *8*; 57, *9*, *10*, *11*; 58, *12*, *13*, *14*; 59, *15*, *16*; 60, *17*, *18*, *19*; 61, *20*; 62, *23*, *24*, n. 1, n. 2; 63, *25*, *26*, n. 3

Teale, Oscar S. (fl. 1865–1927, d. 1934), 154; 163 n. 43

Teulon, S. S. (1812–1873), 123, *3*; 133 n. 3

Thomas, Thomas (1787/8–1871; Thomas & Son), 161 n. 11

Thorp, Alfred H. (1843–1917), 143; 145, *9*; 161 n. 23

Trowbridge, Samuel Breck Parkman (1862–1925; Trowbridge & Livingston), 192

Unwin, Sir Raymond (1863–1940), 291; 294

Vanbrugh, Sir John (1664–1726), 38

Van Brunt, Henry (1832–1903; Ware & Van Brunt), 175; 177

Vaudoyer, A.-L.-T. (1756–1846), 64; 70; 73; 74; 83 n. 20; 84 n. 65

Vaudoyer, Léon (1803–1872), 64; 71–74; 76–80; 82; 84 n. 66

Vaudremer, Emile (1829–1914), 162 n. 28; 249, *4*

Vaux, Calvert (1824–1895; Vaux & Withers), 161 n. 11

Venturi, Robert (b. 1925), 12, *2*; 275; 351; 353; 357 n. 48; 358 n. 51, n. 54; 359 n. 5

Vignola, Jacopo (1507–1573), 300

Vignon, Pierre (1763–1828), 19

Villain, François-Alexandre (1798–1884), 71; 74

Viollet-le-Duc, E. E. (1814–1879), 64; 81; 226; 242 n. 9; 247; 276 n. 9

Wagner, Albert (1848–?), 154; 163 n. 42, n. 43

Wagner, Otto (1841–1918), 294

Walpole, Horace (1717–1797), 27; 47

Ware, William (1832–1915; Ware & Van Brunt), 175, 177

Waterhouse, Alfred (1830–1905), 115

Webb, Sir Aston (1849–1930), 112; 114

Weinbrenner, Friedrich (1766–1826), 68; 81

Wells, Joseph C. (1853–1890), 161 n. 11

White, Horatio Nelson, 175; 177

White, Stanford (1853–1906; McKim, Mead & White), 6; 10; 11, *1*; 140; 150; 151, *17*; 154; 155, *21*; 157, *25*; 158, *26*; 159; 162 n. 28, n. 34; 163 n. 48; 164 n. 54, n. 55; 185–188; 190, *3*; 191; 192, *4*; 193–195; 196, *7*; 197; 198, *9*; 199, *10*; 200, *11*; 201, *12*; 202 n. 2, n. 5; 204 nn. 20–22, n. 26, n. 28; 205 n. 41, n. 45, n. 51; 230; 247; 321; 322; 329; 330; 332, *14*; 334

White, William H. (1838–1896), 114

Wight, Peter B. (1838–1925), 161 n. 15; 162 n. 28; 183 n. 33

Wild, J. W. (1814–1892), 137

Willard, Daniel Wheelock (Babb, Cook & Willard), 150; 152, *18*; 153, *19*; 156, 162 n. 28; 163 n. 48

Withers, Frederick C. (1828–1901; Vaux & Withers), 161 n. 11

Wren, Sir Christopher (1632–1723), 38; 103; 117; 119 n. 98

Wright, Frank Lloyd (1867–1959), 6, *5*; 8 n. 11, n. 17; 11; 12; 172 nn. 1–5; 175; 178; 179, *7*; 181; 182 nn. 1–5; 241 n. 1; 245; 246, *1*; 247, *2*; 248, *3*; 249; 250, *5*; 252, *7*, *8*; 253, *9*; 254, *10*, *11*; 255, *12*, *13*; 256, *14*; 257, *16*; 258; 259; 260, *20*, *21*; 261, *22*; 262, *23*; 263, *24*; 264; 265, *26*; 266, *27*; 267; 268; 269, *29*, *30*; 270; 271, *31*; 272, *32*; 273, *33*; 274, *34*; 275; 276 n. 1, n. 3, n. 5, n. 6, n. 8, nn. 10–13, nn. 15–17; 277 n. 19, n. 22, n. 23, n. 26, n. 27, n. 29, n. 31, n. 32, nn. 34–38, n. 44, n. 46; 321; 341–343; 345; 351; 353; 354; 355 n. 7; 356 n. 18; 357 n. 37, n. 42; 359 n. 56

Wyatt, James (1747–1813), 38; 55

Wyatt, Lewis William (c. 1778–1853), 53

Yamasaki, Minoru (b. 1912), 353; 358 n. 51

Youngs, William Henry Walmsley (d. 1915; Youngs & Cable), 154; 155, *22*; 163 n. 47